Cookery Americana

*C*OOKERY AMERICANA is a series of 27 cookbooks in 15 volumes that chronicles a fascinating aspect of American social life over the past 150 years. These volumes provide unique insight into the American experience and follow the movement of pioneer America from the original colonies to the Great Plains and westward to the Pacific. More than cookbooks, these works were manuals for daily living: household management, etiquette, home medicinal remedies, and much more. See the last pages of this volume for a complete listing of the series.

LOUIS I. SZATHMARY, Advisory Editor for this series, is an internationally known chef, food management consultant, owner of the renowned Chicago restaurant, The Bakery, and author of the best selling *The Chef's Secret Cookbook* (Quadrangle Books, 1971). As a serious student of the history of cookery, he has collected a library of several thousand cookbooks dating back to the 15th century. All of the works in *Cookery Americana* are from his private collection.

PREPARATIONS FOR CATCHING SHAD, A POPULAR 19TH CENTURY FISH

PIERRE BLOT

HAND-BOOK
OF
PRACTICAL COOKERY

Introduction and Suggested Recipes

by

LOUIS SZATHMARY

ARNO PRESS

A NEW YORK TIMES COMPANY

New York • 1973

LIBRARY OF CONGRESS CATALOGING IN PUBLICATION DATA

Blot, Pierre, 1818-1874.
Hand-book of practical cookery.

(Cookery Americana)
Reprint of the 1869 ed.
1. Cookery, American. I. Szathmáry, Louis.
II. Title. III. Series.
TX715.B6465 1973 641.5'973 72-9789
ISBN 0-405-05042-9

Reprint Edition 1973 by Arno Press Inc.

Introduction Copyright © 1973 by Louis Szathmáry

Reprinted from a copy in the private collection of Louis Szathmáry

COOKERY AMERICANA
ISBN for complete set: 0-405-05040-2
See last pages of this volume for titles.

Manufactured in the United States of America

Introduction

Although the author is French, as are some of the cooking expressions and dishes throughout, the *Hand-Book of Practical Cookery* is among the first which can truly be called American. Native American flora and fauna are well represented in many of the recipes which call for such ingredients as bear, buffalo, raccoon, lima beans, pumpkin, and okra. But perhaps more important, Blot often reminds us of how the native Indians cook and prepare the native products. For example, the recipe for Succotash (p. 321) is referred to as a "popular Indian dish." He also approves of Indian methods and suggests their adoption by his readers—New York housewives, housekeepers and servants.

When comparing Blot's expressions and terms to those in English, French, and German cookbooks of the same decade, we find that, although the words are often the same, he interprets them in a strictly American context. The customs he discusses are also definitely American.

The English cookbooks of his contemporaries generally "cook" steaks—with or without potatoes, vegetables, and gravy—in covered pans in the oven, or on top of the stove. "Broiling" (if ever) was mainly a way to prepare tenderloin. For Blot, however, steak and broiling, using a grill or gridiron of some kind, are inseparable.

Blot is very much concerned with nutrition, and his misconceptions regarding it are not his own, but those of his time. He is also quite adventurous; he tells about all the strange creatures which he has tasted through his culinary curiosity—opossum, otter, skunk, fox, woodchuck, and the like.

Although not a unique cookbook, the stories of Blot's adventures which are included among the recipes, are all delightful, American folklore. How to Skin a Skunk (p. 298) is an authentic-sounding story as well as a believable recipe. His Pumpkin and

A FRUIT AUCTION IN NEW YORK

Squash recipes are certainly not original, but definitely American, as is his recipe for Tomato Catsup.

The recipe for Clam Chowder (p. 159) is excellent, and most likely original; he explains that he learned it from a fisherman or boatman on the Harlem River. His Clam Bake recipe (p. 161) originates from "Tom Riley, Harlem River clam-baker."

His section on the packaging, transportation and storage of Game (p. 276) is interesting, and points out the kinetic nature of Americans. This is one of the first books where we read about prefreezing meats for packaging. He explains, however, that as carefully as meat is packed in barrels, even though frozen on the outside, the meat in the middle of the barrel begins to naturally ferment. He fights against the practice of packing game and poultry for freezing in barrels and suggests better ways—for example, the transportation in wicker-baskets with plenty of straw.

TROUT—A HIGHLY ESTEEMED DELICACY OF NEW YORKERS
IN THE 1870s—WAS TRANSPORTED IN GREAT QUANTITIES
FROM SUCH PLACES AS MAINE AND VERMONT TO NEW YORK

"Our Northeastern cities are now supplied by the Western States with game" is a statement which reflects on the difference between the way food was supplied in America and the Old World. In Europe, in 1869, suppliers were still local, but in the United States food sometimes moved thousands of miles from its place of origin to the dining table.

Louis Szathmáry
CHICAGO, ILLINOIS

SUGGESTED RECIPES

*The following recipes have been tested and adjusted to today's
ingredients, measurements, and style of cooking
by Chef Louis Szathmáry.*

ACORN SQUASH (p. 340)

INGREDIENTS FOR 8:

 4 pounds squash
 Enough water to cover
 1 tablespoon salt
 ½ cup of melted butter
 2 tablespoons chopped parsley
 Salt and pepper to taste
 ½ cup milk
 2 egg yolks

METHOD: Cut squash in halves or quarters, and remove seeds. Place
in a large pot, cover with water, then add the tablespoon of salt,
and boil gently until tender. Drain and discard water. Remove the
pulp from the skins, discard skin. Mash the pulp with the melted
butter, or blend in a blender until smooth. Add parsley, salt and
pepper to taste. Warm slowly in a stewing pan, adding the milk in
small amounts, and stirring after each addition of milk. Let it remain on low heat, covered, for 10 minutes. Stir in the 2 egg yolks,
and correct seasoning if necessary. Serve.

CLAM CHOWDER (pp. 159-160)

INGREDIENTS FOR 8:

 6 slices of bacon (thinly sliced)

 4 medium-size potatoes
 (washed, peeled and sliced
 into ¼ inch slices —
 approximately ¾ quart)

 1 cup chopped onions

 1 No. 2 can tomatoes, or 3
 medium-sized tomatoes,
 sliced
 2 8-ounce cans minced clams,
 including juice
 1 small can clam juice
 16 saltines

THE MEAT OF THE BLACK-TAILED DEER OF NORTH AMERICA
WAS USED IN MANY OF THE VENISON RECIPES

INTERIOR OF A RAILROAD DINING CAR
IN THE EARLY 1870s

A BAKER'S SHOP IN 1872

METHOD: Cover the bottom of a soup pot with the thin slices of bacon. Lay ½ of the potatoes over the bacon, sprinkle in ½ the chopped onion, and place 8 crackers, broken into not too small pieces, on top of the onions; add ½ of the clam juice and ½ of the tomatoes. Repeat this, starting with the potatoes and finishing with the tomatoes.

Fill with enough water to cover the whole mixture and place over medium heat. Simmer very gently, just at the boiling point, for 2 hours. Then add the 2 cans of minced clams, including the juice, and stir. Taste and add some salt and freshly ground pepper if desired. Serve with additional crackers.

PUREE OF LIMA BEAN SOUP (p. 81)

INGREDIENTS FOR 8:

1 pound fresh lima beans
    or 1 pound frozen-fresh
    lima beans
	1 10½-ounce can beef broth
	    or beef consomme

1 teaspoon salt	3 cups water
1 10½-ounce can chicken broth	2 ounces butter Croutons (optional)

METHOD: Bring the 3 cups of water with the salt to a boil. As soon as the liquid is boiling, add the lima beans. If the lima beans are fresh, cover and cook over medium heat for approximately 25 minutes; if frozen lima beans are used, follow package instructions. After cooking, drain and discard liquid, and press the beans through a food mill, or blend in small amounts in an electric blender, adding the butter. Return to the pot and stir in the consomme or beef broth, and the chicken broth. Bring to a boil again, reduce the heat and let simmer for 30 minutes. Serve with croutons if desired. If you like a thicker puree of lima bean soup, add less water; if you like it creamy, reduce the amount of water by 1 cup, and just before serving stir in 1 cup half-and-half or cream.

HAND·BOOK

OF

PRACTICAL COOKERY

HAND-BOOK

OF

PRACTICAL COOKERY,

FOR

LADIES AND PROFESSIONAL COOKS.

CONTAINING

*THE WHOLE SCIENCE AND ART OF PREPARING
HUMAN FOOD.*

BY

PIERRE BLOT,

PROFESSOR OF GASTRONOMY, AND FOUNDER OF THE NEW YORK
COOKING ACADEMY.

"If ye be willing and obedient, ye shall eat the good of the land."

NEW YORK:

D. APPLETON AND COMPANY,

90, 92 & 94 GRAND STREET.

1869.

PREFACE.

Food is the most important of our wants; we cannot exist without it. The man who does not use his brain to select and prepare his food, is not above the brutes that take it in its raw state. It is to the physique what education is to the mind, coarse or refined. Good and well-prepared food beautifies the physique the same as a good and well-directed education beautifies the mind. A cook-book is like a book on chemistry, it cannot be used to any advantage if theory is not blended with practice. It must also be written according to the natural products and climate of the country in which it is to be used, and with a perfect knowledge of the properties of the different articles of food and condiments.

Like many other books, it is not the size that makes it practical; we could have made this one twice as large as it is, without having added a single receipt to it, by only having given separate ones for pieces of meat, birds, fishes, etc., that are of the same kind and prepared alike. All cook-books written by mere compilers, besides giving the same receipt several times, recommend the most absurd mixtures as being the best and of the " latest French style."

Although cookery has made more progress within two or three years, in this country as well as in Europe, than it had since 1830, and although all our receipts are complete, practical, wholesome, and in accordance with progress, still they are simple. Our aim has been to enable every housekeeper and professional cook, no matter how inexperienced they may be, to prepare any kind of food in the best and most wholesome way, with economy, celerity, and taste ; and also to serve a dinner in as orderly a manner as any steward can do.

We did not intend to make a book, such as that of CARÈME, which cannot be used at all except by cooks of very wealthy families, and with which one cannot make a dinner costing less than twenty dollars a head. Such a book is to housekeepers or plain cooks what a Latin dictionary is to a person of merely elementary education.

If we give so many different ways of preparing the same article of food, it is not with a view to complicate cookery, but people's taste is in food as in dress, differing not only in the selection of colors, but also in shape ; therefore, by our variety of dishes and our different styles of decorating them ; by the ease that they can be prepared in the cheapest as well as in the most costly way, we think we have met all wants and all tastes. The wealthy, as well as those in limited circumstances, can use our receipts with the same advantage.

Our division of cookery and the system of arranging *bills of fare*, contained in these pages, solve that great and perplexing question, especially for ladies, how to arrange a bill of fare for every season, to suit any number of guests, at a greater or less expense, as they may desire. Every one knows that money alone cannot make good dishes; however good the raw materials may be, they require proper preparations before being palatable and wholesome.

TO HOUSEKEEPERS AND COOKS.

A cook-book cannot be used like a dictionary; a receipt is like a rule of grammar: to comprehend it thoroughly, it is indispensable to understand others. The author, therefore, earnestly recommends to his readers to begin by perusing carefully the directions, etc., at the beginning of the book, and also the explanations given on and heading the different articles of food, before attempting the preparation of a dish for the first time. They will thus soon be able to prepare any dish by merely reading the receipt. If all the explanations necessary were given at every receipt, this work would have filled more than ten volumes like the present.

We are aware that the study of cookery is as uninviting and dry as the study of grammar at first; so is the study of every science and even art; but it becomes comparatively easy and interesting after a while. Mere flourish in a receipt would have the same effect as in a rule of grammar.

TO COOKS.

We think the following friendly recommendations will not be out of place here. They are in the interest of both the housekeeper and the cook:

Make use of every thing good.

Waste nothing, however little it may be.

Have no prejudices.

Be careful, clean, and punctual.

Always bear in mind that routine is the greatest enemy of progress, and that you have agreed to faithfully perform your daily duties for a certain consideration.

PIERRE BLOT.

NEW YORK, *August*, 1867.

CONTENTS.

————•••————

CONTENTS.

COOKING.

THE science and art of cooking may be divided into ten principal parts; the rest is all fancy. These ten parts are : BAKING, BOILING, BROILING, FRYING, MIXING, ROASTING, SAUTÉING, SEASONING, SIMMERING, and STEWING.

Tasting is an adjunct to all.

Baking.—In baking, see that the furnace or oven be properly heated; some dishes require more heat than others. Look at the object in process of baking from time to time, and especially at the beginning, turn it round if necessary, in case it be heated more on one side than on the other, to prevent burning.

In baking meat and fish, besides keeping the bottom of the pan covered with broth or water, place a piece of buttered paper over the object in the pan; it not only prevents it from burning, but acts as a self-basting operation, and keeps the top moist and juicy.

If the top of cakes bake faster than the rest, place a piece of paper on it.

In most of our receipts, we give the degree of heat necessary to bake the different objects; it will, no doubt, be found valuable information.

Boiling.—This is the most abused branch in cooking; we know that many good-meaning housewives and even

1*

professional cooks boil things that ought to be prepared otherwise, with a view to economy; but a great many do it through laziness. Boiling requires as much care as any other branch, but they do not think so, and therefore indulge in it.

Another abuse is to boil fast instead of slowly. Set a small ocean of water on a brisk fire and boil something in it as fast as you can, you make much steam but do not cook faster; the degree of heat being the same as if you were boiling slowly.

If the object you boil, and especially boil fast, contains any flavor, you evaporate it, and cannot bring it back.

Many things are spoiled or partly destroyed by boiling, such as meat, coffee, etc.

Water that has been boiled is inferior for cooking purposes, its gases and alkali being evaporated.

Broiling.—Whatever you broil, grease the bars of the gridiron first.

Broiling and roasting is the same thing; the object in process of cooking by either must be exposed to the heat on one side, and the other side to the air.

Bear in mind that no one can broil or roast in an oven, whatever be its construction, its process of heating, or its kind of heat. An object cooked in an oven is baked.

It is better to broil before than over the fire. In broiling before the fire, all the juice can be saved.

In broiling by gas, there is a great advantage. The meat is placed under the heat, and as the heat draws the juice of the meat, the consequence is, that the juice being attracted upward, it is retained in the meat.

A gas broiler is a square, flat drum, perforated on one side and placed over a frame.

Broiling on live coals or on cinders without a gridiron is certainly not better than with one, as believed by many; on the contrary, besides not being very clean, it burns or chars part of the meat.

That belief comes from the fact that when they partook of meat prepared that way, it was with a sauce that generally accompanies hunters, fishermen, etc.,—*hunger*—the most savory of all savory sauces.

Frying.—That part of cooking is not as difficult as it is generally believed, and properly fried objects are good and do not taste greasy.

To fry requires care, and nothing fried will taste greasy if it has been dropped in fat properly heated and in enough of it to immerse the object.

When an object tastes greasy, it is not because it has been fried in grease, but because there was not enough of it, or because it was not properly heated; for, if heated enough it closes the pores of the object and carbonizes the exterior, so that it cannot absorb any.

Directions for Frying.—Prepare what you intend to fry according to the directions given in the different receipts.

Have fat, lard, or oil in a pan, enough to immerse the object or objects intended to be fried.

When the fat is hot enough (see below), place the object in a kind of wire basket made for that purpose, which drop in the fat and take off when the object is fried. It is handy, and there is no danger of breaking the object in taking it off.

There are objects that require to be stirred or turned over while frying.

Every time you fry any thing, take the fat from the fire, let it stand in a cool place for about five minutes, then turn it gently into a stone jar or pot through a strainer; let cool and put away. In turning the fat, lard, or oil into the jar, pour so that the dregs will be kept in the pan.

To ascertain with accuracy when the fat, lard, or oil is hot enough to lay the things in the pan, dip a fork in cold water, the prongs only, so as to retain but one or two drops of water, which drops you let fall in the fat, and if it crackles, it is hot enough.

Another way is, when jets of smoke come out of the fat.

There are objects that require more heat than others, some that are more sightly when brown, and others when of a pale-yellow hue.

If the object is desired brown, leave the pan on a brisk fire while it is frying; if otherwise, remove it to a slow or less brisk fire.

Fat is not like water, which, no matter how fast you boil it, you cannot augment the degree of heat, while you can that of fat. If water, by boiling it fast, could be heated as much as fat, it would be used to fry in its stead, being cheaper.

Mixing.—In mixing, pay due attention to the quantities we give in the receipts; but as everybody has not the same taste, it is very easy to augment or diminish the quantity of salt, pepper, sugar, butter, etc., so as to suit one's own taste.

When the quantity is left to the judgment or taste of the cook, that is, when the expression *about so much* is made use of, it is not necessary then to have the exact quantity; a. little more or a little less cannot spoil or partly destroy the dish.

Roasting.—When an object is placed on the spit according to directions, remember that it cannot be basted too often.

The time necessary for roasting a piece of meat or any thing else, depends as much upon the fire as upon the nature of the meat. Meat especially requires to be placed very near the fire at first, and then put back by degrees.

There is nearly as much difference between roasted and baked meat as there is between broiled and fried meat.

It is generally admitted here, that English roast-beef is so superior to American roast-beef that it cannot be compared to it. It is not in the quality of the meat that the difference lies, but in the process of cooking.

Meat cannot be roasted in an oven, be it in an ordinary or in a patented one.

That peculiar flavor in roasted meat is produced by the air coming constantly in contact with the heated meat while revolving on the spit.

Cold roasted meat, when desired to be served warm, is enveloped in buttered paper and placed on the spit just long enough to warm it.

Sautéing.—There is no word, that we know, in the English language, corresponding to the French word *sauté*. It differs from frying in this : that to fry any object requires fat enough to immerse that object; while to *sauté* it, requires just enough to prevent it from scorching.

Vegetables, omelets, etc., are *sautéd*, and not fried.

Meat or fish cooked in a frying-pan with a little butter or fat, is *sautéd*, and not fried ; but the term fried is most generally used, the other being only known to practitioners.

To *sauté* requires a brisk fire; the quicker an object is cooked by *sautéing* the better.

Seasoning.—This is the most difficult part in the science of cooking. To season is not difficult, but to season properly is quite another thing.

It is not only necessary to know well how to stew or roast a peace of meat or any thing else, but to know how to season it, to be able to judge what quantity and what kind of spices can be used to season such or such a dish, to what extent all the spices used agree together, and what taste and flavor they will give to the object with which they are cooked; for, if not properly used, they may just as likely destroy the taste and flavor of the object as improve it.

Some-dishes require high and much seasoning, others just the contrary. With a good fire and a good spit, it is not necessary to be a thorough cook to roast a piece well, but the cook is indispensable to mix the gravy or sauce with the proper seasonings.

Simmering.—Simmering differs from boiling only in the amount of heat allowed under the boiler, kettle, or pan. To simmer, is to boil as gently and slowly as possible.

Stewing.—To stew properly it is necessary to have a moderate fire and as even as possible. A brisk fire would cause much steam to evaporate, which steam is the flavor of the object stewed.

Tasting.—This is the most difficult, and at the same time the most delicate, part of seasoning; it is by tasting that we ascertain if we have seasoned properly.

In this only two of the senses are engaged, and one of those much more than the other.

A person may have good feeling, hearing, and sight, and for all that would not be fit for preparing the simplest dish; the senses of smelling and tasting are the ones most required, and without which no one can cook properly.

For these reasons we will take the liberty to recommend to housekeepers, when they have new cooks, to instruct them on their taste, and always let them know when they have seasoned too much or too little. To the cooks we will say, do not season according to your own taste, if the persons for whom you cook do not like it.

If the housekeeper would give his or her candid and frank opinion of the dishes to the cook, and if the latter be not stubborn, the best results might be obtained and both would be benefited by it. That ought to be done every day while making the bill of fare.

To taste a sauce, as well as to know if a thing is good to eat, we cannot trust either our eyes, fingers, or ears; we then have recourse, first to our smelling, and then to our tasting : so do most animals.

We always commence by smelling, and when that sense is satisfied as far as it is concerned, we then apply our tasting qualities; and if that last one is, in its turn, satisfied also, we proceed, that is, we masticate, if mastication is necessary, and then swallow.

DIRECTIONS, EXPLANATIONS, ETC.

ANISE.

ANISE comes from Egypt, and is used as a spice.

APRICOT.

This is a native of Armenia. It is served like plums and peaches; in salad, compote, etc.

BACON.

Never use smoked bacon or ham, except when especially directed. The smoky taste would spoil the dish.

BAIN-MARIE.

A bain-marie is a large vessel of hot or boiling water, in which saucepans, kettles, moulds, etc., are placed to prepare or warm food. It is also used to keep any kind of food warm, when something is ready to serve, and the time has not come; the utensil containing it is placed in hot water, and it not only keeps it warm, but there is almost no evaporation while in it. It does not boil away either.

There are things that are much more delicate when prepared or warmed in hot water.

One utensil made for that purpose, and of brass, with compartments, is more handy, but a large saucepan may be used in its stead.

When any thing is in the bain-marie, the water should

not be allowed to boil fast enough either to upset the pans or get into them.

BAKE-PANS.

A bake-pan for baking meat, fish, or any other object that requires liquor of any kind, must have borders in order to hold that liquor; but a bake-pan for cakes or any other object that does not require any liquor, or that does not turn liquid in baking, is better without borders—that is, a simple piece of sheet iron of a size to go easily in the oven.

BAY-LEAF.

This is known also under its French name *laurier*.

It is used as a spice; it is exceedingly cheap and is excellent to flavor sauces, gravies, etc.

It comes especially from Italy, where it is used to pack figs, oil, and different fruits.

BEETS.

The red beet is much used to decorate different dishes.

It is boiled, then pickled, cut in fancy shapes, either with a knife or with paste-cutters, and tastefully placed on or around the object it is used to decorate.

It is served as a *hors-d'œuvre*, pickled, and cut in slices.

To boil.—Set it on a good fire in a pan, covered with cold water, and boil gently till done.

The beet must not be touched at all with any thing rough, for if the skin or root is cut or broken, all the color goes away in boiling, it is not fit to decorate, and loses much of its quality.

When you buy beets, see that they are not bruised, and that the root is not broken.

BRAISING.

Braising, in cookery, means to cook any thing with fire under and upon the pan, kettle, or other utensil.

A good oven is by far more easy, and answers perfectly the purpose. An oven not only warms the under and upper parts of the utensil, but all around it also.

BUNCH OF SEASONINGS.

It is composed of parsley, thyme, bay-leaf, and cloves, and sometimes a clove of garlic is added. Place the sprigs of parsley in the left hand, rather spread, lay the others on and in the middle of the parsley, and envelop them in it as well as possible, then tie the whole with twine.

As all these seasonings are never served except when chopped, they are more easily taken out than if they were not tied together.

BUTTERED PAPER.

Dip in lukewarm butter a piece of white paper of the size you want, and envelop the piece to broil or roast with it. Tie the paper around with twine or coarse thread.

OILED PAPER. .

The only difference between oiled and buttered paper is, that it is dipped in sweet or olive oil instead of butter.

CATSUP.

Beware of what is sold under the name of catsups and pickles; many cases of dyspepsia, debility, and consumption come from using such stuff.

CAVIARE.

It is made with the rocs, hard and soft, of the sterlet.

It is imported from Russia, and is served as a *hors-d'œuvre*, with slices of lemon and toast.

CERVELAS, SAUCISSONS, ETC.

Cervelas, saucissons, as well as smoked sausages, are pork-butchers' preparations, cut slantwise in very thin slices, and served as *hors-d'œuvre*, with parsley in the middle of the dish.

CHEESE.

Cheese is the first plate of *dessert* to be partaken of. "A dinner without cheese is like a handsome lady with but one eye."—*Brillat-Savarin.*

"Cheese takes away all the taste that might be left from preceding dishes, and by that means prepares the palate for the appreciation of the good things, the delicate flavors of the dessert and wines."

COCHINEAL.

Cochineal, or carmine. Buy the cochineal in powder, prepared for cooking purposes, mix some (say the size of half a split pea) with a few drops of cold water and mix that again with what you wish to color. The quantity of cochineal is according to the quantity of mixture and also according to how deep the color is desired.

CHERVIL.

This comes from Italy, and is used in salad and as a spice.

COLANDER.

Besides the ordinary colander, it is necessary to have a fine one. We mean, by a fine colander, one with holes half the size of the ordinary ones, that is, just between the colander and strainer. A colander should not have holes on the sides; it is handier and more clean with holes at the bottom only.

CURRY.

We think that curry is very good and necessary on the borders of the Ganges River, and for that very reason we think also that it ought to be eschewed on the borders of the Hudson, Delaware, Ohio, and thereabouts.

We cannot describe curry better than by giving here the answer (*verbatim et literatim*) of a gentleman who has lived a few years in Java, to a question on the properties and qualities of curry. He said that he thought it good and even necessary to use some there on account of the climate, but every time he had eaten it he thought he was swallowing boiling alcohol or live coals.

DINING-ROOM.

It must be well ventilated and lighted. The best degree of temperature is about 66 degrees Fahr.

DISH.

A dish ought to be charming to the eye, flattering to the smell, and delicious to the taste.

DRAINING.

To drain, is to put in a colander any thing that has been soaked, washed, or boiled, etc., in water or any other liquid, in order to dry it, or at least to let drop from it the water or other liquid that may be in it.

Salads of greens, as a general thing, are drained after being washed, before putting them in the salad-dish; they must be drained as dry as posible, but without pressing on them, as it would wilt the leaves, and give the salad an unsightly appearance.

DUSTING.

A pan, after being buttered or greased, is dusted with flour, sugar, or even bread-crumbs, to prevent the mixture that is put in it from sticking. Sugar, etc., may also be sprinkled over dishes with a dredger.

DRINKING.

When weary, or cold, or warm, or exhausted, we drink in preference to eating, because we feel the effect instantaneously; while after eating even the most substantial food, we do not feel the effect for some time.

When exhausted and when immediate relief is necessary, the best drinks are broth, chocolate, milk, or water sweetened with sugar. It is more than a mistake to drink wines or liquors at such a time; it is really committing slow suicide.

When only thirsty, without exhaustion, we ought to drink cold water with a teaspoon. When thirsty and heated, the first thing to do is to dip the hands in cold water deep enough just to cover the wrists; then dip a towel in the water, lay it on the forehead, and then drink cold water with a teaspoon.

A few drops of vinegar or lemon-juice may be added to the water. If exceedingly hot, keep your hands in cold water and the towel on your forehead at least one minute before drinking.

HOT WEATHER.

A remark or two on eating and drinking in hot weather are always in season. Green vegetables, properly cooked, are certainly healthful in warm weather; but it is a mistake to think that meat should be excluded from summer diet. The hotter the weather, the more the system wastes, and therefore the more we must supply.

In order to keep the body in a healthful condition, meat ought to be eaten at least once a day in summertime. It would be well to vary this programme by taking one meal of fish on every other day.

Fat should be disused as much as possible. A very little good butter with your fresh radishes at breakfast is as much fat as is necessary.

COLD WEATHER.

Fat meat is good in winter and is relished; so are dry vegetables and saccharine substances.

FOOD.

Nature has provided man with a mind, in order that he should study what kind of food suits his constitution; he who does not do it, is not above the lower animals.

"Good things have been made by the Creator for good people, flowers have certainly not been made for brutes, either quadruped or biped."—*Jefferson.*

"It is from good things that, in a human point of view, we derive the strength necessary to our limbs, let us partake of the same and be thankful."—*Rev. — Chadband.*

Have your food selected and prepared according to constitution, occupation, climate, age, and sex.

Waste in females is greater than in males.

Animals, generally, are very careful in selecting their food.

A temporary bloatedness may be obtained, especially with the young, by eating much farinaceous food, such as pancakes, etc., but it does not last, and is sure to bring on disease or sickness, or both.

Man is omnivorous, and must be fed accordingly.

Extreme leanness comes from want of proper food, either in youth or old age.

It is not the amount that is eaten which nourishes, but the amount that is digested; an excess of food is as bad as a lack of it.

Good and well-baked bread is nutritious and healthful, while unbaked bread is heavy and difficult of digestion.

Take at least half an hour's rest after a hearty meal, for mind and stomach cannot work at the same time.

Never eat when angry, or tired, or when heated; but be as cool and as gay as possible, for food being exposed to a heat of about 100 degrees Fahr, in the stomach, would ferment instead of digesting.

Take a hearty but by no means heavy dinner.

Eat slowly, at regular hours, and masticate well, but do not bolt your food, or eat any thing that does not taste good.

Drink slowly, moderately, and always taste before swallowing.

Vary your food as much as possible.

Always have at least one dish of vegetables for dinner, besides meat, and also ripe fruit.

See that every thing you eat or drink is of a good quality, wholesome and properly prepared.

ECONOMY.

There is not a word so much misused in cooking as the word economy.

Prejudice comes for a large share in the use of it.

How many things are thrown away, or wasted by mere prejudice or ignorance!

It is often from economy that a woman washes meat, because some part of it does not look clean. Instead of washing it, do not buy it; or, if bought, cut off a thin slice and throw it away: it is more economical than washing the whole piece, which you partly destroy by the process.

It is with a view to economy, that an old, bad custom prevails of boiling coffee. What an economy of sending the best part of the coffee (the aroma) to the attic, and the rest to the dining-room. A bad drink can be made cheaper with many things than with coffee.

Tea is also boiled with an eye to economy.

EGG-BEATER.

We have tried five different kinds in Boston, before a large audience and on the demand of an inventor of one, but none could beat eggs as well as a common hand-beater. The whites of the eggs could not be raised with any of the others much more than half as much as with the common one; and besides, could not be beaten stiff.

Many persons do not succeed in making cakes of different preparations in which whites of eggs beaten to a stiff froth are used, because the eggs are not properly beaten.

Any tinsmith can make an egg-beater. It is generally made with tin-wire, but may be made with brass-wire.

With the cut below, as a model, it can be easily made.

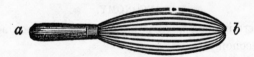

The handle *a* is of tin, into which the tin wires *b* are fastened and soldered.

ERRORS IN COOKING.

Ignorance produces abuse or error, or both. Blissful ignorance may be a fine thing in some cases, but either in preparing or partaking of food, it is certainly more than an abuse, it is a dangerous error.

It is by ignorance or disease that man abuses wine or any other liquor.

It is by ignorance or prejudice that many eschew the best and most healthful of condiments, such as garlics, onions, etc. They dislike them on account of their pungent taste when raw, not knowing that when cooked it is all evaporated. Their pungent taste comes from the volatile oil they contain, and which evaporates in cooking; it cannot be retained, but their sugar is retained, and gives such a good flavor to gravies and sauces.

FENNEL.

This is said to be a native of the Canary Islands; it has a very strong taste, and is used as a spice, especially in blood pudding. The Romans used a great deal of it.

FIG.

The fig-tree comes from Mesopotamia. Figs are generally served as *hors-d'œuvre*, or used in puddings, etc.

FINES HERBES.

Parsley and cives chopped fine, and used for omelets, or with cold meat, sauces, etc., are called thus.

FLOUR.

In cooking, new flour is not as good as old; it does not thicken as well and as fast.

FOIES GRAS.

Foies, or *pâtés de foies gras* are made with geese-livers, fresh fat pork, truffles, ham, *fines herbes*, and spices.

They are always served cold as a *relevé* or *entrée*, but most generally they are used for lunch or supper.

FRUIT-CORER.

There are many sizes in the set, to core from a pine-apple to a cherry.

GALANTINE.

The word galantine means a *boned bird*, or a boned shoulder of veal.

GLAZING.

Glazing is generally done by means of a brush or with feathers. A beaten egg, or syrup, or jelly, or egg and sugar, etc., are used to glaze cakes, etc. It is done by dipping the brush into the egg or jelly, and by spreading it on the cake or other object before baking or before serving, as directed in the different receipts. It is also done by sifting powdered sugar on cakes which are put back in the oven for a short time—that is, the time necessary to melt the sugar.

INDIGESTION.

A cup of tea and camomile, half of each, with a few drops of orange-flower water, and the whole well sweetened and taken warm, is very good after having eaten something difficult to digest.

ITALIAN PASTES.

Macaroni, vermicelli, and the like dry pastes, are called Italian pastes, whatever the shape—round, oval, or star-like.

ISINGLASS.

It is sometimes used instead of gelatine to make jellies.

JELLY-BAG.

Make a conical bag of good white flannel, about twenty inches long, fifteen inches broad at one end when spread on a flat surface, or about thirty inches in circumference, the other end being the point. Sew to it four pieces of white tape at the large end, and at equal distances, so that two sticks may be run into them. The sticks are placed on chairs or something else, in order to have the point of the bag about one foot from the floor. It is then ready to pass the jellies through it.

KITCHEN UTENSILS.

Gastronomists use, in preference to any thing else, crockery or earthen pans; or, for want of these, block-tin pans.

Copper is, in the end, the cheapest of all; but American cooks do not like them because they require too much care and must be examined every day; to prevent any accident, it is necessary to keep the inside properly lined.

Many indispositions are caused by food prepared in copper not properly lined; even food allowed to cool in a well-lined pan would be dangerous.

Pans lined with porcelain are excellent, but the trouble with them is, that they crack, and after that cannot be cleaned; something will always remain between the lining and the iron, and spoil every thing cooked in them.

The tin-lined are preferable, on account of being easily cleaned by means of a small birch-broom, washing-soda, and boiling water.

LAIT DE POULE.

Mix well in a tumbler a yolk of egg and a teaspoonful of sugar; then add a few drops of orange-flower water (*eau de fleur d'oranger*); pour boiling water on the whole, little by little, stirring the while, and drink warm.

The quantity of water is according to taste.

A gill of water to a yolk of egg makes it thick enough.

It makes an excellent drink, to be taken just before retiring, for persons with cough.

LARD.

Never buy lard ready made if you can help it, but take hog's fat, the part enveloping the kidneys, or leaf lard, and chop it fine, put it in a cast-iron or crockery kettle with a bay-leaf and a stalk of thyme to every two pounds of fat; set on a moderate fire, and as soon as it begins to melt, take the melted part out with a ladle, and put it in a stone jar or pot; be careful not to take any pieces of fat not yet melted. Continue that process till it is all melted.

The dry or hard part that remains at the bottom of the kettle when done is no good.

Lard made thus is as white as snow, and may be kept a long time.

When there is water in lard, it flies all over the fire; in that case, boil it a few minutes with a cover on the pan, and then use.

FAT FOR FRYING.

Take beef suet, the part around the kidneys, or any kind of fat, raw or cooked; remove as much as possible fibres, nerves, thin skin, or bones; chop it fine, put it in a cast-iron or crockery kettle; add to it the fat you may have skimmed from the top of broth, sauces or, gravies· Set the pan on a moderate fire; boil gently for about fifteen minutes, skim it well during the process; take from the fire, let it stand about five minutes, and then strain.

Put it in a stone jar or pot, and keep it in a dry and cool place. Cover the jar when perfectly cold.

It is as good as lard and more handy; it does not fly over the pan like lard.

A careful cook seldom buys fat; generally there is enough coming from skimming of broth, sauces, and gravies, for every purpose.

TO CLARIFY FAT.

Set the fat on a moderate fire in a pan, and as soon as it commences to boil, place a slice of bread dried in the oven in it, boil gently for about half an hour; take from the fire, let it settle for a few minutes; remove the bread, turn gently into a jar or pot, leaving the dregs in the pan.

Chicken, Turkey, and Goose Fat.—The fat of the above birds is never used to fry, but to *sauté* instead of butter. To make omelets it is excellent; an omelet is whiter and more sightly made with chicken-fat than when made with butter. It is clarified as directed above.

GAME-FAT.

Game-fat can be used instead of other fat and also instead of butter, to *sauté*, or what is generally called partly fry, game; it may also be used, instead of butter to bake game

It must be clarified longer than other fat, but in the same way.

The boiling of fat with water, as indicated in some cook-books, is only a fancy and extra work, it has no effect whatever on the fat. It is the same by keeping it for hours in a *bain-marie;* it does not change it in the least.

BATTER FOR FRYING.

For frying Vegetables.—Put three tablespoonfuls of flour in a bowl with two yolks of eggs, and cold water enough to make a kind of thin paste, then add salt and half a teaspoonful of sweet oil; mix well. Beat the two whites of the eggs to a stiff froth and mix them with the rest. Put the batter away in a cold place for at least two hours, and use.

It must not be put away longer than for half a day.

Another.—Proceed as above in every particular, except that you use milk instead of water.

For frying Fish.—Make it exactly as the above, except that you do not use any oil.

For frying Fritters.—Mix well together in a bowl three tablespoonfuls of flour with two yolks of eggs and cold water enough to make a thin paste; add a pinch of sugar, rum or brandy, or any other liquor, according to taste, from one to three or four tablespoonfuls, mix well again, and put away for at least two or three hours, but not longer than twelve hours.

Eggs and Crumbs for frying.—The eggs are beaten as for omelets, with a little salt. The objects to be fried are dipped in the eggs first, then rolled in bread-crumbs and fried.

Another.—When rolled in bread-crumbs as above; dip again in the eggs, roll again in bread-crumbs and fry.

Another.—Dip the object in melted butter, then in eggs, and roll in bread-crumbs; fry.

LARDING.

All pork-butchers sell salt pork for larding. Cut it in slices and then by cutting the slices across it makes square strips or fillets.

The strips must be of a proper size to be easily inserted into the larding-needle, and are about two inches and a half long.

When the needle is run half way through the meat, insert the salt pork into it, pull the needle off and leave the salt pork inside of the meat, both ends of it sticking out.

If it were running through, that is, if the salt pork were pulled off with the needle, most likely the strips are too small; then pull slowly, and when the salt pork is far enough into the meat, press on it with the finger and pull the needle, it will then stay in its proper place. It is better to cut a few strips first and try if they are of a proper size.

If, in pulling off the needle, the salt pork does not enter the meat, the strips are too large.

If the strips are of a proper size and break while pulling the needle off, then the pork is not good.

Fricandeau, sweetbreads, birds, etc., are larded in the same way.

For beef *à la mode,* it is described in the receipt.

LARDING-NEEDLE.

The best are made of brass. Those that are sold for steel are generally of iron, and break easily.

Those for beef *à la mode* are of steel, and must be flat near the point, in order to cut the meat.

LEAVEN.

Knead four ounces of flour with baker's yeast, enough to make a rather thick dough; give it the shape of a rather flat apple; with a sharp knife make two cuts on the top and across, and through about one-third of the paste; put the paste in a pan of lukewarm water. In a few minutes it will float; take it off and use then after it has floated about two minutes.

MEAT.

The time it takes to cook meat depends as much on the quality of the meat as on the fire. Some persons like meat more done than others; in many cases you must consult your own taste or that of your guests.

Beef, lamb, mutton, and game, may be eaten rather underdone, according to taste; domestic fowls must be properly cooked; but pork and veal must always be overdone, or else it is very unwholesome, if not dangerous.

The following table may be used as a guide:

Bear and Buffalo,.......................a five-pound piece,...		5 to 7 hrs.
Wild Boar and Woodchuck,............. Do. do.		.. 3 to 4 hrs.
Beef,.................................... Do. do.		.. 1 hr. 30 m.
Do...a ten pound piece,...		2 hrs. 30 m.
Capon,....................................a large one,..........		1 hour.
Chicken,..................................a middling-sized one, 45 min.		
Duck,.....................................a large one,..........45 min.		
Do...a small one,..........30 min.		
Goose, ...a large one,..........		2 hours.
Do ....a small one,..........		1 hr. 30 m.
Grouse, Heathcock, Snipe, and W'dcock, a fat one,.............30 min.		
Do do. do. do....a lean one,...........20 min.		
Guinea Fowl, ...,... ......a middling-sized one, 1 hour.		
Hare,....... ....an old one,..........		1 hr. 30 m.
Do........................... ....a young one,..........about 1 hr.		
Lamb and Kid,...................... ...a large quarter,.......		1 hour.
Do. do....................... ...a small one,..........45 min.		
Mutton,................................a four-pound piece,...		1 hour.
Do..a six " " ..		1 hr. 30 m.
Partridge, Pheasant, and Prairie-Hen,....a middling-sized one, 30 to 45 m.		
Pigeon,............................. .. .. one,. ....30 min.		

Pork,................................a two-pound piece,... 1 hr. 15 m.
Do.............................a four "   "   .. 2 hours.
Quail,................................one,.................20 min.
Sucking-Pig,...........................a large one,.......... 2 hrs. 30 m.
Do.   do............................a small one,.......... 2 hours.
Rabbit,................................a middling-sized one, 30 to 45 min.
Robin, Blackbird, Fig-pecker, High-
    holder, Lapwing, Meadow Lark,
    Plover, Reed-bird, Thrush, Yellow-
    bird, and other small birds,...........................15 to 20 min.
Turkey,..............................a large one,.......... 1 hr. 30 m.
Do..... ....a small one,.......... about 1 hour.
Veal,.............. ....a two-pound piece,.. 1 hr. 15 m.
Venison,..............................a four "   "   .. about 1 hour.

The following table may be used as a guide to know
how long meat may be kept, in a cool, dry, and dark
place ; and protected from flies or other insects :

	In Summer.	In Winter.
Bear and Buffalo,............................	3 to 4 days.	10 to 15 days.
Wild Boar and Woodchuck,.................	3 to 4 "	8 to 10 "
Beef and Pork,..............................	2 to 4 "	6 to 10 "
Capon,.....................................	2 to 3 "	4 to 8 "
Chicken, old one,...........................	3 to 4 "	4 to 10 "
Do. young one,...................	1 to 2 "	2 to 6 "
Deer, Partridge, Pheasant, Prairie-Hen, Quail, Guinea-Fowl, and Turkey,..............	2 to 3 "	6 to 10 "
Duck and Goose,............................	3 to 4 "	4 to 8 "
Hare and Rabbit,............................	2 to 3 "	4 to 8 "
Grouse, Heathcock, Snipe, and Woodcock,..	3 to 4 "	8 to 15 "
Lamb, Kid, Sucking Pig, and Veal,..........	2 to 3 "	3 to 6 "
Mutton,....................................	2 to 3 "	6 to 10 "
Pigeons, Blackbirds, Fig-peckers, High-holders, Lapwings, Meadow Larks, Plovers, Reed-birds, Robins, Thrushes, Yellow-birds, and other small birds,....2 to 3 "		6 to 10 "

The time must be reduced one-half in summer, in
stormy or damp weather, and one-third in winter, in
thawing or rainy weather.

Fish.—When cleaned and prepared as directed, place it
in a crockery stewpan, cover it with cold water, add a little salt, two or three sprigs of thyme, and one or two bay-
leaves. It will keep thus for some time.

2*

MOULDS.

Mould for Meat Pies.—A mould for meat pies may be round or oval; it must be in two pieces, fastened together by a kind of hinge. When the pie is baked, the wire pin holding the mould is pulled, and the mould removed.

Mould for Pies, Jellies, etc.—This mould may be used for any thing that requires a mould; it may also be round, oval, or of any other shape.

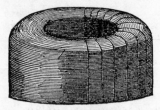

OLIVES.

Fresh and ripe they are served as dessert with other fruit. Preserved, they are served as a *hors-d'œuvre*, and used to flavor and decorate different dishes.

Olives as well as sardines are healthful and considered one of the best *hors-d'œuvre*.

OSMAZOME.

Osmazome is found in beef, mutton, full-grown domestic fowls, venison, and game; in the latter, when the bird or animal is adult.

In meat soup, the osmazome is the soluble part of the meat that dissolves in boiling, and makes nutritious broth.

In broiled or roasted pieces, it is that part which makes a kind of brown crust on the surface of the meat, and also the brownish part of the gravy.

Chicken, lamb, sucking-pig, veal, etc., do not contain any osmazome.

PARSLEY, CHERVIL, THYME, CELERY, SAGE, ETC.,—FOR WINTER USE.

Hang in the shade, under a shed, or in a garret, and in a clean and dry place, some small bunches of parsley, chervil, celery, etc., the roots upward; leave them thus till perfectly dry, then place them in your spice-box for winter use.

The best time for drying them is at the end of October or the beginning of November; dig them up in fine and dry weather, so as to have them clean without washing.

Soak in cold water half an hour before using.

WHITE PEPPER.

This is black pepper decorticated.

Put peppercorns in a bowl, cover with cold water, and leave thus till the skin is tender; then drain. Take the skin off, let it dry, grind it; place with your other spices, and use where directed. It takes many days for the skin to become tender.

QUALITY OF MEAT, FISH, VEGETABLES, FRUIT, ETC.

The quality of meat depends entirely on the quality of food with which the animal has been fed.

For fish, the taste or quality is according to the kind of water in which they have lived; fish from a muddy pond smell of mud, while fish from a clear brook are delicious.

The same difference exists in vegetables and fruit; their quality is according to the quality or nature of the ground in which they have been grown.

PASTRY-BAG.

A bag for pastry is made with thick, strong linen; of a conical shape, about one foot long, eight inches broad at one end when spread on a flat surface, and which makes about sixteen inches in circumference, and only one inch and a quarter at the other end, and in which latter end a tin tube is placed, so that the smaller end of the tin tube will come out of the smaller end of the bag. Putting then some mixture into the bag and by pressing from the upper end downward, the mixture will come out of the tin tube.

RAW MATERIALS.

If American cookery is inferior to any other generally, it is not on account of a want of the first two requisites—raw materials and money to buy them; so there is no excuse for it, both are given to the cooks.

Here, where markets rival the best markets of Europe and even surpass them in abundance, it is really a pity to live as many do live.

SCALLOPED KNIFE.

This knife is used to cut beets, carrots, turnip-rooted celery, potatoes, radishes, and turnips; in slices, round, oblong, or of any other shape; either to decorate dishes, or to be served alone or with something else, or to be fried.

The annexed cuts will give an idea of what can be done

with it. It is understood that the vegetables are peeled
first.

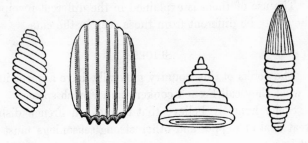

SHALLOTS.

Shallots come from Syria. Shallot is stronger than
garlic and onion; a real Tartar sauce cannot be made without shallot. The small, green onion is a good substitute
for it.

SKEWERS.

The cuts below are skewers. The common ones are
used to fasten pieces of meat together; to roast or bake
small birds, liver in *brochette*, etc., etc.

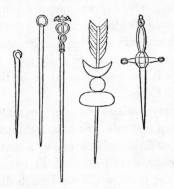

Those to decorate are only used with different flowers
or vegetables, and stuck inside of different pieces of meat

as a decoration. They are removed just before carving.

The use of them is explained in the different receipts. They may be different from those seen in the cuts.

SPICES.

The cooks of this country generally have a queer idea of what they call French cookery and French spices.

Some honestly believe that to make a French dish a great deal of pepper and other strong seasonings must be put in.

Many other persons, who have not been in Europe, really believe also, that French cookery is what is called highly-seasoned. There never was a greater mistake.

If French cooks use several kinds of spices, and may-be more than American cooks, they are not the same; or if some are the same, such as pepper, they use them in much smaller proportions.

They generally use thyme, parsley, bay-leaf, chervil, tarragon, etc., which are aromatic; but never use (in this climate) ginger, curry, cayenne pepper, pimento, catsups, variegated colored pickles made with pyroligneous acids, etc., and which are very exciting and irritating.

Some of our readers may naturally ask: How is it that French cookery is believed by many to be the contrary of what it really is?

Because every eating-house, of no matter what size, pretends to be a first-rate one or a fashionable one—and to be first-rate or fashionable must, as a matter of course, have French cooks, or at least cook French dishes.

You enter the place, ask for a French dish; or, ask if you can have such a dish, *à la Française?*

You are politely and emphatically answered in the affirmative; and very often the polite waiter says that a French cook presides in the kitchen.

Result!—the cook, be he from the Green Isle or of African descent, receiving the order to prepare a French dish, puts a handful of pepper in the already too much peppered, old-fashioned prepared dish, and sends it to the confident customer as a genuine French dish.

Said customer never asks a second time for a French dish, and pronounces French cookery to be—abominable!

STIRRING.

Never use any spoon but a wooden one to stir any thing on the fire or in a warm state.

STRAINING.

To strain, is to pass a sauce or any thing else through a sieve, a strainer, or a piece of cloth, in order to have it freed from particles of every kind.

Broth is strained to make soup, so as to remove the small pieces of bones that may be in it, etc.

SUGAR.

Sugar plays a very important part in cooking. It is added to cereals, vegetables, and fruit, many of which would almost be unpalatable without it, and which are rendered not only palatable but wholesome by its action.

It is the sugar of the carrot and that of the onion, or of the garlic, that gives such a peculiar and delicious flavor to gravies and sauces, to beef *à la mode, fricandeau*, etc.

Pulverized.—When pulverized or powdered sugar can be had pure, it saves the trouble to do it; but often there are foreign matters in it and therefore it is better to make it; you know then what you have.

Break loaf sugar into small lumps, pound it and sift it. With a fine sieve, you can make it as fine as you please.

It was not used in Europe until about the middle of the seventeenth century.

For the cooking of sugar, see PRESERVES.

TARRAGON.

The French name of tarragon is *estragon*. It is excellent in vinegar and in many fish sauces. It is aromatic, sudorific, and stomachic, and grows very well in this country. It grows at least twice as large here as in Europe.

TIN TUBES.

These tubes are put in the pastry-bag, at the smaller end of it, to make *meringues*, ladies' fingers, etc.; they are of tin, and can be made by any tinsmith.

They have the shape of a trapezoid or frustum. Two are enough for any purpose.

No. 1. One inch and a half long; one inch and three-eighths in diameter at one end, and nine-sixteenths of an inch at the other end.

No. 2. One inch and a half long; one inch and a half in diameter at one end, and six-eighths of an inch at the other.

TRUFFLES.

Truffles are found in Europe and Africa, where they were first discovered.

The truffle is neither an animal nor a vegetable, although it has been classed among the fungi, which has root, and the truffle has neither root nor stem.

The truffle is used for stuffing and flavoring only otherwise it is not of much value. On account of their scarcity, and the difficulty in finding them, they are rather costly.

We think truffles may be compared to lace—both are dear, and neither has an intrinsic value.

VANILLA

Is a native of America, extensively used for seasoning creams, pastry, etc., to which it gives a delicious flavor.

Although a native of America, all the extracts of vanilla, as well as others, were formerly imported; but within a few years Americans have found out that they are able to distil also, and "Burnett's Extract of Vanilla" is better known to-day all over the country than any other.

VEGETABLE SPOONS.

Vegetable spoons are used to cut potatoes, carrots, and turnips; there are different shapes, round, oval, carrot-shape, plain, and scalloped. We give here only two, being sufficient to explain their use.

The first (*a*) is of an oval shape, and makes the cut *c*; the second (*b*) is round, and makes the cut *d*.

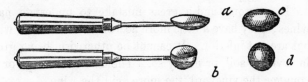

When the vegetable is peeled, place the spoon on it, the convex side up; holding the vegetable in your left hand, press on the spoon with your left thumb, and in order to cause it to cut the vegetable while turning it with the right hand, first half way or rather when the half of it is inside of the vegetable, stop, turn it the other way, causing it to cut the vegetable also, then raise it up without turning at all and you have in the spoon a piece of vegetable of the shape of the spoon, and as seen in the cuts.

WATER.

Rain-water is for cooking purposes, as for other purposes, the best, but is seldom used, especially in large cities, where it is difficult to procure it. Another difficulty is, when procured it soon gets foul.

The next best is river-water, or water from lakes.

By boiling, water evaporates its gases and alkali, and is inferior afterward for cooking purposes, especially for boiling vegetables; therefore, we earnestly recommend to use the water at the first boiling.

When foul water has to be used for want of other, if no filter, charcoal, sand, or paper can be had to filter it, it will improve by boiling it and then exposing it to the air for some time.

WINES.

Native wines, when pure, are just as good as any other for cooking purposes.

It is wrong and a great mistake to underrate native wines; they have a little more acerbity than foreign wines, but are not inferior. It cannot be otherwise, being grown in a virgin soil, or nearly so. The richer the soil or the younger the vineyard, the more acid the wine.

Cold nights during the ripening of the fruit make the wine more acid, not ripening so perfectly.

Wine is a healthy drink, and many invalids would recover much quicker by a judicious use of it.

Different wines are used in cooking, and we give the names of the best ones in the different receipts.

A little vinegar may be used as a substitute for wine,

but it is very inferior, and in many dishes it cannot be used at all.

A few dollars spent during the year in wine for cooking purposes, makes much better and more wholesome dishes.

White wine contains little tannin; it retains nitrogenous matters, and is free from essential oils; hence the superior flavor and quality of brandy made with white wines.

It is more aperient and less nutritive than red wine.

Essential oils pass in red wine while it is fermenting.

Wine and sugar with certain fruits are excellent, and are known to neutralize the crudity of the fruit, such as straw-berries, pears, peaches, currants, etc.

MOTTO.

The motto of the New York Cooking Academy is—

Since we must eat to live, let us prepare our food in such a manner, that our physical, intellectual, and moral capacities may be extended as far as is designed by our CREATOR.

DIVERS RECEIPTS.

ALMONDS.

Two kinds are used in cooking, the sweet and the bitter.

They are shelled first, then by pouring boiling water on them and leaving them in it for two or three minutes, they are easily skinned.

They are sometimes used as soon as skinned, and sometimes dried after being skinned and just before using.

When wanted dried, place them in a pan in a slow oven with the door open, and turn them occasionally.

LEMONADE OR ORANGEADE.

Put two ounces of loaf sugar in a quart of water, also the rind of an orange or one of lemon. Half an hour after strain the whole, and press into it the juice of the orange, and a few drops of lemon-juice. If found too strong, add water and sugar. It is a very good drink in summer, or for evening parties. A little currant jelly may be added to make a variety.

LEMONADE WITH BARLEY.

To the above lemonade or orangeade you add, instead of water and sugar, some barley-water and sugar; it is very good and very refreshing.

Barley-water is made by soaking in lukewarm water a

pint of barley, drain it two or three minutes after; put the barley in a crockery pan, cover it with cold water (about three quarts), set it on the fire, and boil till the barley is perfectly cooked; skim off the scum during the cooking, drain, let cool, and use the water.

BARLEY SUGAR FOR CHILDREN.

Soak a quart of barley in lukewarm water for two or three minutes, and drain. Put the barley in a crockery stewpan, with four or five quarts of water, and set it on a good fire, boil till the barley is overdone, and then take from the fire, mash it as well as possible and strain, throwing away what there is in the strainer, and if the remainder does not make a kind of jelly when cool, the barley has not been boiled enough.

Mix that jelly with sugar and fry it; it is better than any other candy, barley being refreshing, and the principal substance of it.

BAVAROISE WITH CHOCOLATE.

Put in a tin pan a pint of milk, with one ounce of chocolate, and two of sugar; set it over the fire, but do not allow it to boil; stir well with a wooden spoon during the process, and when the whole is well mixed, serve warm in cups.

It is an excellent and wholesome drink in the evening.

The same with Coffee or Tea.—Proceed as above in every particular, except that you put in the pan a small cup of coffee or tea instead of chocolate, and a little more sugar.

BICHOF.

Put in a crockery tureen two bottles of white wine, with an orange and a lemon, both cut in slices; cover, and place it in a warm place for about ten hours; then strain into a vessel, and mix well with the liquor about a pound of loaf sugar, and a little grated cinnamon.

It may be served warm or cold.

Another way.—Melt a pound of loaf sugar in half a pint of cold water, and then mix with it two bottles of white wine, a pinch of grated cinnamon, the juice of an orange, and that of a lemon, and use. It takes only a few minutes to make it.

If found too strong, add water and sugar.

TO PRESERVE BIRDS.

Broil or roast, according to our directions, chickens, ducks, geese, turkeys, partridges, pheasants, prairie hens, quails, etc.; then carve them; take the bones out of the pieces, place them in a crockery pot, which you fill with melted butter or lard, and cover well when cold. Place the pot in a cool and dry place, and they will keep for months.

When you wish to eat them, take out the quantity you want, and place it in a frying-pan, with the butter or lard that is around; fry till warm, and serve.

BREAD-CRUMBS.

Put slices of stale bread in a slow oven till they are perfectly dried up. Break them in pieces and reduce them to coarse powder with a rolling pin; sift them, and they are ready for use.

Bread-crumbs are better than cracker-crumbs; the latter, when reduced to powder, are too floury, and besides, there is always stale bread enough in a kitchen to make crumbs.

The above crumbs are rather brown.

White crumbs.—Cut in rather large dice the soft part of stale bread, put the pieces in a new and coarse towel, rub between the hands so as to reduce the pieces of bread to crumbs; pass through a colander or through a sieve, according to need, coarse or fine, and use.

BURNT SUGAR.

Take an old tin ladle and place it over a sharp fire, with two ounces of loaf sugar in it; stir with a stick or skewer till it is thoroughly black and burnt. Then add, little by little, about one gill of water; stir a little, boil about four minutes, but not fast, lest it should boil over the ladle; strain, and it is made.

As soon as cold, bottle it and use when wanted.

It keeps any length of time.

It is used to color broth, sauces, gravies, etc.

It is called *caramel* in French.

COFFEE.

It is simple to make coffee. Of course, when properly made, with good berries, the liquor is good.

When good roasted coffee can be bought, it saves the trouble of roasting it, and is, or rather ought to be, cheaper than it can be done in a family.

If coffee is roasted a long time before being used it loses much of its aroma, therefore a family ought not to roast more than it can use in about a week, while twenty or twenty-five pounds can be roasted at one time and by one person.

Three or four different kinds, roasted separately, and properly mixed, make better coffee than one kind alone.

A good proportion is: to one pound of Java add about four ounces of Mocha, and four ounces of one or two other kinds.

Good coffee, as well as tea, is said to possess exhilarating properties.

Its use was not known in Europe before 1650. Neither was the use of sugar, tobacco, and brandy.

Good coffee cannot be made but by leaching.

The easiest utensil is what is called a filter, or coffee-pot, or biggin, according to locality, with a top to diffuse the water.

The coffee-pot called "the French balance" makes the best-flavored coffee, but it is an expensive one.

There are several good filters, but the great majority of the people find them too complicated for daily use.

The bottom of the filter should be of silvered brass-gauze instead of perforated tin, as it is generally.

Gauze-holes being much smaller than those of perforated tin, the coffee can be ground much finer, and therefore, all the strength and aroma can be had; while if ground coarse, it is utterly impossible.

Good coffee cannot be made in a utensil often but wrongly called a *coffee-pot*, which is nothing but a pot, and something like a tea-pot.

With such a utensil, the grounds must be boiled; and as no liquor can be boiled without allowing the steam to escape (the steam made by boiling coffee being its aroma), therefore the best part of the coffee is evaporated before it is served.

Never grind your coffee until ready to make it.

No matter how air-tight you keep it, the aroma evaporates or is absorbed.

Coffee can be ground and made as soon as cool; but it is better to let it stand for about twenty-four hours after being roasted.

If kept as air-tight as possible in a tin-box, it will keep very well for about a week.

Never buy ground coffee except when you cannot help it.

By taking a pinch of ground coffee and rolling it between wetted fingers, it will remain in grains, if pure; and will form in a ball if foreign matters are mixed with it.

TO ROAST.

In roasting, good coffee swells about thirty-three per cent., and loses about sixteen per cent. in weight.

Roast once a week or oftener.

Put coffee in the apparatus (cylinder, or drum, or roaster), the quantity to be according to the size of the roaster, or according to how much is needed. Have a rather slow fire at first; when the coffee has swollen, augment the fire, turning, shaking, tossing the roaster, some-

3

times fast, sometimes slowly, and take from the fire a little before it is roasted enough; the roasting will be finished before the coffee gets cold and before taking it from the roaster, which you continue turning and shaking as if it were yet on the fire.

A charcoal fire is the handiest, and more easily regulated.

It is well roasted when it evaporates a pleasing odor and when of a brownish color.

Then take it from the roaster, spread it on a matting or on a piece of cloth, and put it in a tin-box as soon as cold.

It is exceedingly difficult, if not utterly impossible, to roast coffee properly by machinery, and for two reasons: in the first place, there is too much of it in the cylinder to roast evenly, some berries are burned, others not roasted enough; the other is, that being turned by machinery, the cylinder is turned regularly and is neither shaken nor tossed; and even if there were not too much coffee in it, some berries would be much more roasted than others.

TO MAKE.

Set a kettle of cold water on the fire. Place the ground coffee in the filter, and as soon as the water begins to boil, pour just enough of it over the coffee to wet it. Put the kettle back on the fire, and again, at the first boiling, pour it over the coffee rather slowly, and till you have poured enough water to furnish the quantity of coffee required.

If the water does not pass through fast enough, just stop pouring for a few seconds, that is, long enough to put the kettle back on the fire and start the boiling again. As soon as the water has passed through, the coffee is made. The quantity of coffee must be according to the strength you wish it, and the quantity wanted, or according to age and constitution.

Four teaspoonfuls make a quart of very good coffee for breakfast. It would be rather strong for children, but can be diluted to a proper state with milk.

No matter what quantity of coffee is put in the filter, the liquor must be clear; the more is used, the blacker the substance is, but it must never be muddy. If muddy at all, be sure you have not used good coffee.

One pound of good coffee to a quart of water, should make black but clear coffee.

CAFÉ AU LAIT.

This is coffee and milk for breakfast. The milk is set on the fire in a tin saucepan, and taken off when it rises; then mixed with the coffee, either in the cup or any kind of vessel. The proportions are pint for pint.

CAFÉ NOIR.

Café noir is the name given to the coffee taken after dinner. It is generally made rather strong. Gentlemen sometimes put liquor in it—a glass of brandy, or rum, or kirschwasser; and ladies, a little cold milk.

Taken fifteen or twenty minutes after dinner, it helps digestion. It excites the faculties of the mind, and gives what physiologists call "agreeable sensations."

Coffee is nutritious, and to a certain extent prevents waste of the system.

CHOCOLATE.

The quantity of chocolate for a certain quantity of milk is according to taste. Two ounces of chocolate make a good cup of it, and rather thick.

Break the chocolate in pieces, put it in a tin saucepan with a tablespoonful of water to an ounce of chocolate, and set it on a rather slow fire. Stir now and then till thoroughly melted.

While the chocolate is melting, set the quantity of milk desired in another tin saucepan on the fire, and as soon as it rises and when the chocolate is melted, as directed above, turn the milk into the chocolate, little by little, beating well at the same time with an egg-beater. Keep beating and boiling after being mixed, for three or four minutes; take off and serve.

If both chocolate and milk are good, it will be frothy; and no better or more nutritious drink can be had.

CHOCA.

Choca is nothing more nor less than one cup of coffee and milk mixed with a cup of chocolate, and for breakfast.

COCOA.

Put in a tea or coffee cup one or two tablespoonfuls of ground cocoa, pour boiling water or boiling milk on it, little by little, stirring with a spoon the while; sweeten it to taste. A few drops of essence of vanilla may be added, according to taste.

ESSENCE OF SPINACH, OR GREEN ESSENCE.

Put two handfuls of very green and fresh spinach in a mortar and pound it well. Then put it in a saucepan, set on a rather slow fire, and when on the point of boiling take it off, pass it through a sieve and use. It may be kept for some time with a little sugar.

ESSENCE OF BEEF.

The essence of beef of commerce is well known.

To make essence of beef used in cooking and called *glace* in French, set three or four quarts of broth on a slow fire, in a saucepan and reduce it to jelly. Keep it simmering all the time; it may take twenty hours to reduce. When properly reduced, it is of a very dark-brown color and has a very pleasant odor.

When cold, it must be rather hard.

When essence of beef tastes like glue and has an unpleasant odor, it is not made properly, or with good beef.

If properly made, it will keep any length of time.

It is used to thicken sauces, to decorate boned birds, etc.; when in a hurry, it may be used to make soup, but, like every thing preserved, is of course inferior to fresh broth.

ICING.

Put about three tablespoonfuls of pulverized sugar in a bowl with the white of a small egg; and then mix and work well for at least five minutes with a piece of wood. When done it is perfectly white and rather thick.

Make a kind of funnel with thick, white paper; put the mixture in it, and by squeezing it out, you make decorations according to fancy, on cakes, charlotte russe, etc. You make the decorations of the size you please, by cutting the smaller end of the paper-funnel of the size you wish.

The mixture may also be spread on cakes with a knife, according to what kind of decoration is desired.

A charlotte russe may be decorated in the same way, with the same cream as that used to fill it.

MEAT JELLIES.

Put in a saucepan two ounces of gelatine with three eggs and shells, a tablespoonful of salt, the rind of half a lemon, a liquor-glass of rum or brandy, or a wine-glass of sherry, port, or madeira wine; mix well the whole. Add one quart of broth, twelve pepper-corns; beat the whole well with an egg-beater and set on a good fire; stir gently till it comes to a boil; then move it on a rather slow fire;

boil slowly for about eight minutes and turn into the jelly-bag. Have two bowls at hand to be used alternately; have one under the bag before turning the jelly into it; and when it has passed through the bag once, turn it into the bag again, putting the other bowl under; repeat this three or four times, and it will be perfectly clear. Just before turning into the bag the first time, a few drops of burnt sugar are added to give the jelly an amber color. Use the jelly immediately if wanted in liquid form, as to fill a meat-pie, etc., or put it on ice to congeal.

Boned-turkey Jelly.—As soon as the water in which you have boiled a boned turkey is cold, skim off the fat and strain it. Then proceed exactly as for meat jelly, except that you take one quart of the above instead of one quart of beef broth.

Boned-chicken Jelly.—Prepare the water in which the boned chicken has been cooked, the same as above; take a quart of it and proceed as for meat jelly for the rest.

For jelly to decorate any boned bird, the water in which it has been cooked may be used, as described above.

Calves'-feet Jelly.—Scald well four calves' feet, and split each in two lengthwise. Put them in a saucepan with about three pints of water, two onions, two cloves, two cloves of garlic, six sprigs of parsley, one of thyme, a stalk of celery if handy, salt, and half a dozen pepper-corns. Set on the fire, boil gently till well cooked. Serve the feet with a *poulette* or *vinaigrette*.

Strain the liquor; put in it two eggs with their shells, salt, rum or wine, as in meat jelly; beat the whole well with an egg-beater; set on a good fire, and finish like meat jelly.

Calf's-head Jelly.—Proceed as for the above in every particular, except that you use four eggs, having about twice as much liquor, therefore making twice as much jelly. A little gelatine may be added, if not found firm enough.

MEAT GRAVY.

When you are short of gravy, cut a little piece of veal, say half a pound of the breast or neck piece, or trimmings of veal-cutlets; set on the fire with about an ounce of butter, and half of a rather small carrot cut in slices; stir, and when the meat is turning rather brown, add two or three onions in slices also; stir again till the onions are nearly fried; when covered with broth or water, add salt, a dozen whole peppers, a bay-leaf, and two stalks of thyme; boil gently for two or three hours, and strain.

If it is boiling away, add water to fill up.

Trimmings of mutton, lamb, beef, chicken, or turkey, may be added to the veal.

In case of hurry, it may be done quickly and by boiling rather fast, but it is not as good, and there is less of it with the same quantity of meat.

For a grand dinner, the gravy may be made one or two and even three days in advance; then simmer it for five or six hours.

MELONS.

Musk-melons are always served as a *hors-d'œuvre*, but must be eaten immediately after soup, or the first thing of all if no soup is served.

It is a great mistake to serve melons as a dessert.

Water-melons, though eaten abundantly, are considered very unwholesome by the great majority of doctors, chemists, and physiologists.

Musk-melons are served in slices with sugar, or with salt and pepper, according to taste.

MEUNIÈRE.

Mix well together in a cup one teaspoonful of flour with a tablespoonful of cold water.

It is used to thicken sauces and different dishes.

MINT.

Put four sprigs of mint into a quart of brandy, cork well, or cover air-tight if in a pot, and leave thus forty-eight hours; then strain through a cloth. Put half a pound of loaf sugar in a stewpan with a pint of water, set it on the fire, and, at the first boiling, pour it into the quart of brandy; cover with a cloth, let it cool, and again strain the whole through a fine cloth. Bottle and cork carefully, and use when wanted.

A small liquor-glass of it is very good for stomach-ache; it is also useful after having eaten any thing difficult of digestion.

PANADE.

Break in pieces the soft part of a small stale loaf of bread; put it in a tin saucepan, cover it with cold water, and leave thus about an hour; then mash it well, set it on the fire, add salt, butter, and sugar, to taste; simmer about an hour, then add again two yolks of eggs beaten with two tablespoonfuls of cream or milk; mix the whole well together, and serve.

It makes an excellent food for infants.

PAP.

Put an ounce of butter in a tin saucepan, set it on the fire, and when melted, turn into it two tablespoonfuls of flour, thoroughly mixed with half a pint of milk; stir with a wooden spoon, boil gently for about twelve minutes, stirring the while; take off, turn into a bowl, add salt and sugar to taste, and use.

If wanted richer, an egg may be mixed with the flour and milk, or a yolk of egg may be added as soon as taken from the fire.

RAISINS.

When the stems of raisins or of currants are removed, put them in a bowl, dust them well with flour, move them round a little, then turn them into a sieve and shake them well. This process will remove the sand as well as washing them, and will not take away the sweetness.

SANDWICHES.

These are too well known to require any direction.

SAUSAGE-MEAT.

Butchers generally, with an eye to economy, make sausage-meat of bad or tainted pork.

We recommend our readers, as far as possible, never to buy sausage-meat ready made, but to make it themselves, or have it made according to their directions.

A chopping-machine costs very little, and saves a great deal of work, besides chopping much better than can be done by hand.

The proportions are: one pound of lean pork and one pound of lean veal, chopped very fine, well mixed, and both very fresh. Season with salt, pepper, nutmeg and clove grated, and with cinnamon, if liked.

A yolk of egg may be added to a pound of meat.

It may also be made with one pound of veal and half a pound or less of pork, or with veal only or pork only, according to taste.

3*

SOUSE.

Put three ounces of butter in a saucepan, and set it on the fire; when melted, add two carrots and two onions sliced, stir now and then till they begin to turn brown; then add about three pints of warm water, half a pint of vinegar, one clove of garlic, four sprigs of parsley, one of thyme, a clove, a bay-leaf, six pepper-corns, a little grated nutmeg, and salt. Simmer about an hour, strain, and it is ready for use.

Another.—Put two quarts of vinegar and about ten quarts of water in a stone or crockery vessel, with four cloves of garlic, a handful of parsley, six cloves, four stalks of thyme, four bay-leaves, half a nutmeg grated, three or four carrots, and three or four onions sliced, a little salt, and two dozen pepper-corns. Stir and mix the whole well, and it is ready for use.

Pieces of mutton, beef, pork, venison, and bear-meat, may be soaked in one of the above preparations from four to six days before cooking them. A piece of tough meat will be more tender and juicy after being soaked.

More or less may be made, according to the size of the piece of meat.

TEA.

There are many ways of making tea; we might say that every one makes it in his own way; but, after many experiments and much information, we have found the following to be the best:

Warm the teapot either by pouring boiling water in it and emptying it, or by placing it on a corner of the range.

Then put good tea in it (the quantity to be according to the strength and also to the quantity you want), and pour boiling water on the leaves, just enough to wet them; leave thus about one minute, then pour on all the water you want.

Let it steep no longer than about six minutes, and not less than four minutes, before drawing it.

If allowed to steep longer than six minutes, all the astringency of the tea is extracted, and it acts and has a bad effect on the nervous system, besides losing most of its aroma.

Chemists and physiologists generally recommend black tea, as not affecting the nervous system as much as green tea.

Tea being naturally very astringent, should never be served at breakfast.

Taken after dinner, instead of *café noir*, it has the same effect, and brandy may be mixed with it as in coffee.

Tea is excellent in damp climates and marshy countries, but it must be taken after a substantial meal.

Drinking warm tea while eating causes the food to pass through the system without nourishing it, or supplying its waste.

TOAST.

Cut several slices of bread of even size, and spread some anchovy-butter on them; cut anchovies in small strips, lengthwise, lay them on the bread also, and then spread over some hard-boiled egg chopped fine, and on it some parsley also chopped fine, finish with capers here and there.

Place the toast or slices of bread on a dish, tastefully arranged all around, a few sprigs of parsley in the middle, and you have a fine *hors-d'œuvre*.

Sardines, Dutch herrings, or red herrings may be used the same as anchovies.

WELSH RAREBIT.

This dish is not generally understood. It is thought by many to be Welsh rabbit, that is, a rabbit prepared *Welsh fashion.*

It is not a rabbit, but Welsh cheese (a certain kind only, and prepared for that purpose), melted to a certain degree, and then spread on toast of Welsh bread.

Grate some Gloucester or Gruyère cheese and pepper it with Cayenne pepper. Fry some slices of bread with a little butter, but on one side only, until perfectly yellow, then spread a thick coat of grated cheese on the fried side of the bread, place the slices in a baking-pan, put them in a pretty warm oven, take off when it begins to melt, and serve warm.

Then you have as good a Welsh rarebit as can be made here. The receipt was given to us by an English lady.

POTAGES OR SOUPS.

POTAGE is the modern word for soup, and is used in bills of fare everywhere.

Three kinds of liquor are used to make potages: broth, milk, and water.

Besides the liquor, meat, fish, and vegetables are used.

The richest potages are made with *consommé* and some other compounds; such as bread, Italian pastes, vegetables, etc.

Consommé means rich broth; literally, it means consumed, perfect, that is, properly reduced and partly consumed, as it is the case in making it. *Consommé* is broth reduced to a certain point, according to want or taste.

Broth.—Broth is to good cooking what wheat is to bread. Dishes (with some exceptions) prepared without broth are, to those prepared with it, what rye or corn bread is to wheat bread. Broth, and especially *consommé*, are to old age what milk is to the infant. Broth is called *bouillon* in France, and *stock* in England. The word *pot-au-feu* means the meat, vegetables, seasonings, spices, and the " pot " or soup-kettle itself, *i. e.*, every thing made use of in making broth. The popular meaning of the term in France is, the soup and the beef and vegetables served as *relevés;* and, with the working-classes, the only thing (with bread, wine, and fruit) composing the family dinner. The French army is fed on this *pot-au-feu* three hundred and sixty days in the year.

It is a great mistake to believe that bones or veal make good broth; by boiling or simmering bones or veal, you obtain a gelatinous liquid, but not a rich broth with a pleasant flavor. When properly made, broth is clear. If milky, it has been made with bones, veal, or very inferior beef.

Broth for Potages.—Take three pounds of good, lean, fresh beef, from any part except the shin. There must not be more than two ounces of bone to a pound of meat, and the less bone the better. Place the meat in a soup-kettle or iron saucepan lined with tin, with three quarts of cold water and salt, and set it on a good fire. After about thirty minutes, the scum or albumen of the meat will gather on the surface, and the water will commence boiling. Now place the kettle on a more moderate fire, add one gill of cold water, and begin to skim off the scum, which will take only a few minutes. Then add one middle-sized carrot, half as much turnip, one middle-sized leek, a stalk of celery, one of parsley, a bay-leaf, one onion with two cloves stuck in it, and two cloves of garlic. Keep the kettle between simmering and boiling heat for about five hours. Dish the meat with carrot, turnip, and leek around it, and serve it as a *relevé.* Strain the broth, and it is ready for use.

If the broth is required to be richer, use more beef and less water, but follow the same process; if weaker, use more water and less beef, but still follow the same process.

Broth for Sauces and Gravies.—Place in a soup-kettle

or saucepan fresh bones of beef, mutton, lamb, veal, or poultry—of either, or of all; also, bones of the same meats from roasted pieces; also trimmings of the same, if very fresh, with one quart of cold water to every pound of bones or meat; skim it like the preceding, add the same vegetables and seasonings, and simmer for at least six hours. Then skim off very carefully all the fat on the surface, pass the remainder through a strainer or a sieve, and it is ready for use. This broth is certainly very inferior to the preceding one, but it is excellent for sauces and gravies, and is very cheaply made. It may be used for potages also; but, as we have said above, it is very gelatinous, and cannot be compared with the highly nutritious beef-broth.

Broth that is not to be used immediately must be cooled quickly after being strained, as the quicker it is cooled the longer it keeps. As soon as cold, put it in a stone jar or crockery vessel, and place it in a cool, dry, and dark place. It will keep three or four days in winter, but only one day in summer. If the weather is stormy, it will not keep even for twelve hours; it turns sour very quickly.

I do not put parsnips or thyme in broth, the taste of these two vegetables being too strong. They really neutralize the fine aroma of broth. Even in this nineteenth century there are some pretty good cooks who put thyme and parsnip in broth, but they do it by routine. Routine is in every thing the greatest enemy of progress. Ancient cookery used to put in the *pot* (old name for soup-kettle) a burnt onion to give an amber color to the broth. This has exactly the same effect as thyme and parsnip, giving it a bad taste, and neutralizing the flavor given to the broth by the osmazome of the meat. When broth of an amber color is desired, add to it a few drops of burnt sugar, the receipt for making which will be found elsewhere.

Consommé.—There are two ways of making *consommé:* one is to make broth as above, with the exception that five pounds of lean beef, instead of three, are used with three quarts of water, and simmered from seven to eight hours, instead of five, the vegetables and seasonings being the same; or by boiling broth gently till properly reduced.

The other way is to roast, until they are only one-third done, one, two, or three fowls, not under two years old; then place them in a soup-kettle with three pounds of lean beef; wet with three quarts of cold water; skim off as above directed; add the same vegetables and seasonings as for broth for potages. After having simmered the whole for three hours, the fowl or fowls must be taken out of the kettle, and the rest is to be simmered for about three hours longer. The meat, vegetables, and seasonings are then taken from the kettle or saucepan; the liquor is strained, and that liquor is the best *consommé* that can be made; or by boiling the same, gently, in three quarts of good broth, you make *consommé* also.

The reason for directing to use one, two, or three fowls is, that the more fowls used, the better and richer the broth. The fowls after having been thus used may be prepared in salad, and make a very excellent dish.

One pound of beef is enough to make broth for a potage for three or four persons.

Always use fresh meat; meat with a venison taste or tainted would spoil if not entirely destroy the broth.

To clarify Broth.—If not as clear as wanted, beat the white of an egg with a gill of cold broth, and turn into the broth ; boil gently about ten minutes, and strain through a cloth or towel.

Any kind of potage made with broth may be made with *consommé*. It may also be made with water, adding butter. With *consommé* it is richer, and with water much inferior, than with broth.

When a rump-piece is used to make broth, it is better to bone it first, and take it from the soup-kettle after three or four hours; it is served as a *relevé*, or prepared as cold beef. The broth is finished as directed; the bones and vegetables being kept on the fire longer than the meat.

Chicken and turkey broth are often called *potage de santé* (potage of health).

Chicken.—Roast or bake till turning yellow, a chicken over two years old. Put it in a soup-kettle with three pints of water, and set it on a rather slow fire; skim off the scum, add a middling-sized onion, a leek, a few stalks of chervil if handy, a middling-sized head of lettuce, and salt; simmer about three hours. Take out the chicken and vegetables, skim off the fat, strain, and use. This broth is excellent for a weak stomach, and is easy of digestion. The chicken is served in salad.

Turkey.—Procure a rather old turkey and roast or bake it till about one-third done; put it in a soup-kettle with about a pint of water to a pound of meat, and set it on a rather slow fire. As soon as the scum comes on the surface, skim it off carefully; then add two onions, two leeks, two or three heads of lettuce, a small handful of chervil if handy, and salt. Simmer about five hours.

Use the broth as chicken-broth above, and serve the turkey in salad.

Fish (also called *à la Lucullus*).—Slice three middling-sized onions and fry them with one ounce of butter till turning yellow; add three or four pounds of fish (bass, pike, trout, salmon, and the like), any fish having a firm and compact flesh, of one or several kinds; add also two carrots, two onions, and one leek, all sliced; four stalks of parsley, one of thyme, one clove of garlic, a bay-leaf, one clove, six pepper-corns, salt; cover the whole with cold water, set on a good but not brisk fire, boil gently for about two hours. If the water is boiling away, add some more; then strain, and use.

This broth may be used for *bisque* and fish sauces, instead of beef-broth.

It may be made rich; for instance, instead of three pounds of fish, use six, seven, eight pounds, or more, and seasonings in proportion.

Louis XV. was on a visit to the monastery of Saint-Denis one day during Lent; after having walked all over the grounds and gardens, he was offered a cup of broth by the superior.

Being a little fatigued, he took the cup and drank the whole at one draught.

In going back to Versailles, one of his suite, who did not like the monk-superior, adroitly alluded to the cup of broth, and managed to persuade the king that the monk had done it on purpose; that is, had made the king partake of meat-broth, when it was forbidden by the Church.

The next day the monk-superior was sent for and brought before the king. On hearing the object of the summons, he asked the king if the broth had indisposed him. Being answered in the negative, he begged to be allowed to prepare the same broth before the king himself, which he did, and from that time till his death the king used to send several hundred pounds of fish during Lent to the monks of Saint-Denis.

Frog.—Skin and put the hind-legs of two dozen of frogs in cold water for an hour; drain and put them in a saucepan, and set it on a slow fire; stir now and then till they are turning yellow, then take them off and chop the flesh rather fine; put back in the pan with a carrot sliced, a stalk of celery and one leek, both chopped, a little salt, and cover the whole with water. Simmer for about two hours; mash the whole through a colander, add butter which you stir and mix in, and it is ready for use.

This broth, taken warm before retiring, is excellent for persons having a cough or cold.

It is also excellent for consumptive persons, and is only second to snail-broth.

Another.—Take the hind-legs of fifty well-skinned green frogs, put them in cold water and a little salt for half an hour—drain them; then put them in a crockery kettle, with a leek, half a carrot, two stalks of celery, a middling-sized parsnip, a turnip, two onions, one clove of garlic, two ounces of fat bacon, a little salt, and white pepper; cover the whole well with cold water, set on the fire, simmer gently about four hours; strain, pour on *croutons,* and serve.

The hind-legs of the frogs are taken from the strainer, placed on a dish, and served at breakfast the next day, with a white sauce, or in fricassee, as a chicken.

Game.—Roast or bake, till about one-third done, two prairie-hens, and put them in a soup-kettle with about one pound of lean beef, salt, and five pints of water. Set the kettle on a rather slow fire, skim off the scum when it gathers on the surface, and then add half a carrot, two stalks of parsley, one of celery, one onion with a clove stuck in it, a bay-leaf, six pepper-corns, and two cloves of garlic. Simmer about three hours, and take the birds out of the kettle; simmer then two hours longer; strain, and the broth is ready for use.

Game-broth is warming and stimulating; it may be taken alone, or prepared with *croutons*, rice, vermicelli, or other Italian pastes, the same as beef-broth.

The prairie-hens are served in *salmis*, and the beef is served as boiled beef.

Snail.—Clean and prepare twenty-five snails as directed. Put them in a saucepan, with a carrot, an onion, and a head of lettuce, all chopped, a small handful of chervil, a few leaves of sorrel, and a little salt; cover the whole with three pints of cold water. Boil slowly for about three hours, strain the broth, add a little butter to it, and it is ready for use.

A tumblerful of this broth, taken warm before retiring, is certainly the best thing for a consumptive person.

It is also excellent for a cough.

Just salt the snails to taste, and eat them as they are, warm or cold.

Veal.—Procure two pounds of veal, from the neck or breast piece. Put the meat in a soup-kettle with two quarts of cold water and a little salt; set it on a good fire, and skim off the scum as soon as it gathers on the surface. When skimmed, add a head of lettuce, a leek (and a few stalks of chewil if handy); simmer for about three hours; strain, and use.

This broth, as well as chicken and turkey broth, is excellent for convalescent persons.

It may be made richer by putting a little more meat, according to taste; but generally the physician gives directions.

Another.—Soak a calf's liver in cold water for two hours, clean and wash it well; put it in a soup-kettle with about three pints of cold water, salt, boil gently for an hour and a half, and then add a handful of water-cresses; simmer fifteen minutes longer, strain and use.

Another.—Proceed as above in every particular, except that you use a handful of chervil instead of water-cresses.

Another.—Use three or four leeks instead of water-cresses, and proceed as above for every other particular.

The last three especially make a very refreshing drink, and are a great relief in some cases of fever.

Vegetable Broth (called also *Bouillon Maigre*).—Scrape, clean, and slice three carrots and three turnips, peel three onions; fry the whole with a little butter till it turns rather yellow; and then add two plants of celery cut in pieces, three or four leeks, also cut in pieces; stir and fry the whole for about six minutes. When fried, add also one clove of garlic, salt, pepper, two cloves, two stalks of parsley, a little nutmeg grated; cover with about three quarts of water. Keep on a rather slow fire, skim off the scum carefully, and then simmer for about three hours. Strain, and use.

This liquor is called vegetable broth, and is used instead of broth in time of Lent by persons who do not want to use beef-broth.

Another.—Proceed as above, and with the same vegetables till they are fried. Then add salt, pepper, two cloves of garlic, four stalks of parsley, three cloves, a little nutmeg grated, two quarts of white beans previously soaked in cold water for twenty-four hours, and five or six quarts of water. Skim it as above; simmer for about four hours; strain, and use.

The beans, carrots, turnips, and leeks may be mashed through a colander and served in *purée*.

Another.—Proceed as above in every particular, with the exception that instead of using beans, you use peas, lentils, chestnuts, or samp. Peas and lentils are soaked in water only for four or five hours. Chestnuts must be shelled. Some other vegetables may be added, according to taste, and also according to the nature of the vegetables.

Another.—Clean and put in a bowl a head of lettuce, a handful of sorrel, same of chervil, same of purslane, and all chopped fine; pour over nearly a quart of boiling water, add two ounces of butter, cover the bowl with a wet towel; leave thus half an hour, and strain.

When cold it makes a very refreshing drink, and is taken morning and evening with salt, to taste.

It may also be taken warm.

A la Minute, or made quickly.—Cut four ounces of fat salt pork in dice and set it on the fire in a saucepan; stir, and when it is turning rather brown add one onion chopped, and half a middling-sized carrot, sliced; stir, and when they are partly fried, add also two pounds of lean beef cut in small dice; stir and fry for five minutes. Then pour in it about three pints of boiling water, salt, boil gently about forty minutes. Strain, and use.

The beef may be served with the broth, or separately as an *entrée*, with a *piquante*, *ravigote*, or Robert sauce.

Bisque of Lobster.—Boil one or several lobsters as directed, and when cold split the tail in two, lengthwise, take the flesh out of the shell, remove the black vein that is on the back, take out the meat of the two large claws, and keep the flesh of the claws and tail for the following day's breakfast.

For a *bisque*, nothing is thrown away but the head,

stomach, and black vein. The head is the part immediately under the eyes; the stomach is a small, round pouch immediately behind the head ; and the vein runs from the stomach to the end of the tail.

Put all the rest, shell, small claws, all the matter found in the large shell (green, white, or yellow), in a mortar and pound well. Then put a tablespoonful of butter in a saucepan, set it on the fire, and when the butter is melted, put what is in the mortar in, stir with a wooden spoon for about ten minutes, then add one pint of warm broth, stir for about twenty minutes, and strain. Put the liquor back on the fire with about four ounces of toasted bread, boil five minutes, and mash through a colander. Put the liquor back again on the fire, add one quart of broth, boil gently ten minutes, and turn into the soup-dish.

While it is boiling, chop fine the coral-piece of the lobster or lobsters, knead it with a piece of butter of about the same bulk, then rub both through a wire sieve ; put them in the soup-dish with *croutons* and about two or three ounces of the flesh of the lobster cut in very small dice. Turn the broth into the soup-dish also, and as directed above, and serve warm.

When there is no coral in the lobster or lobsters, knead a hard-boiled yolk of egg with butter in its stead.

Use one, two, three, or more lobsters, according to how much soup is wanted. It is not costly, because the flesh, or most of it, is kept to make a salad the next day, for breakfast or lunch.

The salad might be served the same day at dinner, but lobster is a rather heavy food, and it is more prudent not to eat any late in the day.

Bisque of Lobster à la Colbert.—Make a *bisque* as above, and while it is on the fire, poach as directed as many eggs as there will be persons at dinner; put them in the soup-dish instead of *croutons*, and serve as above.

Of Crabs.—Proceed as for a *bisque* of lobster in every particular, except that you use hard-shell crabs instead of lobster.

The same à la Colbert.—Add to the above as many poached eggs as you have guests.

Of Craw-fish (Bisque d'Ecrevisses).—Our readers who have been in Europe will certainly remember the name of one of the best soups that can be made. It is made of craw-fish the same as with lobster, and is certainly more delicate than a *bisque* of lobster or of crabs. (See CRAW-FISH for other particulars.)

A *bisque* of craw-fish may also be served *à la Colbert* the same as a *bisque* of lobster.

Bouillabaisse.—The real *bouillabaisse* is made in Marseilles; they make an imitation of it in Bordeaux, and in many other parts of France and the Continent; but, like a Welsh rarebit prepared out of Wales, it is very inferior to the real one. However, we will give the receipt to make it here, and as good as possible with the fish that can be procured.

Put a gill of sweet-oil in a tin saucepan and set it on a sharp fire; when hot, add two onions and two cloves of garlic sliced; stir so as to partly fry them, and then take from the fire. Put also in the pan three pounds of fish, such as haddock, halibut, turbot, white-fish—of all if possible, but at least of two kinds; also a dozen muscles, just blanched and taken from the shell (some put them whole, properly cleaned). The fish is cut in pieces about two inches long. Then add one gill of Catawba or Sauterne wine, a bay-leaf, two cloves, two slices of lemon, the juice of a tomato, salt, pepper, a pinch of saffron, cover with cold water, and set the pan back on a brisk fire. After about thirty minutes add a teaspoonful of chopped parsley; boil ten minutes longer, and it is done.

The pieces of fish are then placed on a dish and served.

Put in a deep dish, and to be served at the same time, some slices of bread, over which you turn the sauce through a strainer.

One slice of bread and one piece of fish is served to each person, also some sauce.

It is put in two different dishes, to avoid breaking the pieces of fish.

There are over a hundred ways of making a *bouillabaisse ;* the above is one of the best.

There are also about as many ways of spelling the same.

A *bouillabaisse* is served as a soup.

POTAGES.

A la Colbert.—Scrape carrots and turnips and cut them in small dice or with a vegetable spoon; add green peas and string-beans, if handy, the beans cut in pieces; set them on the fire in a pan with cold water and salt; boil gently till done, and drain. Put them back on the fire, covered with warm broth, salt to taste, boil gently about two or three minutes, and turn into the soup-dish, in which you have put as many poached eggs as there are or will be persons at table. A poached egg with soup is served to every person. Proportions of broth and vegetables according to taste.

Julienne.—Scrape two carrots and two turnips and cut them in pieces about an inch and a half long; cut slices lengthwise about one-eighth of an inch thick, then cut

4

again across, so as to make square strips. Put them in a saucepan with about two ounces of butter, three table-spoonfuls of cabbage chopped fine, and half a middling-sized onion, also chopped; set on the fire and stir till about half fried. Add broth to make it as you wish, thin or thick; boil gently till done; salt to taste, skim off the fat, and serve. It takes about two hours.

Julienne with Rice.—Boil two ounces of rice in water and a little salt, till about three-quarters done; drain and put in the *julienne* after having added the broth; finish as above.

Julienne with Barley.—Boil barley till done; add it to the *julienne* at the same time the broth is added, and serve as the above.

Julienne aux Croutons.—Put some *croutons* in the soup-dish, and when the *julienne* is done, pour it over them, and serve.

Brunoise.—Put an ounce of butter in a saucepan on the fire, and when melted, add one carrot, one turnip, a little celery, all cut in dice; stir till they turn yellow, then add about a quart of broth, a middling-sized leek cut in pieces, a few leaves of lettuce and of sorrel, if handy, and a pinch of sugar. Simmer about two hours; skim off the fat; add a few drops of burnt sugar to color.

Have *croutons* in the soup-dish, turn the potage over them, and serve.

Brunoise with Rice.—Proceed as above, except that you add from two to four ounces of boiled rice to the potage ten minutes before taking from the fire. Serve without *croutons*.

Another.—Use boiled barley instead of boiled rice.

A la Monaco.—Put some thin slices of stale bread in the soup-dish, sprinkle pulverized sugar and orange-rind grated all over. Pour boiling milk over; cover the dish for five minutes, and serve.

A la Régence.—Put about two dozen *quenelles* made with chicken into the soup-dish with half a pint of boiled green peas; turn boiling *consommé* over, and serve warm.

A la Royale.—Make a custard with a dozen yolks of eggs, about the same volume of good cream, season with sugar, salt, and a little nutmeg; cook, and when perfectly cold, cut it in slices and again cut in fancy shapes with paste-cutters or with a knife; place it in the soup-dish, pour boiling *consommé* gently over, and serve warm.

Potage Printanier (called also *Jardinière* and *à la Paysanne*).—It is a potage *julienne,* to which is added the top or eatable part of six asparagus, six turnip-rooted red radishes, and two or three tablespoonfuls of green peas. They are fried, boiled, and served with the other vegetables.

Velouté.—Put yolks of eggs in the soup-dish and beat them a little with cold or lukewarm broth; then pour boiling broth over them, little by little, stirring the while, and serve warm.

It is made thin or thick, according to taste.

With Arrow-root.—Set broth in a saucepan on the fire, and as soon as it boils, sprinkle some arrow-root into it, stirring the while with a wooden spoon; boil gently for about half an hour, stirring now and then the while, and serve warm, adding salt to taste.

Milk or *consommé* may be used instead of broth.

If you use milk, add a very little salt and sugar, to taste.

The proportion of arrow-root to a certain quantity of broth is according to taste; it can be made thick or thin.

With Corn-starch.—Proceed as for arrow-root.

With Bread.—This is the simplest of all. Dry some

slices of bread, either stale or fresh, in the oven, place them in the soup-dish, pour boiling broth over them, cover the dish for two or three minutes, and serve.

With Fecula.—Proceed as for arrow-root. Being finer, it does not require more than about twelve or fifteen minutes.

With Barley.—Wash the barley in cold water, then drop it in boiling broth, little by little, stirring the while; when in, keep simmering till perfectly done, which you ascertain easily by tasting; add then salt to taste, a pinch of sugar, and serve warm.

It must be stirred occasionally while on the fire.

With Gruel (*French Gruau*).—It is made as with arrow-root.

With Indian Meal.—Proceed as with arrow-root.

With Sago.—Sago must be boiled gently about an hour; but for the rest, proceed as with arrow-root in every particular.

With Semoule.—With *semoule* it is the same as with arrow-root, except that it is boiled only about fifteen minutes.

With Tapioca.—Tapioca is prepared like arrow-root, but must be boiled about forty-five minutes.

All the above, like arrow-root, may be prepared with *consommé*, or with milk, as well as with broth.

With Giblets.—Throw the giblets in boiling water and a little salt, boil for ten minutes, take off and drain. Drop them in broth, boil gently till done, and turn the whole into the soup-dish, in which you have some leeks, boiled and cut in pieces. Serve warm.

Some *croutons* may be added, and chervil chopped fine, just before turning into the soup-dish; or they may be placed in the soup-dish before pouring in the broth.

With Mackerel.—Clean, prepare, and cut in pieces about one inch and a half long, a mackerel weighing about one pound and a half; fry it with two ounces of butter till it turns rather brown, then cover with nearly a quart of water ; add a few slices of carrot, same of turnip, a small onion, two or three stalks of parsley, salt, pepper, a clove of garlic, and a stalk of celery if handy ; boil slowly for about an hour ; mash gently through a colander, put what has passed through the colander back on the fire, add a little butter, give one more boil, turn into the soup-dish over *croutons,* and serve.

With new Carrots.—Take small, young carrots, clean and wash them, then blanch them for about five minutes. Set them on the fire, cover with broth or *consommé ;* boil gently till done, and serve.

Another.—With carrots and peas. Proceed as above till the carrots are half done, then add blanched green peas; finish the cooking, and serve.

Another.—Make as the above, but using one or two heads of cabbage-lettuce, blanched for two minutes, instead of green peas.

Fancy Potage.—Take twelve very small rolls; cut off one end and remove all the soft part of it ; fill them with *quenelles* of chicken; replace the piece cut off as well as possible; place them in the soup-dish; pour boiling *consommé* or good broth over them ; cover the dish for ten minutes, and serve warm.

With Vermicelli.—Drop the vermicelli in boiling water, and in which you have put a little salt; boil ten minutes, drain, drop again in cold water, drain again and put it in boiling broth ; boil ten minutes; add salt to taste, and serve.

With Macaroni.—Proceed as for vermicelli in every particular, except that it takes twice as long to cook.

With Macaroni and Cheese.—Proceed as for the above, and when done, put grated cheese in the soup-dish, turn the macaroni over it, and serve.

With Italian Pastes.—No matter of what shape are the pastes, proceed as for vermicelli; the only difference is in the time of cooking, which depends on the size.

Consommé may be used instead of broth. If milk is used, sugar must be added.

With Macaroni à la Corinne.—Set two quarts of cold water on the fire, with an ounce of salt, and two ounces of butter; at the first boil, drop into it four ounces of macaroni; boil five minutes, and drain. Immediately drop the macaroni in boiling *consommé*, and boil gently till done. Drain it again and place a layer of it in the soup-dish, over the macaroni; place a thin layer of Parmesan cheese grated; then a layer of *macédoine* of vegetables; then again, a layer of macaroni, one of cheese, etc.; pour *consommé* to taste on the whole, and serve warm.

With Macaroni à la Médici (also called *à la Napolitaine*).—Proceed as for macaroni *à la Corinne* in every particular, with the exception that you put also in the soup-dish a layer of *quenelles* of chicken over that of *macédoine* of vegetables, and serve in the same way.

The *quenelles* are boiled till done, in broth in which you put a few sprigs of mignonette.

Another.—Add to the above about a gill of thick tomato-sauce, just before pouring the *consommé* over the macaroni, etc.

Macaroni à la Romulus.—Prepare eight ounces of macaroni as directed for macaroni *à la Corinne;* place a layer of it in the soup-dish; then over it a layer of *quenelles* of chicken; over the *quenelles*, a thin layer of grated Parmesan cheese; then a layer of thin slices of salt beef tongue, boiled and skimmed; over the latter a layer of sweetbreads boiled in broth and cut in thin slices also; and lastly a layer of thin slices of boiled flounders. Several layers of each of the above may be placed in the soup dish, in the same order; then boiling *consommé* is poured over the whole; the dish is covered, put in a warm place for ten minutes, and served.

Although this dish is a regular potage, and served as such, still many Italians make a meal of it.

With Macaroni à la Rossini.—Proceed as for macaroni *à la Corinne* above, with two exceptions: first, that you add a layer of *quenelles* of partridge; and second, that you use *consommé* of partridge.

With Macaroni à la St. Pierre.—Proceed also as for potage macaroni *à la Corinne* as far as placing a layer of macaroni in the soup-dish; then put over it a layer of boiled soft roe of fish; over which put a thin layer of grated Parmesan cheese; then a layer of *quenelles* of fish; another layer of macaroni; over it, a layer of boiled thin slices of salmon; macaroni again, etc. Pour boiling *consommé* over the whole, and serve.

Although bearing the name of Saint Pierre (St. Peter), the above dish has not been devised by the saint; but, like all the above, save that *à la Corinne*, it has been invented by monks.

With Nouilles.—Set broth on the fire in a saucepan, and at the first boiling take the *nouilles* from the water with a skimmer and put in the broth, stir occasionally and boil gently till done. The proportions are according to taste. The more broth used for a certain quantity of *nouilles* the thinner the soup will be, and *vice versa*. Salt to taste, and serve.

With Potatoes.—Cut about half a pint of potatoes with

a vegetable spoon (it is understood half a pint when cut, the rest being used to make mashed potatoes), and blanch them for three minutes, drain and put them in boiling broth; boil gently till about half done, add then two or three tablespoonfuls of green peas; finish the cooking; and just before serving add a pinch of sugar, salt to taste, turn into the soup-dish, and serve with or without *croutons.*

With Quenelles.—Drop *quenelles* in broth; boil gently till done, and serve.

The proportion according to taste. Half a dozen *quenelles* for each person, and about half a pint of broth, make a good proportion.

With Rice.—Put boiled rice in the soup-dish, turn boiling broth over it, and serve warm.

With Turnips.—When clean, cut the turnips in slices, drop them in boiling water, add a little salt, boil for five minutes, and drain. Set them on the fire in a saucepan, cover them with milk, and boil gently till done. Mash them through a colander, put them back on the fire with milk, butter, a little sugar and salt; stir and boil gently a few minutes; then add a yolk of egg for two turnips, stir in also two or three tablespoonfuls of cream; stir, but do not boil; put some *croutons* in the soup-dish, turn the turnips over, and serve.

Purée of Split Peas.—The proportions vary according to taste; the more peas that are used with a certain quantity of broth, the thicker the potage will be, and *vice versa.*

Soak one pint of split peas in cold water over night and drain. Put them in a saucepan with a few slices of carrot, same of turnip, same of onion and salt. Cover with cold water, set on the fire and boil till done. Drain, and then mash through a colander. Put back on the fire with warm broth to taste—that is, to make the potage thin or thick, season with salt or pepper; boil gently for five minutes, stirring the while; turn into the soup-dish over *croutons*, and serve warm. It may be served without *croutons*.

Purée of Green Peas.—It is sometimes called *à la Chantilly*, or *à la Française*. Put cold water and a little salt on the fire, and at the first boiling throw the peas in; if they are very tender, leave them in only a few seconds; if large and rather hard, boil one or two minutes; drain, mash them through a colander, and finish as the above.

Purée of Dry Beans.—White and dry beans have several names, but no matter what kind, they are prepared alike. If you are not sure that the beans are new, soak them in cold water for about twenty-four hours, and drain. Cook, mash, and serve them the same as split peas.

Purée of Lentils.—Wash the lentils in cold water and proceed as for split peas for the rest.

Purée of Peas.—Proceed as for split peas.

With Lima Beans.—Proceed as with green peas.

With Potatoes.—Steam potatoes, then peel and mash them through a colander. Put them back on the fire with broth, butter, and salt to taste; stir, boil a few minutes, and serve with *croutons*. Water or milk may be used instead of broth.

With Pumpkins.—Peel, take away the seed and cut the pumpkin in small pieces; put them in a stewpan with water just enough to cover them, a little salt and white pepper, set on the fire and take off when cooked; throw away the water, mash and strain the pumpkin, put it back in the stewpan, cover with milk, add a little sugar, set it again on the fire, and take off at the first boiling; pour a little of it on *croutons* in the soup-dish, and keep covered

4*

in a warm place for ten minutes; then pour also the remainder in, and serve.

Another.—Prepare as above, throw the pieces in boiling water with a little salt for five minutes, mash and drain; put butter in a stewpan, set it on the fire; when melted put the pumpkin in, stir about five minutes; have ready in your soup-dish some slices of bread fried in butter, and dusted with sugar, pour on them some boiling milk, keep covered in a warm place two or three minutes; then turn the pumpkin on, at the same time mixing the whole gently, and serve.

With Squash.—It is made as with pumpkin.

With Asparagus.—Proceed as for green peas.

With Jerusalem Artichokes.—It is made like that of potatoes.

With Carrots.—When made with young carrots, it is called potage *purée Crécy*, or *à la Crécy*. Add broth to taste to a *purée* of carrots, turn into the soup-dish over *croutons*, and serve.

With colored Beans.—When made with colored beans, it is called *à la Condé*. Proceed as with beans.

The Prince of Condé devised this potage, and besides cooking the beans in broth, he used to put in one or two partridges also, to give, as he used to say, "a good taste to the beans."

With Cauliflowers.—Make a *purée* of cauliflowers, to which you add broth to taste, and serve with *croutons*.

With Chestnuts.—Add broth and *croutons* to a *purée* of chestnuts, and serve warm.

With Turnips.—It is made as with carrots.

With Wheat.—Cut ears of wheat when full, but not ripe, and put them away to dry. Shell the wheat; wash it in cold water, put it in a saucepan, cover it with broth and boil gently till done. Mash through a colander, put back on the fire with a little butter; add broth if too thick, stir now and then for about fifteen minutes; take from the fire, add two or three yolks of eggs beaten with a little cream and a pinch of sugar; mix them well with the rest, and serve warm.

With Sweet Corn.—Proceed as with wheat in every particular. It makes a healthy and excellent potage.

Water may be used instead of broth, but it is not as nutritive.

With Swallows' Nests, or Chinese Soup.—The nests are made a mucilaginous substance of, and built by the species of swallows called *Hirundo esculenta;* it would require several pages to describe them, together with their compound material, and would be out of place in a receipt book. Suffice it to say, that they sell for $100 a pound in London and Paris (gold of course), and the cheapest potage for one person costs about three dollars.

Soak about four ounces of it in cold water for ten hours, drain and clean. Put it in a saucepan, cover well with chicken-broth, place the saucepan in boiling water for about two hours, add salt to taste, and then drain again. Place the nests in the soup-dish, pour boiling *consommé* over them, and serve warm.

The Chinese are said to use very rich *consommé* of chicken to prepare them.

With Tomatoes and Rice.—Blanch half a dozen tomatoes, and skin them. Put them in a saucepan with a quart of broth, season with an onion sliced, three or four sprigs of parsley, one of thyme, half a dozen pepper-corns, a bay-leaf, two cloves, two cloves of garlic; salt and pepper. Boil gently till reduced to about two-thirds, when mash gently through a colander. It is understood by mashing gently, to mash so that all the liquid part shall pass through the colander, and the seeds and spices shall be retained in it and thrown away.

While the tomatoes are on the fire boiling, set four ounces of rice on the fire with cold water and salt, and boil it till tender. Drain the rice, put it in a saucepan with the tomato-juice after being mashed, set the saucepan on the fire, add one ounce of butter, a teaspoonful of sugar, both according to taste; to make the potage thin or thick, boil gently fifteen minutes, turn into the soup-dish, and serve warm.

The same may be done with canned tomatoes; in that case, set a can of tomatoes on the fire with the same seasonings, and proceed exactly as for the above in every other particular.

The same with Croutons.—Fry some *croutons* with a little butter, put them in the soup-dish; turn the potage, or rather the same mixture as above, over them; cover the soup-dish for two or three minutes, and serve.

With Tomatoes and Croutons only.—Fry the *croutons* and put them in the soup-dish; turn the tomatoes only over them, after being prepared as above; cover the soup-dish for two or three minutes, and serve.

Purée à la Reine.—Procure a rather old chicken and cut it in pieces as for fricassee; set it on the fire in a saucepan with about a quart of cold water, salt, and boil gently about one hour. Then add about four ounces of rice, washed in cold water, continue boiling until the chicken is overdone and tender. Take the pieces of chicken from the pan, scrape the flesh off the bones; cut the white flesh (the flesh that is on both sides of the breast-bone) in dice, and put it in the soup-dish; chop fine all the other flesh, and then mash it through a sieve or strainer, together with the rice. If it be rather too thick to mash through, moisten it with broth. A large iron spoon is the best utensil to mash through with. Then set the rice and flesh back on the fire in a saucepan with broth to taste, stir and add immediately from two to four ounces of butter, a gill of cream, or, if not handy, a gill of milk. Keep stirring on a slow fire for five or six minutes; salt to taste, turn into the soup-dish, and serve.

There is no danger of curdling if kept on a slow fire and not allowed to boil.

The same with Broth.—To make the potage richer, cook the chicken and rice in broth instead of water, and proceed as above for the rest.

The same with consommé.—The chicken and rice may also be cooked in *consommé*, and when mashed through the sieve, add *consommé* also instead of broth, and you have an exceedingly rich soup. This is excellent for persons having throat diseases; it is easily swallowed, and very nutritious.

The same à la Française.—The potage *purée à la française* is the same as that *à la reine*, with the addition of *quenelles* of chicken.

The same à la Princesse.—Add to that *à la reine*, the white flesh of a roasted chicken, cut in dice, and put in the soup-dish.

Purée of Game.—Proceed as for potage *purée à la reine*, with the exception that you use prairie-hen, instead of chicken.

SOUPS.

Maigre, or Vegetable Soup.—Proceed as for *julienne* in every particular, except that water is used instead of broth. Four ounces of butter may be used instead of two.

Beef and Mutton Soup.—Take three pounds of beef and two pounds of breast of mutton; put both pieces in a crockery kettle with four quarts of cold water, salt, and pepper, set on a slow fire; skim carefully, then add half a carrot, two turnips, two onions with one clove stuck in each, two stalks of celery, two leeks, one sprig of parsley, and one clove of garlic. Simmer four or five hours; dish the meat with carrots, turnips, and leeks around, to be served after the soup if you choose; strain the broth, skim the fat off, put back on the fire, give one boil; have *croutons* in the soup-dish, pour over them, and serve.

Mock Turtle.—Put two ounces of butter in a sauce-pan and set it on the fire, when melted, add a tablespoonful of flour, stir, and when turning brown, add three pints of broth (either beef-broth or broth made by boiling a calf's head, according to taste); boil five minutes then add a liquor glass of brandy or rum, from one to three glasses of Madeira, Port, or Sherry wine, about four ounces of calf's-head (the skin only) cut in dice, mushrooms or truffles, or both, also cut in dice; boil five minutes. While it is boiling, cut two hard-boiled eggs and half a lemon in dice and put them in the soup-dish; turn the broth over, and serve.

Made with beef broth it is certainly richer than when made with calf's-head broth, the latter is gelatinous but less nourishing than the former.

Mock Turtle with consommé.—Use *consommé* instead of broth, and you have as rich a soup as can be made.

Mock turtle is an English soup, very rich and very good.

Au Chasseur (*Hunter's or Sportsman's Soup*).—A potage *au chasseur* is always made with game, such as rabbit, prairie-hen, grouse, venison, wild turkey, wild

pigeon, etc., but never with aquatic birds. It might be
made with quail, but that bird is really too delicate to
make soup with. A whole bird or animal is never used,
but the bones and trimmings only. After having cut off
the fleshy parts, the bones are cracked and used to make
the potage.

Take the bones of two prairie-hens after having cut off
the flesh on both sides of the breast-bone, also the legs;
cut the bones in pieces about half an inch long and set
them on the fire with half an ounce of butter, stir for two
or three minutes, cover with broth, or game broth, and
boil gently till well cooked, or about two hours.

Put in another pan, and set it on the fire at the same
time as the above, half a head of cabbage, one carrot, one
turnip, and one onion, all cut fine; about half a pound of
lean salt pork; cover with cold water, and boil gently for
about two hours also.

In case the water or broth should boil away, add a
little more.

After having boiled both vegetables and bones about
two hours, take off the salt pork from the pan in which
the vegetables are, and turn what you have in the other
pan over the vegetables, through a strainer; add some
broth if it is too thick; boil ten minutes, and serve.

Proceed as above with the bones and trimmings of
other birds.

Turtle or Terrapin.—Cut the turtle in dice, throw
it in boiling water for two or three minutes, and
drain; put it in a stewpan with onions and ham, also cut
in dice; season with thyme, parsley, bay-leaf, salt, pepper,
and a wine-glass of Madeira wine or of good brandy;
wet with *Espagnole* sauce or with *consommé*, set on a good
fire, boil about half an hour. Ten minutes before taking

from the fire, chop the eggs of the turtle, after having boiled them, and put them in a stewpan; if the turtle has none, chop and use hard-boiled eggs instead. When done, throw away parsley, thyme, and bay-leaf, turn into bowls, add a little chopped chervil, and a quarter of a rind of lemon, also chopped; the latter is enough for six persons. Serve warm.

It may be strained before putting it in bowls, according to taste.

Turtle-steaks are prepared like beef-steaks.

With Rice and Milk.—Wash half a pound of rice in cold water. Set it on the fire with about one pint of milk, boil gently till done, filling with more milk, so as to keep the rice always covered. When cooked, add a little butter, milk according to taste, sugar or salt, or both, and serve. It will not take more than two quarts of milk.

The French name for the above is *riz au lait.*

With Okra.—Okra or gumbo is little known here; yet it is good in pickles, used like cucumbers. It is much used for soup in the Southern States and in the West Indies.

When green and tender, cut it very fine, cook it in broth, add a few tomatoes or tomato-sauce, according to taste; season with salt, pepper, and a pinch of sugar. When the tomatoes are cooked, serve warm.

If dry, make a potage like that of tapioca, to which you add a little tomato-sauce and pepper.

With Onions.—Put two ounces of butter in a saucepan, and when melted add a tablespoonful of flour, stir, and when turning rather yellow add also four or five onions sliced, stir till fried, when you add broth to taste (about one quart); boil gently about fifteen minutes; mash through a colander, put back on the fire; give one boil, salt and pepper to taste; turn into the soup-dish, in which you have some *croutons*, and serve.

More or less onions may be used, according to taste.

Ox-Tail.—Chop the ox-tail in pieces about one inch long, set them on the fire, with about one ounce of butter, stir till it turns rather brown, and turn the fat off. Then add broth to taste, boil slowly till the pieces of tail are well done; add salt, pepper, and when handy add also three or four tomatoes whole; boil gently about fifteen minutes longer, turn into the soup-dish, and serve meat and all.

Some add wine and liquor, the same as to the mock-turtle soup, but this is according to taste. The soup is excellent served without wine or liquor.

When no tomatoes are used, it is not necessary to boil fifteen minutes longer, serve as soon as done.

Simple.—Use water instead of broth; season with carrot, turnip, parsley, leek, onions, cloves, salt, and pepper. Serve as the above.

Ox-cheek.—An ox-cheek soup is made the same as an ox-tail soup. The broth is made with ox-cheek instead of with other parts of the beef, and the potage or soup made with the broth. A little wine—Madeira, Port, or Sherry—is sometimes added, as for mock-turtle.

Sheep's-tail.—Proceed as for ox-tail in every particular.

Sheep's-neck.—Made the same as ox-cheek soup.

Sorrel.—Put two ounces of butter in a saucepan, set it on the fire, and as soon as melted, put a good handful of sorrel in, stir for about one minute; then add a pint and a half of water, salt; boil two or three minutes; add again a little butter, give one boil and turn into the soup-dish in which you have *croutons*.

As soon as taken from the fire, two, three, or four

yolks of eggs, beaten with a tablespoonful of water, may
be added.

Broth may be used instead of water.

Oyster.—Put one quart of oysters with their liquor in
a saucepan, with one pint of cold water, and set it on a
good fire. Take from the fire at the first boil, and skim
off the scum. Take the oysters from the pan with a skimmer and put them in the soup-dish. By keeping the soup-
dish in a warm but not hot place, the oysters will not
harden. Add to the juice in the saucepan a gill of white
wine; give one boil, and take from the fire. Mix two
ounces of butter with two tablespoonfuls of flour in a bowl;
turn the juice and wine into the bowl also, and mix the
whole well; put the mixture back in the saucepan, and set
it on the fire, adding about half a dozen mushrooms, two
or three stalks of parsley, and pepper to taste. Boil two
minutes, turn over the oysters through a strainer, and
serve.

The mushrooms may also be turned into the soup-dish.

Cabbage.—Put in a kettle with two quarts and a half
of water a pound of salted pork, same of breast of mutton;
also, if handy, the remains of a roasted piece; set on a slow
fire; skim before it boils, and then boil for about an hour
and a half; strain, to remove the small bones, if any; put
back in the kettle broth and meat, also one middling-sized
cabbage, which you must have previously thrown in boiling water and boiled ten minutes; add then two carrots,
one turnip, two leeks, half a head of celery, one onion
with a clove stuck in it, a little salt and pepper, and about
half a pound of sausage (not smoked); then boil gently
about two hours, strain the broth, pour it on *croutons* in
the soup-dish, and serve.

The pork, mutton, and sausage, with the cabbage

around, may be served on a dish after the soup at a family dinner, or kept for breakfast the next day.

Cauliflower.—Clean and cut in small pieces three middling-sized cauliflowers. Put in a stewpan two ounces of butter, and set it on a moderate fire; when hot put the cauliflowers in; stir now and then till it turns brown, then add a sprig of thyme, same of parsley, a bay-leaf, one onion with a clove stuck in it, salt, and white pepper; simmer gently till the whole is well cooked, throw away the onion, clove, thyme, and bay-leaf; mash well the cauliflowers, strain and put back on the fire with the broth; give one boil, pour on *croutons*, and serve.

Cheese.—Put four ounces of butter in a soup-kettle, with an onion chopped fine; set on a brisk fire, stir now and then till it has a yellow color, then sprinkle on it half a tablespoonful of flour, keep stirring till it turns brown; then add two quarts of water, salt, and pepper; boil about five minutes. Have prepared in the soup-dish the following: a thin layer of grated cheese, Gruyère or pine-apple cheese; on it a layer of thin slices of bread, then another of cheese, again another of bread, etc., three or four of each; strain, and pour the liquor in the kettle on the whole; keep in a warm place five minutes, and serve.

Milk.—Put a quart of milk in a tin saucepan and set it on the fire; when it begins to rise, sweeten it to taste; give one boil, pour on toasted bread, or on *croutons*, or on two ounces of boiled rice, and serve.

Yolks of eggs may be stirred in, just before turning the milk into the soup-dish, and when taken from the fire.

Maigre (called *Soup aux Herbes, Herb-Broth,* etc.).— Wash, drain, and chop fine a handful of sorrel, a dozen sprigs of chervil, and half a head of lettuce; put an ounce of butter in a stewpan, set it on a good fire; when melted, put the sorrel, chervil, and lettuce in, add salt and pepper, stir till the whole is cooked; then cover with lukewarm water; boil three minutes, beat well three yolks of eggs with a tablespoonful of water, take from the fire and put the eggs in while stirring; pour immediately on *croutons*, and serve.

With Leeks.—Clean six leeks; cut them in pieces about half an inch long, then fry them with a little butter till turning rather yellow; add then about a pint and a half of water, boil gently till the leeks are perfectly cooked, salt to taste, and it is ready for use.

This broth may be taken warm or cold.

It is a demulcent, and at the same. time the most refreshing drink that can be taken.

With Clams.—Wash and clean the clams well. Then put them in a saucepan with half a pint of water (say one quart of clams), set on the fire, and at the first boil, take off and drain. Put the pan back on the fire with two ounces of butter in it; when melted, fry a chopped onion in the butter, add then the liquor drained, a pint of water, salt, pepper, parsley chopped fine, and the clams; boil two minutes, add also a little butter, and when melted and mixed, turn over some *croutons* in the soup-dish, and serve warm.

With Muscles.—Proceed as for clams in every particular.

Allemande, or German Soup.—Soak four ounces of pearl-barley in tepid water for eight or ten hours, and drain. Put it in a saucepan with one quart of broth, a piece of leek, one of celery, and boil gently about one hour and a half. While it is boiling, mix well together in a bowl one tablespoonful of flour and half a gill of broth, which turn into the saucepan, also grated nutmeg and sugar to taste; boil ten minutes longer, and serve.

Another, called à la Maria Theresa.—Proceed as for the above, except that you mix in a bowl six yolks of eggs with half a gill of broth, and no flour; and finish as in the preceding.

Another way.—Instead of using pearl-barley, use flour that you have dried in a bakepan till it turns yellow.

Indian, or Curry.—Put in a saucepan one ounce of butter and set it on the fire; when melted, fry in it two large onions, one carrot, and half a turnip, all sliced; also one leek, a stalk of celery, and four of parsley, all cut fine. When the whole is fried, cover with about one quart of broth, season with two cloves, a bay-leaf, half a teaspoonful of cayenne pepper, same of pimento, two stalks of thyme; boil gently about one hour and a quarter, and drain. Put the liquor back in the saucepan and add four ounces of boiled rice, a little saffron to color, simmer about fifteen minutes longer, and serve.

This soup is good and healthy for southern countries, but is too highly spiced for this climate.

Polish, or Barscz.—Peel and clean fifteen or twenty red beets, split them in two or four lengthwise, and put them in an earthen vessel with a pail of water and about a pound of rye bread; cover the vessel as air-tight as possible, and set it in a warm place (about 80 degrees Fahr.) for about eight days. After that time the liquor is rather sour, then drain.

Put in a saucepan four pounds of lean beef, one pound of smoked pork, half a pound of ham, four onions, two leeks, and about four quarts of the liquor made as above. Simmer till the whole is done; skim off the scum that may gather on the surface, and then strain.

Roast till half done, three chickens, or one chicken and one rabbit, or one chicken and one duck; put them on the fire in a saucepan with the liquor strained from the beef, pork, etc., as described above. Boil gently about half an hour, strain the liquor again. Then cut the beef, smoked pork, and ham, in small dice, put the whole in the soup-dish, with the strained liquor, and serve warm, as soup.

The chicken, or chicken and rabbit, or chicken and duck, are generally served separately, with some of the beets used to make the liquor, and with the addition of mushrooms, parsley, celery, onions, and sausages, raw or cooked, according to taste; and salt, pepper, and spices, according to taste also.

The poorer classes make this soup with water instead of beet-juice, and very often with mutton instead of beef; but proceed as described above in every other particular.

Russian, or Uka.—The *uka* is made in Russia with sterlets. It may be made here with the sturgeon of the lakes, or with salmon or trout.

Cut the fish in pieces about two inches long, and put them in salt water for one hour, and drain. Cut in small pieces two roots of parsley and two of celery, throw them into boiling water five minutes and drain them. Then fry them with a little butter till they turn yellow, when add a gill of broth, and boil gently till it becomes rather thick. Put the pieces of fish in also, add salt and pepper, to taste, cover the whole with fish-broth, boil gently till the fish is cooked, and serve warm.

Some *caviare* may be added just before serving.

Another, or Tstchy.—Put four pounds of beef in a soup-kettle (the poorer classes always use mutton), with a chicken or a duck, half a pound of smoked pork, same of smoked sausages, four carrots, four cloves, twelve pepper-corns, salt, two leeks, two onions, four stalks of parsley, and one of celery ; cover the whole with fish-broth, and set on a good fire. Skim off the scum carefully, and boil gently till the whole is done. As soon as either the chicken or duck, etc., is done, take it from the kettle. When the whole is cooked, drain.

Put the liquor back in the kettle with a middling-sized head of cabbage cut in four, or about the same quantity of sour-krout, slices of carrots and onions, pearl-barley, *semoule*, or gruel ; simmer about three hours, and it is done.

It is served in two ways : first, all the meat and vegetables are cut in small pieces and served with the broth as soup ; second, the broth is served with the vegetables cut up, and the meat is served after and separately, as a *relevé*.

Nothing is thrown away but the pepper-corns and cloves.

Spanish, or Olla Podrida.—Put four ounces of lean and fat salt pork into a saucepan and set it on a good fire ; when partly fried, add half a pound of beef, same of mutton, same of veal (occasionally a chicken or partridge is added also), and four ounces of ham. Just cover the whole with cold water, and skim carefully as soon as the scum comes on the surface. When skimmed, add a gill of dry peas, previously soaked in water for an hour, half a small head of cabbage, pimento to taste, one carrot, one turnip, two leeks, three or four stalks of celery, same of parsley, two of thyme, two cloves, two onions, two cloves of garlic, ten pepper-corns, and some mace; fill up with water so that the whole is just covered, and simmer for about five hours.

In case the water should simmer away too much, add a little more.

When done, dish the pork, beef, mutton, veal, ham, and

chicken. Put the peas, cabbage, carrots, turnips, leeks, celery, and onions on another dish.

Strain the liquor, pour it on *croutons* in the soup-dish, and serve the three dishes at the same time.

The Spanish peasantry and the lower classes in cities, serve the whole in the same dish, and generally omit the beef and veal. The better class serve the soup first, and then the meat and vegetables afterward.

Another.—Chop very fine two onions, one cucumber peeled and seeded, a little pimento, two cloves of garlic, four sprigs of parsley, same of chervil, and mix the whole in a bowl with the juice of four tomatoes, and to which add two or three tablespoonfuls of bread-crumbs. Then season with oil, vinegar, salt, pepper, mustard, and water to taste, and serve.

The Spanish call it a cool and refreshing soup.

SAUCES.

THERE is no good cooking possible without good sauces. Many excellent pieces of meat, etc., are spoiled by being served with a poor sauce.

Let every one bear in mind that water is no substitute for broth; that vinegar or water is no substitute for wine, etc.

There is no place where the old proverb can be better applied than in the kitchen, "Waste not, spare not."

The *French*, *Italians*, *Spaniards*, and *Germans*, use broth and wine in their cooking, and do not spend as much as the *Americans* for their food; they could not afford it; but they waste not, neither do they lose any thing good through carelessness or prejudice.

Good sauces are not as difficult to make as is generally believed.

This general belief comes from the fact that many, after having partaken of a certain dish somewhere, and liking it much, ask of their own cook to prepare the same.

The cook, most probably, has never heard of it, but nevertheless prepares a dish which is hardly eatable, and is to the other what a crab-apple is to a raspberry.

The most important thing in making a sauce is for the cook to put his or her whole attention and care to it.

5

Most sauces must be stirred continually while on the fire, and especially white sauces, such as *Béchamel, Béchamel* with cream or cream sauce, and white sauce.

It is necessary to stir all sauces now and then, to prevent the forming of a kind of skin on the surface.

The onions, shallots, garlics, and vinegar, used in sharp sauces, may be prepared as described for *piquante* sauce.

Sauces can always be made to suit the taste. A thousand can be made as well as a hundred, by merely adding or subtracting one or more of the compounds, or by proceeding differently. An idea of what can be done in that line can be formed by reading our directions for SUPREME SAUCE.

HOW TO MAKE A SAUCE THICKER WHEN IT IS TOO THIN, AND THINNER WHEN TOO THICK.

Take two fresh eggs, break them gently, and separate the white part from the yolk; be careful to have the yolk free from any white (there is in every yolk a little white spot, which you cannot detach without using a fork, knife, or spoon); mix well the two yolks with two or three tablespoonfuls of the sauce that is too thin, and a piece of butter the size of a pigeon's egg; then take the sauce from the fire, pour the mixture in it, little by little, stirring all the time; when the whole is in, put back on the fire for three or four minutes, but do not allow it to boil; take away and use. When too thick, add broth.

Allemande.—Chop fine and fry in butter four or five mushrooms; then add a little flour, and four or five tablespoonfuls of broth; reduce it to a sauce; put a piece of butter the size of an egg in it, also a sprig of white parsley chopped fine, one of thyme, a clove, a bay-leaf, a clove of garlic, a little nutmeg grated fine, the juice of a quarter of a lemon, and three well-beaten yolks of eggs, boil two or three minutes, and use. If found too thick, add a little broth.

Anchovy Butter.—Strain essence of anchovy through a fine sieve, and knead it with fresh butter, or salt butter that you have kneaded in cold water previously, and it is ready for use.

Anchovy Sauce.—Use butter without salt; if salty, work it in cold water. Set three ounces of butter in a saucepan on the fire, and melt it slowly; then add about two teaspoonfuls of essence of anchovy; stir a few seconds, and it is done. More anchovy may be used if liked. It is served in a boat.

Apple.—Peel, quarter, and core four or six apples, and set them on the fire in a small saucepan, with two tablespoonfuls of water; stir now and then till done; when done, mash through a fine colander; add a little sugar, and it is ready for use.

If found too thin, keep on the fire for some time. If too thick, add a little water.

Cranberry.—Put a quart of cranberries in a saucepan and set it on a rather slow fire; stir occasionally till done; mash gently through a fine colander, or through a strainer; add a little sugar, and use.

Currant.—Proceed as for a cranberry-sauce in every particular, except that it must be mashed through a strainer or through a towel.

Peach.—Stone about a quart of peaches, and proceed as for apple-sauce for the rest.

Raspberry.—Made the same as currant-sauce.

The five sauces above are served with roasted game.

Béchamel.—Mix cold, and well together, in a tin saucepan, two ounces of butter and a tablespoonful of flour; then add a pint of milk, and set on the fire; stir continually, and when turning rather thick, take off; beat a yolk of egg in a cup with a teaspoonful of water; turn it into the sauce, and mix well again; salt and white pepper to taste, and it is ready for use.

Blonde.—Proceed exactly as for white sauce, using broth instead of water.

Bread.—Take the soft part of half a ten-cent loaf of bread; break it in pieces, which put in a saucepan with a quart of good fresh milk, six pepper-corns chopped fine, and a little salt; set on the fire and boil five or six minutes, stirring the while; take off, mash through a strainer or a sieve, and it is ready for use.

A bread-sauce is really a very poor sauce. Its insipidity is concealed by the great amount of pepper that it contains.

Brown Butter, or Beurre Noir.—This is butter set on the fire in a frying-pan and left till it turns perfectly brown, then a few sprigs of parsley are dropped in it, fried half a minute, and it is ready for use.

It is sometimes used with vinegar, but in that case it is described in the receipts.

Caper.—Mix well together, cold, in a small saucepan, two ounces of butter and a tablespoonful of flour; then add a pint of broth, set on the fire, stir, and when thickening, add capers to taste, whole or chopped; give another boil, take from the fire, add salt, the yolk of an egg beaten with a teaspoonful of water, mix and serve.

Celery.—Proceed as for a caper-sauce in every particular except that you add three or four stalks of celery chopped fine, and then boil ten or twelve minutes, and strain it before using.

Colbert.—Set half a pint of meat gravy on the fire, in

a small saucepan with half a dozen mushrooms and one or two truffles chopped fine (the latter, if handy), boil gently five minutes, add one ounce of butter, stir, and when the butter is melted and mixed with the rest, it is ready for use.

Coulis of Fish, or Fish Gravy, is one and the same thing.

Boil hard four eggs, and put the yolks in a mortar. Take a pike weighing about two pounds, clean, prepare, and broil it as directed; split it open, take all the bones and skin off, put the flesh in the mortar with the yolks, and pound the whole, and knead it with a little butter. Place a little butter, of the size of a walnut, in a stewpan, and set it on a good fire; when melted, fry in it till of a golden color, two carrots and two onions cut in slices; after that add also a piece of bay-leaf, two sprigs of parsley, one of thyme, a little isinglass, the eggs and fish, and cover with water; simmer gently about one hour and a half, and strain.

If found too thin after it is strained, set it back on the fire, add a little more isinglass, and simmer fifteen minutes longer.

Coulis of Veal.—Place in a stewpan about one pound of veal, fillet or knuckle, with four ounces of bacon, not smoked, and cut fine; also a carrot cut fine, a little pepper, and grated nutmeg; set on a slow fire, cover well; half an hour after augment the fire, and as soon as you see the meat sticking to the pan, subdue it, leave it so ten minutes, then take from the fire, put the bacon, veal, and carrot on a dish; put butter about the size of an egg in the pan; when melted, sprinkle in it a teaspoonful of flour, stir with a wooden spoon, then put the meat back into it. Cover with warm broth and set on a slow fire for about two hours; take off, throw in it a few drops of cold water, skim off the fat, strain, and use.

Cream.—A cream-sauce is a *Béchamel* made with cream instead of milk.

It is often called *à la crème*, its French name.

Cucumber.—Proceed as for caper-sauce, using pickled cucumbers, chopped fine, instead of capers.

Egg.—Proceed as for caper-sauce in every particular, except that you use two hard-boiled eggs, chopped fine, instead of capers.

Diplomat.—Make a cream-sauce with one pint of cream. When made, put in it nearly half a pound of lobster butter, stir, and when the whole is well mixed, add also about a tablespoonful of essence of anchovy and mix again; pepper to taste, and use.

It is a rich sauce, used with boiled fish and baked or roasted meat.

Espagnole.—This sauce is very seldom made in the kitchen of a family, except of a large and wealthy family, being a rather expensive one. In the kitchen of a family, gravy or even broth is used in its stead; but, when preparing an extra dinner, it should be made, and a little of it used in all the brown sauces, either for meat, fish, or vegetables.

Spread about half a pound of butter in the bottom of a stewpan, lay in it lean ham and veal, partridge, wild rabbit, pheasant, or fowl of any kind, about four ounces of each, a small carrot cut in dice, one onion with a clove stuck in it, half a turnip, and a sprig of thyme; cover the pan and set it on the fire; let it simmer till reduced to a jelly, then mix in it two tablespoonfuls of flour, a wine-glass of white wine, cover with broth, add salt, pepper, a clove of garlic, a sprig of parsley, one clove, a bay-leaf, and two mushrooms cut in pieces; simmer from three to four hours, skim off the scum as soon as it comes on the surface; when done, take it from the fire, throw a few drops of cold water in, and skim off the fat, then strain and use.

It will keep for some time if kept air-tight in a pot or bottle, and in a cool, dry place.

Essence of Spinage, or Spinach.—Soak in water, drain, dry, and pound well two or three handfuls of spinach, put them in a coarse towel and press the juice out, put it in a pan on a moderate fire, and when nearly boiling, take it off, strain, and add to it a little fine-crushed sugar, stir a little, and bottle when cold; it may be kept for months; use it where directed.

Sauce for every kind of Fish, boiled, baked, or roasted. —Boil hard two eggs, take the yolks and pound them well, and place them in a bowl. Have boiling water on the fire, and put in it cives, burnet, chervil, tarragon, and parsley, four or five sprigs of each; boil five minutes, take off, drain and pound them well, then strain them on the eggs, add two tablespoonfuls of cider vinegar, two of French mustard, salt, pepper, and four tablespoonfuls of sweet-oil, which you pour in, little by little, at the same time mixing the whole well with a boxwood spoon, and it is ready for use.

Fines Herbes.—Chop very fine a small handful of parsley, shallots, and chives; and proceed as for making a caper-sauce, except that you use the chopped spices instead of capers.

Génoise.—Put two ounces of butter in a small saucepan, set it on the fire, and when melted, mix in it a tablespoonful of flour; stir for one minute, add one-fourth of a carrot, sliced, stir now and then, and when nearly fried, add also a pint of broth, half a pint of claret wine, a small onion, and a clove of garlic, chopped; two cloves, a bay-leaf, two stalks of parsley, one of thyme, salt, and pepper; boil gently about one hour and forty minutes, and strain. If it boils away, add a little broth. Put it back on the fire with about half an ounce of butter, boil gently for about ten minutes, and it is ready for use.

This sauce is excellent with any kind of boiled fish, but especially with trout, pike, and pickerel.

A trout served with a *génoise* sauce is considered a *recherché* dish.

Hollandaise.—Set one ounce of butter on the fire in a saucepan, and when melted, add half a tablespoonful of flour, stir, and when turning rather yellow, add half a pint of broth, stir for one minute; add also four sprigs of parsley and four mushrooms chopped fine (one truffle sliced, if handy, would be excellent), a liquor-glass of Madeira, Port, or Sherry wine; boil gently ten minutes, stirring the while, and serve.

Indian.—This sauce may be used with fish, in summer and in southern places.

Have a stewpan on a moderate fire, with two ounces of butter in it; when melted, add a teaspoonful of pimento, salt, a pinch of saffron, and one of grated nutmeg, also one and a half tablespoonfuls of flour—the latter you sprinkle in, little by little, stirring the while; cover with broth, boil twelve minutes and strain; afterward add two ounces of butter, stir a little, and use.

Italian.—Tie together two sprigs of parsley, one of thyme, and a bay-leaf; put them in a stewpan with two or three mushrooms cut fine, one shallot, a small onion with a clove stuck in it, a piece of butter the size of a walnut, and half a pint of white wine; set on a gentle fire, and reduce it half; then add about one tablespoonful of olive-oil and half a pint of broth, simmer forty minutes, strain, and use.

Lobster.—Chop very fine or pound some of the flesh of a boiled lobster. Make a white or blonde sauce, and instead of taking it from the fire when done, turn the chopped flesh into it with a little piece of butter; stir, give one boil, and it is ready for use.

Craw-fish, prawn, shrimp, and *crab* sauces are made the same as *lobster* sauce.

Madeira.—Mix cold in a saucepan two ounces of butter with a tablespoonful of flour, set on the fire and stir till it turns rather brown; when add nearly a pint of gravy, stir till it is becoming thick; then add half a pint of Madeira wine, little by little, stirring the while, give one boil only, salt to taste, and then strain and use.

Champagne sauce is made in the same way, except that it must be poured in faster and used immediately.

All wine sauces may be made in the same way. We mean wine sauces for meat or fish.

Maître d'Hotel.—This sauce is sometimes called *butter maître d'hotel.* Mix and knead well together in a bowl, two ounces of butter, a tablespoonful of chopped parsley and the juice of a half lemon; salt to taste and use.

Pepper, grated nutmeg, and chopped chives, may be added if liked. Using vinegar instead of lemon-juice makes an inferior sauce.

Mayonnaise.—In warm weather it is necessary to put the bowl on ice while making it. Put one or two yolks of fresh eggs in a bowl with a small pinch of salt; commence stirring with a box-wood spoon, or, what is still better, a stone or marble pestle. Stir without interruption, always in the same way and describing a circle. It is

5*

more easily done if the bowl is held steady. After having stirred about half a minute, commence pouring the oil in, drop by drop, and as soon as you see that it is thickening pretty well, add also a few drops of vinegar and same of lemon-juice; then continue with the oil in the same way. Every time that it becomes too thick, add a little vinegar, but continue stirring. You put as much oil as you please; two bottles of oil might be used and it would still be thick. Spread it on chicken salad, etc.

Tartar.—Chop some capers and shallots very fine, mix them well with a *mayonnaise* when made, and you have a Tartar sauce.

Mushroom.—Proceed exactly as for caper-sauce, using chopped mushrooms instead of capers.

Piquante.—Take a small saucepan and set it on the fire with two ounces of butter in it, and when melted add a small onion chopped; stir, and when nearly fried add a tablespoonful of flour, stir, and when turning rather brown, add half a pint of broth, salt, pepper, a pickled cucumber chopped, four stalks of parsley, also chopped, and mustard; boil gently about ten minutes, add a teaspoonful of vinegar; give one boil, and serve.

Another way.—Set the chopped onion on the fire with one gill of vinegar, and boil gently till the vinegar is entirely absorbed, or boiled away. Make the same sauce as above in another pan, omitting the onion and vinegar, and when done mix the two together, and it is ready for use.

Another.—Add three shallots, chopped fine, to the chopped onion, and proceed as above for the rest.

Parisienne.—Make a bunch of seasonings with six sprigs of parsley, one of thyme, a bay-leaf, and two cloves; put it in a saucepan with half a pint of chopped truffles, and about a pint of white wine; set on the fire and boil gently till about half reduced, strain, put back on the fire, turn into it, little by little, stirring the while, nearly a pint of gravy or *consommé ;* continue stirring now and then till it begins to turn rather thick, add pepper to taste, strain, and use with fish and game.

Poivrade.—Put a piece of butter the size of an egg in a stewpan, and set it on the fire; when melted, sprinkle in it, little by little, about a tablespoonful of flour, stirring the while; when of a proper thickness, and of a brownish color, take from the fire, add a tablespoonful of vinegar, a wine-glass of claret wine, a glass of broth, a shallot cut in two, a middling-sized onion, also cut in two, with a clove stuck in each piece, a sprig of thyme, one of parsley, a bay-leaf, a clove of garlic, a little salt, and two pepper-corns ; boil about twenty minutes, strain and use.

The vinegar, shallot, and onion may be boiled separately as for a *piquante* sauce.

Polonaise.—Put four ounces of butter in a saucepan on the fire, and when melted add two or three tablespoonfuls of the soft part of bread, bruised in a coarse towel; stir for about one minute, salt to taste, and use.

Like the *Parisienne,* it is used with game.

Poulette.—Set a stewpan on the fire with a piece of butter the size of an egg in it; when melted, sprinkle in it a tablespoonful of flour, stirring the while; pour gently in it also, and little by little, a glass of warm water, and a wine-glass of white wine, or broth instead of both, salt, pepper, a sprig of parsley, one of thyme, a bay-leaf, a chopped shallot, a little nutmeg, four small white onions, and two or three mushrooms (the latter cut fine and fried in butter before using them) ; simmer till the whole is well cooked, strain and use.

In case it should be found too light, add when done,

and before taking from the fire, two or three yolks of eggs, and the juice of a lemon.

Princesse.—Make a cream-sauce with one pint of cream and set it on a moderate fire; immediately turn into it, stirring the while, about half a pint of reduced, good meat gravy; when thoroughly mixed, add two or three ounces of butter, stir for a couple of minutes longer, strain and use immediately.

It is a very rich sauce, used with boiled fish and roasted or baked meat.

Provençale.—Chop fine two or three mushrooms, and two shallots; put the whole in a stewpan with a clove of garlic, and two tablespoonfuls of olive-oil; set on a moderate fire, and leave till half fried; then sprinkle in it half a teaspoonful of flour, stirring the while; add also half a pint of white wine, and as much broth, and two small onions, two sprigs of parsley, one of thyme, half a bay-leaf, salt, and pepper; simmer about half an hour, take from the fire, and a few minutes after skim off the fat; take out the garlic, onions, parsley, thyme, and bay-leaf, and it is then ready for immediate use.

Ravigote.—Chop fine, and in equal proportion, two tablespoonfuls of chervil, tarragon, and pepper-grass, also, in equal proportion, one teaspoonful of burnet and table celery; place the whole in a stewpan with salt and pepper, cover with broth, set on the fire, and boil twenty minutes; after which take from the fire, and strain. Mix two ounces of butter with flour enough to make a paste, put it with the sauce on the fire, add a tablespoonful of cider vinegar; simmer till of a proper thickness, and use.

Robert.—Put about four ounces of butter in a stewpan, set it on a moderate fire; when melted, sprinkle in it about a tablespoonful of flour, stirring the while; when of a brownish color, add three small onions chopped fine, salt, and pepper; stir, and leave on the fire till the whole is turning brown, then add a glass of broth, boil about thirty minutes, and strain; mix well in a cup one teaspoonful of vinegar, one of sugar, and one of mustard, which mix again with the sauce, and it is ready to be used.

Rémolade.—Chop very fine a small handful of chervil, tarragon, and burnet, in equal proportion, and put them in a saucer or boat; add salt, pepper, nutmeg grated, and mustard, to taste; also one or two hard-boiled eggs cut in dice; mix the whole gently and well; then add the vinegar, and lastly the oil. The two latter ones are put in little by little, stirring gently the while. Serve as it is.

Another.—Proceed as for the above, except that you chop fine with the chervil, etc., some parsley, shallot, and garlic; the five spices in equal proportion.

When finished, add also a pinch of sugar.

Roux.—Set a small saucepan on a moderate fire, with two ounces of butter in it; sprinkle into it, when melted, a tablespoonful of flour; stir, and when turning brown, use.

Shallot.—Chop the shallots, and proceed as for caper-sauce, using them instead of capers.

Soubise.—Put about half a pint of good meat gravy in a saucepan; set it on the fire, and when boiling add half a gill of Madeira wine; when well mixed, add also two or three tablespoonfuls of *purée* of white onions, salt, and pepper; boil five minutes, stirring now and then, and it is made.

A *soubise* is an excellent sauce for baked or boiled fish, also for roasted meat.

Supreme.—This sauce is made in several ways. We will give here the three principal ones:

1. Make an *Allemande* sauce; and when done, add to it two ounces of butter and half a gill of *consommé;* stir and mix, and place on a brisk fire to start it boiling at once; take it from the fire as soon as it becomes thick; then add a few drops of lemon-juice, and use.

2. Make a *roux;* add to it about half a pint of chicken gravy; stir or boil five or six minutes; then add two ounces of butter, the juice of a lemon, a pinch of parsley chopped fine; give one boil, and use.

3. This is made like No. 2, except that you use an *Allemande* sauce instead of a *roux*, and besides the pint of chicken gravy, etc., you add also half a gill of white wine.

It is used especially with roasted chicken and game.

Tomato.—If you use fresh tomatoes, blanch them first; if preserved, use them as they are in the can. Put one pint of tomatoes in a saucepan with a small onion and a clove of garlic sliced; also two stalks of parsley, one of thyme, a bay-leaf, one clove, six pepper-corns, and salt; boil gently till reduced about one-third, when mash gently through a strainer or sieve; all the tomato-seed and seasonings must remain in the strainer; put back on the fire, with a little piece of butter; give one boil, and it is done.

Truffle.—This sauce is made like a caper-sauce, using chopped or sliced truffles instead of capers.

Velouté.—This and gravy is nearly the same thing. It is gravy made as directed for gravy, with the addition of a dozen mushrooms chopped fine; and is used for sauces, like gravy, to make sauces richer than with broth.

Vinaigrette.—Put salt and pepper in a saucer (and mustard, if it is to be used with butcher's meat; but with fish, chicken, or birds, it is really too strong; it neutralizes the delicate flavor of the object), and pour vinegar over, little by little, beating with a fork at the same time; then pour the oil, also little by little, and while beating; a little chopped parsley is also added; and serve with cold meat, fish, or vegetables.

It is quickly made, is good, and makes an excellent dish for breakfast, served as we said above.

White.—Put two ounces of butter in a small saucepan and set it on the fire, stir a little, and as soon as melted, remove on a rather slow fire; add a tablespoonful of flour, stir continually till thoroughly mixed (two or three minutes); then add again about a pint of boiling water, pouring gently, and stirring the while, take off when it begins to turn thick; add a yolk of egg beaten with a teaspoonful of cold water, mix it well with the rest, and it is ready for use; after having mixed, also salt and white pepper to taste.

Oyster.—Add to a white sauce some oysters blanched; then stir and mix with the whole the juice of half a lemon.

Muscle.—Boil the muscles about one minute and make as oyster-sauce.

SAUCES FOR PUDDINGS.

Milk.—Put in a block-tin saucepan four tablespoonfuls of sugar, one of flour, four yolks of eggs, one pint of milk; essence to flavor, and mix the whole well; set on a good but not sharp fire, stir continually till it begins to become rather thick; take off, turn over the pudding, and serve.

Madeira.—Set a saucepan on the fire with one ounce of butter in it; as soon as melted, add half a tablespoonful of flour, stir till it turns rather yellow, and add also one pint of water, four ounces of sugar, and a few drops of burnt sugar; boil gently, about twenty-five minutes; add nearly a gill of Madeira wine, boil again ten minutes, and serve in a boat.

Rum.—Proceed as for Madeira-sauce, except you use half a gill of rum instead of Madeira.

Brandy.—Proceed as for rum-sauce, using the same proportion of brandy.

FARCES AND GARNITURES,

CALLED ALSO GARNISH AND GARNISHING, USED TO DECORATE OR ORNAMENT DISHES.

With Bread.—Put in a tureen about a pound of the soft part of bread, and cover with broth; when it has absorbed the broth, place it in a stewpan, set it on a slow fire, and leave till it becomes a thick paste; stir now and then, then mix well with it three yolks of eggs, and it is ready for use.

With Cabbage.—Throw into boiling water a little salt and a middling-sized cabbage; boil it half an hour, take it from the kettle with a skimmer, throw it in cold water, and drain it, pressing it a little in the drainer to force the water out; cut off the stump, and chop the cabbage fine. Have in a stewpan on the fire, three or four ounces of fresh butter; put the cabbage in when the butter is half melted, sprinkling on while stirring a teaspoonful of flour; pour on it, little by little, some broth, stirring the while, and when it has a fine brownish color, wet with broth enough to boil it; season with salt, a little grated nutmeg, and four pepper-corns; boil gently till the sauce is thick enough, take away the pepper-corns, and use.

With Combs of Chicken.—Soak the combs over night in cold water, and then clean them well by wiping roughly with a coarse towel, wetted and salted; wash and drain them; put a dozen of them in a saucepan with two sweetbreads blanched, cover the whole with broth, and boil till done; then add salt, pepper, a few drops of lemon-juice, and it is ready for use.

With Cauliflowers.—Proceed as for cabbage in every particular, except that it does not require as long doing.

With Croutons.—Cut pieces of soft part of stale bread in different shapes, and fry them on both sides in butter or fat.

For potage, they are cut in dice, but for decorating dishes, they are cut either round, square, oblong, or of a heart, star-like, half moon, butterfly, or flower shape, and about one-quarter of an inch thick. Take them off with a skimmer, and turn into a colander to drain.

The cut *d* is used for potage, and *a*, *b*, *c*, etc., are used to decorate.

Duxelle.—Make a *fines-herbes* sauce, and when ready to be used, add half a gill of gravy, and give one boil; add also two or three yolks of eggs, simmer one minute, and use warm.

Mushrooms, whole or in slices, may be added at the same time the yolks of eggs are added.

With Eggs.—Mash and mix well together six hard-boiled yolks of eggs with three yolks not cooked, salt and pepper. Put the mixture in parts on the paste-board, which must be previously dusted with flour; roll each part and give it the shape of a small egg (a pigeon's egg or a little larger). When the whole is thus prepared, drop in boiling water, boil till cooked, and use to decorate meat or fish.

Financière.—A garniture *financière* is the same as a garniture with combs of chicken, to which are added some mushrooms and truffles, both cut in slices.

It is generally served with a roast chicken.

With Livers.—Geese livers are the best, being the fattest. Drop two geese livers in boiling water and a little salt, boil three minutes and drain. Put in a saucepan one gill of broth, same of white wine, Sauterne or Catawba, a tablespoonful of gravy, six pepper-corns, two or three stalks of parsley, salt, and the livers; set on the fire and boil gently for about twenty-five minutes. Take off the livers, boil a few minutes longer to thicken the sauce, turn it over the livers through a strainer, and it is ready.

The same may be done with the livers of poultry or any other kind of birds; the seasonings are the same, and the proportion is according to the size or to the number of livers.

Besides being used as garnishing, it may be served as a breakfast dish.

Macédoine.—Blanch a dozen of Brussels cabbages. Blanch also half a dozen asparagus cut in pieces about an inch long. Put four ounces of butter in a saucepan on the fire, and when melted put it into a gill of carrots, same of turnips, both cut with a vegetable spoon, also a dozen small onions; stir now and then till the whole is about

half done, when add a little over a pint of broth and the
Brussels cabbages; boil about ten minutes.   Then add
again the blanched asparagus, half a dozen mushrooms.
broth just enough to cover the whole, simmer till every
thing is done, salt and pepper to taste, a pinch of sugar
and it is ready for use.

Water may be used instead of broth, but is inferior.

A *macédoine* may be served with any meat—roasted,
baked, or broiled.

With Mushroons.—Chop fine half a pint of fresh
mushroons and two tablespoonfuls of parsley.   Set a
saucepan on the fire with two ounces of fat grated salt
pork in it, as much butter, and as soon as the butter is
melted put the mushrooms and parsley in; season with
salt, pepper, a little grated nutmeg, and a quarter of a pint
of white wine; let boil gently till reduced to a jelly, and
use.

When done, three or four yolks of eggs may be mixed
with it.

With Onions.—Put a dozen onions in a crockery
saucepan and half cover them with broth.   Cover the pan
as well as possible, simmer till cooked, when add a teaspoonful of sugar, salt, simmer again for about ten minutes, basting now and then, and serve warm with beef,
mutton, or venison.

Quenelles.—Chop fine one pound of fresh veal, half
lean and half fat—the fat nearest the kidney is the best;
then pound it well and mash it through a sieve.   Mix two
yolks of eggs with it, and season to taste with salt, pepper, nutmeg grated, and powdered cinnamon.   Spread
flour on the paste-board, put a teaspoonful of meat here
and there; roll gently each part into small balls, using as
little flour as possible.   They may also be rolled of an

olive shape. Throw the balls into boiling broth or boiling water at the first boiling, boil five minutes and drain. As soon as cold they are ready for use.

Boulettes, fricadelles, godiveau, and *quenelles* are one and the same thing.

Whole eggs may be used instead of the yolks only, add also a few bread-crumbs. To the seasonings above some parsley chopped fine may be added.

Make *quenelles* with any kind of meat—butcher's meat, poultry, and game, also with fish well boned.

To the lean meat add the same weight of fat veal, as above directed, or, in its stead, beef suet.

Truffles or mushrooms, or both, may be added to the mixture, either of meat or of fish.

Quenelles are used for garnitures, etc. They may be fried instead of boiled.

Salpicon.—Cut in dice an equal quantity of each, and to weigh altogether about one pound and a half, calf sweetbreads, livers, or flesh of fowls, and ham—three kinds in all; also two mushrooms and two truffles; all must be nearly cooked in water beforehand. Put them in a stewpan, season with salt, pepper, a bay-leaf, a clove of garlic, an onion, a sprig of parsley, and one of thyme; cover with half a pint of broth, and as much of white wine; set on a slow fire; it must not boil, but simmer gently; stir now and then till the whole is well cooked; take out the bay-leaf, onion, garlic, parsley, and thyme. In case the sauce should not be thick enough, add a little fecula, stir, and leave awhile longer on the fire, and it is ready for use.

With Truffles.—Slice the truffles and put them in a saucepan with a pinch of sugar, broth and claret wine enough to cover them, half of each, simmer for about twenty minutes, add a little potato starch, boil gently till it begins to thicken, and use.

Lobster Butter.—Put the flesh of the two large claws of a boiled lobster with a little of the inside, about a tablespoonful, in a mortar and pound well. Add about the same volume of good butter and pound again till the whole is well mixed. It is then mashed through a fine sieve, and is ready for use. When the lobster has coral, it is pounded with the rest, and gives a fine color to the butter.

If the lobster has no coral, a piece of the reddest part of the shell is pounded with the rest, when the butter is to be colored.

This butter may be used instead of ordinary butter for fish-sauces, or for making a *maître d'hôtel* for boiled fish, or for garnishing the same.

To clarify it, just put the butter into a bowl when made, put the bowl in a boiling *bain-marie* for about half an hour, take off and immediately turn it through a cloth into a bowl half full of cold water. The cloth must be rather twisted, to cause the butter to run through. When it is in the bowl, stir it till rather hard; work it in a ball, and wipe it dry.

Thus clarified it is finer than when used merely mixed.

The same butter may be made, and in the same way, with *craw-fish*, *prawns*, and *shrimps*.

Horse-radish Butter.—Grate some horse-radish and mix it well with about the same volume of butter, mash through a sieve, and it is ready for use.

Tarragon and *garlic* butter are made as the above.

If the butter be found too strong, use more butter and less of garlic, etc.

Ravigote Butter (called also *Beurre de Montpellier*).— Blanch the following spices: parsley, tarragon, chives,

chervil—parsley and chervil in equal proportion and about
half as much of the two others, about two handfuls alto
gether—drain dry and put them in a mortar with two
anchovies boned, one shallot chopped and bruised in a
coarse towel, half a dozen capers, a rather small piece of
pickled cucumber, four ounces of butter, two hard-boiled
yolks of eggs, and the juice of half a lemon. Pound the
whole well together, then add a tablespoonful of essence
of spinach, mix well, mash through a sieve, and use.

This butter is excellent to decorate and to eat with cold
fish. It is sometimes used with cold birds.

Hazel-nut Butter.—Pound some hazel-nuts or filberts
and then mix throughly with good butter, mash through
a sieve, and use as ordinary butter. The proportion according to taste. It is easily prepared, and is delicious.

Do the same with *pea-nuts*, or any other nut.

Melted Butter.—Put butter in a crockery vessel and
place it above a pan of water or some other liquid, heated
but not boiling, so that the butter will melt slowly and
gradually. Sometimes the butter may be wanted soft only,
or what is called melted soft, or thoroughly melted. It is
easy to obtain those different states above with heated
liquor, and the butter, though melted, is more firm than
when melted on the fire.

Scented Butter.—Whenever a certain flavor is desired
with butter, put a piece of firm and good butter in a bowl
with a few drops of essence, knead well, and then mash
through a sieve.

PURÉES.

Purées are made with vegetables, but when the flesh
of poultry or other birds is mashed through a sieve after
being cooked, it is sometimes called a *purée* also.

The bones of a ham, after the flesh is disposed of, is the most excellent thing you can put with the vegetables to boil them in order to make *purées*.

One-third of the bones of a middling-sized ham is enough for about a quart of vegetables.

When you have no ham bones, use four ounces of good salt pork, as lean as possible; but never use smoked pork, it gives a disagreeable taste to the *purée*.

Of Dry Beans, white or colored, Kidney, Lima, or any other kind.—Dry beans must be soaked in cold water, or even in lukewarm water, when in a hurry. According to the nature of the beans, they must be soaked for from six to twenty-four hours.

Soak a quart of beans as directed above; drain and put them in a saucepan with one-third of the bones of a ham, or about four ounces of salt pork; cover with cold water, season with a bay-leaf, a sprig of thyme, two of parsley, two middling-sized onions, with two cloves stuck in them, and a carrot cut in pieces; when the whole is well cooked, throw away thyme, bay-leaf, onions, and cloves; mash well through a colander all the rest except the bacon.

While mashing them through the colander, wet them with some of the water in which they have boiled, else it would be difficult and long.

When mashed, put them in a saucepan with a little broth or water, salt, and two ounces of butter; stir now and then till the butter is melted and thoroughly mixed with the rest, and it is ready for use. The quantity of broth or water is according to how thick or thin they are wanted. The salt pork is good to eat.

Of Lentils.—It is made in the same way as that of beans, except that they do not require to be soaked more than five or six hours in cold water.

Of Peas (dry or split).—Proceed as for lentils in every particular.

Of Chestnuts.—Remove the skin of a quart of chestnuts and drop them in boiling water, with a little salt. As soon as the under skin comes off easily, take them from the fire, drain, drop them in cold water, and then remove the under or white skin; put them in a saucepan with about one quart of broth, set on the fire and boil gently till well done, and mash through a colander.

Then put the chestnuts, and what is left of the broth, in a saucepan, set on the fire, stir, add a pinch of sugar and an ounce of butter; give one boil, and it is made.

Of Green Peas.—Wash a quart of green peas in cold water, and drain; put two quarts of cold water on the fire in a saucepan, with a little salt, and at the first boil throw the peas in, season with three or four sprigs of parsley, one of thyme, two onions, and two cloves, a carrot in slices, salt, and pepper; boil till tender. It may take only two minutes, or it may require half an hour, according to how tender the peas are.

Mash through a colander, and finish like *purée* of beans, using either broth or water. With broth it is richer and better.

Of Lima Beans.—Proceed for green Limas as for green peas.

Of Sweet Corn.—It is made like that of green peas.

Of Asparagus.—Cut the eatable part of the asparagus in pieces, and proceed as for *purée* of green peas.

Of Potatoes.—Steam a quart of potatoes, and then mash them well; put them in a saucepan with half a pint of milk, two ounces of butter, and salt; set on the fire, stir now and then, take off and use. It takes about fifteen minutes after being set back on the fire.

6

Another way.—Proceed as above, using broth or water instead of milk.

Of Jerusalem Artichokes.—Prepared as potatoes.

Of Carrots.—Clean well, and cut in slices, a dozen middling-sized carrots; put them in a stewpan with four ounces of butter, and set on the fire; when about half fried, cover with broth or water; season with half a bay-leaf, a small sprig of thyme, one of parsley, a small onion, and a clove stuck in it; when the whole is well cooked, throw away onion, clove, bay-leaf, and thyme, mash the rest through a colander; then put back on the fire, with a little butter; simmer for about two hours, stirring occasionally, and it is made.

In case it should turn too thick, add broth or water.

The longer they are simmered, the better the taste.

Of Turnips.—Proceed as with carrots in every particular.

Of Celery.—It is always made with turnip-rooted celery. Clean the celery well, wash and cut it in pieces, and prepare as *purée* of carrots, adding a teaspoonful of sugar.

Of Cauliflowers.—Separate the branches, and throw them in boiling water and salt; boil two minutes and drain. Put them on the fire with broth or water, enough just to cover them, two or three stalks of parsley, and salt to season.

Boil gently till tender; remove the parsley; mash through a colander; put back on the fire with a little butter and white pepper, simmer about ten minutes, stirring now and then the while, and it is ready for use.

Instead of butter, some cream may be added.

Of Pumpkin.—Made exactly the same as that of cauliflowers, after the pumpkin is peeled and cut in pieces.

Of Squash.—Same as pumpkin.

Of Spinach.—Clean the spinach, and cut off the stem; the leaf only is good; wash and drain it; put cold water and a little salt on the fire, and throw the spinach in at the first boil. When tender, drain and drop immediately in cold water; drain again, and then chop it very fine. After being chopped, it may be mashed through a sieve, to have it finer; put it back on the fire without any water at all, and when it gets rather dry, add a little flour; stir and mix; add again a little gravy or good broth; stir, then salt to taste, and it is ready for use.

If the spinach is young and tender, it takes only two or three minutes boiling before chopping it.

From the time it is put back on the fire, it takes about five or six minutes to finish it.

Of Sorrel.—Proceed as with spinach in every particular.

Of Mushrooms.—Clean well and cut in pieces a quart of fresh mushrooms; soak them in cold water, in which you have put the juice of a lemon; drain, and chop them fine. Put a stewpan on the fire, with a piece of butter the size of a duck's egg; when melted, put your mushrooms in; when half fried, add the juice of a lemon, finish frying, then cover with some roux-sauce; let simmer till it becomes rather thick, strain and use.

Of Onions.—Peel, quarter, and blanch for eight minutes, a dozen onions. Drain and put them in a saucepan with four or six ounces of butter, according to the size of the onions; set on a slow fire, stir now and then till well done; then season with salt, a little flour, stir for two minutes to cook the flour, and mix it thoroughly with the rest; take from the fire; add cream, little by little, stirring the while. It does not require much cream to make the *purée* of a proper thickness. Mash through a sieve or fine colander, add a pinch of sugar, and it is ready for use.

It makes an excellent *purée*, and is good served with nearly every kind of meat.

Made with white onions, and properly mashed through a sieve, it looks like cream, and is almost as white as snow.

FISH.

The Indians bleed the fish as soon as caught, because the flesh is firmer when cooked.

The Dutch and the French bleed the cod, which accounts for the better quality and whiteness of their codfish.

To select.—To be good, fish must be fresh. It is fresh when the eyes are clear, the fins stiff, the gills red, hard to open, and without bad odor.

To clean and prepare for boiling.—The sooner fish is cleaned the better. Cut the belly open, take the inside out, wash well and wipe dry immediately with a clean towel, inside and out. Place the eggs or soft roes inside, and tie with twine. It is then ready to be boiled.

If not cooked as soon as cleaned and prepared, keep it on ice.

To clean and prepare for baking, frying, roasting, and to cut in pieces, etc.—Scale the fish well, holding it by the head or tail; cut the belly open and take the inside out; trim off the fins, gills, and tail; wash well inside and out, and wipe dry immediately.

Keep it on ice if not used immediately.

Same Family, or Kind.—We give only one receipt for all the fishes of the same family, or having the same kind of flesh, as they are cooked alike, and require the same spices.

Almost every kind of fish is boiled, broiled, fried, or stewed. Some are better boiled than broiled, others better fried than stewed, etc. With few exceptions, any eatable fish may be cooked in these four ways. Few are roasted.

To know when cooked enough.—It is very difficult, if not entirely impossible, to tell how long it takes to cook fish, as it depends as much on the size, kind, or quality of the fish as on the fire; but as soon as the flesh comes off the bones easily, the fish is cooked; this is very easy to be ascertained with a knife.

To improve.—Clean the fish as for baking, etc., and lay it in a crockery vessel with the following seasonings under and upon it: parsley and onions chopped fine, salt, pepper, thyme, bay-leaves, and vinegar or oil; turn it over occasionally, and leave thus for two or three hours.

To bone.—Slit the fish on one side of the backbone and fins, from head to tail; then run the knife between the bones and the flesh so as to detach the whole side from the rest; do the same for the other side.

For a flounder, or any other flat fish, slit right in the middle of both sides of the fish so as to make four instead of two pieces.

The head, bones, and fins are not used at all, and are left in one piece.

To serve, when boiled.—The fish is placed on a napkin and on a dish or platter, surrounded with parsley, and the sauce served in a saucer.

To skin.—Take hold of the piece of fish by the smaller end, and with the thumb and forefinger of the left hand; run the knife between the flesh and skin, moving the knife to and fro as if you were sawing. Throw away the skin, and the fish is ready for cooking.

If the skin were breaking, as it happens sometimes, take hold of it again, and proceed as before.

To decorate.—Fish may be decorated with jelly, but it is easier and more sightly with craw-fish. The skewers are stuck in the fish as they are in a *fillet of beef.*

The craw-fish when boiled are red like the lobster, and, besides using them with skewers, some may be placed all around the fish; it is delicate eating as well as sightly. Skewers are never used with fish in *vinaigrette,* or when the fish is cut in pieces. The craw-fish has only to be boiled before using it for decorating fish.

Shrimps and *prawns* are used the same as craw-fish.

Oysters are also used, raw or blanched; run the skewer through a large oyster or craw-fish, then through a slice of truffle; again through an oyster, truffle, etc.; through two, three, or more of each, according to the size of the skewer or of the fish.

Fish-kettle.—A fish-kettle must have a double bottom. It is more handy to take the fish off without breaking it,

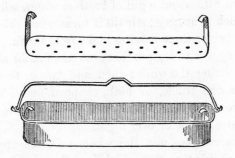

and there is no danger of having it spoiled while cooking. Fish-kettles are found in every house-furnishing store.

Baked.—Clean and prepare the fish, as directed for baking; put it in a baking-pan with salt, pepper, and butter spread all over it; just cover the bottom of the pan with water or broth; place a piece of buttered paper over it and bake. Baste two or three times; take off when done, and serve warm with a sauce.

While the fish is baking you prepare the sauce, put it in a boat, and serve warm with the fish.

A baked fish may be served with its gravy only, adding a few drops of lemon-juice or vinegar, or with any kind of sauce, according to taste.

Balls.—Fish-balls are often called *fish-cakes* or *fish-croquettes.* They are generally made with cold fish, but it may be cooked especially to make balls.

Fish, full of bones, like shad, is not fit to make balls; cod is the easiest.

Commence by chopping the flesh very fine, then chop fine also a small piece of onion and fry it with butter (half a middling-sized onion with two ounces of butter are enough for half a pound of fish); when fried stir in it a tablespoonful of flour, and about half a minute after turn the fish in with about a gill of broth or water, salt, pepper, and a pinch of nutmeg; stir till it turns rather thick, which will take two or three minutes; take from the fire, mix two yolks of eggs with it; put back on the fire for about one minute, stirring the while; then add two or three mushrooms or one truffle, or both, chopped fine. Turn the mixture into a dish, spread it, and put it away to cool for two or three hours, or over night.

Before cooking, mix the whole well, the upper part being more dry than that which is under; put it in parts on the paste-board, roll each part to the shape you wish, either round, oval, or flat; the paste-board may be dusted with bread-crumbs or flour to help in handling the mixture, then boil or fry, according to taste.

It may also be baked in cakes.

When fried, they may be dipped in beaten egg, rolled in bread-crumbs, and then fried in hot fat. (*See* FRYING.)

Boiled.—Clean and prepare the fish as directed, and put it in a fish-kettle; cover it with cold water (sea-water is the best); add the following seasonings to a pound of fish: two stalks of parsley, one of tarragon if handy, one tablespoonful of vinegar, and half a middling-sized onion sliced; salt if boiled in fresh water. Set on the fire, and, for a fish weighing two pounds or under, take off at the first boiling—it is done enough. For a fish weighing five pounds, boil five minutes, etc., that is, about one minute for each pound. If it were a thick slice of fish instead of a whole one, weighing two or three pounds, it should be boiled two or three minutes longer, etc., according to thickness.

Broiled.—Slit the fish on the back and clean it; salt and pepper it; have a little melted butter and spread it all over the fish, on both sides, with a brush, and broil it. (*See* BROILING.)

While the fish is broiling, prepare a *maître d'hotel* sauce, spread it on the fish as soon as dished, and serve.

It may also be served with anchovy butter.

Fried.—Any small fish of the size of a smelt, or smaller, is better fried than prepared in any other way.

Clean and prepare the fish as directed, wipe it dry. Dip it in milk, place in a colander for five minutes, then roll in flour, and fry. It may also be fried just rolled in flour.

Another way.—When wiped dry, dip in beaten egg, roll in bread-crumbs, and fry.

Another.—When wiped dry, dip the fish in butter, and

6*

fry. Then the fish is dropped in hot fat (*see* FRYING), turned into a colander, salted, and served hot, with fried parsley around or in the middle, according to how the fish is arranged in the dish.

Fry the following as above: *carp, tench, frost, bass, perch, black and blue fish, gold, loach, mullet, porgy, weak, flounder, pike, pickerel, smelt, sun, herring,* and *white-fish of the lakes.*

A la Orly.—If it is small fish, like the smelt, it is pre-pared whole; if the fish is larger, it must be boned and skinned, and cut in pieces about two inches long. Roll the fish, or pieces of fish, slightly in flour; dip it in beaten egg, and roll it again in bread-crumbs; then fry it in hot fat as above.

When fried, serve it with a tomato-sauce.

The fish may be served on a napkin in a dish, and the sauce in a boat or saucer.

Roasted.—The following fishes only are roasted: *eel, salmon, shad, pike, turbot.*

Clean and prepare as directed, and then tie with twine. Spread salt, pepper, and melted butter (with a brush) all over the fish, and then envelop it in buttered paper; set on the spit and roast. Baste with a little melted butter, and remove the paper about five minutes before it is done.

When on the dish the twine is cut off and removed, and it is served as hot as possible with the following sauces, to which tarragon is added in making them, if handy: *caper, Hollandaise, Mayonnaise, piquante, poivrade,* and *rémolade.* A roast fish is served after roast meat.

Another way.—Clean, and cut in slices half an inch thick, or leave entire, as it suits you; skin it well; lay it in a crockery vessel, spread over it some chopped parsley, grated nutmeg, salt, pepper, and two gills of white wine (this is for about three pounds), leave thus two hours; then take the fish only, envelop it in buttered paper, fix it on the spit before a good fire, baste with the wine and seasonings from the crockery dish, and when nearly done take the paper off; finish the cooking, basting the while, and serve with the drippings, to which you may add a little vinegar, sweet-oil, and mustard.

If there is any left, you can serve it cold the next day with an oil-sauce.

Sauté.—Scale, clean, and prepare the fish as directed. For one pound of fish put about one ounce of butter in a frying-pan on the fire, and when melted put the fish in; fry it on both sides, and serve it with a *maître d'hôtel.*

Stewed.—Clean and prepare as directed three pounds of fish, cut it in pieces about two inches long. Put in a fish-kettle four ounces of butter, kneaded with a teaspoonful of flour, and the same of chopped parsley, add two or three mushrooms cut in pieces, salt and pepper, then the fish and a glass of claret wine, or a wine-glass of vinegar; cover with water, set on a good fire, boil gently till cooked; dish the pieces of fish, strain the sauce on them, spread the pieces of mushrooms over, and serve.

Stuffed.—When cleansed, cut out the backbone from the head to within two inches of the tail, and fill its place with the following mixture: soak stale bread in cold water and then squeeze the water out; put one ounce of butter into a saucepan and set it on the fire; as soon as melted, fry in it one middle-sized onion, chopped fine; then add the bread; stir for two minutes, add also salt, pepper, a pinch of nutmeg, two or three tablespoonfuls of broth; stir again two or three minutes; take the pan from the fire, add a yolk of egg, put back on the fire for half a minute, stirring the while, take off again, add a teaspoonful of chopped parsley, and use. When full, tie the fish with twine; place it in a baking-pan, salt and pepper it; spread a little butter on it also; cover the bottom of the pan with cold water, bake and serve with its gravy.

If there is not gravy enough, or if it has dried away, add a little broth a few minutes before taking from the oven.

Fish au Gratin.—Bone and skin the fish as directed. For a fish weighing about two pounds, spread one ounce of butter on a tin plate or baking-pan, spread over it half an onion, chopped; place the pieces of fish on them; add salt, pepper, a tablespoonful of vinegar or a wine-glass of white wine, and half an ounce of butter; spread over and bake.

While it is baking, put in a small saucepan one ounce of butter, and set it on the fire; when melted, add half a tablespoonful of flour, stir, and, when it is turning yellow, add also about one gill of broth, two tablespoonfuls of meat-gravy, the juice of the fish when baked (if the fish be not done when the time comes to put the juice in the pan, keep the pan in a warm place, and wait), salt, and pepper; boil gently about five minutes, stirring occasionally. Place the fish in a tin or silver dish, spread three or four mushrooms sliced over it; turn the sauce gently over the whole, dust with bread-crumbs; put half an ounce of butter, in four or five pieces, on the whole; bake ten or twelve minutes, and serve in the dish in which it is.

In Matelote.—Every kind of fish is good in *matelote*, but the following are the best: *bass*, *black-fish*, *blue-fish*, *carp*, *eel*, *perch*, *pickerel*, *pike*, *porgy*, *tench*, *trout*, and *craw-fish*.

A *matelote* may be made of eels alone, but it is better with eels and one, two, or three other kinds of fish.

Eels tasting of mud are not good. There is a sure way of taking away the muddy taste, but it is a rather expensive one. Boil them a few minutes in claret wine and a little salt, before using them.

Clean, and prepare as directed, one pound of eels, one pound of pike, and one pound of trout, or one pound of any of the fishes named above—in all, three pounds. Cut the fish in pieces about two inches long, fry it slightly with a little butter, and put it away for awhile.

Put four ounces of butter in a saucepan and set it on the fire; when melted, add two tablespoonfuls of flour, stir, and, when the flour is turning rather brown, add also about a quart of broth, a pint of claret, a bunch of seasonings, composed of half a dozen stalks of parsley, two of thyme, two bay-leaves, and two cloves, also salt, pepper, two cloves of garlic, and six button onions; boil gently for about half an hour. Then put the fish in with from six to twelve mushrooms, broth enough to cover the whole, if the broth and wine already in do not cover it; boil gently for about half an hour, or till the fish is cooked, tossing the saucepan now and then; dish the fish; place the mushrooms and onions all over; sprinkle the sauce over it through a strainer, and serve warm. *Croutons* may be served around.

Another, or Marinière.—Prepare and cut the fish as for the above, but instead of frying it put it in a saucepan, into which you have put previously about half a dozen sprigs of parsley, two of thyme, two bay-leaves, two cloves of garlic, twelve small onions, two cloves, salt, and pepper; when the fish is placed over the above seasonings, cover entirely with claret wine. Set the saucepan on a sharp fire, and, as soon as it boils, throw into it a glass of French brandy, set it on fire, and let it burn. It will not

burn very long, but enough to give a good taste to it. As
soon as it stops burning, knead four ounces of butter with
a tablespoonful of flour, and put it in the pan; toss
the pan gently now and then till done. It takes about
forty minutes with a good fire.

When done, dish the fish carefully, place the mushrooms all over it, the onions all around, strain the sauce
over the whole, and serve warm.

Croutons may also be served with the rest; put around
the fish one *crouton*, then an onion, and so on, all
around.

Another.—Proceed as for the above, in every particular, except that you cover the fish and seasonings with
broth and white wine, half of each, instead of claret.
Serve in the same way.

A *matelote* may be made three or four days in advance,
and then warmed in boiling water (*bain-marie*) just before
serving it.

Many prefer a *matelote* made four days before eating
it, and prepared in the following way : When made, put
it away to cool as quickly as possible; twenty-four hours
after that, warm it in boiling water; cool, and warm again
in the same way once a day. If the sauce becomes thick,
add a little broth.   Serve warm.

Vinaigrette—Boil a fish as directed, take it from the
kettle and let cool; then dish it.   Chop fine the yolks of
two hard-boiled eggs; do the same with the two whites;
chop also a handful of parsley.   Put a string of the yolks
on both sides of the fish, then along that a string of the
whites, and along these a string of the parsley; along the
parsley, and about half an inch apart, a string of capers.
Cut a lemon in sixteen slices, and in the following way :
first split the lemon in two lengthwise, then split again

each half in two and lengthwise also; by splitting four times, you have sixteen pieces, resembling somewhat the carpels of oranges. After the first splitting, hold the piece of lemon with the nail of the left thumb, the rind downward, and always split lengthwise and in the middle. Place eight pieces on each side of the dish and along the capers, and serve cold, with stalks of parsley on top of the fish, and also two or three in its mouth.

Serve with it a vinaigrette, in a saucer or boat.

The following fishes, *bass, black and blue fish, carp, cat, dory, drum, gar, gurnard, herring, king, lump, mackerel, parr, perch, pickerel, pike, pilot, porgy, roach, rock, scup, sucker, sword, tautog, tench, trout, troutlet, weak,* and *weaver,* after being baked or boiled as directed, may be served with the following sauces: *anchovy, caper, génevoise, génoise, au gratin, Hollandaise, Italienne, matelote, tomato, Tartar,* and *vinaigrette.*

It would be perfectly useless to have a receipt for each fish, since the preparation is the same.

The same fishes are also prepared *au court bouillon.* Clean and prepare about three pounds of fish, as directed for baking, etc. It may be one fish or several, according to size. Place the fish in a fish-kettle, just cover it with cold water and a gill of vinegar, or with half water and half white wine; season with three or four sprigs of parsley, one of thyme, a bay-leaf, one clove, one onion, half a carrot (in slices), two cloves of garlic, salt, pepper, and a little tarragon, if handy. Set on the fire, and boil gently till done. Dish the fish, and serve it warm with a caper or anchovy sauce in a boat, or with currant jelly.

The same—à la Bretonne.—Slit the fish on the back, as for broiling, and clean it. When wiped dry, lay it in a bake-pan in which there is a little melted butter, the inside of the fish under; place thus on a good fire, turn over when done on one side, and, when cooked, spread some *maître d'hôtel* on it, and serve warm.

The same—aux fines herbes.—Clean and prepare as for baking, etc., and also improve it as directed. Envelop the fish in buttered paper, and also the seasonings in which it has been improved, except the thyme and bay-leaves, broil it, and serve with *piquante* sauce.

Cod-fish, cusk, haddock, hake, halibut, pollack, and *torsk,* after being baked or boiled as directed, are served with the following sauces:

Anchovy, Béchamel, caper, cream, egg, Hollandaise. maître d'hôtel, tomato, vinaigrette.

EEL, CONGER, AND LAMPREY

To clean.—When skinned, clean, head, and tail them. Then throw them in boiling water, in which you have put a little salt and a teaspoonful of vinegar; leave them in it about five minutes, take out, and drain.

Broiled.—Clean and cut two pounds of eel, or of either of the others, in pieces about three inches long. Put in a stewpan a piece of butter the size of an egg, and set it on the fire; when hot, lay the eels in, fry about three minutes, turning them over the while; then turn the whole into a crockery vessel, add a teaspoonful of chopped parsley and onions, a pinch of grated nutmeg, a tablespoonful of sweet-oil, salt, and pepper; set on the fire and simmer two hours; take off, roll the pieces in fine bread-crumbs, place them on a gridiron, and on a good fire, and serve when done with *piquante* sauce.

From the nature of their flesh, eels require to be prepared thus; and, when properly done, make really a very good dish.

Roasted.—Prepare the eels as for broiling, and, instead of placing on the gridiron, envelop them in oiled paper and roast before a sharp fire. Serve with *piquante, ravigote,* or Tartar sauce.

Fried.—Prepare as for broiling as far as rolling in bread-crumbs, then dip in beaten-egg, roll in bread-crumbs again, and fry. (*See* FRYING.) Serve with tomato-sauce, or just as it is.

In Maître d'hôtel.—Clean as directed, but boil twenty minutes instead of five. Serve with a *maître d'hôtel* sauce and steamed potatoes, or with muscle, oyster, shrimp, or Tartar sauce.

In Matelote.—(*See* FISH IN MATELOTE.)

Stuffed.—Clean as directed; stuff it with currant jelly, bake or roast, and serve with currant jelly.

Flounder (wrongly called *sole;* the flounder is as good as the sole—the soles that may be found here are imported from Europe or from Newfoundland), *dab-fish,* and *plaice,* after being baked or boiled, may be served with the following sauces:

Allemande, anchovy, anchovy-butter, Mayonnaise, tomato, and *au gratin.*

Baked.—Clean three pounds of the above fish. Put in a crockery dish four ounces of butter, set it on a good fire, and when melted sprinkle in it a teaspoonful of flour, stirring the while; also, a pinch of grated nutmeg, salt, pepper, a saltspoonful of chopped parsley, two or three mushrooms, also chopped, then the fish; pour on it a glass of white wine, and a liquor-glass of French brandy; cover the dish, take it from the fire, and put it in a moderately heated oven, and serve when done just as it is, and in the crockery dish.

A la Normande—Bone and skin the fish as directed.

For a fish weighing four pounds, spread two ounces of butter on the bottom of a baking-pan; spread one onion, chopped fine, over the butter, and as much carrot, cut in small dice. Place the fish over the whole, the pieces as they are, or cut according to the size of the pan, salt and pepper, and bake. Take from the oven when done and dish the fish, leaving the juice in the pan; cut the stems of about a dozen mushrooms; place the heads on the middle of the fish, and the stems around it.

Mix cold a tablespoonful of flour and the same of butter in a saucepan, turn into it a pint of broth, set on the fire and stir continually; when thoroughly mixed, turn into it also, and through a strainer, the juice from the pan in which the fish has baked; stir again two or three minutes; turn gently over the fish, put in the oven for about ten minutes, and serve hot. *Croutons* may be placed around the dish as a decoration.

Another Normande.—Bone and skin the fish as directed; butter well the dish on which the fish is to be served, spread some chopped onion all over, then place the fish over it; sprinkle salt, pepper, and white wine or vinegar (a tablespoonful to a pound of fish), all over the fish, and bake it. It takes about fifteen minutes for a fish weighing two or three pounds. Wine is better than vinegar.

While the fish is baking, set a saucepan on the fire with an ounce of butter in it, and when melted, add half a tablespoonful of flour; stir, and when turning yellow, add also half a pint of broth or water, salt, then the juice from the fish when baked, stir, give one boil, and turn over the fish.

Blanch a dozen or so of oysters, place them all over the fish also.

Have ready two or three potatoes, cut with a round

vegetable spoon; boil till done; place them around the fish as a border for it; dust then the whole with bread-crumbs, put in a warm oven for about fifteen minutes, take off, place half a dozen *croutons* all around the dish also, and serve.

The *croutons* are generally cut of a heart-shape. It will be easily done if the directions are followed properly and carefully.

Commence by cutting the bread, then cut the pota-toes, and set them on the fire with cold water and salt; while they are cooking, prepare the fish and set it in the oven; while this is baking, make the sauce, fry the *crou-tons*, and blanch the oysters. If the fish is baked be-fore the rest are ready, take it off and keep warm till wanted. It makes a sightly and excellent dish.

The same fried.—Small flounders are fried like other small fish, and served either with or without a tomato-sauce or *à la Orly*.

The same, boned and fried.—Bone and skin small flounders as directed; mix together a tablespoonful of oil, a teaspoonful of chopped parsley, the juice of half a lemon, and salt; dip the pieces of fish in the mixture, dust them slightly with flour, and fry. Serve hot.

Pike, Pickerel, and Trout or Troutlet.—Those three fish, besides being prepared as directed for bass, etc., and in all its different ways, they are boiled as directed and served warm, with a *génoise* sauce.

A more delicious dish of fish can hardly be prepared.

Ray, Skate, and Angel or Monk fish.—Ray, though excellent, is very little known; there is only one place at which it can be bought—Washington Market, New York.

It is unquestionably an excellent dish, prepared *au*

beurre noir. When clean, boil the fish as directed, and dish it, sprinkling salt and pepper on it.

While it is boiling, put about two ounces of butter to a pound of fish in a frying-pan, set it on a sharp fire, stir now and then, and when brown, throw into it about six sprigs of parsley, which you take off immediately with a skimmer. As soon as the parsley is taken off, pour the butter over the fish, quickly put two tablespoonfuls of vinegar in the frying-pan and over the fire, give one boil, and pour also over the fish. Frying the parsley and boiling the vinegar cannot be done too fast, as the fish must be served very warm. The warmer it is served, the better it is.

Salmon, sturgeon, and *white-fish,* after being baked or boiled, may be served with a caper, and also with a *Mayonnaise* sauce. They may also be served in *court bouillon,* like bass. They are broiled whole, or in slices, and served with a *maître d'hôtel* or a caper sauce.

The same in Fricandeau.—Cut the fish in slices about half an inch thick, and place them in a saucepan with slices of fat salt pork, carrots and onions under them; set on a good fire; ten minutes after, add a little broth, just enough to cover the bottom of the pan; after about five minutes, turn the slices over; finish the cooking and serve with the gravy strained over the fish, or with a tomato-sauce.

The same in Papillotes.—Fry slices of salmon with a little butter, and until of a golden color; take them from the fire. While they are frying, mix well together parsley chopped fine, salt, pepper, melted butter, grated nutmeg, and a little lemon-juice; spread some of the mixture on both sides of the slices of fish, envelop them in buttered or oiled paper; broil, and serve them hot.

Some mushrooms or truffles, or both, and chopped, may be added to the mixture.

The same à la Génevoise.—Put in a saucepan a thick slice of salmon—from five to six pounds; just cover it with broth and claret wine—half of each; season with a bunch of seasonings composed of six or eight sprigs of parsley, two of thyme, two bay-leaves, two cloves, and two cloves of garlic, salt, a few slices of carrot, and a small green onion, or a shallot, if handy. Boil gently till nearly done, when add about a dozen mushrooms, and keep boiling till done; dish the fish, and put it in a warm but not hot place; mix cold, in a saucepan, four ounces of butter with about two ounces of flour; turn over it, through a strainer, the liquor in which the fish has been cooked, and set on a sharp fire; after about three minutes, during which you have stirred with a wooden spoon, add the mushrooms; stir again for about two minutes, turn over the fish, and serve warm.

The same in Salad.—Boil, as directed for fish, some thin slices of salmon, drain, and serve cold, on a napkin and on a dish.

Serve with it, and in a boat, the following: half a teaspoonful of salt, a pinch of pepper, two tablespoonfuls of vinegar, four of sweet oil, a pickled cucumber chopped fine, two hard-boiled eggs, chopped fine also, two or three anchovies, and a tablespoonful of capers; the anchovies may be chopped fine or pounded. Beat the whole well and serve.

The same in Scallops.—Cut it in round slices, about one-eighth of an inch in thickness; fry them with butter, and serve.

The pieces should be tastefully arranged on a dish, imitating a flight of stairs.

Broiled.—Cut it in rather thin slices, butter both sides with a brush; broil, and serve with a *maître d'hôtel.*

Shad and *sheep's-head*, after being baked or boiled, are served with an anchovy, caper, or tomato sauce. They are also served cold, *à la vinaigrette.*

Broiled.—When cleaned and prepared, salt, pepper, and butter it; broil and serve it with a *maître d'hotel.*

It may be *stuffed* as directed for fish.

In Provençale.—Clean, prepare, and cut the fish in pieces about two inches long; put about three pounds of it in a saucepan, with a pint of claret; six stalks of parsley, a small onion, a clove of garlic, and six mushrooms, all chopped fine; boil till done, when add four ounces of butter, and two of flour, well kneaded together; boil three minutes longer, and serve warm.

Another way, or à la Chambord.—Stuff the fish with sausage-meat, envelop it in a towel, boil, and serve it with a tomato-sauce.

The same with Sorrel.—Broil the fish, and serve it on a *purée* of sorrel or of spinach.

It may also be prepared *au court bouillon, à la Bretonne,* and *aux fines herbes,* like bass, etc.

Sheep's-head may also be prepared like turbot.

Au Gratin.—The shad, after being cleaned, but not split on the back (as is too often the case, to the shame of the fishmongers who begin by spoiling the fish under the pretence of cleaning it), is placed in a bake-pan, having butter, chopped parsley, mushroom, salt, and pepper, both under and above the fish. For a fish weighing three pounds, add one gill of broth and half as much of white wine; dust the fish with bread-crumbs, and set in a pretty quick oven.

Fifteen minutes afterward, examine it. When done,

the fish is dished, a little broth is put in the pan, which is placed on a sharp fire; stir with a spoon or fork so as to detach the bread, etc., that may stick to the pan, then pour this over the fish, and serve warm.

The gravy must be reduced to two or three tablespoonfuls only, for a fish weighing about two pounds.

The fish must be dished carefully in order not to break it.

Sterlet.—This is a fish of the sturgeon family, very plentiful in the Caspian Sea and in many Russian rivers, principally in the Neva and in Lake Ladoga.

Tunny and *bonito*, after being boiled, are served cold in *vinaigrette.*

Turbot and Whiff.—Turbot is among fishes what pheasant is among birds. Rub it with lemon before cooking it.

After being boiled or baked, as directed, it is served with the following sauces: *Béchamel, cream, caper, Hollandaise, Mayonnaise, tomato,* and in *vinaigrette.*

It is also served *au court-bouillon* and *aux fines herbes* like bass.

Au Gratin.—It is prepared and served like shad *au gratin.*

It is also broiled and served with a *maître d'hôtel.*

Bordelaise.—Bone and skin the fish as directed; dip each piece in melted butter, then in beaten egg, roll in bread-crumbs and broil. While it is broiling on a rather slow fire, turn it over several times and keep basting with melted butter; the more butter it absorbs the better the fish.

When broiled, serve the slices on a dish and place some boiled craw-fish all around and in the middle. A dish of steamed potatoes is served with it.

The following sauce is also served at the same time: Chop fine and fry till half done, with a little butter, two small green onions or four shallots. Put half a pint of good meat-gravy in a small saucepan; set on the fire, and as soon as it commences to boil, pour into it, little by little, stirring the while with a wooden spoon, about a gill of Bordeaux wine, then the onions or shallots, and also a piece of beef marrow chopped fine; give one boil, and serve in a saucer.

In Salad.—Proceed as for salmon in salad.

When *boiled*, serve the turbot with anchovy-butter, lobster-butter, lobster-sauce, or muscle-sauce.

Cold.—Any cold piece of turbot is served with a *Mayonnaise* sauce, or in *vinaigrette*.

Cold Fish.—If the fish is with sauce, that is, if the sauce is in the same dish with the fish, warm it in the *bain-marie*, and serve warm. Any other piece of cold fish, baked, boiled, broiled, or roasted, is served with a *Mayonnaise* sauce, or with a *vinaigrette*.

Any kind of cold fish may be prepared in salad. Slice the fish or cut it in pieces and put it in the salad-dish with hard-boiled egg sliced, onion and parsley chopped fine, salt, pepper, vinegar, and oil. Mix the whole gently and well, and serve.

Anchovy.—It is imported preserved. It is used as a *hors-d'œuvre*, to decorate or season.

The essence of anchovy is used for sauce.

The smallest are considered the best.

To serve as a *hors d'œuvre*, wash, wipe dry, and remove the backbone, serve with tarragon or parsley, chopped fine, vinegar, and oil.

They may also be served with hard-boiled eggs, chopped or quartered.

Sprats.—There are none in or near American waters; they are imported under their French name, sardines. Fresh sprats are very good boiled without any grease, and without being cleaned and prepared like other fish; but when on the plate, skin them, which is easily done, as then the flesh is so easily detached from the bones that the inside need not be touched at all; they are eaten with salt and pepper only.

Sardines are served as a *hors-d'œuvre*, with oil and lemon-juice, and properly scaled. They are arranged on the dish according to fancy, together with lemon in slices.

Salt Cod—to prepare.—Soak it in cold water for two days, changing the water two or three times; then scale it well and clean. Lay it in a fish-kettle, cover with cold water, set on a rather slow fire, skim off the scum, let it boil about one minute, take the kettle from the fire, cover it well, and leave thus ten minutes; then take off the cod, and drain it.

In Béchamel.—Prepare it as above, and serve with a *béchamel* sauce, and as warm as possible.

With a Cream-Sauce.—Prepare as above, and serve either warm or cold with a cream-sauce.

In Brown Butter.—When prepared as above, place it on a dish, and keep it in a warm place. Put four ounces of butter in a frying-pan, and on a good fire; when turning brown, add three sprigs of parsley, fry about two minutes, pour the whole on the fish, and serve. You may also pour on it a hot caper-sauce, and serve.

With Croutons.—Prepare and cook as directed, three pounds of cod; take the bones out, break in small pieces, and mash with the hand as much as possible; put it then in a stewpan, beat three yolks of eggs with two table-

7

spoonfuls of cream, and mix with the cod; set on a slow fire, and immediately pour in, little by little, stirring the while, about one gill of sweet oil; simmer ten or twelve minutes, and serve with *croutons* around.

In Maître d'Hôtel.—Lay three pounds of cod on a dish, after being cooked as directed; keep it warm, spread a *maître d'hôtel* sauce on it, and serve.

With Potatoes.—Prepare about three pounds of cod as directed above. Lay the fish on a dish; have a *piquante* sauce ready, turn it over it, and serve with steamed potatoes all around the dish. The potatoes may also be served separately.

In Vinaigrette.—Prepare as directed, and when cold, serve with a *vinaigrette.*

With Cheese.—Prepare the cod as directed, then dip it in lukewarm butter, roll it in grated cheese, lay it in a baking-pan, dust slightly with bread-crumbs; bake, and serve warm. Two or three minutes in a quick oven will be sufficient.

Au Gratin.—When soaked only and wiped dry, but not boiled, prepare it as directed for fish *au gratin.*

With Caper-Sauce.—Prepare it as directed, and serve warm with caper-sauce.

Salt Salmon.—Soak it in cold water for some time, the length of time to be according to the saltness of the fish; scale and clean it well, lay it in a fish-kettle, cover it with cold water, and set it on a moderate fire. Boil gently about two minutes, skim off the scum, take from the kettle and drain it. Put butter in a frying-pan and set it on the fire; when it turns rather brown, put a few sprigs of parsley in it, and immediately pour it over the fish in the dish; add a few drops of lemon-juice all over, and serve warm.

It may also be served with a caper or *maître d'hôtel* sauce; or, when cold, serve *à la vinaigrette*.

Salt salmon is also served like salt cod-fish.

It may also be served on a *purée* of celery or of onion.

Smoked Salmon.—Cut it in thin slices; have very hot butter or oil in a frying-pan, and lay the slices in only long enough to warm them; then take out, drain them, and serve with a few drops of lemon-juice or vinegar sprinkled on them.

Tunny.—This is not a good fish fresh; it is generally preserved, and served as a *hors-d'œuvre*. It comes from Holland, Italy, and the south of France.

Fresh, it is prepared like sturgeon. That prepared in Holland is the best. The Dutch cure fish better than any other nation.

When you serve tunny, take it out of the bottle or jar and serve it on a small plate, or on a dessert-plate. A very small piece is served, generally like every other *hors-d'œuvre*.

Salt Herring.—Soak in cold or tepid water; if soaked in tepid water, it does not require as long; the time must be according to the quality or saltness of the fish. Wipe dry, broil, and serve like salt mackerel.

Another way.—Salt herring may also be soaked in half water and half milk, or in milk only; drain and wipe dry. Bone and skin, cut off the head, tail, and fins, and serve with oil, vinegar, and pickled cucumbers.

They are also served with slices of sour apples, or slices of onions, after being soaked and wiped dry.

They may also be broiled slightly and served with oil only, after being soaked, or served with sour grape-juice.

Salt Pike.—It is prepared and served the same as salt herring; so is pickled trout.

Red Herring.—Wipe or skin them, they are not as good when washed ; cut off the head and tail, split the back open, lay them on a warm and well-greased gridiron, set on a slow fire ; spread some butter or oil on them, turn over, do the same on the other side ; broil very little, and serve with a *vinaigrette* and mustard to taste.

Another way.—Clean and split them as above, soak them in lukewarm water for two hours ; take out, drain, and wipe dry. Mix two or three yolks of eggs with a teaspoonful of chopped parsley, salt, pepper, and a little melted butter ; put some of the mixture around every herring, then roll them in fine bread-crumbs, place them on a gridiron on a slow fire, and when lightly broiled, serve as the preceding one.

Red herring may also be broiled with bread-crumbs like salt herring.

It is also served as a *hors-d'œuvre*, cut in slices.

Salt Mackerel broiled.—If the fish be too salt, soak it for a while in lukewarm water, take off and wipe dry. Have a little melted fat or lard, dip a brush in it and grease slightly both sides of the fish ; place on or inside of the gridiron, the bars of which must also be greased ; set on, or before, or under a pretty sharp fire ; broil both sides ; dish the fish, the skin under ; spread butter on it ; also parsley chopped fine, and serve.

Lemon-juice may be added if liked, or a few drops of vinegar.

When broiled and dished, spread a *maître d'hôtel* on it, and serve.

Another way.—When soaked and wiped dry, dip in melted butter, again in beaten eggs, and roll in bread-crumbs. Broil and serve with parsley and lemon-juice, or with a *maître d'hôtel*.

FROGS.

The hind-legs of frogs only are used as food; formerly they were eaten by the French only, but now, frog-eating has become general, and the Americans are not behind any others in relishing that kind of food.

Fried.—Skin well, and throw into boiling water with a little salt, for five minutes, the hind-legs only; take out and throw them in cold water to cool, and drain. Have hot fat in a pan on the fire (*see* Directions for Frying); lay the frogs in, and serve when done with fried parsley around.

Stewed.—Skin, boil five minutes, throw in cold water, and drain as above. Put in a stewpan two ounces of butter (for two dozen frogs); set it on the fire, and when melted, lay the legs in, fry two minutes, tossing now and then; then sprinkle on them a teaspoonful of flour, stir with a wooden spoon, add two sprigs of parsley, one of thyme, a bay-leaf, two cloves, one of garlic, salt, white pepper, and half a pint of white wine; boil gently till done, dish the legs, reduce the sauce on the fire, strain it, mix in it two yolks of eggs, pour on the legs, and serve them.

LOBSTER.

Never buy a dead lobster.

Large lobsters are not as good as small ones. From about one to two pounds and a half in weight are the best. The heavier the better.

Lobsters are better at some seasons of the year than at others. They are inferior when full of eggs.

It is from mere prejudice that the liver (also called *tom-alley*) is eschewed. This prejudice may come from its turning green on boiling the lobster.

Use every thing but the stomach and the black or bluish vein running along its back and tail.

Boil your lobsters yourself; because, if you buy them already boiled, you do not know if they were alive when put in the kettle.

A lobster boiled after being dead is watery, soft, and not full; besides being very unhealthy, if not dangerous.

A lobster suffers less by being put in cold than in boiling water, and the flesh is firmer when done. In putting it in boiling water it is killed by the heat; in cold water it is dead as soon as the water gets warm.

To boil—Lay it in a fish-kettle; just cover it with cold water, cover the kettle, and set it on a sharp fire.

It takes from fifteen to twenty-five minutes' boiling, according to the size of the lobster.

When boiled, take it from the kettle, break it in two, that is, separate the body from the tail, and place it in a colander to let the water drain.

In the shell.—When the lobster is boiled, divide it in two, taking care not to break the body and large claws. The tail is then split in two, lengthwise, the flesh taken off, cut in small dice, and mixed with the inside of the lobster.

The vein found immediately under the shell, all along the flesh of the lobster, is removed as soon as it is split. The stomach, found near the head, is removed also and thrown away; all the rest is good, including the liver.

When the flesh and inside are properly mixed, season with salt, pepper, vinegar, oil, mustard, and chopped parsley.

Place the body of the lobster on the middle of a dish, the head up, the two large claws stretched out, and the two feelers stretched out also and fastened between the claws. A sprig of parsley is put in each claw, at the end of it, in the small claws as well as in the two large ones. Then the two empty halves of the tail-piece are put around the body of the lobster, the prepared flesh placed around them; hard-boiled eggs cut in eight pieces each are placed around the dish, tastefully arranged; some slices of red, pickled beets and cut with paste-cutters, are placed between each piece of egg, and serve.

It makes a simple, good, and very sightly dish.

Half a dozen boiled craw-fish may be placed around the dish also; it will add to the decoration.

Two middling-sized lobsters prepared thus will fill a very large dish. They should be placed back to back, with only a few craw-fish between, and the rest arranged as the above.

In Salad.—Boil the lobster as directed; break and drain it as directed also. Slice the flesh of the tail, place it tastefully on a dish; also the flesh from the two large claws, which may be sliced or served whole. Lettuce, or hard-boiled eggs, or both, may be arranged on the dish also, and served with the following sauce:

Put in a boat or saucer all the inside save the stomach, with salt, pepper, vinegar, oil, mustard, and chopped parsley, to taste; beat and mix the whole well together, and serve. In case there are eggs, these are also to be mixed with the rest.

Another.—Boil and drain as directed; cut all the flesh in dice, and put it in a bowl with the inside, some lettuce cut rather fine, salt, pepper, vinegar, mustard, and very little oil; mix well, and then put the mixture on a dish, placing it like a mound on the middle of the dish; spread a *Mayonnaise* sauce over it; decorate with the centre leaves of the lettuce, some hard-boiled eggs cut in slices or in fancy shapes, capers, boiled or pickled red beets, cut also in fancy shapes, slices of lemon, and serve.

Anchovies, olives, pickled cucumbers, or any other pickled fruit or vegetable may also be added.

A rose, or two or three pinks, may be placed right on the top, as a decoration. Just before commencing to serve, the rose may be put on a dessert plate and offered to a lady.

In Coquilles, or Scalloped.—It is boiled and then finished like oysters scalloped.

It may be served thus on scallop-shells, on silver shells, or on its own shell; that is, on the shell of the tail, split in two lengthwise, and trimmed according to fancy.

Croquettes.—Lobster croquettes are made exactly like *fish-balls,* and then fried according to directions for frying.

They are served warm. It is an excellent dish for *breakfast.*

Fried.—To be fried, the lobster must be bled; separate the body from the tail, then cut the tail in pieces, making as many pieces as there are joints. Put these pieces in a frying-pan with two or three ounces of butter, and one onion, chopped fine; set on a sharp fire, stir now and then till the whole is fried, then add a bunch of seasoning composed of three sprigs of parsley, one of thyme, a bay-leaf, and a clove; salt, pepper, and three gills of Madeira wine; boil gently till reduced about half; dish the pieces of lobster according to fancy; add two or three tablespoonfuls of gravy to the sauce, stir it, give one boil, and turn it over the lobster through a strainer; serve warm.

Another way.—Proceed as above in every particular, except that you use Sauterne or Catawba wine instead of Madeira, and, besides the seasonings, add half a dozen mushrooms, or two truffles, or both.

Dish the mushrooms and truffles with the lobster, then finish and serve as the above.

Craw-fish.—These are found in most of the lakes, brooks, and rivers.

In some places they are called *river-crabs*, or fresh-water crabs.

They resemble the lobster, and are often taken for young lobsters.

Besides being a beautiful ornament and much used to decorate dishes, they are excellent to eat and very light.

They are dressed and served like lobsters and crabs.

Fishermen are sure to find a ready market for them, though they are, as yet, very little known.

Crabs.—Crabs are boiled like lobsters, and may be served like lobster, *in salad*. They are often eaten, only boiled, without any seasonings.

Like lobsters also, to be good, crabs must be put in the water alive.

When well washed and clean, they may be prepared in the following way: Put them in a saucepan with slices of onions, same of carrots, parsley, chives if handy, thyme, bay-leaves, cloves, salt, and pepper-corns; half cover them with white wine, add butter, set on a good fire, and boil till done. Serve with parsley only.

The sauce may be used a second time by adding a little wine.

The *soft-shell crab* is blanched five minutes, and *fried* like fish.

It may also be *sauté* with a little butter, and served with a *maître d'hôtel*.

Broil it also, and serve it with a *maître d'hôtel*.

Muscles.—These are unwholesome between April and

7*

September. They must be heavy, fresh, and of a middling size. The very large ones are really inferior.

Soak them in water and wash well several times, then drain.

In Poulette.—Put them in a saucepan with a little parsley chopped fine, and set them on a pretty good fire; as soon as they are opened, remove the shell to which they are not attached, and keep them in a warm place.

For two quarts of muscles, put two ounces of butter in the saucepan in which they have been cooked and in which you have left their liquor; set on the fire, stir, and as soon as the butter is melted, add and stir into it a tablespoonful of flour; when turning a little yellow, add also half a dozen pepper-corns, then the muscles; boil gently about ten minutes, stirring occasionally; take from the fire, mix one or two yolks of eggs with it, a little lemon-juice, parsley chopped fine, and serve warm.

Another way.—When clean, put them in a saucepan with a few slices of carrot, same of onion, two or three stalks of parsley, one of thyme, a bay-leaf, two cloves, six pepper-corns, and salt. Set on the fire, and take the muscles from the pan as soon as they open, then remove one shell; put them back in the pan, with as much white wine as there is liquor from the muscles; boil gently about ten minutes, add the yolk of an egg, a little lemon-juice, and dish the muscles; drain the sauce over them, add a little chopped parsley, and serve warm.

Fried.—Fry, and serve the muscles like fried oysters. They may also be served like scalloped oysters.

Prawns and Shrimps.—Wash, boil in water and salt, and serve. They may be used, like craw-fish, to decorate fish after being boiled.

Another way.—Wash well, and put two quarts of them

in a saucepan with four onions in slices, two sprigs of parsley, one of thyme, a bay-leaf, two cloves, salt, pepper, half a pint of white wine, and two ounces of butter, just cover with water and set on a good fire; when properly cooked, drain, and serve warm with green parsley all around. The liquor may be used a second time.

OYSTERS.

The American oyster is unquestionably the best that can be found. It varies in taste according to how it is treated, either after being dredged or while embedded; and also according to the nature of the soil and water in which they have lived. . It is very wrong to wash oysters. We mean by washing oysters, the abominable habit of throwing oysters in cold water, as soon as opened, and then sold by the measure. It is more than a pity to thus spoil such an excellent and delicate article of food.

Oysters, like lobsters, are not good when dead. To ascertain if they are alive, as soon as opened and when one of the shells is removed, touch gently the edge of the oyster, and, if alive, it will contract.

Raw.—When well washed, open them, detaching the upper shell, then detach them from the under shell, but leave them on it; place on a dish, and leave the upper shell on every oyster, and serve thus.

To eat them, you remove the upper shell, sprinkle salt, pepper, and lemon-juice on, and eat.

When raw oysters are served on a table, at which there are gentlemen only, some shallots, chopped fine and gently bruised in a coarse towel, are served with them, on a separate dish. The taste of the shallot agrees very well with that of the oyster.

A Tartar sauce may be served instead of shallots.

To blanch.—Set the oysters and a little water on the fire in a saucepan, take them off at the first boil, skim off the scum from the top, strain them, and drop them in cold water.

The skimming, straining, and dropping in cold water must be done quickly—the quicker the better. If allowed to stay in the warm water, or out of water, they get tough.

In dropping them in cold water, see that they are free from pieces of shell; take them with a fork if necessary.

As soon as in cold water they are ready for use, but they must always be drained again before using them.

When the water used to blanch is employed in preparing them, it is explained in the different receipts.

White wine may be used, instead of water, to blanch them, according to taste.

Fried.—Open the oysters, and put them in a colander for about half an hour. They must be as well drained as possible. Then dip them in egg and roll in bread-crumbs in the following way: Beat one or two, or three, eggs (according to the quantity of oysters to be fried), as for an omelet, turn the oysters into the eggs and stir gently; then take one after another, roll in bread-crumbs; place each one on your left hand, in taking them from the crumbs, and with the other hand press gently on it. Put them away in a cool place for about half an hour, and then dip again in egg, roll in bread-crumbs, and press in the hand as before. It is not indispensable to dip in egg and roll in crumbs a second time; but the oysters are better, and you are well repaid for the little extra work it requires. While you are preparing them, set some fat on the fire in a pan, and when hot enough (*see* FRYING) drop the oysters in, stir gently, take off with a skimmer when fried, turn into a colander, add salt, and serve hot.

Roasted.—Place the oysters on a hot stove or range, or on coals, and as soon as they open take off, remove one shell; turn a little melted butter on each, and serve.

There are several other ways.

When blanched, they are served on toast, a little gravy is added, the toast placed on a dessert-plate, and served thus.

Broiled and roasted as above is the same thing.

Oysters scalloped on their own shell, and placed on the range instead of in the oven, are also called broiled.

Scalloped.—Place the oysters when thoroughly washed on a hot stove, and as soon as they open remove one shell, the flatter one of the two, and take them from the fire. Sprinkle salt, pepper, chopped parsley, and bread-crumbs on them; place on each a piece of butter the size of a hazel-nut; put in the oven about ten minutes, and when done add a few drops of meat-gravy, to each, and serve hot.

Another.—Put a quart of oysters and their liquor in a saucepan, set it on the fire, take off at the first boil, and drain. Set a saucepan on the fire with two ounces of butter in it; as soon as melted, add a teaspoonful of flour, stir, and, when turning rather brown, add the juice of the oysters, about a gill of gravy, salt, and pepper; boil gently for about ten minutes, stirring now and then. While it is boiling, place the oysters on scallop-shells, or on silver shells made for that purpose, two or three oysters on each, turn some of the above sauce on each, after it has boiled; dust with bread-crumbs, put a little piece of butter on each shell, and bake for about twelve minutes in a warm oven.

A dozen silver shells served thus make a sightly and excellent dish.

Some truffles, chopped fine, may be added to the sauce, two minutes before taking it from the fire.

Stewed.—Procure two quarts of good and fresh oysters. Set them on a sharp fire, with their liquor and a little water, and blanch as directed. Put four ounces of butter in a saucepan, set on the fire, and when melted stir into it a small tablespoonful of flour; as soon as mixed, add also a teaspoonful of parsley, chopped fine, and about half a pint of broth; boil gently about ten minutes, then add the oysters, salt and pepper, boil again about one minute, dish the whole, sprinkle lemon-juice on, and serve.

An oyster soup is often called a stew.

In Poulette.—In adding chopped mushrooms to the stewed oysters, at the same time that the oysters are put in the pan, you make them in *poulette.*

A la Washington.—Fried oysters are called *à la Washington*, when two, three, or four very large oysters are put together (they adhere very easily), dipped in egg, rolled in bread-crumbs, and fried, as directed above. It is necessary to have a deep pan, and much fat, to immerse them completely.

Pickled oysters are always served as a *hors d'œuvre.* Place around the oysters some hard-boiled eggs, chopped fine, and serve with oil and vinegar.

Serve them in the same way, with slices of truffles instead of hard-boiled eggs.

They may also be served with lemon-juice only.

Or with shallots chopped fine, and then bruised in a coarse towel. This last one is considered of too strong a taste for ladies.

They are also served with a Tartar sauce.

Scallops.—Blanch the scallops for three minutes, drain them. Put butter on the fire in a frying-pan, and when melted turn the scallops in; stir now and then, take from the fire when fried, add parsley chopped fine, salt, pepper, and serve warm.

On the Shell.—Chop fine a middling-sized onion, and fry it with one ounce of butter. While the onion is frying, chop fine also one quart of scallops and put them with the onion; stir for two or three minutes, or till about half fried, when turn the juice off, put back on the fire, and add one ounce of butter, one gill of white wine, stir for two or three minutes, and if too thick add the juice you have turned off; take from the fire, and mix a yolk of egg with it, add salt, pepper, nutmeg grated, and parsley chopped fine.

Have the scallop shells properly cleaned, or silver shells, spread the mixture on the shells; dust with bread-crumbs, put a piece of butter about the size of a hazel-nut on each, and put in an oven, at about 320 deg. Fahr., for from ten to fifteen minutes.

This is a dish for *breakfast.*

Scallop, scollop, or escalop, are one and the same fish.

CLAMS.

Wash clean with a scrubbing-brush and put them in a kettle; set on a good fire, and leave till they are wide open; then take from the kettle, cut each in two or three pieces, put them in a stewpan with all the water they have disgorged in the kettle, and about four ounces of butter for fifty clams; boil slowly about an hour, take from the fire, and mix with the whole two beaten eggs, and serve warm.

Clams are also eaten raw with vinegar, salt, and pepper.

Chowder.—This popular dish is made in a hundred different ways, but the result is about the same.

It is generally admitted that boatmen prepare it better than others, and the receipts we give below came from the most experienced chowder-men of the Harlem River.

Potatoes and crackers are used in different proportions, the more used, the thicker the chowder will be.

Put in a *pot* (technical name) some small slices of fat salt pork, enough to line the bottom of it; on that, a layer of potatoes, cut in small pieces; on the potatoes, a layer of chopped onions; on the onions, a layer of tomatoes, in slices, or canned tomatoes; on the latter a layer of clams, whole or chopped (they are generally chopped), then a layer of crackers.

Then repeat the process, that is, another layer of potatoes on that of the clams; on this, one of onions, etc., till the pot is nearly full. Every layer is seasoned with salt and pepper. Other spices are sometimes added according to taste; such as thyme, cloves, bay-leaves, and tarragon.

When the whole is in, cover with water, set on a slow fire, and when nearly done, stir gently, finish cooking, and serve.

As we remarked above, the more potatoes that are used, the thicker it will be.

When done, if found too thin, boil a little longer; if found too thick, add a little water, give one boil, and serve.

Another way.—Proceed as above in every particular, except that you omit the clams and crackers, and when the rest is nearly cooked, then add the chopped clams and broken crackers, boil fast about twenty-five minutes longer, and serve.

If found too thick or too thin, proceed exactly as for the one above.

Fish Chowder.—This is made exactly as clam chowder, using fish instead of clams.

Clam Bake.—This is how it is made by the Harlem River clam-baker, TOM RILEY.

Lay the clams on a rock, edge downward, and forming a circle, cover them with fine brush; cover the brush with dry sage; cover the sage with larger brush; set the whole on fire, and when a little more than half burnt (brush and sage), look at the clams by pulling some out, and if done enough, brush the fire, cinders, etc., off; mix some tomato or cauliflower sauce, or catsup, with the clams (minus their shells); add butter and spices to taste, and serve.

Done on sand, the clams, in opening, naturally allow the sand to get in, and it is any thing but pleasant for the teeth while eating them.

BEEF.

HOW TO SELECT.

See if the meat is fine, of a clear red color, with yellowish-white fat.

COW BEEF.

Cow beef must also be of a clear red color, but more pale than other beef; the fat is white.

BULL BEEF.

Bull beef is never good; you recognize it when you see hard and yellow fat; the lean part is of a dirty-reddish color.

The rump piece is generally prepared *à la mode.* For steaks, the tenderloin and the piece called the porterhouse steak, are the best; rump steaks are seldom tender.

The roasting or baking pieces are the tenderloin, the fillet, and some cuts of the ribs.

For soup, every piece is good; to make rich broth, take pieces of the rump, sucket, round, etc., but every piece makes excellent broth, and therefore excellent soup. (*See* Broth.)

A good piece of rib, prepared like a fillet or tenderloin, makes an excellent dish, the bones and meat around them being used to make broth.

A LA MODE.

Take from six to twelve pounds of rump and lard it. To lard it you take a steel needle made for that purpose, flat near the pointed end and much larger than an ordinary larding-needle. It must be flat near the point in order to cut the meat so as to make room for the larger part of the needle to pass, and also for the salt pork. This needle is only used for beef *à la mode*.

Cut the salt pork in square strips to fit the needle, (*see* LARDING), and proceed.

Examine the piece of beef, lard with the grain of the meat, so that when it is carved the salt pork shall be cut across.

If the piece is too thick to run the strip of pork through, so that both ends stick out, lard one side first then the other. We mean by one side first, this: to be easily handled, the salt pork cannot be cut longer than about four inches; as half an inch of it must stick out of the meat, it leaves only three inches inside, and if the piece of meat be six inches or more thick, of course it would be impossible to have the strip of pork stick out on both sides; therefore, you lard one side first; that is, you run the needle through the meat, leaving the salt pork stick out on the side you commence, and when that side is larded, do the same for the other. You have then the salt pork sticking out on both sides of the meat and looking just as if the strips were running through the whole piece.

Some like more salt pork than others in the beef; the strips may be run thickly or thinly.

Thirty strips may be run into three pounds of meat as well as half a dozen; but about half a pound of salt pork to five pounds of beef is a pretty good proportion.

Then take a saucepan of a proper size for the piece of meat; it must not be too large or too small, but large enough to hold the meat without being obliged to bend or fold it; a crockery pan is certainly the best for that purpose, and one that will go easily in the oven.

Put in the saucepan, for six pounds of beef, half a calf's foot, or a veal-bone if more handy, two ounces of butter, half a handful of parsley (cives, if handy), two bay-leaves, a clove of garlic, a sprig of thyme, two onions, with a clove stuck in each, sàlt, pepper, half a carrot cut in slices, the rind of the salt pork you have used, and what you may have left of strips; the whole well spread on the bottom of the pan, then the piece of meat over, cover the pan, set on a rather sharp fire and after about ten minutes add half a gill of water; keep the pan covered to the end.

After another ten or fifteen minutes, add about one pint of cold water, turn the meat over, and after about ten minutes more, place the pan in the oven, a rather slow oven (a little above 220 degrees Fahr.), for five or six hours. Dish the meat, skim off the fat on the top of the gravy, give one boil and turn it over the meat and carrots through a strainer.

When the meat is dished, put some carrots *au jus* all around; serve warm.

Cold.—Serve it whole or in slices, with meat jelly, or with a sharp sauce; such as *piquante, ravigote,* etc.

STEWED.

Stewed beef is called also *daube* or *braised* beef, but it is the same.

It may be larded as beef *à la mode,* or not; it may be put whole in the pan or in large dice, according to taste.

The following is for five or six pounds of rump or even a piece of ribs:

Put in a saucepan two ounces of salt pork cut in dice, four sprigs of parsley, two of thyme, two bay-leaves, a clove of garlic, a sprig of sweet basil, two cloves, three carrots cut in pieces, salt, and pepper; put the piece of beef on the whole, wet with a glass of broth, and one of white wine (a liquor-glass of French brandy may also be added); season with six or eight small onions; place in a moderately heated oven, put paste around the cover to keep it air-tight; simmer about six hours; dish the meat with the onions and carrots around it, strain the gravy on the whole, and serve.

Almost any piece of beef may be cooked in the same way, and will be found good, wholesome, and economical.

ROASTED.

How to improve it.—Put the meat in a tureen, with four tablespoonfuls of sweet-oil, salt, pepper, two table-spoonfuls of chopped parsley, four onions cut in slices, two bay-leaves, and the juice of half a lemon; put half of all the above under the meat, and half on it; cover, and leave thus two days in winter, and about eighteen hours in summer.

It certainly improves the meat and makes it more tender. The tenderloin may be improved as well as any other piece.

Then place the meat on the spit before and near a very sharp fire. Baste often with the seasonings, if you have improved the meat; or with a little melted butter, if you have not. Continue basting with what is in the dripping-pan.

Beef must be placed as near the fire as possible, without burning it, however; and then, as soon as a coating or crust is formed all around, remove it by degrees. Remember that the quicker the crust is formed, the more juicy and tender the meat.

Nothing at all is added to form that kind of crust. It is formed by the osmazome of the meat, attracted by the heat, and coming in contact with the air while revolving.

Beef is more juicy when rather underdone; if good, when cut, it has a pinky color inside.

Roast beef may be served with the drippings only, after being strained and the fat removed.

It may also be served in the following ways:

With Potatoes.—Fried potatoes may be served all around the meat, or on a separate dish. Also, potato *croquettes.*

With Horse-radish.—Grate horse-radish, mix it with the drippings, and serve in a boat.

With a Garniture.—Mix a liver garniture with the gravy, add lemon-juice, place all around the meat, and serve.

With Truffles.—Place the garniture of truffles on and around the meat, turn the drippings on the whole, and serve.

With Tomatoes.—Surround the meat with stuffed tomatoes, strain the gravy on the whole, and serve.

On Purées.—Spread either of the following *purées* on the dish, place the meat over it, strain the drippings on the whole, and serve:

Purées of *asparagus, beans, cauliflowers, celery, Lima beans, onions, green peas, potatoes,* and *mushrooms.*

With Cabbage.—Surround the meat with Brussels cabbages, prepared *au jus;* strain the drippings on the whole, and serve.

With Quenelles.—Place twelve quenelles of chicken around the meat, and serve with the drippings.

TO DECORATE.

When served in any way as described above, one or two or more skewers may be run through craw-fish and a slice of truffle, and stuck in the meat, or through sweetbreads *au jus,* and slices of truffles. It makes a beautiful and good decoration.

The skewers may also be run through chicken-combs, prepared as for *farce ;* first through a comb, then through a slice of truffle, through a sweetbread, again through a slice of truffle, then through a craw-fish, and lastly a slice of truffle, or the reverse, according to fancy.

With Rice.—It is surrounded with rice croquettes, the drippings strained over the whole.

We could put down some twenty or more other ways, but any one with an ordinary amount of natural capacity can do it, by varying the *garnitures, purées, decorations,* etc.

Cold roast-beef is prepared like boiled beef.

BAKED.

Place the meat in a bake-pan, with cold water about a quarter of an inch deep; spread salt, pepper, and a little butter on the meat, cover it with a piece of buttered paper; baste often over the paper, lest it should burn; keep the bottom of the pan covered with juice; if the water and juice are absorbed, add a little cold water and continue basting; turn over two or three times, but keep the paper on the top; if it is burnt, put on another piece. The paper keeps the top of the meat moist, and prevents it from burning or drying.

When done, it is served like roasted beef.

FILLET.

The tenderloin and even the sirloin are sometimes called, or rather known, under the name of fillet, when cooked. It comes from the French *filet*—tenderloin.

Sirloin means surloin; like *stock* and several others, sirloin is purely English. The surloin is the upper part of the loin, as its prefix indicates; it is *surlonge* in French.

A fillet is generally larded with salt pork by means of a small brass larding-needle; the salt pork cut in strips to fit the needle (*see* LARDING).

If you use a tenderloin, trim off the fat. If it is a piece of ribs, prepared fillet-like, shape it like a fillet as near as possible; the rest is used as directed above.

A piece of ribs is certainly cheaper, and can be had at any time, while the other is as difficult to procure as it is dear.

To lard it.—Have a towel in your left hand and place the meat over it, the most flat and smooth side up, holding it so that the upper part will present a somewhat convex surface, and commence larding at either end and finishing at the other, in this way:

Run the needle through the upper part of the convex surface, commencing at about a quarter of an inch from the edge of one side, running through the meat a distance of about one inch and a half, about half an inch in depth at the middle, and the strip of salt pork sticking out at both ends; that is, where the needle was introduced into the meat, and where it came out of it. Repeat this till you have a row of strips across the meat, the strips being about one-third of an inch apart.

Lard row after row in the same way, and till the whole flat side is covered; the ends of the strips of pork sticking out of each row being intermingled.

To cook it.—It may be roasted or baked exactly in the same way as directed above for roast and baked beef. It may also be improved in the same way.

When cooked in either of the two above ways, it is served with its gravy only, or—

With fried potatoes.   With tomatoes.
With potato coquettes.   With quenelles.
With truffles.   With Madeira-sauce.
              With green peas.

The same as roast or baked beef above. It may also be decorated in the same way.

A fillet is also cooked exactly like beef *à la mode*, with the exception that it does not require as long; for a large one, it requires only about three hours.

When cooked thus, it is served with its gravy strained, and decorated with skewers, as above.

With Macaroni.—While the fillet is cooking, prepare a pound of macaroni *au jus*, and serve the fillet on the macaroni spread on a dish; the gravy of the fillet being mixed with the macaroni when both are done.

Fillet à la Brillat-Savarin.—Cook it in a pan as above, and serve it decorated with sweetbreads and slices of truffles, as described for roast-beef, and with a Champagne-sauce.

A la Chateaubriand.—This is prepared and served like the preceding one, with a *Madeira* instead of a *Champagne* sauce.

Sauté.—When cooked in a pan as directed above, cook mushrooms about ten minutes in the gravy, and serve mushrooms and gravy all around the meat.

A fillet *sauté* is always made with a tenderloin.

As is seen by the above receipts, all the good pieces of beef may be prepared in the ways described, ribs as

8

well as other pieces, and from the plainest to the most *recherché* way, from the cheapest to the most costly manner.

Several names are given to the different ways we have described, such as fillet *financière* (fillet served with a ragout of chicken-combs), fillet Richelieu (fillet with half a dozen skewers), etc.

En Bellevue.—This is the best way to serve it cold. It may be served whole, or part of it, that is, what is left from the preceding dinner. For a supper or lunch, it is the most handy dish, as it can be prepared in advance. Make some meat jelly or calf's-foot jelly, put a thickness of about three-quarters of an inch of it in a tin dish or mould, large enough to hold the fillet; then place on ice to cool, and when congealed and firm enough, place the fillet on it, the larded side downward; fill now with jelly till the fillet is covered, and have a thickness of about three-quarters of an inch above it.

The fillet must not touch the sides of the mould, but be perfectly enveloped in jelly. If the thickness of jelly is even on both sides and all around, it is much more sightly. When the jelly is perfectly congealed and firm, place a dish over the mould, turn upside down, and remove it. Serve as it is.

As a tenderloin is very expensive and rather difficult to get, buy a fine piece of ribs, cut the fleshy part of the shape of a tenderloin, and prepare it as directed above; it makes an excellent and sightly dish. The bony part with the rest of the flesh is used to make broth.

RIBS.

With Vinegar.—Put two tablespoonfuls of fat in a saucepan, and set it on the fire; when melted, put the beef in; say a piece of three pounds, from the round, rump, or rib-piece; brown it on every side; add one gill of vinegar, salt, and a teaspoonful of pepper, cover the pan, and keep on a rather sharp fire for fifteen minutes; then add one carrot and one onion, both sliced, a stalk of thyme, three cloves, two bay-leaves, and six pepper-corns, a pint of broth, and same of water; boil gently till done; dish the meat, strain the sauce over it, and serve.

Ribs may also be broiled like steaks, and served either with a *maître d'hôtel*, mushrooms, potatoes, or water-cress. The low cuts of beef are generally used to make broth, or stewed.

STEAKS.

The best piece of beef for a steak is the tenderloin.

What is called a porter-house steak is the tenderloin, sirloin, and other surrounding parts cut in slices.

A steak should never be less than three-quarters of an inch in thickness.

It should always be broiled; it is inferior in taste and flavor when cooked in a pan (*sauté*), or other utensil, but many persons cook it so, not having the necessary fire or utensil to broil; broiled or *sauté*, it is served alike.

The same rules are applied to steaks of venison, pork, etc.; turtle-steaks are also prepared like beef-steaks.

A good steak does not need any pounding; the object of pounding a steak is to break its fibres. A pounded steak may appear or taste more tender to a person not knowing or never having tasted a good steak, but an experienced palate cannot be deceived.

It is better to broil before than over the fire. (*See* BROILING.)

To cook a steak in an oven or drum, or any other

badly-invented machine or contrivance, is not to broil it, but to spoil it.

To make tender.—When cut, trimmed, salted, and peppered, put them in a bowl, and sprinkle some sweet-oil or melted butter over them; turn them over in the bowl every two or three hours for from six to twelve hours.

To cut and prepare.—Cut the meat in round or oval slices, as even as possible, of any size, about one inch in thickness, and trim off the fibres and thin skin that may be around. Do not cut off the fat, but flatten a little each slice with a chopper.

To broil.—When the steaks are cut and prepared as directed, they are slightly greased on both sides with lard or butter (if they have not been in a bowl with oil or butter before cooking them), placed on a warmed gridiron, set before or on a sharp fire, turned over once or twice, and taken off when rather underdone. Salt and pepper them, dish, spread a *maître d'hôtel* over them, and serve very warm.

Cooks and epicures differ about the turning over of steaks; also about broiling them with or without salt; some say that they must not be turned over twice, others are of opinion that they must be turned over two or three, and even more times; some say that they must be salted and peppered before broiling, others say they must not; we have tried the two ways many times, and did not find any difference; if there is any difference at all, it is in the quality of the meat, or in the person's taste, or in the cook's care.

When the steak is served as above, place some fried potatoes all around, and serve hot. Instead of fried potatoes, put some water-cress all around, add a few drops of vinegar, and serve. The water-cress is to be put on raw and cold.

When the steak is dished, spread some anchovy-butter on it instead of a *maître d'hôtel*, and serve warm also. It may also be served with lobster-butter instead of a *maître d'hôtel*. Steaks are also served with horse-radish butter, and surrounded with fried or *soufflé* potatoes.

With a Tomato-Sauce.—Broil and serve the steak as directed above, and serve it with a tomato-sauce instead of a *maître d'hôtel*.

With a Poivrade or Piquante Sauce.—Broil and serve with a *poivrade* or *piquante* sauce, instead of a *maître d'hôtel*.

With Egg.—When the steaks are cut and prepared as directed, dip them in beaten egg, roll them in bread-crumbs, then broil, and serve them with either a *maître d'hôtel* or tomato-sauce, or with potatoes, etc.

With Truffles.—Set a saucepan on the fire with one ounce of butter in it; as soon as melted add half a table-spoonful of flour, stir, and, when turning brown, add also about a gill of broth; stir again for five or six minutes, when mix three or four tablespoonfuls of good gravy with the rest; boil gently ten minutes, take from the fire; slice two or three truffles, mix them with the rest; add salt and pepper to taste; give one boil, turn over the steak which you have broiled as directed, and serve.

With Mushrooms.—Proceed as for truffles in every particular, except that you use mushrooms.

Fancy Steak.—Cut the steak two or three inches thick, butter slightly both sides, lay it on a gridiron well greased and warmed; set it on a moderate fire and broil it well; to cook it through it must be turned over many times, on account of its thickness. Serve like another steak, with a *maître d'hôtel*, *poivrade*, potatoes, or water-cress, etc.

BOILED BEEF.

This is understood to be beef that has been used to make broth—a rump-piece or a rib-piece, boned and tied with twine before cooking it.

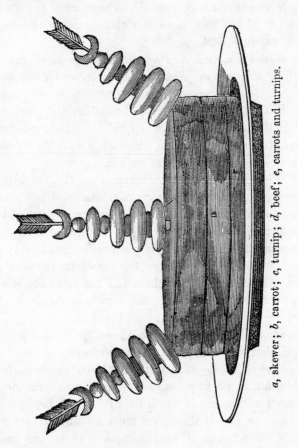

a, skewer; *b*, carrot; *c*, turnip; *d*, beef; *e*, carrots and turnips.

With Carrots and Turnips.—Remove the twine, and place the piece of beef on the middle of a dish, with carrots and turnips, cut with a fruit-corer, prepared *au jus* or glazed, and arranged all around it; also, some skewers run through pieces of carrot and turnip, and then stuck in the piece of beef. (See cut p. 174.) Serve warm.

With Brussels Cabbage, or Sprouts.—Serve the beef as above, surrounded with sprouts *au jus,* and also ornamented with skewers run through sprouts, with a piece of turnip between each.

In Bourgeoise.—Serve the piece of beef warm, decorated if handy, and surrounded with fried potatoes cut with a vegetable spoon or in fillets, and gravy spread over the whole.

If not decorated, a few sprigs of parsley may be spread on the beef.

With Onions.—Serve the beef as above, and surround it with glazed onions.

With Celery.—When served as above, the meat is surrounded with a *purée* of celery.

With Cauliflowers.—Serve warm, with a garniture of cauliflowers all around. It may be decorated with skewers.

With Chestnuts.—Glaze chestnuts as for dessert; run the skewers through a chestnut first, then through a fried potato, and then through a slice of carrot, and stick one at each end of the piece of beef; put chestnuts all around, spread some gravy over the whole, and serve warm.

In Croquettes.—Proceed as for *croquettes* of chicken.

Hollandaise.—Cut the meat in fillets and put it in a saucepan, with about two ounces of fat or butter to a pound of meat; set on the fire and stir for ten minutes. Then add a tablespoonful of flour and stir about one minute, with warm water enough to half cover the meat, and boil about five minutes, stirring now and then.

Mix together in a bowl two yolks of eggs, the juice of half a lemon, and two or three tablespoonfuls of the sauce from the saucepan in which the beef is; turn the mixture into the saucepan, stir and mix, add salt and pepper to taste, give one boil, and serve warm.

Broiled.—Cut the meat in slices about one inch in thickness, broil, and serve like steaks.

Au Gratin.—Put two ounces of butter in a saucepan on the fire, and when melted sprinkle into it two table-spoonfuls of bread-crumbs, two or three mushrooms chopped, a teaspoonful of chopped onions, same of parsley, a pinch of allspice, salt, and pepper; stir for about two minutes, add a little broth to make the whole rather liquid. Cut one pound of boiled beef in slices, place them in a tin or silver dish, turn the mixture over them, dust with bread-crumbs; put half a dozen pieces of butter here and there on the top, and bake for about fifteen minutes.

Take from the oven when done, add a few drops of lemon juice all over, and serve warm in the dish in which it was baked.

With a *maître d'hôtel*, *piquante*, *Mayonnaise*, *Robert*, *ravigote*, *Tartar*, or *tomato* sauce.

Cut it in slices, place them on a dish, spread on them some chopped parsley and slices of pickled cucumbers, and send thus to the table, with either of the above sauces in a saucer to be used with it.

IN MIROTON.

Put a piece of butter the size of an egg in a stewpan (this is for about two pounds), and set it on the fire; when melted, put in it four middling-sized onions, cut in slices;

when nearly cooked, sprinkle on them a pinch of flour, and stir till it takes a golden color; then add half a glass of white wine, and as much of broth, also salt, pepper, and a little grated nutmeg; boil until well cooked, and till the sauce is reduced; then add the boiled beef, cut in slices, and leave it fifteen minutes; dish it, pour on a few drops of vinegar, and serve.

Hashed.—Proceed exactly as for *miroton*, except that the beef is cut in strips or chopped, and that no wine is used.

IN SALAD.

Cut it in very thin and short slices, and place them on a dish with chopped parsley; put in a saucer sweet-oil and vinegar, according to the quantity of beef you have, two tablespoonfuls of oil to one of vinegar, salt, pepper, and some mustard; beat the whole a little, pour on the slices, and serve.

CORNED BEEF.

Corned beef is generally boiled. Soak the corned beef in cold water for some time, according to how salt it is.

Set it on the fire, covered with cold water, and boil gently till done.

With Cabbage.—Blanch the cabbage for about five minutes, and drain. Then put it to cook with the corned beef when the latter is about half done; serve both on the same dish, or separately, according to taste.

Corned beef, when boiled as above, without cabbage, can be served and decorated, in every way, like boiled beef. It certainly makes sightly as well as good dishes for a family dinner.

A piece of corned beef, surrounded with a garniture

8*

as we have described above, decorated with skewers, is very often served as a *relevé* at an extra dinner.

Cold Corned Beef.—A whole piece, or part of it, may be served *en Bellevue*, the same as a *fillet en Bellevue;* it is also excellent.

TONGUE.

Clean and blanch it for about ten minutes—till the white skin can be easily removed. After ten minutes boiling, try if it comes off; if not, boil a little longer, then skin it well.

To boil.—When skinned, put it in your soup-kettle with the beef, etc., to make broth, and leave it till done. When boiled, the tongue may be served and decorated exactly the same as boiled beef, in every way.

Stewed.—Cut square fillets of bacon, which dredge in a mixture of chopped parsley, cives, salt, pepper, and a little allspice; lard the tongue with the fillets. Put in a crockery stewpan two ounces of bacon cut in dice, four sprigs of parsley, two of thyme, one of sweet basil, two bay-leaves, a clove of garlic, two cloves, two carrots cut in pieces, four small onions, salt, and pepper; lay the tongue on the whole, wet with half a glass of white wine and a glass of broth; set on a moderate fire, and simmer about five hours—keep it well covered; then put the tongue on a dish, strain the sauce on it, and serve. It is a delicious dish.

It may also be served with vegetables around, or with tomato-sauce.

Another way.—When prepared as above directed, put it on the fire with the same seasonings as the preceding one; simmer four hours and take from the fire; put the tongue on a dish and let it cool, then place it on the spit before a good fire, and finish the cooking; serve it warm with an oil, or *piquante* sauce.

If any is left of either of the two, put in a pan the next day, wet with a little broth, set on the fire, and when warm serve it on a *purée ;* do not allow it to boil.

BRAIN.

Soak it in lukewarm water and clean well, so as to have it free from blood, fibres, and thin skin; then soak it again in cold water for twelve hours in winter and six in summer. Put in a crockery stewpan one ounce of bacon cut in slices, one carrot cut in pieces, two sprigs of parsley, one of thyme, a bay-leaf, a clove, four small onions cut in slices, a teaspoonful of chopped cives, salt, pepper, a pint of white wine, as much of broth, and then the brain; set on a moderate fire for half an hour and take it off; dish the brain and place it in a warm place; then strain the sauce, put it back on the fire with the brain in it, add two or three mushrooms cut in pieces, leave on the fire from ten to fifteen minutes, and serve it, parted in two, with fried parsley around.

Another way.—When the brain is cleaned and prepared as above, cut it in eight pieces. Mix well together a little flour, chopped parsley and cives, also a pinch of allspice; roll the pieces of brain in it, so as to allow the mixture to adhere to them; have some butter in a frying-pan on the fire, and when hot put the pieces of brain in it; fry gently, and serve with fried parsley around.

HEART.

Soak it in lukewarm water for two hours, free it from blood and skin, drain and wipe dry; then stuff it with sausage-meat, to which you have added three or four onions chopped fine, put it in a rather quick oven, or on the spit before a good fire (if on the spit, envelop it with buttered paper), basting from time to time ; it takes about an hour and a half to cook a middling-sized one ; serve it with a *vinaigrette*, *piquante*, *poivrade*, or *ravigote* sauce.

It may also be fried with butter, and cut in slices, but it is not as good as in the above way ; it generally becomes hard in frying.

KIDNEYS.

First split the kidneys in four pieces, trim off as carefully as possible the sinews and fat that are inside, then cut in small pieces.

Sauté.—The quicker this is done the better the kidney. For a whole one put about two ounces of butter in a frying-pan and set it on a very sharp fire, toss it round so as to melt the butter as fast as possible, but without allowing it to blacken ; as soon as melted, turn the cut kidney in, stir now and then with a wooden spoon for about three minutes, then add a tablespoonful of flour, stir again the same as before for about one minute, when add a gill of white wine and about one of broth ; stir again now and then till the kidney is rather underdone, and serve immediately.

If the kidney is allowed to boil till perfectly done, it will very seldom be tender.

It may be done with water instead of wine and broth ; in that case, add a few drops of lemon-juice just before serving it.

Prepare and serve it also as calf's-kidney, in every way as directed for the same.

LIVER.

Cut the liver in slices a quarter of an inch in thickness, sprinkle on them salt and pepper, place them on a gridiron, and set on a sharp fire; turn over only once, and serve rather underdone, with butter and chopped parsley, kneaded together and spread between the slices.

A few drops of lemon-juice may be added.

Another way.—When the liver is cut in slices, as above, put a piece of butter in a frying-pan on the fire, and when melted, lay the slices in; turn over only once, then serve, with salt, pepper, vinegar, and chopped parsley.

TAIL.

Cut the tail at the joint, so as to make as many pieces as there are joints; throw the pieces in boiling water for fifteen minutes, and drain them. When cold and dry, put them in a saucepan with a bay-leaf, two onions, with a clove stuck in each, two sprigs of parsley, and one of thyme, a clove of garlic, salt, pepper, half a wine-glass of white wine, and a few thin slices of salt pork; cover with broth or water, and set on a moderate fire for two hours. Dish the pieces, strain the sauce on them, and serve with a garniture of cabbage, or with any *purée.*

TRIPE.

How to clean and prepare.—Scrape and wash it well several times in boiling water, changing the water every time, then put in very cold water for about twelve hours, changing the water two or three times; place it in a pan, cover it with cold water; season with parsley, cives, onions, one or two cloves of garlic, cloves, salt, and pepper; boil gently five hours, take out and drain.

In case the water should boil away, add more.

You may save all the trouble of cleaning and preparing, by buying it ready prepared, as it is generally sold in cities.

Broiled.—When prepared, dip it in lukewarm butter, roll in bread-crumbs, place on a gridiron, and set it on a moderate fire; turn over as many times as is necessary to broil it well, and serve with a *vinaigrette, piquante,* or Tartar sauce; also with a tomato-sauce.

Stewed.—Put in a stewpan two ounces of salt pork, cut in dice, three carrots cut in slices, eight small onions, four cloves, two bay-leaves, two cloves of garlic, a piece of nutmeg, four sprigs of parsley, two of thyme, a dozen stalks of cives, six pepper-corns, the fourth part of an ox-foot cut in four pieces, salt, pepper, about two ounces of ham cut in dice, then three pounds of double tripe on the whole; spread two ounces of fat bacon cut in thin slices on the top; wet with half white wine and half water, or water only if you choose; put the cover on, and if not air-tight, put some paste around; set in a slow oven for six hours, then take the tripe out, strain the sauce, skim off the fat when cool, then put the sauce and tripe again in your pan, warm well, and serve in crockery plates or bowls placed on chafing-dishes, as it is necessary to keep it warm while eating. It is good with water only, but better with half wine. This is also called *à la mode de Caen.*

In Poulette.—When cleaned and prepared as directed, cut one pound of tripe in strips about one and a half inches broad, then cut again contrariwise, so as to make small fillets. Put one ounce of butter in a saucepan with half a tablespoonful of flour, and mix cold; add two gills of water, mix again, set on the fire, stir now and then, give one boil, put the tripe in, salt and pepper to taste; boil two minutes and dish the whole; put a teaspoonful of chopped parsley all over, and serve hot.

Aux Fines Herbes.—Broil the tripe, and serve it with sauce *fines herbes.*

Tripe may be bought pickled; it is then served at breakfast and lunch.

SMOKED BEEF'S TONGUE.

Soak the smoked tongue in cold water for at least three hours, change the water once or twice during the process. Then take off the thin skin or strip around if there is any; put the tongue in a saucepan with two sprigs of thyme, two of parsley, a bay-leaf, two cloves, six small onions, and a clove of garlic; fill the pan with cold water, and let simmer about six hours. If the water is boiling away, add more. Take from the fire, let cool as it is, then take it out of the water; clean it, let dry, and serve it when cold.

Cut the tongue, when prepared as above, either in slices or in strips, and use for sandwiches, or serve it whole, with a cucumber, *piquante*, *poivrade*, or tomato sauce, at breakfast or lunch. It may also be served in *vinaigrette*.

When prepared as directed above, serve it as a fillet of beef *en Bellevue*, for supper, lunch, or breakfast. It makes a fine and delicious dish.

It is used also to stuff boned turkeys and other birds, as directed in those receipts; always boil it as directed above, before using it.

When served with any of the above sauces, it may be decorated with skewers the same as boiled beef.

Larded.—When boiled, lard it with salt pork, and bake it for about one hour in a moderately heated oven, and serve it with the same sauces as above.

Cut in slices and served with parsley, it is a *hors-d'œuvre*.

MUTTON.

HOW TO SELECT.

You may be sure that mutton is good when the flesh is rather black, and the fat white; if the fat breaks easily, it is young.

The wether is much superior to the ewe.

You will know if a leg of mutton comes from a wether, if there is a large and hard piece of fat on one side at the larger and upper end; if from a ewe, that part is merely a kind of skin, with a little fat on it.

ROASTED.

A piece of mutton to roast must not be too fresh, it is much more tender when the meat is rather seasoned, but not tainted, or what is sometimes called "high." When on the spit, place it near the fire, baste immediately with a little melted butter, and then with the drippings. As soon as you notice that a kind of crust or coating has formed around the piece of meat, remove it a little from the fire by degrees; and continue basting till done. The quicker the crust is formed, though without burning the meat, the more juicy and tender it will be.

Roast mutton, like roast beef, is better served rather underdone, but should be a little more done than beef. When properly roasted, the meat, whatever piece it may be, either a loin or saddle, a leg, shoulder, or a breast, may be served with its gravy only ; that is, with what is in the dripping-pan after having removed all the fat, also on a *soubise* or on a *purée* of sorrel. The above pieces may also be served in the following ways :

With Potatoes.—When dished, surround the meat with potatoes, either fried, mashed, or in *croquettes.*

With Quenelles.—Dish the meat, place half a dozen *quenelles* around it, and decorate it with skewers which you have run through a *quenelle* and then through a crawfish and stuck in the meat.

With Carrots.— When dished, put all around the meat carrots *au jus,* or glazed and cut with a vegetable spoon.

With Spinach.—Spinach *au jus* when done is spread on the dish, the meat is put on it, and served warm. Do the same with a *purée* of cauliflowers.

BAKED.

All the above pieces are baked as well as roasted; and when done, served exactly in the same and every way as when roasted.

Put the meat in a baking-pan with a little butter spread over it; cover the bottom of the pan with cold water, then put in a quick oven. After it has been in the oven for about fifteen minutes, baste and place a piece of buttered paper on the top of the meat. If the bottom of the pan is getting dry, add a little more water, but it is seldom the case except with inferior meat. When you see rather too much fat in the pan, take from the oven, turn the fat off, put cold water instead, and put back in the oven to finish the cooking. If the paper burns, put on another piece; but by basting often over the paper, it will remain pretty long before burning.

With a small knife or a skewer you ascertain when done enough or to your liking; never cook by guess or by hearsay; the oven may be quicker one day than another, or slower; the meat may be more tender, or more hard; remember that if you cook by guess (we mean, to put down, as a matter of course, that it takes so many hours, or so many minutes, to bake this or that), and stick to it, you will fail nine times out of ten. When done, serve as directed above.

In Croquettes.—Make and serve as chicken *croquettes.*

In Haricot or Ragout.—Take a neck or breast piece of mutton, which cut in pieces about two inches long and one broad. Put them in a saucepan (say three pounds) with two ounces of butter, set on the fire and stir occasionally till turning rather brown, then add a tablespoonful of flour, stir for one minute, cover with cold water, add one onion whole, salt, a bunch of seasonings composed of four sprigs of parsley, one of thyme, a bay-leaf, and a clove, one clove of garlic, chopped fine. Boil gently till about two-thirds done, stirring now and then; add potatoes, peeled, quartered, and cut, as far as possible, of the shape of a carpel of orange. The proportion is, about as many pieces of potatoes as of meat. Boil again gently till done, place the pieces of meat in the middle of the dish, the potatoes around, the juice or sauce over the whole, and serve. Skim off the fat, if any, before turning the sauce over the rest.

BREAST BOILED.

Put the breast entire in a saucepan, with a sprig of thyme, two of parsley, a bay-leaf, a clove, salt, and pepper, cover with water, set on the fire, boil gently till cooked, and then drain. Put in a frying-pan three table-spoonfuls of sweet-oil, a teaspoonful of chopped parsley, salt, and pepper; when hot lay the breast in and fry it all around for five minutes; then take it off, roll it in bread-crumbs, place it on a gridiron, and set on a good fire for five minutes; turn it over once only, then serve it with a *piquante*, *poivrade*, or tomato sauce. It may also be served on a *purée* of sorrel.

NECK BROILED.

Prepare and serve exactly the same as a breast broiled.

A breast or a neck piece broiled may be served on a *soubise*. It may also be served with a *maître d'hôtel* or mushroom sauce, also with a *piquante* or any other sharp sauce.

CHOPS.

Broiled.—Trim and flatten the chops with a chopper, sprinkle salt and pepper on both sides, dip them in melted butter, place them on a gridiron, and set on a sharp fire, turn over two or three times to broil properly, and when done, serve them around a dish, one lapping over the other, etc., and serve with the gravy. It takes about twelve minutes to cook with a good fire.

Another way.—When trimmed and flattened, dip them in beaten egg, roll them in bread-crumbs and broil, either as they are, or enveloped in buttered paper, and serve them with a *maître d'hôtel* sauce.

Sautés.—When trimmed and flattened, fry them with a little butter on both sides; then take the chops from the pan and put them in a warm place. Leave in the pan only a tablespoonful of fat, add to it three times as much broth, a teaspoonful of parsley and green onions,

two shallots, two pickled cucumbers, all chopped fine, and
a pinch of allspice; give one boil, pour the whole on the
chops, also the juice of half a lemon, and serve.

The same, with Vegetables.—Put in a frying-pan a
piece of butter the size of two walnuts for four chops, set
on a good fire, and when hot lay the chops in, after having flattened them with a chopper, and having sprinkled
salt and pepper on both sides; add a clove, and a teaspoonful of chopped parsiey and green onions; leave thus five
minutes, turn over once or twice; then add also half a
wine-glass of broth, same of white wine, and finish the
cooking. Take the chops off the pan and put them in a
warm place. Boil the sauce in the pan ten minutes, turn
it on the chops, put a garniture of vegetables around, and
serve. Throw away the clove just before serving.

Another way.—Have a piece of butter the size of an
egg for eight chops in a crockery vessel, and set it on a
good fire; when melted take from the fire, lay the chops
in, after having flattened them; then cover them with a
sheet of buttered paper; place the vessel in a rather hot
oven, and when cooked serve them on a *maître d'hôtel*,
provençale, or tomato sauce. They may also be served on
a *purée* of sorrel, or one of potatoes.

The same, in Papillote.—Cut the chops rather thin,
beat them gently and flatten them; then proceed as for
veal cutlets in *papillotes* in every particular.

Financière.—Broil the chops, either with or without
egg and crumbs, and serve them with a *financière* garniture.

Soubise.—The chops are either broiled or fried; either
broiled only dipped in lukewarm butter or in beaten egg
and crumbs and then served on a *soubise*. A little lemon-
juice may be added when they are on the dish.

Jardinière.—Cut two carrots and two turnips with a vegetable spoon and set on the fire with cold water and salt; boil gently till tender, and drain. Boil also in the same way, in another pan and till tender, two tablespoonfuls of green peas, or string-beans cut in pieces, and drain also. Then put carrots, turnips, peas, or beans, back on the fire, in the same pan with a little gravy and broth, enough to cover them, salt, and pepper; boil gently five minutes; then put the chops in after being fried as directed below; boil another five minutes; take from the fire, place the chops around the dish, one lapping over the other, and so that an empty place is left in the middle; turn the carrots, turnips, and peas, with the sauce in that empty place, and serve. Salt and pepper the chops on both sides; fry them in a little butter till about three-quarters done; then take off and put with the vegetables as directed above. They may be broiled instead of fried, which is better.

A la Princesse.—Trim the chops as usual and salt and pepper both sides. Chop very fine a piece of lean veal, about half a pound for six or eight chops, according to size, then pound it and mix it with half a teaspoonful of flour, a pinch of nutmeg, salt, pepper, a yolk of egg, two tablespoonfuls of bread-crumbs and one ounce of butter. If too firm the butter must be melted so as to mix better. Put the mixture in a saucepan, set on a good fire, stir for ten minutes, and take off. Then grease the paste-board slightly with butter, put a teaspoonful of the mixture here and there on it, roll and make small balls of it, drop them in boiling broth or water, boiling about fifteen minutes, and take off with a skimmer. Dip the chops in melted butter, then in beaten eggs, and roll in bread-crumbs; fry them with a little butter. Fry the balls also. Place the chops on the dish, the bones toward the edge, and the balls between the chops; serve warm. A few balls may be placed in the middle.

With Mushrooms.—Broil and serve them with a *purée* of mushrooms, or with a mushroom garniture.

Mutton chops, broiled, may be served with every kind of butter, every garniture, and every sauce, according to taste; they may also be served with every *purée*.

A French cook once said he could serve mutton *chops* in three hundred ways, *apples* in two hundred ways, and *eggs* in four hundred ways. The culinary science and art is advanced enough to-day to double the above figures, and have plenty to spare.

LEG.

Besides being prepared as directed for roast mutton, a leg of mutton, roasted or baked, may be served in the following ways:

Boil white beans and drain them as directed, then put them on the fire with the drippings of the leg of mutton for ten minutes, stirring now and then, and serve them with it. They may also be kept in the dripping-pan for ten minutes, when boiled and drained, before the leg is done. If the leg of mutton is baked, set them on the fire for about ten minutes, with the gravy, stirring occasionally. Serve either on the same or on a separate dish.

With Currant Jelly.—Roast or bake the leg of mutton, and serve it with currant jelly or with a *purée*.

Provençale.—With a sharp-pointed knife, make a small cut in the leg of mutton here and there, and large enough to stick into the cut a clove of garlic. Make as many cuts as you please, from six to twenty, according to taste, and in each cut stick a clove of garlic. When prepared thus, roast or bake, and serve it with either of the following sauces: *piquante, poivrade, ravigote, rémolade,* Robert, shallot, Tartar, tomato, and in *vinaigrette.*

Decorated.—A leg of mutton may be decorated the same as a fillet of beef.

Stewed.—Take the large bone out, leaving the bone at the smaller end as a handle; cut off also the bone below the knuckle, and fix it with skewers; then put it in a stew-pan with a pinch of allspice, four onions, two cloves, two carrots cut in four pieces each, a small bunch of parsley, two bay-leaves, three sprigs of thyme, salt, pepper, two ounces of bacon cut in slices, a quarter of a pint of broth, and water enough just to cover it; set on a good fire, and after one hour of boiling add a liquor-glass of French brandy. Let simmer then for about five hours, in all about six hours; then dish it, strain the sauce on it, and serve.

We would advise those who have never tasted of a leg of mutton cooked as above, to try it.

It may be served also with white beans cooked in water and fried in butter, or on fried potatoes.

The next day.—If you have a piece left for the next day, cut it in thin slices after dinner, place the slices on a dish, with parsley under, in the middle, and above, and keep in a cold place.

A while before dinner you put in a stewpan a piece of butter (the quantity to be according to the quantity of meat), and set it on a good fire; when melted, sprinkle in, gradually, a little flour, stirring with a wooden spoon; when of a proper thickness, and of a brownish color, add a glass of broth, salt, pepper, a few pickled cucumbers cut in slices, and two or three mushrooms; boil ten minutes; lay the slices of meat in, subdue the fire, simmer twenty minutes, and serve.

The same, in another way.—Chop fine the slices of leg of mutton, put a piece of butter in a stewpan, and set it on the fire; when melted, place the chopped meat in, keep stirring with a wooden spoon for about ten minutes; then add two or three tablespoonfuls of broth, salt, pepper, and a pinch of allspice; simmer fifteen minutes, and serve with fried eggs all around the dish.

Boiled.—Set a saucepan on the fire with cold water enough to cover the leg of mutton, add salt; at the first boil put the leg of mutton in, wrapped up in a towel. Boil gently till done. For a middling-sized one, it takes about two hours. Remove the towel, dish the leg of mutton, spread a caper-sauce over it, and serve hot. The sauce may also be served in a boat or saucer.

Cold.—What is left of it may be prepared like cold mutton in *vinaigrette.*

SHOULDER.

Shoulder boned.—Split the shoulder just in the middle, on the inside, lengthwise and following the middle of the bones; remove the flat bone at the larger end first. This is easily done by scraping the meat off the bone on both sides, and then pulling it off. Do the same with the remaining bone. Spread the shoulder open on the table, the inside up, salt and pepper it, then spread on it the same stuffing as for a chicken stuffed with sausage-meat. Roll the shoulder round, tie it with twine, and roast or bake it. When roasted or baked, serve with the gravy.

On a Purée.—Bone and roll the shoulder as above directed, but do not stuff it; roast or bake it, and serve it on a *purée* of potatoes, beans, peas, lentils, or any other vegetable; place the shoulder in the middle of a dish, cut it in slices, and place them all around the *purée*, one lapping over the other; turn the gravy over the whole through a strainer, and serve hot.

With a Sauce.—When baked or roasted as above, with or without stuffing, serve it with a *piquante, ravigote,* or *Robert* sauce.

Boiled.—Boil, and serve it with a caper-sauce, the same as the leg.

SADDLE.

Prepare, cook, and serve the saddle in the same way as the leg—roasted or baked, warm or cold.

COLD MUTTON.

Served cold, à la Vinaigrette.—A shoulder of mutton, roasted or baked, after being boned, makes a handsome dish served cold. Cut any piece of cold mutton that you may have, in thin slices, as evenly as possible. Place a paste-cutter, about an inch and a half in diameter, in the middle of an oval dish; then place the slices of meat all around the dish, one slice lapping over another; the dish being oval, the slices of meat will touch the paste-cutter on two sides, but there will be two empty places on the two other sides, which you fill with hard-boiled white of egg chopped fine, and hard-boiled yolk of egg chopped fine also; they must not be mixed, and the yolk must be farther from the paste-cutter, the white touching it. Put a string of chopped yolk of egg all around the meat, and outside of it one of chopped white of egg around the yolk, and one of chopped parsley around the white. Remove the paste-cutter, and put a rose, or two or three pinks, in its place, or a small bunch of violets. Place one or three capers on each small heap of yolk of egg that is on the middle of the dish, and also some capers here and there on the string of white of egg.

9

Place a rose at each end of the dish, as indicated in the cut opposite; six radishes around the dish, also as indicated in the cut, and you have a dish as sightly as can be made, and an excellent one, too. Serve with the following sauce in a boat or saucer: Put in a bowl half a teaspoonful of mustard, a little pepper and salt; then pour one or two tablespoonfuls of vinegar on, little by little, beating with a fork at the same time; again, three or four tablespoonfuls of oil, and in the same way; and when the whole is well mixed, serve.

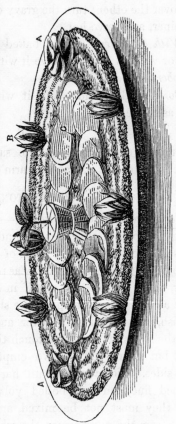

A, two roses, one at each end; B, six radishes around; C, slices of meat; D, eggs; E, yolks of eggs; F, parsley.

SHEEP'S BRAIN.

Prepare, cook, and serve as calf's brain.

FEET.

Broiled.—Throw them in boiling water for ten minutes, clean and scrape off the hair and take out the large bone. Put in a saucepan a bay-leaf, one clove, a tablespoonful

of vinegar, a clove of garlic, two sprigs of parsley, two
green onions, salt, pepper, a piece of butter the size of
two walnuts, half a pint of broth, then a dozen feet on
the whole; set on a s.ow fire, simmer one hour, stir now
and then, take from the fire and let cool. Then dip each
foot in beaten egg, and roll it in bread-crumbs; place them
on a gridiron ; turn over to broil both sides properly, and
serve them with the sauce in which they have been
cooked, after having strained it. They may also be served
on a *piquante, poivrade, ravigote,* or *Robert* sauce.

In Poulette.—Prepare and clean them as directed
above. Put in a saucepan four ounces of salt pork cut in
dice, two ounces of lard, salt, and white pepper; when
warm, add three sprigs of parsley, two of thyme, a bay-
leaf, one clove, four onions, and one carrot, cut in slices,
a quarter of a lemon, also cut in slices, free from rind and
seed, two tablespoonfuls of flour ; this last must be added
by sprinkling it little by little, stirring the while with a
wooden spoon ; five minutes after, place the feet in, cover
the whole with warm water, and let simmer gently for
five or six hours. After that time see if the meat can be
easily detached from the bones, and if so, they are cooked ;
if not, leave them a little longer, and take from the fire
as soon as it is easily detached, but do not detach it.
Put in a stewpan a piece of butter the size of two walnuts ; when melted, sprinkle in it a tablespoonful of flour,
stir with a wooden spoon, then put the feet in, add a teaspoonful of chopped parsley and green onions, a little
piece of nutmeg, salt, pepper, and two or three mushrooms cut in slices or pieces; wet with broth; simmer
half an hour, take from the fire, and throw away the
piece of nutmeg; mix with the whole two yolks of eggs
well beaten and a tablespoonful of vinegar, and serve.

SHEEP'S KIDNEYS, BROILED.

Split them in two, and put them in cold water for five minutes; trim off the pellicle or thin skin, run a skewer through, sprinkle salt and pepper on, place them on the gridiron, and set on a good fire; turn over, and when broiled, serve them with a piece of butter and chopped parsley kneaded together, and placed on each kidney; add also a few drops of lemon-juice.

You may also, when broiled, serve them on a *maître d'hôtel* sauce.

The same, in Brochette.—Proceed as above in every particular, except that you place the kidneys on the spit instead of on the gridiron. Serve them in the same way.

The same, with Champagne.—Cut the kidneys in slices, each in ten or twelve pieces. Put in a stewpan a piece of butter the size of two walnuts, and set it on the fire; when melted, add a teaspoonful of chopped parsley, same of mushrooms, a pinch of grated nutmeg, salt, pepper, and the kidneys; keep tossing till they become stiff, then sprinkle on them a saltspoonful of flour, stirring with a wooden spoon the while; add also a wine-glass of Champagne, or of good white wine; subdue the fire, and let simmer till cooked; take from the fire, add about one ounce of fresh butter, and the juice of half a lemon, and serve. This is a very delicate dish.

SHEEP'S TAILS.

Put in a stewpan two ounces of bacon cut in slices, with a bay-leaf, two sprigs of parsley, one of thyme, one clove, six small onions, one carrot cut in four pieces, then about six tails; cover the whole with broth and white wine, half of each; add salt and pepper. Place the pan in a moderately heated oven; it will take about four hours to cook them. After that time, take the tails from the pan, and put them in a warm place, then strain the sauce in which they have cooked, skim off the fat if too much of it, put the sauce back in the pan, and set on the fire; let it reduce till rather thick, place the tails on a *purée*, turn the sauce on them, and serve.

SHEEP'S TONGUES.

Soak the tongues in cold water for two hours in winter, and one in summer, and drain. Throw them in boiling water, and leave till you can easily take the skin off; then skin and clean well, split in two lengthwise, and let cool. Put in a stewpan two ounces of bacon cut in thin slices, a bay-leaf, two sprigs of thyme, four of parsley, two cloves, three green onions and six small red or white ones, one carrot cut in four pieces, salt and pepper, then the tongues; add also half a pint of broth, same of water, same of white wine; set in a moderately heated oven, and simmer about four hours; have the stewpan covered as nearly air-tight as possible. Then take the tongues from the pan and drain them; knead well together two ounces of fresh butter, with two teaspoonfuls of chopped parsley, a little salt and allspice; spread some on each of the tongues as soon as they are cold; envelop each in oiled paper, broil them gently on a slow fire, and serve with the paper.

You may also when prepared and cooked as above directed, and instead of broiling them, place a *purée* on a dish, and serve them on a *purée*, pouring on the whole the sauce in which they have cooked, and straining it at the same time.

They are really more delicate when broiled.

LAMB.

To select.—The flesh must be like that of mutton, rather black, and the fat white.

There is no difference in the wether and ewe. The shorter the quarters are the better the meat, and the fore as well as the hind quarter. With the exception that the breast-piece is prepared also in *épigramme*, and that it is cut in quarters instead of dividing it like mutton, lamb may be prepared in the same and every way like mutton. The quarters may be prepared like shoulder, leg, and saddle of mutton.

Chops may be cut and prepared the same as mutton-chops.

Fore-Quarter.—According to the opinion of a great many epicures, the fore-quarter is the best part of the lamb; but, as we have previously said, every one to his liking.

Lard it slightly, and envelop it with buttered paper, place it upon the spit before a good fire; when done take from the fire, and take the paper off, sprinkle on it salt, pepper, and chopped parsley; put back on the spit before a sharp fire, just long enough to allow it to take a fine color; then take off, run a knife under the shoulder to make a small hole, pour *maître d'hôtel* sauce in it, and serve either as it is, with its gravy, or on a *purée* of sorrel.

To bake it.—Put it in a baking-pan, spread a little salt, pepper, and butter over it; cover it with a piece of buttered paper; have the bottom of the pan covered with cold water and put in a warm oven, baste often till done. If the paper burns, put on another piece. Run a small knife or a skewer into the meat, to ascertain when properly done.

It may be served with the gravy only, after having removed the fat, or with a *piquante*, *poivrade*, or *maître d'hôtel* sauce.

It is also served with a garniture of mushrooms or onions, or with a *macédoine*, or on a *purée* of spinach, or of sorrel.

Hind-Quarter.—Throw it in boiling water for five minutes, and drain. Put in a stewpan a piece of butter the size of an egg, and set on the fire; when melted, mix in it a tablespoonful of flour; after which, pour in, little by little, a pint and a half of boiling water, stirring with a wooden spoon all the time; then put the meat in the pan, add four onions, a bay-leaf, two cloves, three sprigs of parsley, two of thyme, salt, and pepper; about fifteen minutes before it is done, add two or three mushrooms cut in slices, take from the fire when cooked, place the meat on a dish with the mushrooms and onions around, or if preferred, without either; strain the sauce on the meat, and serve.

If the sauce is not thick enough, mix the yolk of an egg in it just before serving.

Roasted.—Roast and serve the hind-quarter in the same way as directed for the fore-quarter.

Baked.—Bake and serve it also in the same and every way like the fore-quarter.

Epigramme.—Put a breast of lamb in a saucepan, cover it with cold water, season with a small onion and one clove stuck in it, two stalks of parsley, a piece of carrot, one of turnip, and salt. Boil gently till you can pull off the bones easily. It may also be boiled in the soup-kettle while making broth. When the bones come off easily, take from the fire, pull out all the small bones and cut out the large one. Place the breast in a large bakepan, with some weight over so as to flatten it, and leave it so till perfectly cold. Then cut it in pieces of rhombic shape about four inches long and two inches broad; salt and pepper each piece on both sides; dip them in beaten egg, roll in bread-crumbs and fry them with a little butter, and serve on a tomato, *piquante, ravigote*, or *soubise* sauce, or on any *purée*.

When the sauce is spread on the dish, place the pieces of lamb all around it, one lapping over the other, and forming a kind of oblong string, and serve warm.

Another.—When the *épigramme* is prepared as above and ready to be served, have as many mutton-chops as you have pieces of meat from the breast; dish in the same way, except that you put one piece of the breast and then a mutton-chop fried in the same way as the pieces of meat; the chops lapping over the pieces of breast, and *vice versa*.

Broiled.—The same may be broiled instead of fried, and served in the same way.

Roasted entire.—Skewer a lamb properly on the spit, envelop it with buttered paper, place before a good fire, baste often with melted butter first, and then with the drippings; when nearly done take the paper off, let the lamb take a fine color around, and serve it with the gravy. It may be served with a garniture around and decorated with skewers, the same as directed for fillet of beef; it then makes a sightly as well as a delicious dish.

Served with a garniture and decorated as directed for a fillet of beef, it is served as a *relevé* at a grand dinner, and as an *entrée* at a family dinner.

Cold.—Cold lamb is served in every way like cold mutton. A part left from a roasted piece may be enveloped in buttered paper, put on the spit just long enough to warm it, and served just in the same way as roast lamb.

Lamb's head, feet, kidneys, etc., are prepared and served like the same parts of the sheep, and as directed in the different receipts.

KID.

Prepare, cook, and serve kid the same as lamb.

9*

VEAL.

NEVER buy too young veal. It is very easy to know it; when too young, the bones are very tender; they are more like nerves than bones; the meat is gluish, and has little or no taste. Epicures say that if a calf is killed before it is two months old, or at least six weeks, it is not fit for eating. We are of that opinion, although, perhaps, very few are allowed so long a life. We will therefore recommend our readers to beware buying too young veal; many diseases, especially in children, come from eating it.

When you broil or roast a piece of veal, baste often. Veal is better when a little overdone; it is not good, and operates like physic, if underdone.

The best veal is that of a greenish color and very fat. It is fresh when the eyes are full and smooth, and when the meat is firm. If the meat is yellowish or contains yellowish spots, it is not fresh. The veins must be red.

To improve.—Chop fine a tablespoonful of parsley, a teaspoonful of shallots, same of green onions, a bay-leaf, two sprigs of thyme, two or three mushrooms, add to them, salt, pepper, a little grated nutmeg; cover the bottom of a tureen with half of each, put on it the piece of veal you wish to improve, cover with the other half of the seasonings; then pour gently on the whole two tablespoonfuls of sweet-oil; leave the veal thus about four or five hours in winter and about two in summer.

ROASTED.

The pieces of veal that are roasted are the *loin, leg,* and *shoulder.*

It may be improved as directed above or not, according to taste; but we earnestly recommend it as not a little improvement, but as a marked one, as everybody can try it and judge, veal being naturally tasteless.

There are three ways of roasting veal. We will describe them, so that it can be done according to taste.

1. Spread a thin coat of butter around the piece of veal after being salted all around, put on the spit before a good but not very sharp fire; near it, but not too much so: veal being more tender than beef, it would also burn much quicker. Baste often with melted butter first, and then with the drippings, and from the beginning to the end. When done, that is, when overdone, as veal must always be, serve with the gravy only, or in the different ways described below.

2. Lard all the fleshy parts of the piece of veal with a larding-needle and strips of salt pork, the same as a fillet of beef, but which strips you roll in a mixture of parsley chopped, salt and pepper, before running them into the meat, and proceed as above for the rest. Serve also like the above.

3. After the piece of veal is improved as directed, spread the seasonings in which it has been improved all around it, then envelop the whole in buttered paper, which you fasten with twine, put it on the spit, and baste often with melted butter. It must be basted often to prevent the paper from burning. About fifteen minutes before it is

done, remove the paper, put the meat a little nearer the fire so as to give it a fine yellow or golden color, finish the cooking till overdone, and serve also like the first, or No. 1.

No matter which of these three ways the piece of veal is roasted, it is served in the same manner.

With Asparagus.—When the roasted piece of veal is dished, put a *purée* of asparagus all around, and serve warm.

With Peas.—Spread one pint or one quart (according to the size of the piece of meat) of green peas *au jus*, on a dish; place the meat on the peas, spread the gravy over the whole, and serve as warm as possible.

With Quenelles.—Dish the roasted piece, place around it six or eight *quenelles* of chicken or of veal, strain the gravy on the whole, and serve warm.

With Vegetables.—When roasted and dished, put any kind of vegetables, prepared *au jus*, all around the piece of meat, and serve warm.

With Sweetbreads.—Roast the piece of veal as directed, and when dished, place six sweetbreads, prepared *au jus*, tastefully around the meat; strain the gravy over, and serve very warm.

Decorated.—Every piece of roasted veal may be decorated with skewers, either served *au jus* or in any of the above ways. The skewers are first run through either of the following and then stuck into the piece of meat: slices of truffles; chicken-combs, prepared as for garniture; slices of sweetbreads or whole ones, prepared *au jus; quenelles* of chicken or of veal; slices of carrots, turnips, beets, all prepared *au jus;* and mushrooms. One, two, three, or more to every skewer; for instance: one slice of truffle, then one of turnip, a chicken-comb, then a slice of sweetbread or a whole one, and then stick in the meat. From two to six skewers may be used. On a large piece never put less than two, and no matter how many you use, always have even numbers of them.

BAKED.

All the parts of veal that are roasted, that is, the loin, leg, and shoulder, can be baked. They may be improved in the same way as to roast them. Put the piece of veal in a bakepan; spread salt, pepper, and butter on it; cover the bottom of the pan with cold water, about a quarter of an inch in depth; place a piece of buttered paper on the meat, and put in a warm oven. If the meat has been improved, the seasonings are spread over it before placing the buttered paper. Baste often with the water and juice in the pan and over the paper, which you need not remove till about ten minutes before taking from the oven, or in case it should burn; then you must replace it by another. It keeps the top of the meat moist, and it is more juicy when done.

When properly baked (overdone, as every piece of veal must be), serve either *au jus*, or with the same garnitures, the same decorations, as directed for roasted veal.

The gravy in the bakepan is strained, the fat skimmed off, and then it is turned over the meat and garnitures when dished, the same as the drippings or gravy of roast meat. In case the water in the bakepan, or the juice, or both, should boil away or be absorbed, put more cold water in it, so as to be able to baste.

BLANQUETTE.—(*Also called Poulette.*)

Take about two pounds of neck, breast, shoulder, or any other piece, which cut in pieces, two inches square, throw them in boiling water, with a little salt, for five minutes, and drain them. Put in a stewpan a piece of butter the size of an egg, set it on a good fire, and when melted mix in a tablespoonful of flour, stirring all the time, and when turning yellow pour gently and slowly in the pan a pint of boiling water; add a teaspoonful of chopped parsley and green onions, salt, pepper, six small white or red onions, two or three mushrooms, and then the meat; boil gently about three hours, and serve.

CROQUETTES.

Proceed as for chicken croquettes in every particular, except that you use cold veal instead of cold chicken.

RAGOUT.

The neck and breast pieces are generally used to make a *ragout*, but any other piece may be used. Take about three pounds of veal, which cut in pieces about two inches square. Put two ounces of butter in a saucepan, set it on the fire, and as soon as the butter is melted, lay the meat in, stir now and then till of a golden color, and then take the meat from the pan. Leave the pan on the fire, and put in it a tablespoonful of flour, little by little, keep stirring about five minutes; add also half a pint of broth, same of warm water, one onion with a clove stuck in it, a bay leaf, two sprigs of thyme, two of parsley, a clove of garlic, a small carrot cut in two or three pieces, salt and pepper, then the meat, and cover the pan. Half an hour after your meat is in, fry in butter in a frying-pan six small onions, which you also put in the stewpan as soon as fried. When the whole is cooked, place the meat on a dish, strain the sauce on it, surround the whole with the six small onions, and serve warm.

In Scallops.—Take a piece from the loin or leg of

veal, cut it in pieces about three inches long, two inches broad, and one-third of an inch thick, as evenly as possible, and flatten them with a chopper. Salt and pepper them on both sides, and fry them with a little butter till about half done, on both sides alike. Add a little broth and chopped parsley, and boil gently till done. Place the pieces of veal all around the platter, one lapping over another, turn the sauce in the middle of them, and serve.

Another.—Cut the veal in pieces as for the above; beat one or two eggs in a plate with salt, pepper, and chopped parsley; dip each piece into it and then roll in bread-crumbs; butter a bakepan, place the veal in with a small lump of butter on each piece, and bake; turn over to bake evenly. Serve as the above, with a *piquante* or tomato sauce in the middle.

BREAST, STEWED.

Cut in dice two ounces of bacon, put it in a stewpan and set on a good fire; add two ounces of butter, and two onions cut in slices; when melted, lay the breast in, turn it over and leave till of a golden color on both sides; add then two small carrots cut in pieces, one teaspoonful of chopped green onions, three sprigs of parsley, half a turnip, salt, and pepper; moisten with half a pint of warm water; leave thus about three hours on a moderate fire. Strain the juice in a dish, put the meat on it, and serve.

The pieces of carrots and of bacon may be served with the meat, if you choose.

The same, with Green Peas.—Cut the breast in square pieces about two inches in size. Put in a stewpan a piece of butter the size of an egg, and set it on the fire; when melted, mix in it a teaspoonful of flour, then lay the meat in, and wet with half a glass of broth, same of warm water, also two sprigs of parsley, salt, and pepper; stir now and then. One hour after add green peas, and leave on the fire till the whole is cooked, when skim off the fat on the surface, and serve.

In Matelote.—To make a *matelote* of veal any piece can be used, but most generally it is made with a breast or neck piece. Cut the veal in square pieces about two inches in size; have in a stewpan and on a good fire a piece of butter about the size of an egg; when melted, put the meat in, stir now and then till of a golden color; then take the meat from the stewpan, which you leave on the fire, and in which you put half a pint of warm water, same of claret wine, same of broth, a bay-leaf, two cloves, two sprigs of parsley, one of thyme, a clove of garlic, salt, and pepper; when turning brown, put the meat back in the pan, and fifteen minutes before it is cooked add also ten small onions fried in butter beforehand and four or five mushrooms, then have a brisk fire to finish the cooking; place the meat on a dish, strain the sauce on the meat, put the ten small onions around it, and serve.

Broiled.—Salt and pepper both sides of the breast of veal, grease it all over with melted butter, by means of a brush, and broil till overdone. Serve with a *maître d'hôtel*, *piquante*, or *poivrade* sauce.

CUTLETS.

Broiled.—When properly trimmed, they may be improved as directed for veal. Salt and pepper both sides; spread a little melted butter on both sides also by means of a brush; place them on, before, or under the fire (*see* BROILING); baste now and then with melted butter; turn over one, two, or three times, and when rather overdone serve with a *maître d'hôtel* sauce spread all over.

The above way of serving them is sometimes called *au naturel.*

With Crumbs.—When trimmed, dip them in egg beaten with salt, pepper, and chopped parsley, roll them in bread-crumbs, and then broil and serve them as the above, with a *maître d'hôtel.*

Fines Herbes.—Broil the chops as above, either with or without crumbs, and serve them with sauce *aux fines herbes.*

A l'Italienne.—When broiled as above, serve them on a layer of *macaroni Italienne.*

With Mushrooms.—When broiled and dished, surround them with a garniture of mushrooms, and serve warm. When there are several cutlets on the dish, and placed all around overlapping, the garniture may be put in the middle of the chops.

Do the same with the following garnitures: chicken-combs, *croutons, duxelle, financière, Macédoine,* and onion. They may also be served on any *purée.*

Baked.—Trim six cutlets. Mix well half a pound of sausage-meat with two eggs. Put a piece of buttered paper large enough to cover the bottom of a bakepan in which the six cutlets may be laid easily. Spread half the sausage-meat on the paper in the pan, then lay the cutlets in it; put the other half of the sausage-meat over the cutlets, and place the whole in a rather quick oven. Baste every five minutes with melted butter and broth, using them alternately, and serve warm with the gravy when done. A few drops of lemon-juice may be added to them when on the dish, if liked.

Sautées.—Trim, and fry them with a little butter. When done on both sides, add a little broth, salt, pepper, and mushrooms and parsley chopped fine ; chopped truffles may be added, if handy; boil gently for about ten minutes. Place the cutlets around the dish, one lapping over the other, turn the sauce in the middle, sprinkle some lemon-juice over the whole, and serve warm.

With Sauce.—When broiled, baked, or *sautéd*, they máy be dished and served with either of the following sauces: *fines herbes*, *maître d'hôtel*, *piquante*, *poivrade*, *ravigote*, *tarragon*, tomato, or truffle.

En Bellevue.—Proceed the same as for fillet of beef *en Bellevue*.

In Papillotes.—Trim six veal-chops, spread salt and pepper on them, and fry them with a little butter till about half done. Take from the fire, and cut a small hole in the middle with a paste-cutter. While they are frying, fry with a little butter one onion chopped fine; as soon as fried, add half a pound of sausage-meat; stir now and then for about five minutes; add also a pinch of cinnamon, same of nutmeg; take off and mix with the whole one yolk of egg, a tablespoonful of chopped parsley, salt, and pepper. Cut six pieces of white paper of a heart-like shape, and large enough to envelop a chop; grease them slightly with butter or sweet-oil; place some sausage-meat on one side of the paper (say half a tablespoonful), place a chop on it; put some sausage-meat on the chop and in the hole; fold the paper in two; then, by folding all around the border, the chop and seasonings are perfectly enveloped in the paper; put the chops in a baking-pan, spread a few drops of oil all over, and bake for about fifteen minutes in an oven at about 250 deg. Fahr. Instead of baking them, broil them carefully turning them over often and basting them to prevent the paper from burning, and serve with the paper on. They may be served on a *duxelle* garniture, or with a *purée*.

Fricandeau.—Take a piece of veal of any size, from the leg, loin, or cutlet piece, about three-quarters of an inch in thickness, lard one side with salt pork, the same as a fillet of beef. Put in a saucepan (for two pounds of meat) one ounce of butter, half a middling-sized onion, and as much carrot in slices, two or three stalks of parsley, one of thyme, a bay-leaf, six or eight pepper-corns, and rind of the pork you have used; spread all these seasonings on the bottom of the saucepan, put the piece of veal on them, the larded side up, set on a good fire for about fifteen minutes; after which you look if the under side of the meat is well browned; if so, add a gill of broth, put in the oven and baste often, if not, leave a little longer on the fire. Add a little broth once in a while, to keep the bottom of the pan wet, and to have enough to baste till a little overdone, and serve with the gravy strained all over it. It is then called *au jus.*

With Spinach.—Prepare and cook the *fricandeau* as above; and when done, put some broth in the pan after having taken off the meat; give one boil; turn in the spinach *au jus;* stir on the fire one minute; dish the spinach; place the *fricandeau* on it, and serve.

With Sorrel.—Proceed as with spinach in every particular, except that you serve on sorrel *au jus* instead of spinach. It makes a more delicate dish with sorrel, although excellent with spinach.

It may also be served with green peas *au jus* or *à l'anglaise.*

Financière.—When prepared, cooked, and dished as directed, surround it with a *financière* garniture, and serve warm.

Jardinière.—After being cooked and dished, put a *Macédoine* garniture around it, and serve warm.

SHOULDER.

Boned.—Lay the shoulder on the table, the inside up, split it just in the middle, lengthwise, and following the middle of the bones; remove the flat bone at the larger end first. Do the same for the remaining bone. Then spread the shoulder open, and salt and pepper it. Fill the inside with sausage-meat; roll it of a round shape, and when properly tied with twine, roast or bake it, as directed for roasted or baked veal. It is then dished, decorated, and served in the same and every way as directed for roasted pieces of veal.

It is an excellent dish served on either of the following *purées: beans, celery, lentils, peas, potatoes, sorrel, spinach,* or *tomatoes.*

When served on a *purée,* it may be decorated with skewers, the same as when served with a garniture.

It may also be served with a *piquante* or *poivrade* sauce.

Stuffed.—Bone the shoulder as directed above; spread it open, and salt and pepper it, also as directed. Spread a coat of sausage-meat on it, about one-third of an inch in thickness, then put a layer of salt pork on the sausage-meat; then a layer of boiled ham; again a layer of sausage-meat; on this a layer of beef or sheep's tongue, boiled. The ham and tongue are cut in square fillets, about one-fourth of an inch broad and about two inches long. The tongues may be fresh or salted, according to taste. When filled, roll it so as to give it a round shape; wrap it up in a towel and drop it in boiling water, to which you have added salt. Boil gently for about four hours, take the kettle from the fire and let cool. When cold take the shoulder off, wipe it dry and serve with meat jelly. The jelly is chopped, or cut in fancy shapes, or both. Some chopped jelly may be placed all around the meat, and some cut in fancy shapes with a paste-cutter or with a knife, and placed over it.

It may also be decorated with skewers, as directed for roasted pieces of veal.

En Bellevue.—When boiled and cold, prepare it like a fillet of *beef en Bellevue*, and serve.

LOIN OR LEG STEWED.

Have in a stewpan and on a slow fire three or four tablespoonfuls of sweet-oil; when hot put the loin in, turn it over till of a yellow color all around, then add a bay-leaf, salt, pepper, and a pint of warm water; simmer four hours, and serve with the following sauce, which you must have prepared at the same time: Fry in butter till of a golden color ten middling-sized onions, then add to them half a glass of claret wine, two tablespoonfuls of broth, and two of the juice of the loin, ten mushrooms (if handy); simmer till cooked, and strain. Mix the sauce with the juice of the loin, and put it on a dish, place the loin upon it, and serve with the onions and mushrooms around the meat.

In case the juice of the loin should be found too fat, throw in it (and before mixing it with the sauce) a few drops of cold water, and skim off the fat.

The only thing to throw away before mixing is the bay-leaf.

Another way, or prepared with a Garniture of Cabbages. —Put in a stewpan and set on a good fire a piece of butter the size of an egg; when melted, add four onions and two small carrots, cut in slices; fry them two or three minutes, then put the loin in, with half a bay-leaf, wet with warm broth; then subdue the fire, let simmer about two hours and a half; strain the sauce on a dish, place the meat on it, and serve with a garniture of cabbages around.

COLD VEAL.

Cut the meat in slices and serve them on a dish, arranged according to fancy, and serve with a *piquante, poivrade, Mayonnaise, Provençale, ravigote,* or *rémolade* sauce. It may also be decorated and served like cold mutton, in *vinaigrette.*

Another way.—Put a piece of butter the size of an egg in a stewpan and set on a good fire, mix in when melted two teaspoonfuls of flour, stir till of a brownish color, when add a saltspoonful of chopped parsley, four leaves of tarragon, salt, pepper, and half a pint of broth (more or less of the above according to the quantity of meat you have left), boil the whole fifteen minutes; then, if what you have left is from an entire piece, cut it in slices, lay them in the pan, and serve when warm enough, as it is.

If what you have left is in pieces or slices, you merely place them in the pan and serve with the sauce when warm.

BRAIN.

To prepare.—Put the brain in a bowl of cold water and a tablespoonful of vinegar and leave it in from one to two or three hours, that is, till you are ready to use it, but do not leave it more than five or six hours and not less than one hour. Take it off, remove the thin skin and blood-vessels that are all around.

To boil.—When prepared, put the brain in a small saucepan, cover it with cold water; add two tablespoonfuls of vinegar, half an onion sliced, three stalks of parsley, one of thyme, a bay-leaf, six pepper-corns, one clove, salt, boil about five minutes and take off the fire. Cut each half of the brain in two, from side to side; place the four pieces on a dish, the part cut upward.

Au Beurre Noir.—When dished as above directed, put two ounces of butter in a frying-pan and when melted turn into it two tablespoonfuls of vinegar, boil two or three minutes, then throw into it half a dozen stalks of parsley, take them off immediately with a skimmer, turn the butter and vinegar over the brain; spread the parsley around, and serve.

Stewed, or in Matelote.—When prepared as directed, put it in a small saucepan and cover it with claret wine; add half an onion sliced, one clove of garlic, one clove, two sprigs of parsley, one of thyme, salt, a bay-leaf, six pepper-corns, and boil gently for about fifteen minutes. Cut and dish it as directed above; turn the sauce over it through a strainer and serve—it is understood, the sauce in which it has been cooked.

Fried.—Prepare as directed, cut in about six slices, dip them in batter, and fry in hot fat. (*See direction for* FRYING.)

In Poulette.—Prepare and boil it as directed, split each half of the brain in two or four pieces, place them tastefully on a dish, spread a *poulette* sauce all over, and serve warm. It may also be prepared and served with a *piquante* sauce. When the *piquante* sauce is made, put the brain or brains in, boil ten minutes, and serve as it is.

EARS.

They are prepared in every way like calf's head.

FEET.

To boil.—Throw them in boiling water for five min-utes, split them in the middle and lengthwise after having taken off the large bone and hair, and tie them with a string. Put a piece of butter the size of two walnuts in a stewpan and set it on the fire, when melted add a teaspoon-ful of chopped parsley and green onions, half of each, a quarter of a lemon cut in slices, salt, and pepper, then the feet; wet with a glass of warm water; boil gently two or three hours, take from the fire and when nearly cold dip them in bread-crumbs, place them on a gridiron and set on a good fire, baste slightly with the juice in which they have cooked, and serve with fried parsley around.

The same, in Poulette.—Prepare and cook them as above. When you take them from the fire, instead of dipping them in bread-crumbs, put them in a *poulette* sauce, simmer ten minutes, and serve.

Fried.—When boiled and drained dry, dip them in beaten egg, roll in bread-crumbs, fry in hot fat, and serve with green parsley all around.

In Vinaigrette.—Boil them as directed and drain them dry. When perfectly cold, serve them with a *vinaigrette.*

CALF'S HEAD.

How to prepare.—When the hair is off and the whole head well cleaned (this is generally done by butchers; but if not, throw the head in boiling water for five min-utes and scrape the hair off with a knife immediately after taking it from the water), put it then in cold water for twenty-four hours in winter and ten in summer, changing the water two or three times.

To boil.—It may be boiled whole or after it is boned. If boiled whole, cut a hole on the top of the head and take off the brain without breaking it; put it in cold water immediately and as directed. Then set the head on the fire in a saucepan, covered with cold water, salt, one onion sliced, half a lemon, four stalks of parsley, one of thyme, a bay-leaf, two cloves, two cloves of garlic, ten pepper-corns, and two tablespoonfuls of vinegar; boil gently till done. Bone it before using it.

When boiled after being boned, the brain is taken off in the same way as above and put in cold water also; then the tongue is cut out and boiled with the skin of the head, etc., with the same seasonings as when boiled whole. It is then ready for use, but leave it in the water till wanted; it would become tough if exposed to the air.

In Poulette.—Put about two ounces of butter in a saucepan, set it on the fire, when melted turn in one table-spoonful of flour; stir, and as soon as it commences to turn yellow add half a pint of broth, stir again, and when thickening, add the calf's head cut in rather large dice, give one boil, take from the fire, add the yolk of an egg and about a teaspoonful of chopped parsley, stir, give another boil, and serve.

In Vinaigrette.—Leave it in the water till perfectly cold; or, if wanted immediately, as soon as boiled, take it off and put in cold water to cool, and use. Cut the head in large dice and serve it with oil, vinegar, salt, pepper, mustard, and parsley chopped.

Broiled.—Prepare and boil the calf's head as directed. As soon as cool, cut it in about half a dozen pieces, dip them in beaten eggs, roll them in bread-crumbs, and broil both sides till turning of a golden color; serve warm with a *maître d'hôtel* sauce, or with anchovy or horse-radish butter.

Fried.—Calf's head may be fried as soon as prepared and boiled; but most generally, it is only what has been left from the day before that is fried. Cut it in small pieces about two inches square, dip them in melted butter,

10

roll them in bread-crumbs, and fry them in hot fat. Serve hot, adding lemon-juice when the pieces of calf's head are on the dish.

En Tortue, or Turtle-like.—There are two ways of preparing calf's head *en tortue :*

1. When it is prepared and boiled as directed above, drain it dry, cut it in pieces as for frying it; put them in a saucepan with once ounce of butter, set on the fire, stir for two minutes, add nearly a pint of Madeira wine, simmer gently for about half an hour ; dish the meat, add a little lemon-juice all over, and serve warm. Some *quenelles* of chicken may be placed all around, as a decoration ; or a garniture of mushrooms.

2. Prepare and boil the calf's head ; drain it dry and cut it in pieces about two inches square. Dish the pieces either mound-like, or around the dish, one lapping over the other, and turn the following over it, and serve warm : Put a *financière* garniture in a saucepan with a pint of Madeira wine, set on the fire and boil gently for about twenty minutes ; take from the fire, spread over the pieces of calf's head, and serve.

Some hard-boiled eggs cut in four or eight pieces, lengthwise, may be placed all around the dish ; or some pickled cucumbers, cut in fancy pieces, or some *quenelles* of veal or chicken.

HEART.

To prepare.—Soak it in lukewarm water for about three hours, trim it and free it from skin, blood, and small fibres ; then drain and wipe it dry. Stuff or fill it with sausage-meat, to which you add previously two or three onions chopped fine.

To cook.—When thus prepared, envelop it in buttered

paper, set on the spit before a good fire, baste often, remove the paper a few minutes before taking it from the fire, then serve warm with a *piquante, poivrade,* or *ravigote* sauce. It may also be served with a *vinaigrette.*

To bake.—When prepared as directed above, put it in a baking-pan; spread a little butter over, put a little water in the bakepan and set in a quick oven, baste and turn over two or three times, and when done, serve with the gravy and the same sauces as if it were roasted.

In Gratin.—Soak, drain and wipe it dry as directed.

Cut it in slices and put them in a crockery or other pan; turn a white sauce all over, then sprinkle on half a gill of vinegar or the juice of a lemon, dust with bread-crumbs, put half a dozen lumps of butter, each about the size of a hazelnut, all over; bake in a rather quick oven.

KIDNEYS.

Sauté.—When prepared as directed below, cut it in pieces as directed for kidney in *brochettes.* Then put a piece of butter the size of half an egg in a frying-pan and set it on the fire; when melted, sprinkle in a teaspoonful of flour, stirring with a wooden spoon the while, add half a wine-glass of white wine, a tablespoonful of broth, a pinch of chopped parsley, salt and pepper, boil ten minutes and lay the fillets in; have a quick fire, and as soon as cooked dish them, spread the sauce over, sprinkle on a few drops of lemon-juice, and serve.

To prepare.—Never cook a kidney except it be very fresh. Prepare in the following way, a beef, sheep, or calf's kidney. Pig's kidneys are excellent if they have no disagreeable taste, but it is very often the case. The bad taste may be partly taken away by blanching the kidney, but it makes it tough and tasteless; it is better to throw it away.

In Brochettes.—Split the kidney in four lengthwise, and then cut it in rather small pieces. Cut fat salt pork in pieces of the same size as the pieces of kidney—the fatty part of the kidney must not be used—then salt and pepper the pieces of kidney; take a common skewer and run it through a piece of kidney, then through a piece of salt pork; repeat this till the skewer is full. Fill as many skewers as are necessary till the whole kidney is used; and then roast before a good fire, basting often with melted butter. Serve warm.

Another way.—Prepare as above, and instead of roasting, put the skewers in a bake-pan, spread a little butter over the kidney and salt pork, cover the bottom of the pan only with cold water, and bake. While in the oven, turn over and baste occasionally.

Serve as the above, with its gravy, and warm.

Another.—Skewer the kidney, or rather pieces of kidney and salt pork as above; dip them in beaten egg, roll them in bread-crumbs, and fry them in hot fat. Serve warm, but without gravy.

LIGHTS.

Cut them in four pieces, soak and wash them three or four times in lukewarm water, changing the water each time; press them with the hands to extract all the blood. Place the lights in a stewpan, cover them with cold water, and set on a good fire; boil two minutes, take them off, throw them in cold water, and drain them; cut the lights in dice. Have butter in a stewpan on the fire, and when melted, lay the lights in, fry five minutes, keeping them tossed the while, then sprinkle on a tablespoonful of flour, stirring all the time with a wooden spoon; pour on, little by little, about a pint of warm broth, also a saltspoonful of chopped parsley, a pinch of allspice, salt, pepper, a bay-leaf, and sprig of thyme; have a brisk fire, and when about half done, add four or five mushrooms, and eight small onions. When the whole is cooked, take off bay-leaf and thyme, then take from the fire, beat two yolks of eggs with a tablespoonful of vinegar, and mix with the whole, turn on a dish, and serve.

CALF'S LIVER.

How to prepare.—Have water, with a little salt, on the fire, and at the first boiling, throw the liver in for about five minutes, and drain it.

How to improve the Liver before cooking it.—Put in a tureen two tablespoonfuls of sweet-oil, a bay-leaf broken in four pieces, two sprigs of thyme, four of parsley chopped fine, a green onion also chopped fine, salt, and pepper; lay the liver on the whole, and leave it from four to six hours, turning it over two or three times.

How to cook, roasted.—Envelop the liver with buttered paper, place it on the spit before a good fire, baste often with the oil from the tureen, after having taken off bay-leaf and thyme. A few minutes before it is done, take the paper off, baste continually with the drippings till well cooked, and serve it with the gravy.

It may also be served with a *piquante* or *poivrade* sauce.

It takes from thirty-five to forty-five minutes to roast it.

The same, sauté.—Put two ounces of butter in a frying-pan, and set it on a sharp fire; when melted, add a teaspoonful of chopped parsley and green onions, then the liver cut in slices (after having been prepared as above); sprinkle on a saltspoonful of flour, then half a wine-glass of warm broth, same of claret wine, salt, pepper, and a pinch of allspice; serve when done.

It takes only from ten to twelve minutes for the whole process.

The same, in the Oven.—Put two ounces of butter in a frying-pan on a sharp fire; when hot, put the liver in (after having been boiled as directed above, and after having cut it in pieces); fry it five minutes, turning over once only; then take from the fire, salt both sides of the slices, place them on a warm dish, putting on each slice a little butter kneaded with chopped parsley, salt, and pepper; put two or three minutes in a warm oven, take off, sprinkle on the whole the juice of half a lemon, and serve in the dish in which it has cooked.

The same, stewed.—Boil the liver as directed above, and when drained and cold, lard it well. Have butter in a frying-pan on a brisk fire; when hot, put the liver in for about five minutes, turning it over on every side. Have in a stewpan four ounces of bacon cut in dice; set it on a good fire, and when hot, lay the liver in; then add a glass of warm broth, same of white wine, a bay-leaf, a sprig of thyme, two of parsley, a clove of garlic, two cloves, and a small carrot cut in two; cover the stewpan, subdue the fire, and let simmer three hours; stir now and then, place the liver on a dish, strain the sauce on it, and serve.

CALF'S PLUCK.

Put the pluck in cold water for twelve hours in winter and four in summer; change the water once, drain, and throw it in boiling water for ten or fifteen minutes; take off and throw in cold water to cool, and drain it. Cut the pluck in pieces, and cook it like calf's head, and serve with the same sauce.

CALF'S TAIL.

Take two tails, cut each in two, throw them in boiling water for three minutes, and drain. Cut a cabbage in two, trim off the stump, throw the two halves in boiling water, with a little salt, for fifteen minutes, and drain it. Put in a tureen the tails, cabbage, six ounces of lean bacon, two sprigs of parsley chopped fine, same quantity of green onions, two cloves, a little piece of nutmeg, a clove of garlic, salt, and pepper; cover the whole with half broth and half water, and boil gently till cooked. Then take off cloves, nutmeg, and garlic, turn the remainder on a dish, and serve.

TONGUE.

Prepare, cook, and serve a calf's tongue, in the same and every way like a fresh beef's tongue. The only difference is, that, being smaller, it is seldom decorated.

It may be split in two, lengthwise and nearly through, opened and served thus, with slices of pickled cucumbers.

SWEETBREADS.

To prepare.—Soak them in cold water for about an hour. Take off and remove the skin and bloody vessels that are all around. For two sweetbreads set about one pint of water on the fire in a small saucepan with salt, a tablespoonful of vinegar, a few slices of onion, six peppercorns, a clove of garlic, two cloves, six sprigs of parsley, one of thyme, and a bay-leaf; boil two minutes, drop the sweetbreads in, boil one minute and take them off. Drop them immediately in cold water and leave them in for from two minutes to an hour. Put them on a flat surface with a board over, and leave them thus till they are perfectly cold and rather flattened.

Au Jus.—Trim them a little, so as to give them a better appearance. Lard the top or smooth side, then butter the bottom of a pan, spread a few slices of onion on the butter; add a bay-leaf, a clove, two stalks of parsley; place the sweetbreads on the whole, the larded side up, cover the pan and set on a good fire, or in a rather warm oven; about ten minutes after, add two or three tablespoonfuls of broth, baste now and then till done. If the broth is absorbed before the sweetbreads are done, add some more. Dish the sweetbreads, turn the gravy over them through a strainer, and serve.

Another way.—Prepare as above directed; then, instead of larding it, you knead well together two ounces of butter, a teaspoonful of shallots and parsley well chopped, half a clove of garlic, salt, and pepper; place the whole in a stewpan, with the sweetbreads on it, and thin slices of bacon on the sweetbreads; set the pan on a good fire, and add then half a glass of broth, same of white wine; simmer till cooked; dish the sweetbreads, throw a few drops of cold water in the sauce, skim off the fat, strain the sauce on the sweetbreads, and serve.

When the sweetbreads *au jus* are dished as directed, place tastefully, all around, either of the following garnitures: *cauliflower, chicken-combs, duxelle, financière, mushrooms, liver, Macédoine, quenelles,* and *truffles.* Besides these garnitures, the sweetbreads may be decorated with small skewers, run through a boiled *craw-fish* and a small *quenelle* of chicken or of veal. One or two skewers may be stuck in each sweetbread.

The sweetbreads, when several are served at a time, may be placed on the dish, either around it, forming a kind of crown, or forming a pyramid, or in any other way, according to fancy. They may also be served with a sauce *fines herbes*.

10*

PORK.

————◆————

TO SELECT.

WHEN the rind is tender and thin, the pork is young; when thick and hard, it is old.

To be good, the meat must be soft, and have a fresh and good appearance.

We do not think it necessary to indicate here how to make black puddings, chitterlings, Bologna, and other sausages. It is nearly, if not quite impossible, for a person having no practice in it, to make them edible; it is better to buy them ready made at pork-butchers' shops, or to hire an experienced person to make them.

CHINE AND FILLET.

Take a good chine of pork, place it on the spit before a sharp fire, baste often with a little melted butter first, and then with the drippings; when properly cooked, serve it with a *vinaigrette*, *Robert*, *piquante*, or *poivrade* sauce. It will take from two to three or four hours to roast, according to the size of the chine.

HOW TO IMPROVE THE CHINE OF PORK.

Place it in a crockery vessel, pour on it two table-spoonfuls of sweet-oil, then sprinkle on two teaspoonfuls of chopped parsley, also salt and pepper, two onions chopped fine, four cloves, and two bay-leaves; leave thus twenty-four hours in winter, and ten in summer, turning over two or three times. The taste of the meat is much improved by that process. The oil may be used for basting instead of butter.

Baked.—Put the chine in a bakepan, sprinkle salt over it, cover the bottom of the pan with cold water, and put in a rather quick oven, baste often, and in case there should be much fat in the pan, take it off and add a little cold water.

When overdone, serve with any of the following *purées:* beans, lentils, Lima beans, onions, peas, potatoes, sorrel, or spinach.

It may also be served with the following sauces: *fines herbes, piquante, poivrade, Provençale, ravigote, rémolade, Robert, tarragon, Tartar,* and *vinaigrette.*

It is served also with a tomato-sauce. Make more sauce for pork than for other dishes, and make the tomato-sauce rather thick by boiling it gently for some time; it tastes better so with pork.

Always use mustard with pork, if you like it. Horseradish, also, is good with it.

CUTLETS.

Flatten the cutlets with a chopper (they may be improved in the same way as the chine), place them on the gridiron and set on a sharp fire; turn over two or three times, and when properly done, serve them with a *piquante, Robert,* or tomato-sauce, adding to them some slices of pickled cucumbers just before serving.

The same, sautées.—Instead of broiling them, when prepared as above, place them in a frying-pan with a little butter, turn over two or three times during the cooking, and serve as the above, or on a *purée* of sorrel.

LEG, ROASTED.

How to improve it.—Take the skin or rind gently off, put the leg in a crockery vessel, pour on it the following mixture: a pint of white wine, two tablespoonfuls of sweet-oil, a bunch of sage, salt, pepper, and a pinch of grated nutmeg. Leave it thus two days in winter and one in summer, turning it over two or three times during the process.

Place the leg on the spit and put before a very sharp fire, baste often with the mixture from the crockery vessel, or with melted butter, and serve when cooked, with the gravy strained. It will take about two or two and a half hours to roast it.

Baked.—Bake and serve the leg in the same and every way as the chine, with *purées* and sauces. Any part of pork is prepared like chine.

Ham in Hors-d'œuvre.—Cut the ham in small and thin slices, place the slices tastefully on a dish, either overlapping or in pyramid, or in any other fancy way, and serve with parsley in the middle or around. Slices of lemon may also be served with it, either with the parsley or without it.

HAM.

To boil.—Sugar-cured are preferred to others.

Scrape off the outside gently, soak in cold water for from six to twenty-four hours, take off and wipe dry.

Envelop it in a towel and tie it. Place it in a kettle large enough to hold it without bending it; cover with cold water; season with six small onions, two carrots, four cloves, two bay-leaves, a handful or two plants of parsley, two or three stalks of thyme, two of celery, two cloves of garlic (a handful of hay and half a bottle of white wine, if handy would improve the taste); boil gently for four or five hours, according to the size (four hours for a ten-pound one, five for a fifteen-pound one). Pay no attention to the old saying that " it takes half an hour to every pound."

Take from the fire, remove the towel, break off and remove the small bone at the larger end of it, and without tearing the meat. Remove the rind also, leaving only about two inches of it near the smaller end, cutting it so that it will be dentilated.

To decorate.—It is decorated in several ways, according to taste and fancy. If the fat is not white after having removed the rind, spread a very thin coat of lard over it, place the ham on a dish, the fatty side up. Cut carrots, turnips, and beets, boiled tender, in fancy shapes, with paste-cutters or with a knife; place them tastefully all over the ham; place also all over it some parsley, capers, and olives. Chop some meat-jelly and put it all around the dish, and serve. In carving it, scrape back the lard and vegetables, slice, and serve.

Another.—When boiled, trimmed, and the rind removed, put it in the oven for about twenty minutes, basting the while with a Madeira sauce. Serve with the sauce. Any kind of *purée* may be served with it.

Another.—When trimmed and soaked in water as directed, boil it with half wine and half water: the same seasonings as when boiled in water. Use either Catawba, Sauterne, or Rhine wine. It makes it more expensive, but it is excellent. It is served as when boiled in water.

Another.—Boil it in claret wine, and when trimmed and decorated, serve it with a mushroom or a *truffle* sauce.

Another.—Boil, trim, and cut off the rind as described in the above cases; place the frill, and serve with *spinach au beurre.*

Another.—Boil and
trim the ham as above,
cut the rind in the
same way. What is
left of the rind is cut
as seen in the cut op-
posite: that is, some
small square pieces are
cut off, from place to
place, so that it re-
sembles a checker-
board; stick two or
more skewers in it,
glaze it with essence
of beef or with su-
gar, and serve either
on a tomato-sauce
or on *peas à l'An-
glaise.*

*Ham English fash-
ion.*—Soak it in water
and trim it as directed.
Make some paste with
water and flour only;

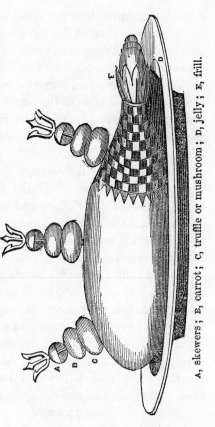

A, skewers; B, carrot; C, truffle or mushroom; D, jelly; E, frill.

spread a coat of this paste all over the ham, and then envelop it in buttered or oiled paper. Put it on the spit and
baste with fat while it is roasting. Roast it for three or
three and a half hours, according to size; remove the paper
about two hours after it has been taken from the fire; cut
a hole in the paste about an inch in diameter and on the
lean side; pour into it, little by little, half a pint of good
Madeira wine, cover the hole with some paste, placing a
band of paper on it to prevent it from falling; put the

ham back on the spit for about twenty minutes, and serve whole with Madeira sauce. We mean, by serving whole, with the paste around it, but not the paper.

Besides the sauce, some green vegetables, boiled only, are served on separate dishes, but eaten with the ham.

It is also served like game, with currant-jelly, apple-sauce, etc.

Champagne Sauce.—Proceed as for the above in every particular, except that you use Champagne instead of Madeira wine, and when done serve it with a Champagne sauce.

Another.—It may be boiled as directed above, and served with a Champagne sauce also.

Another.—When soaked and dry, put it in a crockery vessel; put on and all around it four onions chopped fine, two bay-leaves, two sprigs of thyme, a piece of nutmeg, and pour on the whole a bottle of white wine; cover the vessel as nearly air-tight as possible, leave it thus for about twenty-four hours, turning it over two or three times, so as to let every side take the seasonings. Place the ham on the spit before a good fire, baste often with the seasonings from the crockery vessel, and when done take it off, dust it with fine raspings of bread, place it fifteen minutes in a slow oven, strain the drippings, boil them till reduced to a proper thickness, dish the ham, pour the drippings on it, and serve.

SALTED PORK.

The best and only proper way to cook salted pork, is, to put it in a kettle, entirely cover it with cold water, boil gently till cooked, and serve it with a *purée* or with a garniture of cabbage. Any thing else that you might put with it would rather spoil than better it.

PIG'S EARS.

How to prepare.—Soak them in warm water for a few minutes, then wash and clean them well, and scrape the hair off, if any.

Boiled.—When prepared, you throw them in boiling water for two minutes and take from the fire; add four onions for four ears, one carrot, salt and pepper; leave just water enough to cover the whole, and when cooked, drain. Serve them on a *purée* of beans or of lentils.

The same, broiled.—When cleaned, prepared, and cooked as above, just dip them in beaten eggs, roll them in bread-crumbs, place on the gridiron and on the fire, broil for about two or three minutes; then serve them with a *maître d'hôtel* sauce.

PIG'S FEET.

Broiled, or à la Sainte Menehould.—Split six feet in two, lengthwise, and soak them in tepid water for ten minutes, then envelop each in a piece of linen well tied or sewed; place them in a kettle or stewpan with four small onions, four sprigs of parsley, two of thyme, two of sweet basil, two bay-leaves, two cloves of garlic, two cloves, two small carrots cut in pieces, salt, pepper, and half a pint of white wine; cover with cold water, simmer about six hours, skim them properly, fill with boiling water so as to have them covered all the time; take from the fire when cooked, and when nearly cool take the feet from the kettle, untie them, throw away the linen, and let them cool. Dip each in melted butter or in sweet-oil, roll in bread-crumbs, and place on a gridiron and on a good fire; serve them as they are, when properly broiled.

Stuffed.—Prepare the feet and cook them as above. When perfectly cold, remove the long bone of each half, fill the place with sausage-meat; dip each in melted butter and yolk of egg, mixed and seasoned with salt and pepper, roll in bread-crumbs, and broil. While they are broiling, baste them with melted butter. Serve as they are, or with meat-jelly, or gravy.

Stuffed with Truffles.—Proceed as with the above in every particular, so far as removing the long bone of each half, so as to be ready for stuffing them.

Cut truffles in small dice, enough to half fill the feet, and put them on the fire in a small saucepan, just covered with Madeira wine; toss and stir till the wine is absorbed and nearly boiled away, then add a little gravy, stir half a minute, take from the fire and let cool. When cold, fill each half foot till half full, and finish with sausage-meat; then dip in butter and egg, roll in crumbs, broil and serve as the above.

They may be filled with truffles only, and served with meat-jelly.

PIG'S HEAD.

Soak in water and clean it well; take all the bones and flesh out; then cut the flesh and about one pound of salt pork in strips, which you put inside of the head, well mixed with salt, pepper, half a dozen middling-sized onions chopped, two teaspoonfuls of chopped parsley, half a saltspoonful of allspice, two bay-leaves, two sprigs of thyme, a little sage, and the juice of half a lemon; lay it in a crockery vessel for from four to six days. Envelop the head in a towel, place it in a kettle with eight small onions, two carrots cut in pieces, salt, pepper, four sprigs of parsley, four of thyme, four bay-leaves, two cloves, and a pint of white wine; cover with water, set on the fire, and simmer from six to eight hours; take from the fire and drain, take the towel off and drain again till dry and cold. Serve it with sprigs of green parsley around.

Wild-Boar like.—Prepare, stuff, cook, and allow it to cool as the one preceding; then place it on an oval dish, the ears up, with one or two skewers to hold them in place, and also two or three decorated skewers in the middle of the head and between the eyes—not across, but lengthwise. Glaze it with essence of beef, by means of a brush; make eyes with meat-jelly, which you cut with a vegetable spoon, and imitate the tongue, teeth, and tusks with butter colored with cochineal and kneaded with flour. Cover the back part with jelly and skewers ornamented with flowers or slices of truffles, or with both. Some jelly, chopped, may also be placed all around, and flowers in the ears and on the eyes. It is served as an *entrée,* or for supper, lunch, or breakfast.

PIG'S KIDNEYS.

Prepare, cook, and serve like calf's kidneys.

PIG'S TAIL.

Prepare, cook, and serve like pig's ears.

PIG'S TONGUE.

Prepare, cook, and serve like beef tongue.

Head-cheese.—Soak a pig's head in cold water for two or three hours, clean, and then cut the whole of it, ears and tongue included, in strips one or two inches long, and then put the whole with about two pounds of salt pork, cut in strips also, in a crockery bowl, season with salt, pepper, chopped onion, chopped parsley, thyme, bay-leaf, and sage, chopped also, the juice of a lemon, and leave thus for about two or three days, turning it over occasionally. Then put the mixture in a mould or wrap it in a towel and boil till done. It must be immersed in the water.

Some beet or sheep's tongue, together with the flesh of chicken, may be added to the head.

When cooked and cold, if there are any empty places, they may be filled with meat-jelly.

It is served at late suppers, or at lunch and breakfast. It is always served cold, with parsley around.

SUCKING-PIG.

A sucking-pig, to be good, must be fat.

When properly cleaned, and hoofs off, clean the inside, leaving the kidneys; skewer it, put in it half a pound of butter kneaded with chopped parsley and green onions, four or five mushrooms, and two white onions with a clove stuck in each; place it on the spit before a good fire, baste often with melted butter first, and then with the drippings, and when done serve on a *vinaigrette*.

Some truffles may be added to the seasoning, if handy; it gives it a good taste.

Baked.—Stuff it as the above, place it in a baking-pan with just cold water enough to cover the bottom of the pan; put it in a quick oven, baste often, and when done serve with a *rémolade* or *vinaigrette* sauce.

When roasted or baked, place it on a dish with slices of truffles, mushrooms, and parsley all around. Run some skewers through slices of truffles and whole mushrooms, and plant them in it like the one represented in the cut on the following page.

A small red apple is placed in the mouth after it is cooked, to make room for which a stone is placed in the mouth before cooking it, in order to keep the mouth open.   It is served as warm as possible.

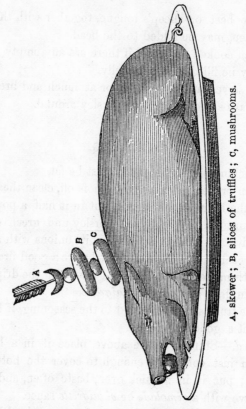

A, skewer; B, slices of truffles; c, mushrooms.

Boned.—A sucking-pig can be boned and filled just the same as a turkey, and cooked and served alike also.

POULTRY.

CHICKENS, ducks, turkeys, and geese must be killed not less than twenty-four hours, and not more than three days in summer, nor less than two days nor more than six days in winter, before cooking them.

HOW TO PREPARE AND CLEAN.

To transport poultry, *see* GAME.

Poulterers are of the opinion that the best and quickest way of killing poultry is by cutting the throat or the tongue. Tie the legs of the bird, hang it by the legs, then kill and let bleed. Some cut the head off and throw it away on the ground, but the poor things do not die so fast, and therefore suffer more.

As soon as the throat or tongue is cut, if the head is held down the bird dies sooner, as it allows the blood to run more freely, preventing the bird from bending and twisting its neck, and also from swallowing its blood.

It is much better to pick the bird dry. By scalding, the skin is spoiled, and very often the flesh of a young and tender chicken is spoiled also, being blanched. When picked, singe the bird carefully, in order not to burn the skin.

Split the skin on the back of the neck, from the body

to near the head; then detach the skin from the neck by pulling it downward and the neck upward; it gives you plenty of room to pull the crop out, which you do. Cut the skin off at about the middle of the neck, and the neck close to the body; that part of the skin of the neck is left to cover the place where the neck was cut off, by turning it on the back of the bird, and holding it with twine in trussing.

Make an incision under the rump, lengthwise, and large enough to draw the bird easily.

When drawn, wipe the inside of the bird with a towel, but do not wash it, except when you have broken the gall-bladder. If that should happen, cut the bird in pieces immediately and wash well in lukewarm water; never roast or prepare whole a bird that has had the gall-bladder broken in it in drawing it. *Sauté* it or prepare it in fricassee.

If there should be any thing unclean on the outside, wipe it off, if possible, or otherwise cut the place off, or wash only the unclean place. A washed bird is a very inferior article. If you see that a bird cannot be cleansed properly except by washing it, do not buy it.

CHICKEN.

To select.—Buy a chicken with white flesh and pale-yellow fat. If young, the cock has small spurs, the hen has the lower part of the legs and feet rather soft and smooth; those parts are rough in old ones.

If the rump is hard and stiff, they are fresh enough; but if soft, it is necessary to examine the bird carefully; it might be tainted.

To truss.—When prepared as directed for poultry,

put the bird on the table on its back, and with a chopper or with a round stick flatten the breast-bone, which you break at a single blow if possible; the bird is much more sightly when served. Cut the legs off just above the first joint, or cut off only half of the claws and trim off the ends of the wings. Place the bird on a table, the breast up and the rump toward you. Push the legs under the skin, so that, by holding them perpendicularly and pressing on them, the part from the second to the third joint is alongside the chicken, or horizontally. Then run a trussing-needle, with twine attached to it, just above the bone of the leg, as near the second joint as possible, on the side (toward you) of the bone of the leg that is perpendicular, through the leg (which leg is the left one of the bird), body, and also through the bird, and at the same place, that is, as near the second joint as possible. Turn the bird upside down and the neck toward you; turn the ends of the wings on the back, as seen in the cut (p. 240), turn the skin of the neck on the back also, between or under the wings and in order to cover the place where the neck has been cut off, then run the needle again through the right wing, the skin of the neck and part of the body, and through the other wing. Tie the ends of the twine fast together.

As it is, the legs of the bird, when on its back, are pointing upward. Bend them gently down till they are perpendicular and as seen in the cut, run the trussing-needle through both and also through the body, above the bones of the legs and under the end of the breast-bone; run it again the other way, but under the bones of the legs, tie the two ends of the twine together, and you have a bird trussed exactly like the one represented in the cut on next page.

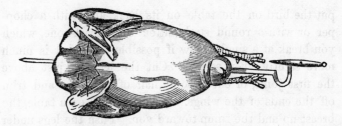

Another way to truss is, to cut only half of the claws, instead of cutting the legs at the first joint; but, to truss thus, the first joint must be partly cut as represented below. If the nerve were not cut, it would contract in cooking, and instead of being straight, the legs would point upward.

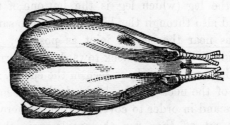

A bird stuffed is trussed exactly in the same way as above, with the exception that the skin of the neck must be sewed up with a trussing-needle before commencing to truss the legs, and the incision must also be sewed up as soon as filled and before trussing.

The twine used to sew and truss the bird is removed just before dishing it.

Some experiments have been made lately, in France, to find out the best way to kill chickens and make them tender. Those killed by electricity were more tender than any other, but they must be cooked immediately, as they become tainted in a very short time.

To blanch.—When cut in pieces as directed, throw it in boiling water to which a little salt has been added; boil two minutes and drain.

To cut.—To make a chicken *sauté* or in fricassee, it is generally cut into eight pieces; the two legs, the wings, one piece of the breast-bone, and three pieces of the back-bone. The ends of the wings, the lower part of the legs after being skinned by warming them, the neck, gizzard, heart, kidneys, and head, are put in the soup-kettle. Generally the bones of the legs above the second joint are removed by breaking them with the back of a knife just above the second joint. The ends of the small bones of the three pieces of the back-bone are trimmed off also.

To dish and serve.—Dish the pieces in the following order: the neck, gizzard, the fore part of the back and the low part of the legs in the middle; then one leg on each side of the dish, with one wing beside each, then the breast and hind part of the back, and lastly the ends of the wings at the top. If cut in eight pieces only, place the breast-bone on the middle of the dish, the hind part of the back-bone at one end of it and the two others at the other end; the legs and wings on each side.

Boiled.—A chicken is boiled only when it is an old one, whose tenderness is doubtful, and which is not needed to make broth or *consommé.*

Clean, prepare, and truss it as directed for poultry. Brown the bird in a saucepan with about one ounce of butter, then half cover it with cold water; season with a few slices of onion, same of carrot, two cloves, two stalks of parsley, salt and pepper. Boil gently about one hour and a half, and when done, dish the bird, strain the sauce over it, and serve warm.

11

If the sauce boils away, add a little cold water; and if there is any fat on it, skim it off.

An old chicken may be cooked especially to make a salad.

Boned.—Pick, bone, fill, cook, and serve a boned chicken exactly like a boned turkey; the only difference is, that it requires less filling, being smaller.

For an extra, legs of large chickens may be boned and filled like the chicken, the rest being used for a fricassee.

Broiled.—Young, or what are called *spring chickens,* are broiled; an old one would not be as good.

To broil, a chicken is split in two lengthwise, or the back only is split, so as to open it. Salt both sides and butter them slightly, then broil on a good but not sharp fire. Serve with a *maître-d'hôtel, piquante,* or *ravigote* sauce.

Broiled hunter-like.—When cleaned and prepared, split the chicken in two lengthwise and place it in a crockery dish with the following seasonings: a teaspoonful of parsley chopped fine, a middling-sized onion in slices, two cloves, salt, pepper, a tablespoonful of sweet-oil, and the juice of half a lemon. Half an hour after turn the chicken over, and after another half hour place the above seasonings all around the chicken, fasten them with paper, tie the paper with twine, and broil carefully on a rather slow fire, and turning over two or three times. When done, remove the paper in which they are enveloped, scrape off the slices without scratching the meat, and serve as warm as possible with a *maître-d'hôtel, ravigote,* or *Madeira* sauce.

When an older chicken is prepared hunter-like, it is generally served with a *Tartar* sauce.

Another way.—Clean and prepare a chicken as directed.

Cut the neck off, also the legs at the first joint, split the breast in two so as to open the chicken, and flatten it with a chopper. Put about two ounces of butter in a sauce-pan and set it on the fire; when melted, add a teaspoonful of chopped parsley, stir for half a minute with a wooden spoon, then put the chicken in with salt and pepper; when about half fried on one side, turn it over and half fry the other side; then take off the chicken, roll it in chopped parsley and bread-crumbs mixed together, broil it properly and serve on a *Tartar* sauce.

A chicken broiled either way above described may also be served on a *Béchamel* or on a *cream* sauce.

Croquettes.—The proportions that we give below are for half a middling-sized chicken.

A chicken may be cooked especially to make *croquettes*, but it is generally made with cold meat.

Chop the meat fine. Chop fine also half a middling-sized onion; fry it with one ounce of butter, then add half a tablespoonful of flour, stir for half a minute, then add also the chopped meat and a little over a gill of broth, salt, pepper, a pinch of nutmeg, stir for about two minutes, take from the fire, mix two yolks of eggs with it, put back on the fire for one minute, stirring the while; lastly you add four mushrooms chopped, or two truffles, chopped also, or both, according to taste; do not put back on the fire, but turn the mixture into a dish, spread it and put it away to cool.

When perfectly cold, mix it well, as the upper part is more dry than the rest; put it in parts on the paste-board, about a tablespoonful for each part. Have bread-crumbs on the paste-board, roll each part of the shape you wish; either round like a small sausage, or flat, or of a chop-shape; then dip each *croquette* or part in beaten egg, roll in bread-crumbs again, and fry in hot fat. (*See* FRY-ING.)

The best way to shape them, is to roll each part round first with a few bread-crumbs, then with a knife smooth both ends, while with the left hand you roll them gently, and if wanted flat, strike gently on them with the blade of a knife. If wanted of a chop-shape, when flat, shape with the hands and strike again to flatten them.

Croquettes are made with any kind of cold meat.

In Fricassee.—Clean, prepare, and cut as directed. If the flesh is not white, blanch it. Put it in a saucepan, cover it with broth or cold water (broth is better than water), set it on the fire, and add one onion whole, and if covered with water, add also a bunch of seasonings, composed of three stalks of parsley, one of thyme, a bay-leaf, and one clove, boil gently till done. Put about two ounces of butter in a saucepan with one tablespoonful of flour, set on the fire, stir and mix while the butter is melting; then turn the broth or water in which the chicken has been cooked into this pan through a strainer, add salt, six mushrooms sliced, then the pieces of chicken; give one boil, dish the pieces as directed, mix a yolk of egg in the sauce, turn it over the chicken, and serve with or without a border of paste.

Border of Paste.—Knead well together, so as to make a rather thick paste, two whites of eggs with flour; spread it with a rolling-pin in a long strip about two inches and a half broad and one-fifth of an inch thick. Trim the sides if not straight; cut three rows of holes in the middle with a fruit-corer, then cut the strip of paste in two, lengthwise and in the middle of the middle row of holes. Cut it again across in pieces about three or four inches long. Put it in a warm place to dry till hard enough to keep in shape and still be pliable; warm the dish on which you wish to place it; beat the white of an egg just a little with a pinch of sugar, glaze the straight side of the paste with it; place it all around and on the border of the dish with the dentilated side up. Place the pieces of chicken inside of the border as directed above, and serve.

The cut below represents the border. One, *a*, is the border before being cut in two, and *b* when cut.

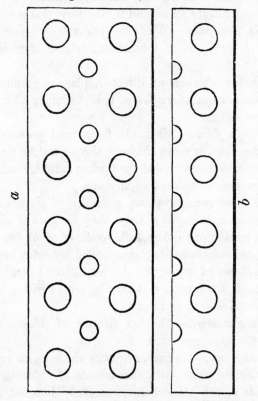

It may seem difficult to place the border at first, but it will be easily done after having tried once or twice, and following the directions previously given. It is better to try when not in a hurry and before being wanted; that is, before you wish to serve it. The border may be made and placed on a dish without a chicken, it will be better for an experiment.

In Fricassée à la chevalière or Parisienne.—While the chicken is cooking as directed for *fricassée,* prepare a garniture of *chicken-combs,* and, when the chicken is dished, place the garniture all around it, and serve warm.

A la Française.—While the *fricassée* is being made, prepare a *garniture* of mushrooms or one of truffles, or both.

Dish the chicken as directed, place a garniture of *mushrooms* or one of *truffles,* or both, tastefully all around, and serve warm.

When a *fricassée* is made for several persons, with two, three, four, or more chickens, three garnitures may be placed around the same dish, and, when carefully and tastefully arranged, it makes a sightly one.

The three garnitures are, generally, of *chicken-combs, mushrooms,* and *truffles;* they may be also of *chicken-combs, quenelles* of chicken, and *croutons;* or, of *financière, truffles,* and *chicken-combs;* or a boiled *craw-fish* here and there, and two of any of the above-mentioned garnitures.

Instead of a garniture, it may be served with a border of rice. (*See* RICE IN BORDER.)

A la financière.—This is a *fricassée* of chicken served with a *financière* garniture.

Au suprême.—Chicken, or rather chickens, *au suprême* is a *fricassée* made with the breasts of chickens only. Each side of the breast-bone is carefully detached in two long pieces called *fillets;* so that, with two chickens, there are eight pieces.

To detach them properly, split the skin right on the breast-bone from the neck to the rump, then pull it off on both sides so as to have the whole breast skinned. Take hold of one wing with the left hand, and, with a sharp knife in the right, split or cut the joint off carefully, we mean the third joint of the wing, or that near the body; as soon as the joint is cut, by merely raising the back of the knife, leaving the edge on the cut joint and pressing gently on the chicken, you easily pull off the larger part of the half breast; detach the end of the other half with the point of the knife and pull it off also.

Do the same for the other side.

When the breasts or fillets are thus detached, prepare them as chicken in *fricassée*, and serve with a border of paste, or with one of rice, as directed in the receipts above, and serve warm.

What is left of the chickens is put in the broth-kettle, or used to make *consommé*.

Another suprême.—Detach the breasts of two chickens as above directed, then prepare the eight pieces or fillets as directed for chicken *sauté*. Ten minutes before taking from the fire, add and mix with the whole two or three truffles, weighing at least six ounces, and sliced; finish the cooking, and serve.

To serve.—Dish the pieces tastefully and according to fancy, and put the dish away in a warm place, then mix a *suprême* sauce with what you have left in the pan, sauce, truffles, etc., boil the whole till rather thick, stirring continually while it is boiling, turn over the pieces of chicken, and serve. The *suprême* sauce used in that case is generally made with very rich chicken gravy.

Chickens *au suprême* is considered a very *recherché* dish, and it is a rather expensive one. For a grand dinner, the breasts of six chickens are used, and all the other parts of the chicken are used to make chicken gravy with rich broth, and that gravy is, in its turn, used to make the *suprême* sauce that is mixed with the liquor in which the chicken has cooked.

The broth used to *sauté* the chicken is generally rich, and very often two pounds of truffles are used with six chickens.

A la Bourguignonne.—This is a *fricassée* also, but instead of covering the chicken with broth or water, it is covered with white wine.

Proceed, for the rest, and serve as *fricassée*.

With Carrots.—While you are cooking a chicken in *fricassée*, prepare a dish of carrots *au jus* or *glazed*, for ornamenting the dish; cut the carrots with a vegetable spoon before cooking them.

Dish the chicken as directed, place the carrots tastefully all around the meat, and serve warm. This dish was devised by a monk, and is often called *à la Saint Lambert*.

A la Royale.—This is nearly the same as *au suprême ;* the only difference is, that the pieces of breast or fillets are larded with salt pork, and then cooked, served and decorated the same as described for *au suprême*.

Marengo.—Clean, prepare, and cut up the chicken as for *fricassée*. Put in a stewpan five teaspoonfuls of sweet-oil, and set on a good fire; when hot, put the chicken in with salt and pepper; turn over once in a while, till every piece is of a golden color, and nearly cooked, when add two sprigs of parsley, one of thyme, a bay-leaf, and one clove, tied together with twine; add also three or four mushrooms cut in slices, and if handy three or four truffles also cut in slices; when the whole is cooked, dish the pieces of chicken thus: the neck and gizzard, with the fore part of the back, and the low part of the legs in the middle, one leg on each side of the dish with one wing beside each, then the breast and hind part of the back, and the ends of the wings at the top. Have an Italian sauce ready, pour it on the chicken, place on the whole the pieces of mushrooms and truffles, also some *croutons* fried in butter, and serve.

With Green Peas.—Clean, prepare, and truss the bird as directed for poultry, then cook it whole as a stewed chicken above. When done, dish the chicken, place peas *à l'Anglaise* all around, strain the sauce over the whole, and serve.

Larded with Truffles.—Clean, prepare, and truss a fat chicken. Make about two dozen small pegs, with truffles, about half an inch long and one-eighth of an inch in diameter. Take a skewer, make a hole in the flesh of the breast of the chicken, and put a truffle-peg into it. Put a dozen pegs in the same way on each side of the breast-bone, and cook and serve the chicken. It is either boiled, stewed, or roasted, and served as directed for either.

With Tarragon.—Proceed as for a stewed chicken, with the exception that it is cooked whole after being trussed as directed for poultry, and after having stuffed it with two ounces of butter kneaded with half a dozen stalks of tarragon chopped fine. Serve with a few stalks of tarragon around the dish.

Roasted.—Clean, prepare, and truss the chicken as directed. Place it on the spit slightly salted and buttered all around, or envelop it in buttered paper, or merely cover the breast with thin slices of salt pork tied with twine. Baste often, at first with melted butter, and then with the drippings.

11*

If the bird has been enveloped with paper, the latter must be removed about ten minutes before taking the chicken from the fire; do the same with the slices of salt pork.

It takes from twenty-five minutes to one hour to roast a chicken, with a good fire. The time depends as much on the quality of the bird as on the size. With a skewer or a small knife, or merely by pressing on it with the fingers, any one can learn how to tell when done, after having roasted only two or three. Even by the look of it, many persons can tell.

With Water-cress.—Dish the chicken when roasted, put fresh water-cress all around, remove the fat from the gravy, which you turn over the whole; add salt and pepper to taste, a little vinegar or lemon-juice, and serve warm.

With Sauces.—When roasted, serve with the following sauces: *soubise, tarragon, oyster, tomato,* and *Provençale.*

With Garnitures.—Dish the bird when roasted as directed, and place one of the following garnitures around, and serve warm: *quenelles* of chicken or of veal, *Macédoine,* and *cauliflowers.*

With Macaroni.—Spread four ounces of macaroni *au jus* on a dish, place the roasted chicken on it, and serve the whole warm.

With Butter.—It may be served with its gravy and craw-fish or lobster-butter.

With Chestnuts.—When dished, surround the chicken with chestnuts glazed, and serve.

With Pigeons.—Dish the bird, place four roasted pigeons around, one at each end and one on each side; fill the intervals with green peas *au jus,* and serve warm.

All the above may be decorated with skewers. Run the skewer in a *chestnut* and then in a *craw-fish;* or, in a

quenelle and then in a *chestnut* or *craw-fish ;* or, in a
chicken-comb, and in a *quenelle,* and stick it on the chick-
en. Two skewers only for a chicken make a fine decoration. Slices of *truffles,* of *mushrooms,* and *chicken-combs,*
make fine as well as delicious decorations.

Baked.—Put the chicken in a baking-pan, after being
cleaned, prepared, and trussed. Salt and butter the breast,
which must be upward, place a piece of buttered paper
on it, and a little cold water in the bakepan. Set it in a
warm, but not too quick oven; baste often with the
liquor in the pan. If the water and juice are absorbed
by the heat, add a little cold water, so as to have liquor to
baste with. Remove the paper about ten minutes before
taking from the oven. It takes about forty minutes to
cook a chicken of middle size.

Serve a baked chicken with *sauces* and *garnitures,* and
decorated the same as if it were roasted, and as described
in the above receipts.

Sauté.—After being cleaned and prepared as directed,
cut the chicken in pieces as for *fricassée.* Put it in a
saucepan with about an ounce of butter; set on the fire,
stir now and then till it is of a golden color and pour off
the fat, if any is in the saucepan. Add a tablespoonful of
flour and stir half a minute, then add also broth enough
to nearly cover the meat, half a pint of white wine, a
bunch of seasonings composed of four stalks of parsley,
one of thyme, half a bay-leaf, and one clove, the four tied
together with twine; add salt, and one onion whole. Boil
gently till done. Ten minutes before serving, add half a
dozen mushrooms.

Dish the pieces of chicken as directed for *fricassée,*
place the mushrooms over them, strain the sauce all over,
and serve warm.

If the chicken is done before the sauce is reduced or is rather thick, dish the meat and put it away in a warm place, boil the rest slowly till reduced, and then turn it over the meat. Serve with or without a border, as in a *fricassée*. Truffles may be used instead of mushrooms, if handy, or liked. Water may be used instead of broth, but it is inferior.

Another.—To be good *sauté*, the chicken must be young and tender. Clean, prepare, and cut as directed. Put about one ounce and a half of butter in a frying-pan, set it on the fire, and when melted put the pieces of chicken in, stir now and then till all the pieces have a golden hue; add a tablespoonful of flour, stir again for about one minute; then add also salt and pepper, half a pint of broth, or one gill of broth and one gill of white wine; boil gently for five or six minutes. Add again a teaspoonful of parsley chopped fine, five or six mushrooms cut in slices, keep it boiling gently till done, and serve warm.

If the sauce is boiling away, or is found too thick, add a little broth. Use *Champagne, Sauterne,* or *Catawba* wine. It is much better with wine than without.

Another.—Clean, prepare, and cut the chicken as for *fricassée.* Put it in a saucepan with about an ounce of butter, set on the fire, stir once in a while till all the pieces are of a fine golden color; then pour off the fat that may be in the pan. Sprinkle a tablespoonful of flour all over it, and stir for about half a minute, then add three or four shallots, or two or three small green onions, chopped fine, parsley, and three or four mushrooms, both cut in small pieces, a bunch of seasonings composed of four sprigs of parsley, one of thyme, a bay-leaf, and one clove, salt, and pepper.

Stir often till cooked, and serve with a few drops of lemon-juice sprinkled on it when dished.

Dish as directed for *fricassée*.

Stewed.—Clean, prepare, and cut the chicken in pieces as for *fricassée*. Brown them in a saucepan with about one ounce of butter, then take the pieces off, add half a tablespoonful of flour to the butter, stir for one minute, then add also three or four mushrooms in slices, a small onion, and half a dozen sprigs of parsley chopped fine, stir for two or three minutes, then cover with half a pint of white wine and the same of broth, boil for ten minutes, put the pieces of chicken back into the pan, boil gently till done, and serve warm as it is.

The pieces of chicken are dished as directed for *fricassée*.

Stuffed with Bread.—Soak stale bread in cold water, and then squeeze the water out of it. Put one ounce of butter in a saucepan and set it on the fire; as soon as melted, add one middling-sized onion chopped fine, and stir till it turns rather yellow, when add the bread, stir two minutes; add again salt, pepper, a pinch of nutmeg, two or three tablespoonfuls of broth; stir again two or three minutes, take from the fire, mix in it a yolk of egg, put back on the fire for half a minute, stirring the while, take off again, add a teaspoonful of chopped parsley, and use. Fill the crop (we mean the place where the crop was) and also the body or inside of the bird with the above mixture, truss it as directed; roast or bake it, and serve with the gravy.

Stuffed with Sausage-meat.—Set a saucepan on the fire with about half an ounce of butter in it; when melted add an onion chopped fine, stir, and, when nearly fried, add also the heart and liver of the bird, chopped fine, four, six, or eight ounces of sausage-meat (according to the size of the bird), stir for about twelve minutes, take from the fire, mix a yolk of egg with it, also four or five mushrooms chopped, or one or two truffles, chopped also, put back on the fire for five minutes, stirring the while, take from the fire again, fill the prepared bird with the mixture, and as above, roast or bake it, and serve it with its gravy.

Stuffed with Chestnuts.—Roast chestnuts and skin them, removing also the white envelope that is under the outside skin. Fill the inside of a cleaned and prepared chicken till half full, add about one and a half ounces of butter, finish the filling; truss, roast or bake as directed, and serve the bird with its gravy.

Stuffed with Truffles.—The truffles, being preserved, do not require any preparation, half a pound is enough for a middling-sized chicken; it is not necessary to put any where the crop was.

Salt and pepper the inside of the bird, and put in it also about a teaspoonful of parsley chopped fine, then the truffles; sew the incision made to draw it; truss it as directed, and roast or bake.

The same, stewed.—When stuffed, put four ounces of salt pork cut in dice in a saucepan, with slices of onion and carrot, place the chicken on them, season with four stalks of parsley, one of thyme, a bay-leaf, and one clove tied together; half cover it with broth and white wine, of equal parts, set on the fire, boil gently till done, turning it over several times. Dish the bird, strain the sauce over it, and serve warm.

After being stuffed with truffles, it may be kept two days before cooking.

Cold.—What is left from the previous day's dinner is known under the name of cold meat.

For about half a chicken put one ounce of butter in a saucepan, and, when melted, turn into it a *financière* garniture, and half a pint of Madeira wine, boil gently about eight minutes, put the cold chicken cut in pieces in it; leave just long enough on the fire to warm it, and serve.

If not a roasted or broiled chicken, or part of either, you merely warm it in the *bain-marie* if possible, or on the fire, and serve as it is.

If roasted or broiled, it is served in *blanquette*, thus:

Cut up the meat in slices, have in a stewpan and on a good fire a piece of butter the size of two walnuts; when melted, sprinkle in it a pinch of flour, stirring with a wooden spoon the while; then pour in also, little by little, two gills of warm broth, same of boiling water, half a teaspoonful of chopped parsley, salt, pepper, and two or three small onions fried in butter; boil fifteen minutes. After that time subdue the fire, place the slices of chicken in the pan, and serve as it is when well warmed.

Instead of onions, slices of pickled cucumbers may be used.

Another way.—Cut up the chicken or part of it as for *fricassée.* Put a little butter in a stewpan and set on the fire; when melted, sprinkle in it a little flour, half a teaspoonful of chopped parsley, same of chopped mushrooms, stir with a wooden spoon the while, two or three minutes after which add two gills of white wine, boil the whole fifteen minutes; then subdue the fire, put the pieces of chicken in the pan, and serve as it is when warm.

It may also, after it is cut up, be served cold, with an oil, *piquante,* or *poivrade* sauce.

The same, in Fricassée.—An old chicken that has been used to make broth, either alone or with beef, when cool, or the next day, may be prepared just as a spring chicken in *fricassée.*

In Salad.—It is made with cold chicken, roasted or baked, with a whole one or part of it.

Cut all the meat in dice and put it in a bowl.

Cut just as much roasted or baked veal in dice also, and put with the chicken.

Cut also about as much table celery as chicken, which put with the meat also. Season with salt, pepper, vinegar, and very little oil; stir and mix the whole well. Add also some lettuce, and mix again gently. Put the mixture then on a platter, making a small mound with it; spread a Mayonnaise-sauce all over it; decorate with hard-boiled eggs, cut in four or eight pieces, lengthwise; also with centre leaves of lettuce, capers, boiled beets, and even slices of lemon.

A hard-boiled egg is cut across in two, then with a sharp knife scallop each half, invert them and run a small skewer through both, so as to leave the smaller end of both halves in the middle and touching; place the egg right in the middle of the dish, when the Mayonnaise is spread all over; plant the centre leaves of a head of lettuce in the middle of the upper half of the egg, with a few capers in it, and serve.

Some use mustard with a chicken salad; it is really wrong, because chickens and Mayonnaise-sauce are too delicate to use mustard with them.

CAPON.

A caponed chicken is cleaned, prepared, cooked, and served in the same and every way as a common chicken.

A capon is almost always fat, larger than an ordinary chicken, and has a more delicate and tender flesh.

Roasted and served in the different ways described for chicken, it makes a *recherché* dish, also when stuffed with chestnuts or truffles, as a common chicken.

Boiled.—Clean and prepare as directed above; rub the fleshy part with lemon, envelop it with slices of bacon, place it in a stewpan with one sprig of parsley, one of thyme, a bay-leaf, one clove, a small carrot, two onions, salt, and pepper; cover with half water and half broth, and set on a moderate fire. When cooked, take the capon off, place it on a dish, and set it in a warm place; then boil the sauce till it is rather thick, when strain it on the capon, and serve.

The same, with Rice.—When cleaned and prepared as above, you place the capon in a stewpan, cover it with water, add one glass of broth, a bay-leaf, one clove, a sprig of parsley, one of thyme, a small carrot, two onions, salt, and pepper; boil ten minutes, then add also about four ounces of rice, soaked in lukewarm water before using it, and let simmer for two hours. Take the capon off, and in case the rice should not be found to be cooked enough, finish the cooking of it; then take off clove, parsley, thyme, bay-leaf, carrot and onions, pour the remainder on the capon, and serve.

TURKEY.

Tame and wild are prepared and served alike.

The legs of a young hen-turkey are black; the cock has small spurs, and also black legs.

The shorter the neck the better and fatter the bird.

An old hen has red and rough legs; the cock also has long spurs.

The fatter they are the better; they cannot be too fat. The broader the breast the better; the skin must be white.

It is fresh enough as long as the legs are not stiff.

Boiled.—Clean and prepare a turkey as directed for poultry.

Put in a stewpan, large enough to hold a turkey, a piece of butter the size of a duck's egg, also a teaspoonful of chopped parsley, same of green onions, and four or five mushrooms; set it on a good fire, and, as soon as the butter is hot, lay the turkey in; turn over now and then till of a fine golden color, then take it from the pan, cover the breast with slices of bacon tied with twine, and put it back in the pan; add a pinch of allspice, six small onions, salt, pepper, a glass of white wine, and a pint of broth; simmer till cooked, dish it, strain the sauce on it, and serve. It takes about two hours to cook a turkey of middling size. A little warm broth should be added, in case the sauce boils away during the cooking.

Roasted.—Clean, prepare, and truss a turkey as directed for poultry, and, if the turkey is not fat, the breast may be larded with salt pork. Place it on the spit before a sharp fire, basting often with melted butter at first, and then with the drippings. It may be enveloped in buttered paper and tied with twine before placing it on the spit; the paper is removed ten or fifteen minutes before taking from the fire; serve with the gravy, after having skimmed the fat off.

Some fresh water-cress is placed all around it, and on which you sprinkle vinegar or lemon-juice.

A turkey may be served in every way as a roasted chicken—with sauces, garnitures, and decorated with skewers.

Baked.—When cleaned, prepared, and trussed, put the turkey in a baking-pan, spread a little butter on it, put a little cold water in the pan, the depth of about two-eighths of an inch, sprinkle salt all over, place a piece of buttered paper on it, and put in a quick oven. Baste often and turn the bird over and round, if necessary. It takes from one hour and a half to two hours to cook a turkey, according to size, quality, and also according to the degree of heat.

It is served with the gravy only, after having removed the fat, or with sauces, garnitures, and decorations, described for roasted chicken.

Oyster-Sauce.—When roasted or baked as directed, serve warm with an oyster-sauce.

With Currant Jelly.—Roast or bake it, and then serve it with currant-jelly.

It is also served with a cranberry-sauce.

Stewed.—An old turkey is more tender stewed than cooked in any other way.

The fleshy parts may be larded with salt pork, if found too lean.

Put in a large stew-kettle half a pound of bacon cut in slices, four ounces of knuckle of veal, three sprigs of parsley, two of thyme, a bay-leaf, six small onions, one carrot, cut in four pieces, three cloves, one clove of garlic, salt, pepper, and then the turkey; wet with a pint of white wine, same of broth, cover as nearly air-tight as you can, place in a moderately heated oven or on a moderate fire, let simmer (not boil) about two hours and a half, then turn it over, put back on the fire or in the oven for another two hours and a half, after which dish the turkey; strain the sauce and put it back on the fire to reduce it to a jelly, which you spread on it, and serve.

Many *connoisseurs* prefer the turkey served thus when cold; it does not cost any thing to try it, and it is very handy for a grand dinner, as it may be prepared one or two days in advance, and is just as good, if kept in a refrigerator.

Stuffed with Chestnuts.—Roast chestnuts enough to

fill the bird. Skin them and remove also the white skin under the outer one. Fill the turkey with them, after having cleaned and prepared it; when about half full, put in it also from four to six ounces of butter; finish the filling with chestnuts; sew it up, truss it as directed, and roast or bake it. Serve with the gravy only.

Stuffed with Truffles.—Chop fine about four ounces of truffles, and put them in a stewpan with about a pound of salt pork cut in dice; set it on a moderate fire; add salt, pepper, a little grated nutmeg, a bay-leaf, a pinch of allspice, and a pinch of dried thyme; when hot, add also about two pounds of truffles, boil fifteen minutes, tossing now and then, and take from the fire. When nearly cool, put the whole in the turkey and sew it up; leave it thus, if fresh, four days in winter and one or two in summer; if not fresh, leave it a shorter time.

Roast or *bake* it as directed above, and serve with the gravy, freed from the fat part. This dish is considered exquisite by epicures.

Stuffed with Sausage-meat.—Proceed as for chicken stuffed, in every particular.

With Salt Pork.—Place thin slices of salt pork on the breast of a prepared turkey, covering it entirely, and fastening the slices with twine; then the turkey is roasted or baked, and served with the gravy. The slices may be removed a little before taking from the fire, in order to color the meat.

Boned.—Buy a good turkey, neither too old nor too fat, and picked dry. Singe the bird, but do not draw it. Cut the neck off about one inch and a half from the body. Cut also the wings off just above the second joint, and the legs just above the first joint; the third joint is the one nearest the body. Split the skin from the end of the neck to the rump; use a small sharp-pointed knife; commence to run the knife between the bones and flesh, on one side, till you come to the third joint of the wings and legs. By twisting and raising both wing and leg, but one at a time, you easily crack the joint, and then separate it from the body with the knife. Continue to run the knife between the bones and flesh, on the same side, till you come to the breast-bone. Do the same on the other side. Pull out the crop and cut off the rump from the body, but without touching the skin, as the rump must come off with the skin and flesh. Then by taking hold of the bird by the neck with the left hand, and pulling the skin gently down with the right, you partly uncover the upper part of the breast-bone; then again run the knife between that bone and the flesh, on both sides, till you come nearly to the end or edge of the bone. Then lay the bird on its back, have somebody to take hold of it by the neck, having the breast of the bird toward you. All along the edge of the breast-bone there is no flesh between the bone and the skin. The bird being held as described above, take hold of the skin of the neck with your left hand, pulling gently downward, and with the knife detaching the skin carefully from the bone, the carcass coming off whole. Place the bird on the table, the inside up, pull out the bones of the wings and legs, scraping the flesh all around so as to leave it attached to the rest; pull or scrape off all the tendons of the legs; push legs and wings inside the bird; see that the rump is clean; cut off the ring under it if necessary. We warrant that anybody, with an ordinary amount of natural capacity, can bone a turkey or other bird by following our directions with care. We recommend persons doing it for the first time not to attempt to do it fast. Now have at hand about two pounds of sausage-meat seasoned as directed, two pounds of boiled ham, half a dozen boiled sheep's tongues or a smoked beef tongue (but really the former is better), a pound and a half of salt pork, and half a pound of truffles sliced (the latter if handy and if liked). Cut the ham, tongues, and salt pork in strips about four inches long, one inch broad, and a quarter of an inch thick. Spread the bird on the table, the inside up and the rump toward you; salt and pepper it; place three or four slices of salt pork here and there on it, then a layer of sausage-meat, strips of ham and tongue and salt pork alternately on the sausage-meat, slices of truffles if used, again sausage-meat, ham, etc., till there is enough to fill the bird well; that is, by bringing the two sides of the skin together, giving the bird a round form, it is perfectly full. It is impossible to give exact proportions; it depends not only on the size of the bird, but also on the quality and degree of fatness of the bird. In two of the same weight, one may require more than the other to fill it. When filled, and when the two sides of the skin are brought together as described above, sew up the cut with a trussing-needle and twine. Wrap up the bird tightly in a towel, tie the towel with a string, and run the string all around the towel to prevent it from opening at all. Take a kettle or saucepan of an oval shape and large enough to hold the bird, put enough cold water in it to cover the bird, also all the bones of the bird (broken in pieces), a small piece of lean beef, say one pound, a few stalks of parsley, two of thyme, two cloves, two cloves of garlic, a bay-leaf, twelve pepper-corns, a middling-sized carrot sliced, half a turnip, and salt. Set on the fire, and at the first boiling put the bird in; boil gently for about three hours if it is a turkey of middling size, two hours for a middling-sized chicken. When done

it partly floats; that is, the upper part is above the liquor.
Take it from the pan, take the towel off and rinse it in
cold water; wrap the bird up in the towel again and in
the same way as before; place it on a large dish, with the
seam or back under; put another plate or dish over it with
a weight on it, and leave thus overnight in a cool place.
The next morning the bird will be perfectly cold and
rather flattened; then remove the towel, also the twine
with which it has been sewed, place it on the dish on
which it is to be served, the breast upward; glaze it with
essence of beef or glace; decorate with meat-jelly, and
serve.

How to decorate with Jelly.—When the jelly is congealed and can be cut with a knife, chop some of it on a
coarse towel and put it all around the bird, about half
an inch thick; cut some in slices about a quarter of an
inch in thickness; cut these again with paste-cutters in
different shapes, according to fancy, and place it over the
bird, also according to fancy; again cut some of it in slices
about one inch broad, a quarter of an inch thick and of
any length, and cut out of these last ones pieces of a
triangular shape, which put all around the border of the
dish, placed so that one point of each piece is turned
toward the edge of the dish and the two other points
touch the other pieces on both sides; then you have an
indented border of jelly. When the jelly is fancifully and
tastefully arranged, it makes a sightly dish.

It is always served cold for breakfast, lunch, or supper.

In summer the jelly melts, and cannot be used as a
decoration. A boned bird is then served without jelly.
The bird is cut in slices, and some jelly is served with each
slice.

Cold.—A turkey, being a large bird, is seldom entirely

eaten the day it is served, and very often more than half of it is left for the next day. What is left may be prepared in different ways.

In Vinaigrette.—Cut the flesh in slices and serve them with a *vinaigrette.* It is not understood here for a boned turkey, which is always eaten cold, but either a roasted, baked, stewed, or stuffed turkey.

In Croquettes.—Proceed in every particular as for chicken *croquettes.*

In Salad.—A salad of turkey is made also exactly the same as a salad of chicken, with cold meat. It is covered with a Mayonnaise-sauce and decorated in the same way.

Besides the above ways of preparing cold turkey, it may also be prepared as directed for cold chicken in general.

A caponed turkey is prepared as a caponed chicken, boiled or with rice; and also like a turkey, as described in the above receipts. They are generally larger, fatter, and more tender and juicy than others. They are very much appreciated here, and every year more and more are supplied, and, as in Europe, the greater the supply the better the quality. There is a ready market for caponed turkeys in all the large cities of the United States, and they command a high price.

DUCKS.

Ducks and ducklings, tame and wild, are prepared alike. To be good, a duck must be fat, be it a *canvasback, gadwell, black-duck, garganey, poachard, wood-duck, pintail, shoveller, spirit-duck, summer-duck, teal, widgeon, shelldrake,* or any other.

How to select.—A young duck has the lower part of the legs soft, and the skin between the claws soft also;

you will also know if it is young by taking hold of it by the bill (the under bill only), if it breaks or bends, the duck is young.

If the breast of the duck is hard and thick, it is fresh enough.

How to prepare.—A duck is cleaned and prepared as directed for poultry.

Roasted.—Clean, prepare, and truss the duck as a chicken, with the exception that the rump is pushed inside; the duck being much longer than a chicken, it is more sightly when so trussed.

Place inside of the duck two sage-leaves, two bay-leaves, and two sprigs of thyme, and leave it thus in a cool place for two or three hours, and then roast it as directed for chicken.

When roasted, serve it with any of the following garnitures: cabbage, cauliflower, *Macédoine*, onion, or truffles.

The fatty part of the gravy or drippings must be carefully and totally removed before turning it over the duck and garniture. It takes from thirty to forty minutes to roast.

Baked.—When cleaned, prepared, and trussed as directed for turkeys and chickens, put the duck in a bake-pan, salt and pepper it, cover the bottom of the pan with cold water, and place it in a rather quick oven.

A duck, being generally very fat, requires to be turned over and over several times and to be basted very often. It is not necessary to cover it with buttered paper. In case there is much fat in the pan, remove it while it is cooking.

It is served as directed for roast duck, with garnitures.

When roasted or baked, it is also served with apple or cranberry-sauce, or with currant-jelly.

12

With Peas.—Cut in dice about one ounce of salt pork and put it in a saucepan ; set it on the fire, and, as soon as the butter is melted, brown in it a duck trussed as directed and take from the fire. Put one ounce of butter in a saucepan and mix it cold with a tablespoonful of flour, set it on the fire, and, when the butter is melted, put the duck in with about a quart of green peas, blanched for one or two minutes only ; add about a pint of water or of broth, a bunch of seasonings composed of three or four stalks of parsley, one of thyme, a bay-leaf, and one clove, salt, and pepper ; boil gently till the whole is cooked, and serve warm.

Remove all the fat carefully before serving.

If the water should boil away while it is cooking, add a little more.

With Oranges.—Roast or bake a young duck as directed, and serve it with carpels of orange all around ; and sprinkle some orange-juice all over just before serving it.

With Olives.—Roast or bake the duck as directed. When done, turn the gravy into a small saucepan with about two dozen olives ; stir gently, and keep on the fire for about five minutes. Dish the duck, place the olives all around ; turn the gravy over the whole, and serve warm.

Sauté, served with a Border.—When cleaned and cut in eight pieces as directed, set it on the fire with one ounce of butter, stir occasionally till turning brown, then pour off the fat from the saucepan, add broth enough just to cover the pieces of duck ; also one onion with a clove stuck in it, a bunch of seasonings tied with twine and composed of four stalks of parsley, one of thyme, and a bay-leaf, salt, and pepper ; boil gently till done. Place the pieces of duck inside of a border of rice, strain the sauce over the duck only, and serve hot.

The rice must be cooked, moulded, and placed on the dish while the duck is cooking, so as to serve the whole warm. (*See* RICE IN BORDER.)

To cut.—A duck is generally cut in eight pieces, the two legs and wings, the breast in two, and the back-bone in two.

With Turnips.—Truss the duck as directed for birds. Put one ounce of butter in a saucepan, set it on the fire, and, when melted, put the duck in, turn over now and then till it is brown on every side. Then add a piece of onion chopped fine, stir, and, when turning brown also, add water enough to half cover it; also a bunch of seasonings composed of three sprigs of parsley, one of thyme, a bay-leaf, and a clove; boil gently till done, when add salt to taste.

While the duck is cooking, cut two turnips in dice or in round pieces with a fruit-corer, or with a vegetable spoon, set them on the fire with cold water and salt, boil till tender, and drain them.

Put them back on the fire with the sauce or gravy from the saucepan in which the duck has cooked, give one boil, dish the duck, place the turnips around, and serve.

Another way.—Cut the duck in pieces. Set a saucepan on the fire with an ounce of butter in it, when melted, add half a tablespoonful of flour, stir, and, when turning brown, add half a dozen small turnips or two large ones, cut with a vegetable spoon; stir, and, when they are all browned, take them off and brown the pieces of duck; then put the turnips back in the pan, add broth enough just to cover the whole; also two sprigs of parsley, one of thyme, a bay-leaf, a clove, salt, and pepper · boil gently till cooked; dish the duck and turnips, turn the sauce over them through a strainer, and serve warm.

Cold.—What is left from the preceding day's dinner is prepared in *salmis.*

Very often a duck is baked, especially to make a *salmis* with it. (*See* SALMIS.)

Boned.—Bone, fill, cook, and serve as turkey boned.

Cold duck may also be prepared in *croquettes* and salad, like chicken.

Stuffed.—It is stuffed with sausage-meat and chestnuts, also like a chicken.

GEESE AND GOSLINGS—TAME OR WILD.

A young goose has much down and soft legs of a yellow color; an old one has little down and rough legs of a reddish color. When fresh, the legs are soft; and stiff and dry when not fresh.

Geese and goslings are prepared, cooked, and served like ducks, in the following ways: roasted and baked, and served with garnitures, with cranberry-sauce, currant-jelly, apple-sauce, with a border, olives, oranges, peas, or turnips; in *croquettes* and in *salmis.*

It is boned, cooked, and served, like a boned turkey.

In Civet.—Clean, prepare, and cut the goose in pieces, removing most of the fat, and then cook, and serve it like rabbit in civet.

It takes a little longer than to cook a rabbit, but makes a very good dish.

When the civet is properly made, it does not taste like goose.

GUINEA-FOWLS.

A young Guinea-bird is good, but an old one is hardly fit to be eaten.

Guinea-fowls are prepared and served like prairie-hens.

PIGEONS.

The stall-fed or squab is prepared the same as the wild one.

To select.—If the legs are not red, they are young; and if not stiff, they are fresh. When not fresh, the rump is of a bluish color.

Clean and prepare them as directed for fowls.

Broiled.—Split the backs of the pigeons so as to open them, flatten them a little with a chopper. Put two ounces of butter (for six pigeons) in a saucepan, and set it on a good fire; when hot, add to it a teaspoonful of chopped parsley and green onions, salt, and pepper; then the pigeons. When half cooked, take them from the fire, roll them in bread-crumbs, place them on the gridiron and set on a moderate fire, turn over once or twice, and, when done, serve on a *maître d'hôtel, piquante,* or *poivrade* sauce.

Another way.—When cleaned, prepared, and split open as directed above, salt and pepper them, grease them slightly with melted butter, by means of a brush; then broil them till underdone, and serve with a *maître d'hôtel* sauce.

In Chartreuse.—A *chartreuse* with pigeons is made and served as a *chartreuse* of prairie-hens.

In Papillotes.—When cleaned and prepared as directed, bake the pigeons till about half done, then split them in two, lengthwise, and then proceed as for *veal cutlets* in papillotes.

They may be fried with a little butter, instead of baked.

With Vegetables.—Clean and prepare as directed for poultry, four pigeons. Cut them in four pieces each.

Put in a saucepan two ounces of butter, and set it on the fire; when melted, brown the pigeons in it, and then take them from the pan.

The pigeons being taken off, put into the pan, which is kept on the fire, half a carrot and two onions sliced, half a turnip, sliced also; four or five stalks of parsley, one of thyme, one of celery, a bay-leaf, two cloves; the latter five tied together. Cover the whole with broth or water; boil gently till about half done, then add the pieces of pigeons, and salt and pepper; continue boiling till the whole is done.

Dish the pigeons, throw away the seasonings, mash the carrot, onions, and turnips through a colander, which you mix with the sauce. Place the mixture around the pieces of pigeons, and serve warm.

Stuffed.—It is stuffed, cooked, and served like a stuffed chicken.

The same, stewed.—Put a piece of butter the size of a walnut in a stewpan, and set it on a good fire; when hot, add two ounces of bacon cut in dice, then place in four pigeons, leave thus till of a fine golden color, and then take pigeons and bacon off the pan. Put again in the stewpan the same quantity of butter as before; when melted, sprinkle in, little by little, a teaspoonful of flour, stirring with a wooden spoon, and when of a proper thickness, and of a brownish color, put the pigeons and bacon back in, add four small onions, two sprigs of parsley, one of thyme, a bay-leaf, a pinch of allspice, salt, pepper, half a glass of broth, same of claret wine; simmer about an hour, take off parsley, thyme, and bay-leaf, and send to the table.

The same, roasted.—Envelop each pigeon in thin slices of bacon tied with twine, place them on a spit before a moderate fire, baste often with the drippings, and, when cooked, serve them with the gravy, at the same time sprinkling a few drops of lemon-juice on them. It takes from thirty to thirty-five minutes to roast them.

To roast or bake they are trussed like a chicken, as seen in the cut below. To carve pigeons is easy, they are merely split in two, lengthwise.

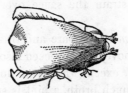

Baked.—Place a thin slice of fat salt pork or bacon on the breast of each pigeon, after being cleaned, prepared, and salted ; place them in a bakepan, on their back ; cover the bottom of the pan with cold water and put in a hot oven, baste often, and when done serve them with water-cress and lemon-juice.

The pigeons are placed on the dish the same as they were in the bakepan ; place water-cress between each, also all around and in the middle of them ; sprinkle lemon-juice all over, and serve warm.

With Green Peas.—When cleaned and prepared, truss the pigeons and put them in a saucepan with about two ounces of butter for half a dozen, stir now and then till turning rather brown all around and take off; then put in the saucepan about two ounces of salt pork cut in dice, stir, and, when partly fried, take it off also. The pan being still on the fire, put into it a good tablespoonful of flour, stir till it turns brown, when you add about a quart of broth, stir and mix ; put pigeons and salt pork back into the pan, season with a bunch of seasonings, composed of half a dozen stalks of parsley, one of thyme, two bay-leaves, a clove, and one clove of garlic. Boil gently till nearly half done, and then add a quart of green peas, blanched previously; boil again gently till the whole is done; remove the bunch of seasonings and the clove of garlic; dish the pigeons, turn the peas in the same dish, but in the middle of the pigeons, which can be tastefully placed all around the dish; strain the sauce over the whole, and serve warm.

With Mushrooms.—Prepare and truss the pigeons the same as for the above, and proceed also as for the above in every particular, except that you do not put in the saucepan quite as much broth, a pint is sufficient, and boil gently till done, but do not add peas.

Ten minutes before taking from the fire, add a dozen mushrooms, whole or sliced, and half a gill of claret wine, if handy.

Dish the pigeons, place the mushrooms in the middle of the dish, strain the sauce over the whole, and serve warm.

Fried.—Take four pigeons, cut each in four pieces, put two ounces of butter in a stewpan and set it on the fire; when melted, put the pigeons in with two or three sprigs of parsley, a small sprig of thyme, a bay-leaf, a pinch of allspice, salt, pepper, and half a pint of broth. Take the pigeons off when half cooked, and, as soon as they are cool, dip each piece in beaten eggs and roll it in bread-crumbs. Strain the butter that may be left in the stew-pan, and put it in a frying-pan with about an ounce more, and fry the birds for about two minutes; serve with water-cress or parsley all around.

In Compote.—Roast six pigeons as directed. Then cut one of them in dice, put it in a mortar and pound it. Put half an ounce of butter in a saucepan, and, when melted, fry half an onion chopped fine in it; then add to the pounded pigeon about a gill of gravy, a gill of good broth, salt, pepper, a bunch of seasonings, composed of three stalks of parsley, one of thyme, a bay-leaf, and a clove; also about a gill of Madeira wine or white wine, boil gently till reduced about one-third, strain. Put back on the fire, add butter, and when melted stir and set it on the corner of the range to keep warm while the rest is prepared. Cut the other five pigeons in two, lengthwise. Cut ten pieces of bread square, or of an oval shape, and about the size of a half pigeon, fry them with a little butter, and place them on a dish. While the bread is frying, put the pigeons in an oven to warm them; place half a pigeon on each slice of bread, or one lapping over the other; have the slices and pigeons so arranged that they fill the dish, leaving only a small space in the middle, into which you pour the sauce; serve the whole hot.

In Crapaudine.—When prepared, split open the backs of the pigeons; cut the legs at the first joints and run them through the skin so that the ends come out on the inside; dip the birds in beaten eggs, roll them in bread-crumbs, and broil them.

While they are broiling, knead butter, chopped parsley, and lemon-juice together; spread some on the pigeons when they are dished, and serve warm.

GIBLETS.

By giblets are understood the gizzards, heads, legs, livers, necks, and ends of the wings of chickens, ducks, geese, turkeys, and other birds, tame or wild.

You begin by cleaning them well, cut off the bills, take the eyes out, warming the legs on live coals, so that

12*

you can take off the outer skin and spurs; place the giblets in a tureen, turn boiling water and a little salt on them, leave them thus five or six minutes, then wash well and drain them.

In Fricassée.—Put a piece of butter in a stewpan (the size to be according to the quantity of giblets you have), set it on a good fire; when melted, sprinkle in it, little by little, a teaspoonful of flour; stir the whole with a wooden spoon; when of a proper thickness, and of a brownish color, add half a gill of warm broth, same of warm water, a sprig of parsley, a small pinch of grated nutmeg, two small onions, salt, and pepper; then the giblets. About half an hour after add also two mushrooms, cut in pieces. It takes about two hours to cook them properly. Dish the pieces, strain the sauce, mix in it one well-beaten yolk of an egg, and a few drops of lemon-juice; pour it on the giblets, place the pieces of mushrooms over the whole, and serve.

The same, stewed.—Put the giblets in a stewpan with butter, and set it on a good fire; when they are of a fine yellow color, add one or two sprigs of parsley, a clove of garlic, a sprig of thyme, one clove, half a bay-leaf, two mushrooms cut in pieces, two small onions, and a pinch of flour; wet with broth, let simmer gently for half an hour, and add also two parsnips cut in slices, and previously half fried in butter; simmer again for about an hour; dish the pieces of meat, strain the sauce, put it back on the fire to reduce it a little, pour it on the giblets, place the pieces of mushrooms at the top, and serve hot.

Sauté.—They may also be prepared and served as a *chicken sauté.*

ASPIC OF MEAT.

Cut four middling-sized onions in slices, lay them in a stewpan with a quarter of a pound of bacon (not smoked); then add about a quarter of a pound of each of the following meats: chicken, game (any kind), mutton, and beef, also a calf's foot split in two, two ounces of rind of bacon, two sprigs of parsley, two of thyme, a clove of garlic, two carrots cut in two, one clove, and four small onions; wet with half a pint of water, and set on a brisk fire; cover the pan well. When nearly cooked, take the grease off with a ladle; add then boiling water enough just to cover the whole, and finish the cooking. Strain the juice, skim off the fat, if any, and let it cool; if it is not found clear enough when strained, beat well two whites of eggs, put them in the stewpan with the juice, set it on a sharp fire for about ten minutes, stirring the while, and take from the fire; add to it a few drops of lemon-juice, and strain again.

Put in a mould some of the above juice, about two-eighths of an inch in depth; place the mould on ice, and leave till the juice has turned into a jelly. Lay on that jelly some of the following meats, free from bones, and not allowing the pieces to touch the sides of the mould: chicken, game, tongues of beef, calf, and sheep, of all or of either of them (the meats must be cooked beforehand). Cover the whole with the remainder of the juice, so as to have about the same thickness at the top as at the bottom. Place the mould in a refrigerator to cool, and turn into a jelly; then dip the mould in very warm water, turn over on a dish, remove the mould, and you have a fine *entrée.*

GAME.

————◆————

GAME, comparatively, is appreciated only by a few.

When the country was first settled, every one was his own provider, and of course game was not sent to a market several hundred miles from the place where it was shot or caught. But settlement and civilization have the same effect on game as they have on barbarians or savages— they drive it away.

Our Northeastern cities are now supplied by the Western States with game. In winter time, game may be kept for weeks without being spoiled or losing its natural flavor and taste, when kept where it is killed; but when transported, it is very different. To transport it requires packing. As soon as packed, it naturally ferments; and even if packed when frozen, the middle of the barrel will ferment and become injured, if not entirely rendered unfit for the table.

The packing of game or poultry in barrels is a bad practice. Nothing requires more ventilation than game while being transported. Many dealers have their game sent to them in wicker-baskets with plenty of straw, but the greater part is still sent in barrels; hence the musty taste when cooked.

To keep game for some time when fresh, open the animal or bird under the rump, just enough to take the inside out, also the crop of birds, being very careful about the gall-bladder; if it bursts, it is better not to try to preserve the piece, but to clean, wash, and use it as soon as possible. Birds must be left in their feathers, and animals in their skins. Fill the inside with dry and clean oats, and put the piece in a heap or barrel of oats. It will keep thus for many days.

Another way is to envelop the piece well in a towel, and bury it in charcoal dust in a cool and dry place.

How to clean and prepare.—Clean and prepare the birds as directed for poultry in general.

After having carefully skinned, take out the inside, and cut the legs off at the first joint of animals; wash the inside with lukewarm water, and wipe it dry with a clean towel immediately after; wipe also the outside, but do not wash it if possible; that is, if you can clean it well by wiping only.

Wild ducks, *geese*, *pigeons*, and *turkeys*, are prepared, cooked, and served like tame ones.

Bear-meat and Buffalo.—The meat of all large animals is better roasted, than dressed in any other way. Prepare, cook, and serve bear and buffalo meat like venison, beef *à la mode*, or stewed.

Bear-meat has highly nutritive qualities, and is very warming.

Buffalo-steaks are said to be better broiled on cinders without a gridiron, than on or before coals with one; that is, Indian fashion and even hunters' fashion.

Indians often use wood-ashes as a substitute for salt, and never use salt with buffalo-meat; but their liking or preference comes from their habit of invariably broiling buffalo-meat on wood cinders or buffalo-chips.

Bear-hams, so well appreciated everywhere, are prepared and served like common hams. A bear-ham, tastefully decorated, is considered a *recherché* dish at supper for evening parties.

Blackbird, Bobolink, and Small Birds.—The cut below represents six small birds on the spit, ready for *roasting.* When the birds are prepared, cut off the ends of the wings and the legs above the first joint. Instead of cutting the legs above the first joint, the ends of the claws only may be cut off, according to taste. Cut thin slices of fat salt pork, of a proper size to cover the breast of the bird ; place the slice on the breast of it, run a skewer through the middle of the bird, so that it will run through the two ends of the slice of salt pork also, as seen in the cut.

Have a skewer, or merely a piece of wire, long enough to hold six birds; fix the skewer on the spit, and roast.

When the six birds are on the skewer, fasten them with twine, to prevent them from turning round, as seen in the cut.

Small birds are cleaned and prepared as directed for poultry, but they are not trussed, their legs being tied while tying the salt pork. While roasting, they are basted often with the drippings. Some water-cress and lemon-juice sprinkled upon them may be served with the birds. The twine is removed before serving, and they must be served hot ; if allowed to cool at all, they lose their taste. It takes from ten to fifteen minutes to roast.

Baked.—Prepare them exactly as for roasting: place the wire or skewer across a baking-pan, turn them round and baste often; serve also as above, with the gravy, and with or without water-cress.

The *bobolink*, *reed-bird*, and *rice-bird* are the same; they are called under these different names at different seasons and in different localities; it is the American ortolan, the most delicate of small birds; the robin comes next.

To eat it à la Brillat-Savarin.—Take hold of the bird by the bill; open your mouth wide enough to introduce the whole bird into it easily; then shut it, at the same time biting off the bill just at its base; chew properly and swallow.

While the birds are roasting or baking, place as many small slices of bread in the dripping or baking pan, and serve a bird over each slice. Cut the slices either square, round, or oval, about one-fourth of an inch in thickness, and large enough to hold the bird.

Hunter-like.—Prepare small birds as described for quails, hunter-like; it makes an excellent dish.

In Salmis.—Roasted or baked small birds can be prepared in *salmis* when cold. Many amateurs prefer small birds not drawn; that is, the crop only is taken off, but nothing of the inside is disturbed; they pretend that they have a better taste when cooked thus; of course, every one to his taste.

High-holders, lapwings, meadow-larks, plovers, rails, robins, snipes, thrushes, woodcocks, woodpeckers, and *yellow-birds* are prepared as above.

Small birds have a better flavor when cooked after being somewhat seasoned than when cooked fresh, but they must not be tainted. As long as the rump is stiff, they are good; if soft, they must be examined carefully, as they might be tainted. When young, there is no stiffness in the legs. Small birds are generally put by the half dozen on the same skewer, as seen in the cut (p. 278); but when a little larger, like the robin or plover, they may be trussed as directed for snipes.

Grouse or Heathcock.—These are good as long as the legs are flexible; if not, examine them carefully, they might be rotten inside.

Lard them well, envelop each in buttered paper, and place on the spit before a good fire; baste often, remove the paper after twenty or twenty-five minutes; leave two or three minutes more, basting continually with the drippings; dish the birds; mix with the drippings a few drops of lemon-juice, and a little salt and pepper, and serve with the birds.

Baked.—Lard the bird as for roasting; that is, the fleshy parts only are larded with salt pork, then truss them as directed for chicken, place them in a baking-pan, cover the bottom of the pan with cold water, put a piece of buttered paper on each bird, place in a hot oven, baste often till done. Serve with the gravy some water-cress, and lemon-juice, or vinegar.

It is also prepared, cooked, and served in the different ways described for prairie-hen, either in *chartreuse*, *salmis*, salad, or any other way.

Hare.—No hares have yet been found in the United States, except in California. The reported hare of the Western prairies is, as far as known, a species of rabbit. That found in the Eastern markets comes from Canada and Europe. The Canadian hare is very inferior in quality.

To select.—When young it has rather soft paws, and not much opened, and also soft ears; but if old, the paws are hard and much worn, and the ears stiff and hard. If fresh, the body is stiff; it is soft, and the flesh is nearly black, if tainted. Save the blood as much as possible; it improves the sauce very much.

In Civet.—When the hare is cleaned as directed for game, cut in pieces. Have in a saucepan and on a good fire two ounces of butter and one of salt pork cut in dice. Stir, and when the salt pork is fried take it off the pan, and put the pieces of hare in it; stir with a wooden spoon now and then, till of a fine golden color; then sprinkle on it a teaspoonful of flour, add ten small onions, four sprigs of parsley, two of thyme, two cloves of garlic, a bay-leaf, salt, pepper, about a pint of claret wine, same of broth, three or four mushrooms, and a little grated nutmeg; boil gently till done; dish the pieces of hare; throw away parsley, thyme, bay-leaf, and garlic; mix the blood of the hare, if any, in the sauce, boil it about ten minutes longer, turn it on the hare, and serve warm.

Many epicures like a civet better when prepared one or two days in advance, and only warmed before serving. When the civet is done, and ready to serve, place the dish in a cool, dry place, and when you want to eat the civet, place the dish in a *bain-marie*, or in an oven, and serve when warm.

The same, roasted.—Lard the hare well; place it on the spit before a good fire; baste often with the drippings, and when properly cooked serve it with the following sauce : put in a stewpan a piece of butter the size of a walnut, and set it on a good fire; when melted, put in it the hare's liver well pounded, then the blood, if any, also the drippings, salt, pepper, a tablespoonful of white wine, same of broth, and one teaspoonful of vinegar; when of a proper thickness, serve with the hare.

It takes about an hour to roast it well.

In a small family, the hind part is roasted, and the fore part of the hare is dressed in civet.

Baked.—Lard it with salt pork and bake it, basting often; serve in the same way as a roasted one.

The same, next day.—If any is left from the day before, warm it and serve, if in civet; cut in slices and serve cold, with an oil-sauce, if roasted.

Leveret.—Cook and serve like a hare.

A leveret may also be *sautéd* like a chicken.

Pheasant, to select.—When young, the claws are short and round at the end, while they are long and sharp when old. They are not fresh when the rump is of a bluish color, but some amateurs like them then; in that state, they are said to have a venison taste. Some hang the bird by the feathers of the tail and leave it so till it falls; then they prepare and eat it. It does not fall until very " high," or rather when tainted. They ought not to be cooked when very fresh, as they have not as delicate a taste then as when rather " high."

Pheasants are prepared, cooked, and served like *prairie-birds* in every way.

Crane, Ostrich, Peacock, Pelican, or other Large Birds.—These birds are seldom eaten. When old, they are tough, and of a disagreeable taste. When young, they are not so bad, and may be prepared like a *turkey* stuffed or stewed.

Prairie-bird, Prairie-hen, and Partridge.—An old prairie-hen has a white bill and bluish legs; when young, the bill is of a rather dark-gray color, and the legs are yellowish. As long as the rump does not turn bluish, it is fresh enough.

To prepare.—Clean and prepare a prairie-hen as directed for poultry in general.

Baked.—Clean and prepare the bird as directed, then cut off the claws to about half their length. Truss the prairie-hen as directed for chicken, and then cover its breast with a thin slice of fat salt pork, but do not cover the back of the bird. Tie the salt pork with twine. Place the prairie-hen on its back in the baking-pan, with a piece of butter the size of a walnut on it; set it in a quick oven (about 400 deg. Fahr.), baste often, and serve when rather underdone. While the bird is baking, prepare some fresh water-cress, place some of it all around the bird; mix lemon-juice with the gravy and turn it over the bird and water-cress, and serve warm. It may also be served after being baked, the same as directed for a roasted one.

Broiled.—Clean and prepare as directed, then split the back of the prairie-hen so as to open it; salt, pepper, and butter it by means of a brush; place it on the gridiron over a good fire; turn over three or four times; as soon as done, sprinkle on it a little allspice, dish the bird, spread a *maître d'hôtel* sauce on it, and serve warm. It is also served with a *piquante, poivrade,* or *ravigote sauce.*

Another way.—Split the prairie-hen in two lengthwise so as to make two equal pieces. Put one ounce of butter in a stewpan and set it on a good fire; when melted, lay the two halves of the bird in; turn over and leave them till a little more than half cooked, when take them off. Envelop each piece in buttered paper, place them on the gridiron, and set it on a rather brisk fire for about fifteen minutes, turning over once only, and serve with the following sauce: Put with the butter in the pan in which was the bird, about a teaspoonful of chopped parsley, same of chopped mushrooms, salt, pepper, and a pinch of allspice; sprinkle in and stir at the same time a teaspoonful of flour; add a gill of white wine, same of broth; boil gently till of a proper thickness, and serve the bird with it, either on the same dish or separately. Serve as warm as possible.

With Cabbage.—Clean and truss the prairie-chicken as directed for birds; fry it a little with butter, just enough to color it; then place a cabbage, previously blanched, cut in four pieces, all around it; also about four ounces of lean salt pork, one onion whole; just cover the whole with cold water (it requires about one pint of it if the pan is of a proper size); when the cabbage is boiled down, baste occasionally with the juice, and if it boils away add a little broth or water; keep enough to baste till done, when dish the prairie-chicken with the cabbage around, also the salt pork if liked; turn the juice all over through a strainer. In case it is not salt enough, add salt while basting. The flesh of a prairie-chicken is naturally dry, and by being cooked with cabbage it is kept moist all the time and is juicy when done. For those who have no prejudice against cabbage, it is the best way to prepare a prairie-bird.

Another way.—Lard two prairie-birds as directed for larding, after being cleaned and prepared as directed. Put in a stewpan half a pound of bacon cut in slices, with four onions, two carrots cut in pieces, a small dried or Bologna sausage, two sprigs of parsley, one of thyme, two cloves, a bay-leaf, a little grated nutmeg, and a cabbage cut rather fine, and which is to be previously thrown in boiling water and boiled ten minutes; then the two partridges or prairie-hens; place over the whole four ounces of bacon cut in thin slices, cover with broth, set the pan on a sharp fire, and when it has boiled about fifteen minutes, subdue the fire, or put the pan in a moderately heated oven, simmer about two hours if the partridges are old, and one hour if they are young; then take from the fire, place the partridges on a dish with the sausage cut in pieces around them, drain the cabbage and put it on another dish with the bacon, strain the sauce on both dishes, and serve.

In Chartreuse.—It is made in a mould for *Charlotte russe,* or in one like the cut following. Clean the prairie-hen as directed for birds; put it in a baking-pan with one ounce of butter spread on it, also salt and pepper, and a gill of cold water in the pan, and bake till underdone, when cut it in seven pieces, making three slices in the breast, lengthwise. Peel and slice two carrots and two turnips; cut the slices about an inch thick; then cut again in small round pieces, with a fruit-corer, about half an inch in diameter; set them on the fire with cold water and salt, boil gently till done, drain and turn immediately in cold water, and they are ready to be used. Put a small head of cabbage in a saucepan with half a pound of lean salt pork, just cover it with cold water, and boil gently till done. The prairie-hen, carrots, and turnips, and the cabbage, may be cooked at the same time, but separately, as directed. When the cabbage is done, turn it into a colander, cut it rather fine with a spoon, press gently on it to get the water out as much as possible without mashing it through the colander, and it is ready to be used. Butter the mould well; place slices of boiled beets on the bottom; some letters or flowers may be cut in beet, the intervals or holes filled with turnips and carrots; when the bottom is lined with beets, carrots, and turnips, lay horizontally a row of pieces of carrots all around and against the sides of the mould; place a similar one of turnips on the carrots, and so on, the last row being as high as the top of the mould. Then put a layer of the cabbage on the bottom, about half an inch thick—that is, on the carrots, turnips, and beets—place a like layer on the sides with a spoon; put the pieces of prairie-hen in the middle, cover with a layer of cabbage, and bake about fifteen minutes in an oven at about 350 deg. Fahr. The meat must not touch the carrots or turnips, but be entirely surrounded with cabbage, else it would crumble down in removing the mould. As soon as the mould is taken out of the oven, place a dish over it and turn it upside down, leave it so about ten minutes to allow the juice to come out, then remove the mould carefully, and serve.

The cut below represents a *chartreuse* made exactly like the one described above, with the exception that instead of having a row of carrots and a row of turnips, they are mixed, that is, placed alternately, the white spots representing pieces of turnips and the black spots pieces of carrots—the top being decorated according to fancy.

According to the size of the mould, two, three, or more prairie-hens may be prepared at one time and in the same mould.

Roasted.—Rub the stomach and legs of the birds with lemon, then envelop those parts with slices of bacon tied with twine, or fixed with small skewers; after which envelop the whole bird in buttered paper tied with twine; place them on a spit before a good fire, take the paper off after twenty or thirty minutes, according to the age of the bird; leave two or three minutes longer, baste often during the process of roasting, with the drippings; dish the birds without removing the slices of bacon; mix in the gravy the juice of half a lemon, or half an orange, a little salt and pepper, and serve it with the birds. It may also be served with water-cress and lemon-juice or vinegar. When roasted or baked and dished, place carpels of oranges all around, and serve.

A roasted or baked prairie-hen is also served with the following sauces: anchovy, caper, Champagne, cranberry, and *ravigote* or tomato, and currant-jelly.

With Mushrooms.—When roasted or baked, serve it with a garniture of mushrooms. It is also served with a garniture of cauliflowers, *financière*, *Macédoine*, and of truffles.

In Fricassée.—Prepare, cook, and serve it like chicken in *fricassée.*

In Crapaudine.—Proceed as for pigeons in *crapaudine*, the only difference being that it takes a little longer to cook. It is also prepared and served as a quail, *hunter-like.* It takes longer to cook than a quail.

Sauté.—Clean, prepare, cut, cook, dish, and serve the prairie-bird as a chicken *sauté.*

Stewed.—Clean, prepare, and truss the bird as directed. Put about one ounce of butter and two ounces of fat salt pork, cut in dice, in a saucepan, and set it on a quick fire; toss gently, and when the butter is melted, put the bird in and brown it all around; then add four small onions, half a carrot in slices, salt, and pepper; stir till the onions and carrot are partly fried; then add half a pint of broth, same of white wine, a bunch of seasonings composed of four or five stalks of parsley, one of thyme, one bay-leaf, and a clove; boil gently till done; dish the bird, turn the sauce over it through a strainer, and serve warm. Thus stewed, it may be served with the following *purées :* asparagus, beans, lentils, lima beans, mushrooms, and peas.

Cold.—A whole bird or part of it left from the preceding day's dinner, if it has been broiled, baked, or roasted, is prepared and served in salad, like a chicken salad; or in *salmis*.

Boned.—A boned prairie-bird makes an excellent dish and a most nutritious and warming one. Persons having a phlegmatic constitution ought to partake of it at least twice a week during hunting-time. Always select a very fresh and fat bird to bone. Pick, bone, fill, cook, and serve it as described for boned turkey. A prairie-hen is more easily boned, when fresh, than an ordinary chicken. The addition of truffles (about half a pound for one bird) makes it still richer and warmer.

In Croquettes.—Prepare, cook, and serve as chicken croquettes.

Quails.—A quail, like a prairie-bird, is old when it has a white bill and bluish legs; when young, the bill is of a rather dark-gray color, and the legs are yellowish. Quails are just the contrary of pheasants; the more fresh they are when cooked, the better.

To prepare.—When cleaned and prepared as directed for poultry, cut off the end of the claws, and then truss it as a chicken, sprinkle salt and pepper on the breast. Cut thin slices of fat salt pork, somewhat square, and of a proper size to cover the breast of the bird, but not the back. Tie it to the bird with two pieces of twine, then roast or bake.

Another way to prepare them.—When cleaned, prepared, and trussed as above, envelop the bird with grape-vine leaves, then in thin slices of salt-pork, and roast or bake them. They may also be enveloped in buttered paper, after being prepared, instead of salt pork or grape-vine leaves, or instead of both, but only to roast them; if baked, the buttered paper is placed over the birds.

Baked.—Place the birds on their backs in a baking-

pan, with a piece of butter the size of a hazel-nut on eacn ,
just cover the bottom of the pan with cold water, and set
in a quick oven (about 400° Fahr.) and baste now and
then. When about half done, put the liver of the birds,
well pounded, in the baking-pan, and continue basting till
done. While the quails are baking, cut as many square
slices of stale bread as you have quails, about three inches
broad and one-fourth of an inch thick; fry them in hot
fat, place them on the dish, place a quail with the breast
upward on each slice; remove the twine, turn the gravy
over them and serve warm. Water-cress may be placed
between each bird, as well as all around, and in the middle of the dish, with vinegar or lemon-juice sprinkled all
over. It must also be served warm.

Hunter-like (*au Chasseur*).—Clean and prepare as directed for birds. Set a saucepan on the fire with two
ounces of butter to melt, then put in it four quails trussed
as for roasting; turn them round in the pan to color every
side; add then half a dozen stalks of parsley, salt, pepper,
and nearly cover them with broth and white wine, half of
each; boil gently till done. Dish the quails, and put them
away in a warm place. Strain the sauce and put it back
on the fire with a tablespoonful of *meunière*, boil rather
fast till it commences turning thick, turn over the quails
and serve warm.

Roasted.—When cleaned and prepared as directed,
envelop the birds in grape-vine leaves and salt pork, or in
buttered paper, as directed above, and place them on the
spit before a moderate though good fire. Have slices of
roasted bread in the dripping-pan, baste often with the
drippings, and when done remove the twine, or the twine
and paper, but neither the salt pork nor the grape-vine
leaves, and serve warm. The slices of bread are placed

13

on the dish, then a quail on each slice. Water-cress may also be served as above.

Quails roasted with grape-vine leaves are considered one of the most *recherché* dishes. When about half roasted, the liver of the birds, well pounded, is put in the dripping-pan, and the drippings are turned over the birds when dished. When pounded, the livers may be spread on the slices of bread before placing them in the dripping-pan.

With Green Peas.—When the quails are roasted or baked, they may be served with green peas *au jus*. They may also be served on a *purée* of celery or of mushrooms.

In Chartreuse.—Proceed exactly as for a *chartreuse* of prairie-bird. Quails may be served in every way like prairie-hens, stewed, in *salad*, in *salmis*, etc.

Rabbit—to select.—A rabbit, like almost every other kind of game, has a better taste when a little seasoned, but not too much so. As long as the body is rather stiff, it is good; but when soft, and when the flesh has a black-bluish appearance, it is necessary to examine it carefully, as it might be tainted. A young rabbit has soft paws, and are not much opened; but an old one has them open, hard, and worn out. The ears of a young one are very soft, while those of an old one are stiff and comparatively rough. The blood of the rabbit is a great improvement when mixed with the sauce or gravy accompanying it when served; therefore, we emphatically and earnestly ask of hunters, when they kill rabbits, to place them in their game-bags in such a position that the place where the shots have penetrated and through which the blood is escaping, be upward, and consequently stop the spilling of it.

Tame rabbits, unless they have been kept in a large

place, well fed, free from any manure or dirt, and having also plenty of room to burrow in a dry soil, are very seldom fit to eat.

To lard.—The fleshy parts of a rabbit are larded with salt pork in the same way as described for a fillet of beef.

Baked.—To bake it, it may be larded or not, according to taste. When cleaned and prepared as directed for game, place the rabbit in a baking-pan, with a few slices of onion and carrot; salt, pepper, and butter it; cover the bottom of the pan with cold water and set it in a quick oven. After ten or fifteen minutes, turn the rabbit over, baste and cover it with a piece of buttered paper. Continue basting till done. When about half done, if the water and juice are boiling away or absorbed, add more water or broth, and when done turn the gravy over the rabbit through a strainer, and serve with water-cress and a few drops of lemon-juice or vinegar.

It is also served with a *cranberry, fines herbes, mushroom, piquante, ravigote, tomato,* and *truffle* sauce.

In Chartreuse.—A rabbit is prepared in *chartreuse* the same as a prairie-chicken; the only difference is, that it requires a larger mould; the rest of the process is the same.

In Civet, or stewed.—Cut the rabbit in pieces, and fry them with a little butter till turning rather brown, when add half a pound of lean salt pork cut in dice; stir and fry two or three minutes, stir in also a tablespoonful of flour; one minute after add a half pint of broth, same of claret wine, salt, twelve small onions, and a bunch of seasonings, composed of three or four sprigs of parsley, one of thyme, a bay-leaf, a clove of garlic, one clove. Boil gently till done; throw away the bunch of seasonings, and serve warm. In case it is not handy to use claret wine, use a gill of Madeira, or Port, or Sherry wine, and one gill of water. Without wine at all it makes an inferior dish.

A civet made three or four days in advance, and warmed in a *bain-marie* for ten minutes, once every day, is better than if eaten as soon as made.

In case the sauce is becoming too thick, after warming the rabbit several times, add a little broth, and also a little butter; stir gently, and always serve as warm as possible.

In Crapaudine.—When cleaned and prepared as directed, cook and serve the rabbit as described for pigeon in *crapaudine,* with the exception that it takes a little longer to cook.

In Croquettes. What may be left from the preceding day's dinner of a baked, roasted, or stuffed rabbit, may be prepared in *croquettes,* in the same way as chicken *croquettes.*

With Currant-Jelly.—A rabbit served with currant-jelly makes a sightly dish, but it requires care and taste. Skin the rabbit carefully, leaving the ears unskinned. Cut the legs at the first joint, then dip the ears in hot (but not boiling) water, and scrape off the hair carefully. Draw it and wash the inside carefully also, putting away the liver, heart, and lungs. Chop fine one middling-sized onion, and fry it with about one ounce of butter; then add to the onion, and fry them also, the heart, liver, and lungs of the rabbit, after being chopped fine, when add a teaspoonful of chopped parsley, salt, pepper, nutmeg grated, and a piece of clove also grated. Stir for about one minute, take from the fire, mix with it two yolks of eggs and one ounce of butter. Fill the rabbit with the mixture, sew up the incision made to draw it, and then truss it in the following way : Put the rabbit on the paste-board so that it appears as if it were resting, lying on its belly. Skewer the ears so that they seem to be naturally bent on the back of the neck. With a trussing-needle fasten the forelegs so that they look also as if naturally bent by the animal when at rest. Roast or bake it, and serve it with the gravy and *currant* or *raspberry jelly.*

It is placed on the dish lying on its belly, the skewers and twine are removed, and a few sprigs of parsley are placed in its mouth. The currant-jelly may be served in a saucer and the gravy in another.

In Gibelotte.—The only difference between a *gibelotte* and a civet is that the latter is made with claret wine and the former with Sauterne or Catawba. Other white wine may be used, but the two kinds above mentioned are the best.

Marengo.—When cleaned and prepared as directed, cut the rabbit in pieces; keep the head, neck, and trimmings, to make a potage *au chasseur,* and cook and serve the rest as a chicken *à la Marengo.*

In Papillotes.—The four legs and two pieces cut on both sides of the backbone may be prepared, cooked, and served as veal cutlets in *papillotes.* The rest is used to make a potage *au chasseur.*

With Olives.—When baked or roasted, serve it as a duck with olives, putting three dozen olives instead of two.

Roasted.—It may be roasted with only a little butter spread all over it, or enveloped in buttered paper; or larded with salt pork; or larded and enveloped in buttered paper. It must be basted often, and if enveloped with paper, the paper must be removed about fifteen minutes before taking the rabbit from the fire. Ascertain when done by means of a skewer or a small sharp-pointed knife. It takes about forty-five minutes to roast, according to size and fire. When roasted it may be served with its gravy or drippings only, or with a *cranberry, fines herbes, mushroom, piquante, Provençale, ravigote, Tartar, tomato, or truffle* sauce.

With Green Peas.—When baked or roasted, serve it with green peas *au jus.*

Sauté.—When the rabbit is cleaned and prepared as directed, proceed as for a chicken *sauté* in every particular.

Sportsman-like.—Clean and prepare the rabbit, then cut off the neck, head, and the end of the legs, which you keep to make a potage *au chasseur.* Put the rest in a crockery vessel with the juice of a lemon, salt, and pepper. Leave thus for at least one day, turning it over two or three times. Then bake or roast it, and serve with the gravy and water-cress.

Stewed.—When cleaned and prepared, cut the rabbit in pieces. Put in a saucepan three ounces of butter and set it on the fire ; as soon as melted, put the pieces of rabbit in, stir now and then till they are turning rather brown, then take them from the pan but keep it on the fire. Put in it a rather small carrot and two or three onions, both sliced, a few slices of turnip, half a dozen sprigs of parsley, two of celery, one of thyme, the last three tied together with twine, and two or three cloves, also half a pint of Madeira or Sherry wine, salt, and pepper ; cover the whole with broth or water ; boil gently till half done, when add the rabbit, and continue boiling till the whole is done, stirring once in a while. Dish the rabbit, mash the onions, carrot, and turnip, through a colander, which you put all around the pieces of rabbit, strain the sauce over the whole, and serve warm.

Cold.—What is left is warmed and served, if from a civet, gibelotte, stewed, etc., and served with a *vinaigrette,* if from a roasted or baked piece. It may also be served with a *piquante, poivrade,* or *ravigote* sauce.

Snipe—to truss.—Prepare as directed for poultry. Cut the wings off just above the second joint, as seen in the cut below. The head and legs must be cleaned very carefully. By heating the lower part of the legs and the claws, the skin can be easily removed, but this is not necessary, they may be singed and washed only. Fold the legs and run the bill of the bird through the two legs and the body. Put a slice of fat salt pork on the breast of the snipe, which you fasten there with twine, as seen in the cut below. The cut represents the bird on the spit, ready for roasting.

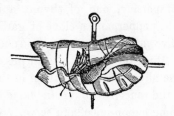

Stewed.—Take four snipes and pound the livers, hearts, and lungs well with about the same amount of fat salt pork; then add to them about a teaspoonful of parsley chopped fine, and the yolk of an egg; divide the mixture in four parts and put each part in a bird, which you sew and truss as directed. Line the bottom of a stewpan with slices of salt pork and lay the snipe on them; set on a slow fire for ten minutes, add about half a pint of white wine, same of broth; simmer till done, dish the birds, strain the gravy on them, sprinkle a few drops of lemon-juice over the whole, and serve warm. Snipes are served in several ways, as described for bobolinks and other small birds.

Salmis.—A salmis is made with tame ducks and any kind of game birds.

Birds may be roasted or baked to make a *salmis*, but most generally it is made with cold birds, that is, what is left from the previous day's dinner. It is certainly the best way to make use of cold birds. The proportions of the different seasonings are according to the proportion of meat. We give below the proportions for a whole bird; it will be easy to augment or reduce. Put two ounces of butter in a saucepan and set it on the fire; as soon as melted stir into it a tablespoonful of flour; when turning rather yellow add one pint of broth, same of claret wine, a bunch of seasonings composed of four or five sprigs of parsley, one of thyme, a bay-leaf and a clove, also salt, pepper, and a clove of garlic; boil gently about thirty-five minutes. Strain the sauce into a saucepan. Cut the bird or part of bird in pieces, the same as they are generally carved; put them in the pan with the sauce; place the saucepan in a *bain-marie* till the meat is warm, add some lemon-juice, and serve. While the meat is warming, cut some stale bread in *croutons*, fry them with a little butter.

To serve.—A *salmis* is served in two ways: first, the *croutons* are placed on the dish, a piece of meat is put on each, and then the sauce is poured all over; second, dish the meat and sauce, place the *croutons* all around the dish, with a piece of lemon or bitter orange between each *crouton*. When the *croutons* are served under the pieces of meat, you must have as many as there are pieces; when served around the dish, have enough of them, and of slices of lemon, to surround the dish. The *croutons* and slices of lemon are always placed around the meat and on the border of the dish. The lemon or orange is first split in two lengthwise, then cut in eight, twelve, or sixteen slices, always commencing to cut on the inside and finishing by the rind. Chop fine the bones, heart, and liver of the bird, and put them in the saucepan at the same time with the broth. Truffles or mushrooms sliced may be added to the sauce, if liked, but only when strained.

Another.—Carve the bird or part of it, and serve cold with the following sauce pound the liver of the bird and put it in a saucer; add to it a little vinegar, salt, pepper, and stir and mix the whole; then add about three times as much oil as vinegar, mix again, then lemon-juice, stir, and serve. It may be made without vinegar at all, using lemon-juice instead of vinegar to mix at first.

OPOSSUM, OTTER, RACCOON, SKUNK, FOX, WOODCHUCK, AND OTHER LIKE ANIMALS.

We cannot say that we have had much experience in cooking the above animals, but they are all eaten by many persons, in different parts of this and other countries. We have tasted of all of them except the raccoon, and we must say that we found them palatable. It is well known that when our soldiers retook possession of Ship Island, they found plenty of raccoons on it, and ate all they could catch. One day we happened to meet a sub-officer, who was there at the time, and inquired of him about it. He said he had never eaten any raccoons before, and did not know that they were eatable; but now he could eat them as readily as rabbits, as they were quite as good.

13*

The best time to eat any of the animals enumerated above is from Christmas to the 15th of February.

How to prepare them.—As soon as the animal is killed skin it, take the inside out, save the liver and heart, and wash well with lukewarm water and a little salt, inside and out; then wipe dry with a towel, put inside a few leaves of sage, bay-leaves, mint, and thyme, and sew it up. Hang it outside in a place sheltered from the sun, such as the northern side of a building; leave it thus five or six days, then take off, and cook.

How to skin a Skunk.—We were hunting one day in New Jersey, northwest of Paterson, with a friend and two farmers living there, when one of them shot a skunk. We asked him how much he could get for the skin. He said it was not worth while to take it to town, but that he would eat the animal, as it was very good.

We thought at first that he was joking; but putting his gun and game-bag to the ground, he looked at us earnestly, and said, "Gentlemen, you seem to doubt; I will show you how it is done." We soon saw that we had been mistaken.

He made a fire, took hold of the skunk by the head with one hand, and with a stick in the other held the skunk over the fire. He burnt off nearly all the hair, taking care to avoid burning the skin, commencing at the hind legs; then with his hunting-knife he carefully cut off the bag containing the fetid matter, and skinned and cleaned it.

We then examined the skunk, and although it had not been washed, we could not find any part of it with a bad smell, and if we had not seen the whole operation we certainly would not have thought that it was a skunk, the very name of which is repulsive.

The following week we dined with the farmer, ate some of that identical skunk, and found it very good.

How to cook the above-named Animals.—Take out the leaves of sage, etc., which you put in the animal before exposing it to the weather. Pound well the liver and heart with about the same quantity of bacon, then mix that with two or three teaspoonfuls of chopped parsley, a pinch of grated nutmeg, salt, and pepper; stuff the animal with that mixture, and also with six small onions fried in butter, and a bunch of seasoning composed of four sprigs of parsley, three of thyme, two cloves, two cloves of garlic, and two bay-leaves, and sew it up again. Butter it well all over, place it on a spit before a very quick fire; put three or four sage-leaves in the dripping-pan, and baste often with the drippings. Serve it when cooked with the gravy, throwing away the sage-leaves.

It may also be served with a *Mayonnaise, ravigote,* or *Tartar* sauce.

Squirrel.—A squirrel is prepared as a rabbit in every particular.

VENISON.

If young, the hoof is not much opened, and the fat is thick and clear; when old, the hoofs are wide open. To know if it is fresh enough, run a knife or a skewer through the leg or through the shoulder, and if it does not smell bad and stale, it is good. It is not as delicate when fresh as when it has been killed for five or six days. If fresh when you buy it, keep it from three to eight days before cooking it.

To improve.—Put the piece of venison in a crockery vessel. For about six pounds put a pint of vinegar in a saucepan with two bay-leaves, two cloves, two cloves of garlic, one onion sliced, two stalks of thyme, four of parsley, and twelve pepper-corns; set it on the fire, give one boil, and turn over the piece of venison. Turn the piece of meat over occasionally for one or two days, and then cook it.

Another way.—Lard the piece of venison and put it in a crockery vessel; spread all over two or three onions and a clove or two of garlic (both sliced), half a gill of sweet-oil, same of claret wine, a pinch of allspice, four cloves, and two sprigs of thyme; baste twice a day for two or three days, and then cook.

To bake.—Put the venison in a baking-pan with the seasonings in which it has improved ; spread some butter on it, and bake in a rather quick oven; baste now and then, and turn over if necessary. When baked, serve with a *ravigote* sauce, to which you have added the gravy from the pan in which it has been baked. Serve it also with a cranberry, *piquante*, *Robert*, or *Tartar* sauce, or with currant-jelly.

In Civet.—Shoulder, neck, and breast-pieces are cut and prepared in civet, in the same way as a civet of rabbit.

It may also be kept three or four days and warmed in a *bain-marie ;* it improves it as much as that of rabbit.

With Mushrooms.—Any piece of venison, baked or roasted, may be served with a garniture of mushrooms.

Cutlets, broiled.—The cutlets are much better when improved as directed. The seasonings are spread all over. They are then wrapped up in buttered paper and broiled on a quick fire. They may also be larded with salt pork, and then broiled with or without being enveloped in paper. When broiled and dished, serve them warm with a *maître d'hôtel* or *ravigote* sauce.

Sautées.—Put six cutlets in a stewpan, larded or not,

with salt, pepper, eight small onions, two carrots, four sprigs of parsley, two of thyme, two cloves, a bay-leaf, a gill of broth, and same of water; set it on a good fire and boil gently till cooked. Dish the cutlets so that every small end or bone rests on the larger end of another, and serve with the sauce strained on them. If more sauce is desired, add to it any of the following: cranberry, *piquante*, *ravigote*, *Robert*, or *Tartar*.

Haunch, roasted.—After being improved, if liked, remove the thin skin around it and lard it with salt pork; it may be roasted without larding, but it is certainly an improvement, the meat being naturally dry. Place it on the spit before a brisk fire and near it; baste with melted butter first, and then with the drippings till done. If it is larded, it will require less butter. As soon as a kind of crust forms around the meat, remove it a little from the fire by degrees. Ascertain with a skewer or small knife when done. Venison is generally served rather underdone, when roasted or baked.

To make the dish more sightly, the skin and hair of the lower part of the leg, together with the hoof, are left untouched. To prevent them from burning while it is roasting, envelop these parts with a wet towel, which you cover with several sheets of buttered or oiled paper. It may be necessary to dip the towel in water two or three times during the process of roasting. When roasted, serve with any of the following sauces: cranberry, *piquante*, *poivrade*, *ravigote*, *Robert*, or *Tartar;* also with currant-jelly. If served with the gravy only, add water-cress and lemon-juice or vinegar.

Baked.—Prepare it as directed for roasting; then place it in a bakepan with a little cold water, just enough to cover the bottom of the pan; sprinkle salt and pepper all over, spread some butter on the upper side and put in a quick oven. Turn over and baste now and then till done. If the water is absorbed, add more. When baked, serve with the same sauces as if roasted, and also with currant-jelly and water-cress.

Saddle.—Roast or bake the saddle, and serve it as directed for a haunch, with the same sauces, and also with water-cress and currant-jelly.

Shoulder.—Cut the shoulder in fillets and lard them slightly. Put in a stewpan four ounces of butter and set it on a brisk fire; when hot, lay the fillets in, and when of a golden color add the seasonings in which you have improved the saddle, or the same ones if you have not done it; then subdue the fire, wet with a little warm broth, simmer till cooked, dish the fillets, strain the sauce on them, and serve. It may also be dressed entire, with the bones off; but it is more generally done in fillets. It is boned like a shoulder of mutton, and roasted or baked, and served like a haunch, with the same sauces and with currant-jelly or water-cress.

Stewed.—Cut the meat in square pieces, about two inches in size. Have in a stewpan, and on a good fire, a piece of butter the size of a duck's egg; when melted, sprinkle in, little by little, a tablespoonful of flour, stirring the while with a wooden spoon; when getting rather thick, add two ounces of bacon cut in dice, also half a pint of claret wine, same of warm water, salt, pepper, a pinch of allspice, two shallots chopped fine, or two green onions, four or five mushrooms, two cloves of garlic, and six onions; then lay the meat on the whole, and boil gently till cooked. Dish the meat, boil the sauce till of a brownish color, skim off the fat if there is too much of it, take out the cloves of garlic, turn the sauce on the meat, and serve hot.

With Truffles or Mushrooms.—Any part of venison, baked or roasted, may be served with a garniture of mushrooms, or one of truffles.

Cold.—When you have some left for the next day, warm it before serving it, if from a stew; but if from a roasted haunch, cut in slices and serve cold with a *vinaigrette.*

SNAILS.

A good many are now imported from Europe.

How to clean and prepare.—Throw them in boiling water, in which you have put some wood-ashes; leave them in till they have thrown their cover wide open, which will take about fifteen minutes; then take them off, pull them out of the shell by means of a fork, place them in lukewarm water, and leave two hours; next, rub them in your hands, and then soak in cold water; rub them again in your hands in cold water, two or three times, changing the water each time, so as to take away most of their sliminess. Wash the shells in lukewarm water with a scrubbing-brush, and drain them when clean.

Broiled.—Knead together and make a paste of a sufficient quantity of butter, parsley chopped fine, salt, pepper, and grated nutmeg; say about two ounces of butter, a tablespoonful of parsley, a saltspoonful of salt, a pinch of pepper, and the same of nutmeg (for two dozen). Put a piece of the above paste, the size of a kidney bean, in each shell, then the snails, and at the top again the same quantity of paste; lay them one by one close together, in a crockery or cast-iron kettle, the mouth of the snails up, and not one upon another; cover the kettle well; set it on a moderate fire, or in a moderately heated oven, and leave thus till cooked, which is easily seen by the parsley beginning to turn black, or as if fried. Lay them on a dish in the same order, and if there is any gravy in the kettle, put a part of it in each shell, and serve hot.

In eating them, be careful after having taken off the snail and eaten it, to turn down the shell, for there is some juice in the bottom of it which is delicious; the best way is to drink it as if from the bottom of a glass.

They can be broiled on a gridiron, but they are not as good as in a kettle; some of the juice is lost, and also the flavor.

Stewed.—Put in a stewpan four ounces of butter for fifty snails, and set it on a good fire; when melted, sprinkle in it a teaspoonful of flour, stirring a while; then add a teaspoonful of parsley chopped fine, two sprigs of thyme, a bay-leaf, a pint of white wine, and then the snails, which you have previously put back into their shells; cover the whole with warm broth, boil gently till the sauce is reduced and the snails are cooked, and serve them mouth upward, and filled with the sauce.

VEGETABLES.

Green vegetables must look fresh, and have nothing rotten about them.

To boil or blanch Green Vegetables.—Whatever they are, spinach, green peas, asparagus, etc., put some cold water and a little salt on the fire; clean the vegetable, wash it if necessary, then drop it in the water at the first boil; keep boiling for a time or till done; drain, and immediately drop it in cold water; drain again before using. It is impossible to tell how long it takes to boil; it depends entirely on the nature of the vegetable: for instance, spinach, as well as peas or any other vegetable, according to how tender it is, may take from three to twenty minutes to cook properly. Dry vegetables, such as beans, peas, lentils, etc., are washed or soaked in cold water, drained, and then set on the fire with cold water and no salt. Salt renders beans much harder and retards their cooking. Other vegetables that are neither green nor dry, such as carrots, turnips, etc., are generally set on the fire with cold water and salt. If prepared in other ways, it is explained in the receipts.

Potatoes are generally steamed; when they must be boiled, it is explained. We recommend to drop the green vegetables in the water at the first boil, because, in boiling, water evaporates its gases and alkali, and is therefore inferior for cooking purposes. Green vegetables are more acid here than in Europe, on account of the newness and richness of the soil; so is some fruit.

Artichokes.—The artichoke we refer to here is the plant somewhat resembling a thistle, having a large, scaly head, like the cone of the pine-tree; the lower part of the leaves composing the head, with the broad receptacle underneath, is the eatable part. It is a native of Sicily, and is an excellent and delicate vegetable. It grows well here, and the reason why it is not more generally known is because some persons who are used to live on coarse food have underrated it—their palates not being fit to appreciate its delicate flavor. We recommend gardeners and farmers to cultivate it; they will find a ready market.

How to eat them raw.—Quarter them, take off the outer leaves and choke, and serve with oil, vinegar, mustard, salt, and pepper.

How to cook.—Clean them and take off the outer leaves, throw them into boiling water, with parsley, salt, and pepper (they are cooked when the leaves come off easily), then take from the fire and drain, taking care to put them upside down.

The same, fried.—When cooked as above, cut the upper part of the leaves, and then cut them in eight pieces, take the choke off, dip each piece in a thin paste made of flour, sweet-oil, beaten egg, vinegar, salt, and pepper, and fry them with a little butter. Serve them with sprigs of fried parsley around.

The same, stewed.—When cooked as directed above, cut them in four pieces, and trim off the upper part of the leaves, take off the choke, and lay them in a stewpan; cover them with broth and set on a moderate fire; add then one ounce of butter for six artichokes, one sprig of parsley, and two mushrooms cut in slices ; boil ten minutes, take the parsley off, and serve the artichokes with the mushrooms around; pour the sauce on the whole.

In Vinaigrette.—Cook, and serve with a *vinaigrette.* The Jerusalem artichokes are dressed like potatoes.

Asparagus.—This is thought to be a native of Asia. The white asparagus sells dearer than the other kinds, but we cannot say that it is on account of its better quality, it is most likely for being more sightly when served. If it is kept for some time before boiling it, place the bunch in about half an inch deep of cold water, the top upward, and keep in a cool place. There are only four ways of preparing asparagus without changing or destroying the natural taste of the plant. The large ones, or what is called the first cut, is prepared in *vinaigrette,* *white sauce,* and *fried ;* the small one, or second cut, is cooked *en petits pois*—like green peas. It is better and has more taste when boiled rather underdone, that is, taken from the water when still firm ; if boiled till soft, it loses its taste and is not crisp.

To boil.—Cut off some of the white part, so as to have the whole of one length if possible ; then scrape the white end a little, soak in cold water for a few minutes, and drain. Tie it in small bunches of half a dozen or a dozen, according to size, and drop them in boiling water and a little salt, at the first boil of the water. Boil till rather underdone, take off, drain and drop in cold water immediately. Drain again, and it is ready to serve.

En Petits Pois.—Cut small asparagus in pieces about half an inch long, and blanch them for three minutes. Take off and drain ; then put them in a saucepan on the fire with two or three tablespoonfuls of broth, stir now and then for about two minutes, add a teaspoonful of flour; stir again, and as soon as mixed with the asparagus add also about one ounce of butter, salt, pepper, and chopped parsley, stir, and, when the butter is melted, serve.

Fried.—Blanch the asparagus two minutes, drain it; dip each in batter and fry in hot fat. Take off with a skimmer when done; and turn into a colander, salt it, and serve hot.

In Vinaigrette.—Boil it as directed. When cold, serve with a *vinaigrette*. (This is also called *à l'huile*.)

With White Sauce.—While it is boiling, make a white sauce; drain the asparagus and serve both, sauce and vegetable, warm. The asparagus is not dropped in cold water.

With Cream Sauce.—It is prepared and served as with a white sauce.

In Omelet.—Boil the asparagus as directed, and when cool cut it in small pieces about half an inch long, and when the omelet is ready to be folded in two, a little while before taking from the fire, place the asparagus in the middle, then fold and serve the omelet as if there were nothing in it.

Green or String Beans, Dwarf or Snap Beans, French Haricots, Pole Beans, Kidney Beans, etc.—*To prepare them when green and cooked with the pods.*—Remove the string or thread that is on both sides, by partly breaking one end of the pod and pulling lengthwise, repeat the same for the other side; cut them in pieces half an inch long, soak them in cold water, and throw them into boiling water with a little salt. Boil them till cooked, which you will know by pressing one between your fingers to see if tender; take them from the fire, throw them into cold water to cool, and drain them.

Au jus.—Cook a quart of beans. Put two ounces of butter in a stewpan and set it on the fire; when melted, put the beans in with a teaspoonful of chopped parsley; stir five minutes; then add a gill of broth, salt, and pepper; simmer twenty minutes, and, just on taking from the fire, mix in it two well-beaten yolks of eggs, with the juice of half a lemon, and serve.

Maître d'hôtel.—Put in a stewpan two ounces of butter, and set it on a good fire; when melted, put in it a quart of beans cooked in water, with a pinch of grated nutmeg, half a pint of milk, salt, pepper, and a teaspoonful of chopped parsley; keep stirring continually, boil ten minutes, take from the fire, mix in it two beaten yolks of eggs, and serve.

The same, with Onions.—Put two ounces of butter in a stewpan and set it on the fire; when hot, put in it two onions cut in slices, and fry them. Then add salt, pepper, a pinch of grated nutmeg, a saltspoonful of chopped parsley, and a quart of beans cooked in water; also half a pint of boiling water; boil ten minutes, stir with a wooden spoon, take from the fire, sprinkle in it a few drops of vinegar, and serve.

The same, in Salad.—Cook the beans in water, as directed above; then put a layer of them in a crockery vessel, the layer to be about one inch thick; then sprinkle on it salt and pepper; repeat the same process till all your beans are in; cover and leave thus three or four hours; then throw away the water, or drain if convenient; place the beans in a salad-dish, with the sweet-oil, vinegar, and parsley necessary; move like a salad, and serve cold.

Green, shelled, Lima, or other Beans.—Shell the beans, throw them in boiling water with a little salt, and when cooked drain them. Put two ounces of butter for a quart of beans in a saucepan, and when melted put the beans in with salt and pepper; toss gently now and then for three or four minutes, then add about a teaspoonful of vinegar, or the juice of half a lemon, and half a teaspoonful of parsley chopped. Mix and serve warm. They may also be prepared as string-beans, either *au jus*, in *maître d'hôtel*, or in *salad*.

Dry Beans, Lima, White or Colored.—Dry beans must be soaked in water for some time. Some require to be soaked twenty-four hours, others only five or six hours. Those that require to be soaked long are not from the last harvest, but have been kept for two or more years. If you are not sure that the beans (especially the white) are from this year's crop, soak them for twenty-four hours in cold water, and then drain them.

To boil.—Put the beans in a saucepan with cold water, and boil gently till tender. If the water boils away, fill up with cold water, but never put any salt to boil dry beans, it prevents them from cooking. As soon as boiled tender, drain them, and they are ready for use.

Au jus.—When boiled as above, set them on the fire in a stewpan with a few tablespoonfuls of gravy or broth, salt, and a little butter, stir for two or three minutes, then add a little chopped parsley, and serve warm.

Maître d'hôtel.—When boiled as above, drain and put them in a saucepan with about three ounces of butter for a quart of beans, stir now and then, and when the butter is melted, add salt, pepper, a teaspoonful of chopped parsley, and a few drops of vinegar; just mix and serve.

With Salt Pork.—Boil a quart of beans as directed above, and drain them. Cut in dice about half a pound of bacon and put it in a saucepan on the fire; when about half fried add the beans, mix and stir for one minute, then put in a warm oven for about twenty minutes, stirring occasionally; when done, sprinkle on it some parsley chopped fine, pepper and salt to taste, if not salt enough. There are several ways of preparing "pork and beans," but the one we give above is the most general in New England. The pork must neither be too fat nor too lean. It may be done also with ham and fresh pork.

With Mutton.—Boil as directed about three pints of white beans and drain them. When the leg of mutton is about half roasted, put the beans in the dripping-pan, and stir occasionally till the meat is done, and serve them with it. It makes a very nourishing dish, but it would be rather heavy for persons having sedentary avocations. Two quarts of beans would not be too much for a good-sized leg of mutton. It may also be prepared with any other piece of mutton; shoulder, saddle, etc.

Boiled with Mutton or Pork.—Prepare a quart of beans as directed, and then boil them ten minutes and drain them. Cut in rather large dice about two pounds of breast or neck of mutton or the same of pork, and of the same pieces, and put meat and beans in a stewpan, cover well with cold water; season with a bunch of seasonings composed of five or six sprigs of parsley, one of thyme, a bay-leaf, and two cloves, salt, pepper, a little nutmeg grated, a carrot cut in three or four pieces, two onions, and a piece of turnip. Boil gently till the whole is thoroughly cooked; remove the seasonings, and serve meat and beans together. This makes also a nourishing dish and not an expensive one. The nutritive qualities of beans are very well known, and very much exaggerated too. Even Professor Liebig once said that "four quarts of beans and two pounds of corned beef or pork boiled to rags, in fifty quarts of water, will furnish a good meal for forty men."

We must say that we have not been able to try the experiment, but we should like very much to see what kind and how much work forty men would do, and for how long, with such a diet. There are many things that look or seem well, and even magnificent in theory, though entirely impracticable. It sounds well, especially to those who do not understand the meaning of it, to say that we feed mostly on gluten, albumen, gelatine, etc., and that we require so many ounces of carbon, oxygen, etc., in twenty-four hours. Every thing that we eat may be, with the exception of salt, turned into charcoal; but no one has yet been known to feed on it.

Colored Beans, stewed.—Soak, boil five minutes, and drain a quart of beans. Put in a stewpan half a pound of bacon and set it on the fire; five minutes after, put the beans in, with four small onions, salt, and pepper, boil gently till cooked, and drain. Put two ounces of butter in a stewpan on the fire; when melted, sprinkle in it a teaspoonful of flour, same of chopped parsley, then the beans, without the bacon and onions; toss now and then for ten minutes, then add half a pint of claret wine, the same of the water in which they were cooked, boil gently twenty minutes; then put in it also the bacon and onions, boil five minutes longer, and serve the whole on the same dish.

Beets, stewed.—Clean and wash well, but do not skin them. Put in a crockery vessel a layer of rye straw, moisten it slightly, place the beets on it, cover the vessel, and place it in a slow oven for five or six hours; cool and skin them. When cooked, cut them in thin slices. Put butter in a stewpan, and when melted sprinkle in it a pinch of flour, a teaspoonful of chopped parsley, salt, and pepper, then the beets; simmer twenty minutes, add a few drops of vinegar, and serve.

Cabbages—to boil.—Take off the outer leaves, clean, cut in four pieces, free it from stump and stalk, and drop it in boiling water with a little salt and a piece of charcoal. Boil slowly till tender, and drain. Cabbage contains some sulphur, and evaporates an unpleasant odor while boiling, and especially while boiling fast. By putting a piece of charcoal in the pot, it does not smell as much.

With Bacon.—When boiled and drained, put the cabbage in a stewpan with bacon, sausage, and a piece of breast of mutton ; cover with cold water, season with three or four sprigs of parsley, a carrot, a clove, a little nutmeg, salt and pepper; boil till the whole is well cooked, remove the seasonings and drain ; dish the cabbage, put the meat on it, and serve warm.

With Milk, or à la Crème.—Boil and drain the cabbage as directed above. Put two ounces of butter in a saucepan, set it on a good fire, and when melted put the cabbage in with · salt and pepper. Sprinkle on it a teaspoonful of flour, add half a pint of cream or good milk; keep stirring with a wooden spoon during the whole process ; boil gently till the sauce is reduced, and serve warm.

Stewed.—Boil and drain two large heads of cabbage, and cut them very fine. Put about three ounces of butter in a saucepan on the fire, and when melted put the cabbage in and stir for five minutes ; then add salt, pepper, and a pinch of flour ; wet with a pint of broth, boil till cooked and the sauce reduced, then serve warm.

A l' Allemande.—Blanch for ten minutes some white or green cabbage and drain it. Put six ounces of salt pork, cut in dice, in a saucepan on the fire, and when partly fried put two or three small heads of cabbage in, stir, and when done, add a little gravy, and serve warm.

With Apples.—Blanch for about ten minutes a head

14

of cabbage and drain it. Put two or three ounces of butter in a saucepan on the fire, and put the cabbage in when the butter is melted with four or five apples peeled, quartered, and cored; also a little salt and a little sugar, about half a pint of water or broth, boil gently till done, and serve as warm as possible. Generally, cabbages are better when prepared at least one day in advance, and then warmed in a *bain-marie* before serving; a little butter may be added while it is warming. Any kind of cabbage is prepared as directed in the above ways.

Red Cabbage in Salad.—Take a hard head of red cabbage, and when all the outer leaves are removed, see if it is clean, but do not wash it; if a cabbage is not clean, do not use it for salad (as you want a hard one, and a hard one is always clean when the outer leaves are taken off). Then cut it in four pieces, trim off the stump and coarse ends of the leaves; cut it as thin as possible, as in making sour-krout, put it in a crockery vessel, with salt, vinegar, and pepper sprinkled on, cover and leave thus from four to six hours; then throw away the water or vinegar, dress as another salad, with oil and vinegar, and serve.

The same, stewed.—Blanch the cabbage for about ten minutes and drain it; then put it in a saucepan with about an ounce of butter and stir for five minutes, when add a little salt, a little sugar, a gill of claret wine, and same of broth or water. Boil gently till done, and serve.

Stuffed.—Remove the outer leaves of either a green, white, or red cabbage, see that it be clean, then put it in a bowl, and pour boiling water on it. Leave it so till the leaves are soft and pliable, when take off and drain. Cut off the stump carefully, place the cabbage on the table, the top upward, then open it gently by spreading the leaves all around without breaking them; then, commencing with the centre leaves, put some sausage-meat between the leaves, finishing with the outer ones and raising them; that is, bringing the cabbage to its original shape as much as possible, and then tie it all around with twine. Put in a saucepan large enough to hold the cabbage easily, but not too large, a little salt pork, cut in small dice, rind of salt pork and trimmings of butcher's-meat that you may have, but if none at all, put a little lean salt pork or bacon, and cut in dice also, half a carrot in slices, two onions in slices also, and then the cabbage on the whole. Half cover it with broth; water may be used instead of broth, but it makes a very inferior dish, while with broth it is unquestionably an excellent one for those who like cabbages. Simmer for two or three hours, according to the size of the cabbage. A piece of sausage may be placed on the cabbage also and cooked with it. Then dish the cabbage, remove the twine tying it; place the sausage around and also the salt pork if liked, strain the sauce on the whole, and serve warm. If the water or broth boils away while it is cooking, add more.

Sour-krout.—Soak in cold water for some time, changing the water three or four times; then put it in a stewpan with a pound of bacon, two ounces of sausages, and two ounces of lard to every quart of sour-krout, salt, and pepper; wet with broth, or with water, boil from five to six hours, and serve with the bacon and sausages on it. When cooked as above, but with water instead of broth, drain it well, put the bacon and sausages away in a warm place; then put the sour-krout in a stewpan with about one pint of white wine to a quart of sour-krout, set it on the fire and boil gently till the wine is nearly all absorbed or boiled away. Serve as above with the bacon and sausages on it. It is almost always prepared with wine in many parts of Germany.

Cardoons.—The white part only is good to eat. Clean well and scrape the sides; cut in pieces two inches and a half in length, and throw them in boiling water with a little salt; boil them till their sliminess comes off easily; then take from the fire, pour cold water in, and by means of a towel remove the sliminess; soak in cold water and drain them. Lay a few slices of bacon in a stewpan, place the cardoons on them, and again lay slices of bacon on; season with two onions, two sprigs of parsley, one of thyme, a bay-leaf, and a clove, salt, pepper, and the juice of half a lemon; cover with water and set on a good fire; boil till cooked; take from the fire and drain the cardoons only, throwing away the seasonings. Put the cardoons back in the stewpan, in which you have left the bacon; add two or three tablespoonfuls of broth, and two of Espagnole sauce; set on a slow fire, and simmer till the sauce is reduced to a proper thickness. Have at the same time in a pan on the fire a piece of ox-marrow, and when melted mix it with the sauce at the moment you take the cardoons from the fire, and serve hot either with or without the bacon.

Carrots—how to clean and prepare them.—Trim off all the small roots, wash them well, scrape them gently, taking care to scrape the skin only; then wash well, drain, and cut them either in slices a quarter of an inch thick, in fillets or strips, or with a vegetable spoon, according to fancy.

To boil.—When prepared, put them in a saucepan with a little salt, more cold water than is necessary to cover them, set on the fire, boil gently till tender, and drain. It is impossible to tell how long it takes, as it depends how young and tender they are.

In Béchamel.—Clean, cut, and boil about a quart of

carrots as directed and drain them. Mix well together in a saucepan, on the table, about two ounces of butter with a tablespoonful of flour, add about one pint of milk, set on the fire, stir slowly till it comes to a boil, when turn the carrots in, stir for about one minute, add also a little salt, same of sugar, two yolks of eggs; stir and mix well, give one boil, and serve warm.

A la Crème, or with Cream.—Proceed as for a *Béchamel* in every particular except that you use cream instead of milk.

In Poulette.—Proceed as in *Béchamel* with the exception that you use broth instead of milk, and add a little parsley, chopped fine, just before serving.

Fines Herbes.—Clean, cut, and boil as directed, about a quart of carrots. Set a saucepan on the fire with two ounces of butter in it, and when melted fry in it a piece of onion chopped fine. When the onion is fried add a pint of broth or water; boil about five minutes, put the carrots in with a teaspoonful of chopped parsley, give one boil, take from the fire, add a few drops of lemon-juice, and serve as warm as possible, with salt to taste.

Au jus.—Proceed as for *fines herbes*, except that you do not use onions, and put half a pint of broth or gravy.

Glazed.—Clean, cut with a vegetable spoon, and boil as directed, about a quart of carrots, and drain them. Put three ounces of butter in a frying-pan and set it on the fire. As soon as the butter is melted turn the carrots in, toss gently for five or six minutes, then add a little over a gill of rich gravy, sugar to taste, toss again now and then till the gravy is half boiled away, and use. Glazed carrots are seldom served alone, but most generally used as garnishing around a piece of meat.

Stewed.—Clean, and cut carrots in slices, and then

blanch them for about five minutes, and drain them. Set a stewpan on the fire with about two ounces of butter in it; as soon as melted put the carrots in with salt, pepper, a pinch of sugar, half a pint of broth; boil gently till cooked, take from the fire, add and mix with the carrots a little chopped parsley, and serve warm.

With Sugar.—Clean and slice about a quart of carrots, and blanch them for five minutes, and then drain them. Put two ounces of butter in a stewpan, and set it on a good fire, and when melted lay the carrots in with salt, pepper, a pinch of grated nutmeg, and about half a pint of broth; sprinkle in it, while stirring with a wooden spoon, about a teaspoonful of flour, and boil gently till cooked. Take from the fire, mix a good tablespoonful of sugar with two yolks of eggs, and those again with the rest, and serve.

Cauliflowers and Broccoli—how to prepare and cook them in water.—Clean and wash them well, throw into boiling water with a little salt and a little flour, boil till cooked, and drain them.

How to serve with Cheese.—Put them on a crockery dish when prepared; pour on a white sauce, in which you have mixed a little grated cheese; then dust the whole with fine bread-crumbs; after which you take a soft brush or a feather, which you dip in lukewarm butter, and put a thin coat of it all over the cauliflowers; then place the dish in a quick oven for ten minutes, and serve as they are, *i. e.*, in the dish in which they have been cooked. This is also called *au gratin.*

In Béchamel.—Boil the cauliflowers till done to your taste, drain immediately and place them on the dish, the top upward. While it is boiling make a *Béchamel* sauce and turn it over the cauliflowers as soon as dished, and serve as warm as possible. Cauliflower, like asparagus, has a better taste when rather underdone; it is more crisp.

Au Beurre Noir (with Brown Butter).—When boiled, drained, and dished, turn a brown butter over them, and serve warm.

With a Cream-Sauce.—Clean, prepare, boil, and drain the cauliflowers as directed above, then dish them also with the top upward. While they are boiling, make a cream-sauce and turn it over the cauliflowers as soon as they are dished, and serve warm. As they must be served warm, if the sauce is ready before the cauliflowers are cooked, keep it in a *bain-marie;* if the cauliflowers are cooked before the sauce is ready, keep them in a warm place.

With a White Sauce.—Proceed as with a cream-sauce in every particular, turning a white instead of a cream-sauce over them; serve warm.

Fried.—Clean, prepare, and boil them for about five minutes, that is, till they are about half cooked; then dip them in batter for frying vegetables, and fry them in hot fat. Take them off with a skimmer, turn them into a colander, sprinkle salt all over, and serve as hot as possible. They are excellent fried, but they must not be allowed to cool.

With a Tomato-Sauce.—Commence by making a tomato-sauce, as it requires longer than preparing the cauliflowers. When the sauce is nearly made, boil the cauliflower as directed, dish it, and then turn the sauce over it, and serve warm.

Au jus, or stewed.—Prepare, boil the cauliflowers till half done, and drain them. Place them carefully in a stewpan, the top upward, and set on the fire with a little fat. The fire must be rather slow. Stir gently and very carefully in order not to break them, and, about five minutes after they are on the fire, add half a gill of broth for a middling-sized cauliflower, salt, and pepper; simmer till done, stirring now and then during the process; dish them, turn the sauce all over, and serve warm.

In Salad.—When boiled and drained, leave them in the colander till perfectly cold, then put them in the salad-dish with salt, pepper, vinegar, and oil, move carefully in order not to break it, and serve. A salad of cauliflowers is not served as a salad of greens, but as an *entremet*, like other vegetables, and as if prepared in any other way. It is an excellent dish for breakfast.

Celery—stewed.—Cut off the green part or top of about half a dozen heads of celery; cleanse and trim them, but leave them whole. Set a saucepan of cold water and a little salt on the fire, and at the first boil drop the heads of celery in, boil till tender and drain. Put the celery back in the pan with about half a pint of broth; boil gently about five minutes, when add two or three tablespoonfuls of good meat-gravy, a teaspoonful of *meunière*, salt to taste, give one boil, and serve warm.

Fried.—Cut the celery in pieces about two inches long, wash, drain, and wipe dry. Dip them in batter for frying vegetables, drop in hot fat, and turn them into a colander when fried; sprinkle salt over, and serve hot. Soup or turnip-rooted celery, after being cleaned and properly scraped, is prepared like table celery as above, either stewed or fried.

Chiccory.—Chiccory, or succory, or endive, is generally prepared as a salad, if it be that with the broad leaves, or the curled endive.

Stewed.—Clean, wash, and drain it. Blanch it for about one minute, and drain again. Then put it in a stewpan with a little broth, and simmer till cooked; then add a little gravy, salt and pepper to taste, and serve. It makes a good *entremet*. The wild chiccory is prepared in the same way.

With Milk.—Remove the outer leaves and see that it is perfectly clean, cut in two or four, wash well in several waters, and throw into boiling water with a little salt; boil half an hour, take it out, throw into cold water, leave two minutes, and drain; press on it the drainer so as to extract all the water from it, after which chop it fine. Put about two ounces of butter in a stewpan; when melted, sprinkle in it a teaspoonful of flour, also salt and pepper; then put the endive in, say three or four heads, stir with a wooden spoon for ten minutes, after which time you beat two eggs with milk, and put them in the stewpan; keep stirring fifteen minutes longer, and serve.

Corn—sweet.—The simplest and best way is to boil it, and then eat it with butter, salt, and pepper. When boiled with any meat-soup, or with *pot-au-feu*, it is delicious to eat, and gives a good taste to the broth; it is also eaten with butter, salt, and pepper, as above.

Stewed.—Shell it and then drop it in boiling water and a little salt, boil till nearly done; then drain and put it back on the fire with a little broth; boil gently for about ten minutes, add a little gravy, salt and pepper to taste, and serve warm.

In Succotash.—This popular Indian dish, is very simply made by boiling corn and green Lima beans together, with salt and pepper. The two can be prepared together as stewed corn, but it makes a very inferior dish.

Cucumbers.—Peel them, split them in four, take the seeds out, cut in pieces about one inch long, throw them into boiling water, with a little salt; boil till cooked, drain,

14*

and put them on a towel so as to dry them well; then put
butter in a frying-pan, and set it on a good fire; when
hot, put in it some chopped parsley, salt, and pepper, two
minutes after put the cucumbers in it, fry a few minutes,
tossing them now and then, and serve.

The same, stewed.—Cook in boiling water, and dry
them as above; then put them in a stewpan with a little
butter kneaded with flour, add salt, pepper, and a pinch
of grated nutmeg; moisten with broth, simmer to reduce
the sauce; take from the fire, mix the yolks of two eggs
in the sauce; add to it a few drops of vinegar, and serve
them.

Stuffed.—Soak a piece of bread in cold water and
then squeeze the water out of it, the size to be according to
how many cucumbers are to be stuffed, or how large they
are. Split large cucumbers in two, lengthwise, remove
the seeds and some of the fleshy parts inside, by means
of a small iron spoon. Put a little butter in a saucepan
on the fire, and when melted fry in it a piece of chopped
onion. When the onion is fried, put in the pan what
you have removed from the inside of the cucumbers, and
which you have chopped a little, stir for about five minutes, and then add the soaked bread, stir and mix well
with the rest; add also salt, pepper, a little grated nutmeg and a little gravy; stir again for about one minute,
take from the fire; fill the cucumbers, that is, each half
with the mixture; place them in a pan, the mixture upward; dust with bread-crumbs, put a little butter on the
top of each, and bake. Before serving, a little gravy may
be sprinkled all over; serve warm.

In Hors-d'œuvre.—Peel the cucumbers, cut them in
slices slantwise, and salt them for two or three hours.
Drain them, and then season with oil, vinegar, pepper,
and parsley chopped fine.

Pickled cucumbers are served whole with small onions, also pickled, as a *hors-d'œuvre*.

Dandelion.—Dandelion is a very healthy greens in the spring, either cooked or raw. Clean and wash them well several times, as it nearly always contains fine sand between the leaves; leave them in cold water about two hours, and drain them; throw them into boiling water and salt; boil twenty minutes if young, and thirty minutes if full grown; then put them in a colander, press on them so as to extract all the water, after which chop them fine; put about two ounces of butter in a stewpan, for two quarts, and set it on a quick fire; when melted, sprinkle in it a teaspoonful of flour, salt and pepper, then put the dandelion in, stir for ten minutes, after which wet it with broth; keep stirring for about fifteen minutes longer, and serve.

Egg-Plant—broiled.—Split the egg-plant in two lengthwise, peel it and remove the seed. Put it in a crockery vessel and sprinkle salt on it; leave it thus nearly an hour, then take it off, dip it in egg beaten with salt, pepper, and chopped parsley, then boil it; serve with a *maître d'hôtel* sauce.

Fried.—Peel and cut in slices, lay the slices in a vessel, sprinkling salt over every layer, and leave thus half an hour and drain. Dip the slices in batter for frying vegetables, drop them in hot fat, and turn them into a colander when fried; sprinkle salt all over, and serve.

Sauté.—Put the slices with salt half an hour in a vessel as directed in the above. Drain them, and then fry them on both sides with a little butter in a frying-pan. Serve warm, with salt and pepper to taste.

Stuffed.—Proceed as for stuffed cucumbers in every particular.

Hominy.—Hominy is prepared in different ways, some make it in cakes, others like mush. The following is, however, the general way of preparing it: boil it for about three hours with water or milk, also butter, salt, and pepper; then mix with it some well-beaten eggs, fry or broil, or even cook it in an oven, and serve for breakfast.

Leeks.—Clean, wash, and drain; throw them in boiling water with a little salt, boil fifteen minutes, and drain; press on them in the drainer, so as to extract all the water, then chop them fine. Put two ounces of butter in a stewpan; when melted, sprinkle in it a teaspoonful of flour, salt, and pepper, then add the leeks. Stir with a wooden spoon for ten minutes; after that beat two eggs with milk, and put them in a stewpan; keep stirring fifteen minutes longer, and serve.

Lentils.—This excellent vegetable, much superior to beans or peas, is not generally known. Most of what we have here comes from Germany; a little comes from France and Switzerland. Many persons think them much dearer than beans or peas, not knowing that they swell three or four times their size when soaked in water before cooking them. They are prepared like dry beans in every way. A *purée* of lentils is excellent with almost every kind of meat, and it also makes a good potage. It has all the nutritive qualities of the bean.

Lettuce.—Cos lettuce, cabbage lettuce, butter lettuce, curled Silesia, white or green lettuce, etc. Besides being served as salad, all the above, when properly dressed, make an excellent *entremet.*

To prepare.—Take off the outer leaves, that is, all those that are too green or too hard, then clean and wash well, but without cutting it off, or without detaching the leaves. To stew lettuce, select hard heads, so that they can be cleansed without detaching the leaves. When cleaned, drop the heads in boiling water and a little salt, boil about five or ten minutes, according to how tender the lettuce is, and drain dry.

Stewed.—When cleaned and prepared, sprinkle on the top of each, salt, pepper, and a little grated nutmeg; then tie each head with a string. Place in a stewpan two or three slices of bacon, put the heads of lettuce in, season with two sprigs of parsley, one of thyme, a bay-leaf, and a clove, also salt and pepper; cover with water, and simmer about two hours in an oven; then take them from the pan, drain, pressing on them to extract all the water, and put them on a dish, the top upward. Have butter in a stewpan, and on a good fire; when melted, sprinkle in it a teaspoonful of flour, stirring with a wooden spoon; subdue the fire, add a little milk, and stir and simmer ten minutes longer; take from the fire, mix in the beaten yolks of two eggs, pour it on the lettuce, which you have kept warm, and serve.

Another way.—When prepared, chop it fine. Put in a stewpan, for four heads of lettuce, three ounces of butter, and set it on the fire; when melted, put the lettuce in with a little chopped chervil, stir now and then till cooked; then sprinkle in it a pinch of flour, wet with broth, boil ten minutes longer, keeping it stirred, and serve. (For a salad of lettuce, see SALAD.)

Stuffed.—Proceed as for a stuffed cabbage.

Mushrooms.—Preserved mushrooms are used for sauces only. The first thing to consider very attentively in mushrooms is, not to eat any that you do not know to be good to eat. There are so many kinds of good and bad ones, that it is necessary to be very careful about even the edible ones, or the ones known as such when young;

it is better and safer never to use them when old; they are considered old when the comb underneath is black before picking, while when young it is of a pink color.

How to clean and prepare them.—Cut off the lower part of the stem; skin them with a steel knife, commencing at the edge and finishing at the top; cut in pieces, put them in cold water, to which you have added a few drops of vinegar; leave them in it two hours, moving them occasionally; then wash well in two or three waters, and drain.

When cleaned and prepared thus, they are ready to be used in sauces, or to cook.

Broiled.—If you have large mushrooms, clean and prepare as above, except that you do not cut them; but when drained, put them upside down on a greased gridiron, and on a moderate fire; place a little butter around the stem upon the comb, and when done place them on a dish which you have warmed in advance, and in the same position they had on the gridiron; put again around the stem some butter kneaded with a little chopped parsley, salt, and pepper, and serve. They must be served warm.

As an ornament, you may make, with common white note-paper, as many little square boxes as you have mushrooms to broil; grease them with butter, put the mushrooms in, set them on the gridiron, and on a moderate fire, and serve them in the boxes when done.

The same, stewed.—When cleaned and prepared as directed, and drained, throw a quart of them in boiling water, to which you have added a few drops of vinegar; boil five minutes, take them out, put them in cold water to cool, drain and dry them in a towel. Put two ounces of butter in a stewpan and set it on a good fire; when melted, sprinkle in it a pinch of flour, add also a sprig of parsley, two small onions, a little piece of carrot, a bay-leaf, salt, and pepper, cover with broth, and boil till the onions are cooked; then take from the pan onions, parsley, and bay-leaf, and put the mushrooms in instead; boil slowly about twenty minutes, take from the fire, add to the sauce the yolks of two eggs well beaten with a few drops of vinegar, and serve warm.

Mushroom Catsup.—Clean and wash them well, stems and all; cut them in two or four pieces; then place the pieces in a crockery vessel, sprinkling salt on every layer of mushrooms, and leave thus twenty-four hours. Take them out and press them well, so as to take all the juice out, which you bottle at once, and cork. Put the mushrooms back in the vessel, and twenty-four hours after press them again; and again put the juice in bottles, and the mushrooms in the vessel, and repeat this process again after another twenty-four hours. Then mix well together the juice of the three pressings; add to it pepper, allspice, one clove (or more, according to the quantity) broken in pieces; boil the whole, skim off the scum as long as you see any on the surface, and strain. Bottle when cool; put in each bottle two cloves and a pepper-corn, cork air-tight, put in a cool and dry place, and it will keep for years.

Dried.—Dried mushrooms are imported from Italy, they come cheaper than the preserved ones in cans, and are as good for brown sauces. Soak them in water over night; drain them, and they are ready for use.

Onions à la Crème.—(*With Cream.*)—Only small white onions are prepared *à la crème.* Have water and a little salt on the fire, and drop two dozen small white onions into it at the first boil. When cooked, drain, and wipe them dry carefully, in order not to bruise them. Set a saucepan on the fire with about two ounces of butter in it, and when melted put the onions in, stirring gently for two or three minutes, then turn about a gill of cream in, little by little, stirring the while, and as soon as the whole is in take from the fire, salt to taste, and serve hot.

Glazed.—Peel a dozen of middling-sized onions and put them in a saucepan with four ounces of butter, and set them on a slow fire; stir occasionally till they are about three-quarters done, when add about two ounces of powdered sugar, stir now and then and finish the cooking. When done and well browned all around, add one or two tablespoonfuls of good meat-gravy, keep a few minutes on a rather brisk fire in order to reduce the sauce, but keep stirring and use. Onions prepared that way are excellent, and generally used to decorate meat.

Stewed.—Clean a quart of small onions, throw them in boiling water, add two sprigs of parsley, one of thyme, a clove, a bay-leaf, a little piece of nutmeg, a clove of garlic, salt, and pepper; boil twenty minutes, drain the onions only, and throw away the seasonings. Put two ounces of butter in a stewpan on a good fire, and when melted sprinkle in it a teaspoonful of flour; then add the onions, cover with half broth and half white wine, boil gently till well cooked and the sauce reduced, serve warm. It is a very wholesome dish.

Parsnips.—*Sautées.*—Scrape, wash, drain, and put about two quarts of parsnips in a saucepan with cold water and a little salt, set on the fire and boil till done, then drain. Cut the parsnips in slices, put two ounces of butter in a frying-pan, and when melted put the sliced turnips in, toss gently till they are of a fine golden color, then add salt and pepper to taste, turn over a dish, sprinkle chopped parsley all over, and serve warm.

Stewed.—Scrape, clean, wash, boil, and drain as above directed, about two quarts of parsnips. Put them immediately into a stewpan with salt, pepper, and broth enough to about half cover them, boil gently for fifteen minutes, and serve the whole as it is. They may also be prepared in *poulette*, the same as turnips.

Peas with Bacon.—Put in a stewpan on the fire four ounces of bacon cut in dice (for one quart of peas), and toss and fry it for about five minutes, then add the peas after having blanched them from five to ten minutes, according to how tender they are; stir for two minutes and add half a pint of broth or water, also a bunch of seasonings composed of two or three sprigs of parsley, half a one of thyme, and a piece of bay-leaf; stir again and mix, and then add also two or three small onions, salt, and pepper; boil half an hour, remove the seasonings, and serve peas and salt pork. A small sausage may be added for those who like the taste of it.

Plain boiled.—Put a saucepan on the fire with water and salt in it, and at the first boil drop two quarts of peas in it; boil gently till done, and then drain. As soon as they are in the colander, just toss them a little, turn them over a dish, and put four ounces of butter on the top, salt, and pepper, then place the dish in the oven with the door open, that is, just to keep them warm and allow the butter to melt, stir for one or two minutes, and serve warm.

With Lettuce.—Blanch a quart of peas for about five minutes, and drain them. Blanch a head of lettuce for one minute. Put peas and lettuce in a saucepan with one ounce of butter, stir gently on the fire for about one minute, and then add a little broth or water, two or three sprigs of parsley, salt, and pepper; boil slowly till done, and serve warm. The parsley may be served, or removed just before serving, according to taste. The lettuce is always served with the peas.

Au jus.—Boil the peas as directed for *plain boiled*, then put them back on the fire with a little butter, stir for one minute, add about three tablespoonfuls of gravy to a quart of peas, salt and pepper, give one boil, and serve.

With Ham.—Blanch two quarts of peas and drain them. Put them in a saucepan with half a pound of ham, cut in dice, half cover them with water, and boil gently till done. If the water boils away, add a little more; serve warm.

Canned peas are prepared in the same way as above.

A l'Anglaise.—If the peas are fresh, blanch them; if they are preserved, drain them only. Put the peas in a saucepan with about one ounce of butter for a pint, set on the fire, stir gently till thoroughly warm, add chopped parsley and a yolk of egg, and serve.

Au Sucre (with Sugar).—Set the peas on the fire, the same as above, add about one ounce of sugar, stir also till warm; take from the fire, stir a yolk of egg in, and serve.

Dry Peas and Split Peas.—Dry and split peas are prepared and served in the same and every way like dry *beans*, with the exception that they require to be soaked only for a few hours before cooking them.

Potatoes.—*To select.*—As a general rule, the smaller the eye the better the potatoes. By cutting off a piece from the larger end you ascertain if they are sound; they must be white, reddish, bluish, etc., according to the species. If spotted, they are not sound, and therefore very inferior. There are several kinds, and all of them are good when sound or coming from a proper soil. Use the kind you prefer, or those that are better fit for the way they are intended to be served. To mash or to make a *purée*, etc., every kind is good. To serve whole or in dice, or in pieces like carpels of oranges, those called *Mercers* and the like, are preferable, because they do not bruise so easily.

To boil.—Being naturally watery, potatoes should never be cooked by boiling except when wanted very white, as for *croquettes*. When boiled whole, put them of an even size as much as possible, in order to cook them evenly. They are better, more mealy, when steamed or baked, but those who have no steamer must, of course, boil them. Cover them with cold water, set on the fire and boil till done, then pour off all the water, put the pan back on a slow fire for five minutes and well covered; then use the potatoes.

To steam.—Place them above a kettle of boiling water, in a kind of drainer made for that purpose, and adapted to the kettle. The drainer must be covered tight. They cook as fast as by boiling, the degree of heat being the same. When steamed the skin is very easily removed.

To prepare.—If they are to be boiled, or steamed, or baked, it is only necessary to wash them. If wanted peeled, as for frying, etc., then commence by cutting off the germs or eyes; if young and tender, take the skin off with a scrubbing-brush and drop immediately in cold water to keep them white; if old, scrape the skin off with a knife, for the part immediately under the skin contains more nutriment than the middle, and drop in cold water also. If wanted cut, either in dice, or like carpels of oranges, or any other way, cut them above a bowl of cold water, so that they drop into it, for if kept exposed to the air they turn reddish and lose their nutritive qualities.

A l'Allemande.—Steam, peel, and slice the potatoes. Cut some bread in thin slices, and fry bread and potatoes with a little butter and turn the whole in a bowl, dust well with sugar, pour a little milk all over and bake for about fifteen minutes; serve warm.

A l'Anglaise.—Steam or boil about a quart of potatoes and then peel and slice them. Put two ounces of butter in a frying-pan on the fire, and put the potatoes in when melted, toss them for about ten minutes, add salt, pepper, a little grated nutmeg, and serve hot.

A la barigoule.—Peel some potatoes and cook them whole in broth; when done take them off carefully, so as not to break or bruise them, and drain. Have some oil in a frying-pan and on a quick fire, and when hot lay the potatoes in; move gently to fry them all around, and then dish them, sprinkling salt, pepper, and vinegar, all over; serve warm.

Béchamel.—Steam or boil and peel some potatoes, then slice them and place on a dish; have a *Béchamel* sauce ready, turn it over the potatoes, and serve warm.

Broiled.—Steam, peel and slice the potatoes. Lay the slices on a gridiron, and place it over a rather slow fire; have melted butter, and spread some over the slices of potatoes with a brush; as soon as the under part is broiled, turn each slice over and spread butter over the other side. When done, dish, salt, and serve them hot. A little butter may be added when dished, according to taste.

A la Parisienne.—Chop an onion fine and partly fry it with butter, then put in it some potatoes cut in dice, add a little water or broth, salt, and pepper; boil gently till done, take from the fire, add chopped parsley, and serve.

Fried.—To be fried, the potatoes are cut either with a

vegetable spoon, in fillets, in slices, with a scalloped knife, or with an ordinary one, or cut in pieces like carpels of oranges, or even in dice. When cut, drain and wipe them dry. This must be done quickly, so as not to allow the potatoes to turn reddish. Have a coarse towel ready, then turn the potatoes into a colander, and immediately turn them in the towel, shake them a little, and quickly drop them in hot fat. (*See* FRYING.) When done, turn them into a colander, sprinkle salt on them, and serve hot. Bear in mind that fried potatoes must be eaten as hot as possible. Fry only one size at a time, as it takes three times as long to fry them when cut in pieces as when sliced or cut in fillets.

To fry them light, or swelled.—When fried, turn into the colander, and have the fat over a brisk fire; leave the potatoes in the colander only about half a minute, then put them back in the very hot fat, stir for about one minute and put them again in the colander, salt them, and serve hot. If the fat is very hot, when dropped into it for the second time they will certainly swell; there is no other way known to do it. It is as easily done as it is simple. Potatoes cut in fillets and fried are sometimes called *à la Parisienne;* when cut in slices or with a vegetable spoon, they are called *à la française.*

Potatoes cut with a vegetable spoon and fried, make a good as well as a sightly decoration for a dish of meat or of fish. They may be fried in oil also, but it is more expensive than in fat. They may be fried in butter also, but it is still more expensive than oil, and is not better than fat; no matter what kind of fat is used, be it lard, beef suet, or skimmings of sauces and gravy, it cannot be tasted.

Hollandaise.—Steam or boil the potatoes, and then

peel and mash them. Season them with a teaspoonful of chopped parsley, salt, and pepper, add also two tablespoonfuls of gravy to a quart of potatoes, then make small balls about the size of a walnut, round or of an olive-shape, dip them in beaten egg, roll in bread-crumbs, and fry in hot fat. Serve hot.

Another.—Proceed as for the above one in every particular, except that you use milk or cream instead of broth, and sugar instead of salt and pepper.

Lyonnaise.—Potatoes *Lyonnaise* are prepared according to taste, that is, as much onion as liked is used, either in slices or chopped. If you have not any cold potatoes, steam or boil some, let them cool, and peel and slice them. For about a quart of potatoes, put two ounces of butter in a frying-pan on the fire, and when melted put as much onion as you please, either sliced or chopped, into the pan, and fry it till about half done, when add the potatoes and again two ounces of butter; salt, pepper, and stir and toss gently till the potatoes are all fried of a fine, light-brown color. It may require more butter, as no vegetable absorbs more than potatoes. It makes an excellent dish for those who do not object to the taste of the onion (the onion can be tasted, not being boiled or kept long enough on the fire to evaporate). Serve warm. Oil may be used instead of butter.

Maître d'Hôtel.—Steam or boil about a quart of potatoes, and then peel and cut them in slices. Put one ounce and a half of butter in a saucepan on the fire, and when melted add a small tablespoonful of flour; stir, and when turning yellow add also about a quart of milk, salt to taste, give one boil and take from the fire. Then add the potatoes, put back on a slow fire, stir for ten minutes, mix in the whole a teaspoonful of parsley chopped fine, also a yolk or two of eggs, and serve warm.

Another Maître d'Hôtel.—Take two quarts of potatoes, prepare and cook them by steam, peel carefully, and cut them in thick slices; place them on a dish and keep warm. Put four ounces of butter in a stewpan and set it on a slow fire; add, when melted, a teaspoonful of chopped parsley, the juice of half a lemon, salt, pepper, and a pinch of allspice, stir ten minutes; afterward, put for five minutes on a quick fire, keep stirring, then pour on the potatoes, and serve.

Mashed.—Peel and quarter about three pints of potatoes as directed; put them in a saucepan with more water than is necessary to cover them, and a little salt; set on the fire and boil gently till done, drain, put them back in the saucepan, mash them well and mix them with two ounces of butter, two yolks of eggs, salt, pepper, and milk enough to make them of a proper thickness. Set on the fire for two or three minutes, stirring the while, and serve warm. When on the dish, smooth them with the back of a knife or scallop them, according to fancy.

Mashed and baked.—Put two ounces of butter in a stewpan and set it on the fire; when hot, add a teaspoonful of parsley chopped fine, and a little salt; five minutes after, put in it a quart of potatoes, prepared, cooked, peeled, and mashed, as directed; then pour on the whole, little by little, stirring continually with a wooden spoon, a pint of good milk; and when the whole is well mixed, and becoming rather thick, take from the fire, place on the dish, then set in a brisk oven for five minutes, and serve.

Polonaise.—Wash well about two quarts of potatoes, put them in a saucepan and cover with cold water, season with salt, half a dozen whole peppers, a bay-leaf, a sprig of thyme, and two or three onions in slices; boil gently till done, and drain. Peel the potatoes, cut them in two, dish and turn a *caper* sauce over them. Serve warm.

Provençale.—Peel and quarter about three pints of potatoes as directed. Put in a saucepan about a gill of oil with the potatoes, salt, pepper, a pinch of nutmeg, six sprigs of parsley, two cloves of garlic, and half the rind of a lemon; the three latter spices well chopped; set on a good fire, stir now and then till cooked, dish the whole, sprinkle the juice of one or two lemons on, and serve warm.

Another way.—Put in a stewpan three tablespoonfuls of sweet-oil, a teaspoonful of chopped parsley, two cloves of garlic chopped very fine, a pinch of grated nutmeg, the juice of half a lemon, salt, and pepper; set on a good fire, and when hot put in it a quart of potatoes prepared and cooked by steam, and cut in thick slices; subdue the fire, simmer about ten minutes, and serve.

Sautées.—Take a quart of young and tender potatoes, peel them with a brush, and cut in slices. Put two ounces of butter in a frying-pan on a quick fire; when hot, put the potatoes in, and fry them till of a golden color; place them on a dish without any butter, sprinkle chopped parsley and salt on, and serve. They may also be served without parsley, according to taste.

Soufflées.—Steam a quart of potatoes, then peel and mash them in a saucepan and mix an ounce of butter with them; set on the fire, pour into it, little by little, stirring the while, about half a pint of milk, stir a little longer after the milk is in and until they are turning rather thick; dish the potatoes, smooth or scallop them with the back of a knife, and put them in a quick oven till of a proper color, and serve.

Another way.—Steam three pints of potatoes and peel

and mash them in a saucepan, then mix with them four ounces of butter, salt to taste, half a pint of milk, and eight yolks of eggs; set on the fire for two minutes, stirring the while, and take off. Beat six whites of eggs to a stiff froth, and mix them gently with the rest. Place the mixture on a dish, smooth with the back of a knife or scallop them, according to fancy, and put in a quick oven. As soon as the top gets a little dry, which will be in two or three minutes after being in the oven, take them off and quickly spread some melted butter all over, by means of a brush, and put back in the oven for two or three minutes longer, when take off again, spread butter over the same as the first time, etc. Repeat the same process two or three times, and serve warm.

Stuffed.—Steam two or three potatoes and peel and mash them in a bowl, then chop fine a small green onion or two shallots with two ounces of fat salt pork and six or eight sprigs of parsley; mix the whole with the potatoes; add also and mix with the rest about two ounces of butter, and salt and pepper to taste. If the potatoes are not warm enough to melt the butter while mixing, it should be melted first. Clean and wash well six potatoes of an even size and split them in two lengthwise; then with a small iron spoon remove the middle part of each half, so as to leave only a thickness of about one-eighth of an inch. You have then a kind of shell, which you fill with the prepared mixture above, filling more than full, so that the top is convex, and which you smooth with the back of a knife. When the twelve halves are thus prepared, butter the bottom of a bakepan, lay the potatoes in with the mixture upward, and put in a warm oven. Take from the oven when about half done, and spread some melted

15

butter all over by means of a brush; put back in the oven, finish the baking, and serve warm.

In Cakes.—Prepare and cook by steam a quart and a half of potatoes, peel and mash them; mix with them the yolks of five eggs, half a lemon-rind grated, and four ounces of fine white sugar. Put four ounces of butter in a stew-pan and set it on the fire; when melted, put the mixture in, stirring with a wooden spoon continually; as soon as it is in the stewpan, add the whites of the five eggs, well beaten; leave on the fire only the time necessary to mix the whole well together, and take off; when nearly cold, add, if handy, and while stirring, a few drops of orange-flower water; it gives a very good flavor; then put the whole in a tin mould greased a little with butter; place in a quick oven for about thirty-five minutes, and serve.

In Croquettes.—Peel, quarter, and boil about a quart of potatoes as directed. Mash them in a saucepan and mix them with four yolks of eggs, two ounces of butter, salt, and about half a gill of milk; set on the fire, stir for about two minutes, take off, spread on a dish and leave thus for two or three hours, and even over night when for breakfast. When left over night, they may be rather too dry to work them; then mix with a few drops of milk. No matter how long they have been left on the dish, it is necessary to mix them, that is, to mix the top, which is the driest part, with the rest. Dust the paste-board slightly with bread-crumbs, put the potatoes on it, in parts of about a tablespoonful each; then, with the hands and a knife, shape them according to fancy, either round, flat, or oval, etc. When shaped round they look like a piece of sausage about two inches and a half long. If wished flat, when shaped round, just flatten them a little with the blade of a knife. Then dip each part in beaten egg, roll in bread-crumbs, and fry in hot fat. (*See* FRYING.) Take them off the fat when done, turn them into a colander, and immediately dish, and serve them as warm as possible. Potato *croquettes* are sometimes called potato-balls. When the *croquettes* are shaped flat, they are also called "*à la duchesse.*"

Another Duchesse.—When the potatoes are ready to be spread on the dish to cool, put them in the pastry-bag and squeeze them out of it like lady's fingers, bake, and serve warm. It makes a sightly dish.

In Matelote.—Prepare and cook a quart and a half of potatoes, and peel and cut them in thick slices. Put in a stewpan a piece of butter the size of an egg, and set it on the fire; when melted, sprinkle in it a teaspoonful of flour, also the same of chopped parsley, salt, and pepper, then the potatoes, wet with half a pint of claret wine, same of broth; boil gently till the sauce is reduced, and serve.

With Butter, or English Fashion.—Put water on the fire with considerable salt in it; at the first boil, drop a quart of washed potatoes in and boil till done, when take off, peel, and put them whole in a saucepan, with butter, salt, pepper, and a little nutmeg; set on a rather slow fire, stirring gently now and then till they have absorbed all the butter. Serve warm. They absorb a great deal of butter.

With Bacon or Salt Pork.—Peel and quarter about a quart of potatoes. Set a saucepan on the fire with about four ounces of fat salt pork cut in dice in it. When fried put the potatoes in. Season with a bunch of seasonings composed of two sprigs of parsley, one of thyme, and a bay-leaf; salt and pepper to taste, and about half a pint of broth or water. Boil gently till cooked, remove the bunch of seasonings; skim off the fat if any, and serve warm. It is served at breakfast, as well as *entremets* for dinner.

With Cream or Milk.—Peel and mash a quart of potatoes, when prepared and cooked. Put two ounces of butter in a stewpan and set it on a good fire; when melted, sprinkle in it a teaspoonful of flour, same of chopped parsley, a pinch of grated nutmeg, and salt; stir with a wooden spoon five minutes; then add the potatoes, and half a pint of milk or cream; keep stirring ten minutes longer, take from the fire, sprinkle in them half a tablespoonful of sugar, and serve as warm as possible.

With White Sauce.—Clean, wash, and throw a quart of potatoes in boiling water, with a sprig of thyme, two onions, a bay-leaf, two sprigs of sweet basil, two cloves, salt, and pepper; when cooked, take the potatoes out carefully, peel and cut them in two, place them on a warm dish, pour on them a white sauce, and serve warm.

Sweet Potatoes.—They are prepared in the same and every way like the others above.

Pumpkins and Squashes.—Peel, take out the seed, cut in pieces, and throw them in boiling water with a little salt; drain when cooked and mash through a colander, put butter in a stewpan on the fire, when melted, add chopped parsley, salt, pepper, and the pumpkin or squash, and simmer ten minutes; after which pour in it half a pint of milk, little by little, stirring the while; leave ten minutes longer on the fire, and take off; mix well in it two or three yolks of eggs, and serve warm. The quantity of milk, butter, eggs, etc., to be according to the quantity of squash.

Purslain.—Clean, wash well, and drop it in boiling water with a little salt, boil till cooked, take off and drain. Put butter in a stewpan on the fire, and when melted lay the purslain in, stir a little and sprinkle on it, little by little, a pinch of flour; season with salt, pepper, and chopped parsley, stir and simmer about ten minutes, take from the fire, mix in it one or two beaten eggs, and serve. Purslain is much more used in Europe than here; there it is cultivated as other vegetables, but it does not grow as well as here.

Rhubarb.—Scrape and cut it in pieces about one inch long, and then blanch it for two minutes. Put it in a saucepan with two or three tablespoonfuls of cold water and set it on a rather sharp fire, toss or stir now and then till done, when sweeten to taste, dish, let cool, and serve. Rhubarb is very wholesome, and ought to be partaken of at least every other day. When prepared as above, it may be used to make pies.

Radishes.—The cuts below are turnip-rooted red radishes, cut with a small knife, put in cold water for about an hour, and served with butter, as a *hors-d'œuvre.* Ro

move the outer leaves, leaving only four or five of the small centre ones, cut off the root close to the radish, and wash clean in cold water. Take the radish with the left hand holding it by the centre leaves, cut the skin from the top downward to near the leaves, in several parts, but without detaching it, and as seen in the cuts above; do the same carefully with the body of the radish, and it will look more like a rose than like a radish. After having prepared two or three, it will be comparatively easy. The centre leaves must be eaten, as well as the body of the radish; they contain a substance that helps the digestion of the radish itself.

Salsify, or Oyster-Plant.—Scrape them, and throw one by one as they are scraped into cold water, with a few drops of vinegar; when they are all scraped, move them a little, take out of the water, and throw them in boiling water with a little salt, boil till tender, and drain; place them warm on a warm dish, and serve with brown butter, a *maître d'hôtel*, or white sauce.

Fried.—When boiled as above, drain them. Then dip each in batter for frying vegetables, drop them in hot fat, and take them off with a skimmer when done, turn into a colander, salt them, and serve hot.

In Béchamel.—While the salsify is boiling as directed above, make a *Béchamel* sauce; drain the salsify when done, and turn it into the *Béchamel* sauce as soon as the latter is finished; keep on the fire for about two minutes, stirring the while, and serve warm. They are prepared and served in the same way with the following sauces: *cream, poulette,* and *white.*

Skirret.—Prepare, cook, and serve in every way like parsnips.

Sorrel.—Sorrel is found in a wild state nearly everywhere; that is, where green plants vegetate. It is an excellent vegetable, good to eat all the year round, but especially in the spring and summer. It is very healthful, containing the pure oxalic acid as it is formed by Nature. Sorrel is the greatest neutralizer of acrid substances. A few leaves chewed, take away from the teeth that disagreeable feeling left after having eaten a tart apple or other tart, unripe fruit. Cultivated in a rich soil, the leaves grow nearly as large as those of the rhubarb. It is cut to the ground several times during the spring and summer.

To boil.—Take a peck of sorrel, separate the stalk from the eatable part, by taking hold of it with one hand and tearing off the rest with the other, so that only the stalk and fibres attached to it will remain after the tearing, and which you throw away. Wash it well, drain and set it on the fire in a saucepan with two tablespoonfuls of water; stir occasionally, and when nearly done, take off, mash through a colander, and it is ready for use.

Au jus.—Put a piece of butter the size of an egg in a saucepan, set it on the fire, and when melted, put the sorrel in after being boiled and mashed as above, stir half a minute, add a tablespoonful of flour; stir another half minute, add also half a gill of gravy, same of broth, salt, stir two minutes, and serve. Hard-boiled eggs, split in four pieces, lengthwise, may be placed around the dish, if the sorrel is served as an *entremets.*

To preserve for Winter Use.—When boiled and mashed as above, put it in stone or glass jars; when cold, turn melted butter or lard over it; cover as tightly as possible with paper, and when perfectly cold, put away in a dark, dry, and rather cool place, and it will keep very well during the whole winter. The best time to preserve it is at the beginning of November, just before the cold weather sets in.

Purée of.—When prepared as for *au jus,* but without gravy, it is a *purée.*

Spinach—to boil.—When cleaned and washed, throw it in boiling water at the first boiling, with a pinch of salt, and boil till done. It will take from one to ten minutes to boil, according to how tender it is. Turn into a colander; press on it to force the water out, put on the paste-board and chop it fine.

Au jus.—When chopped, set the spinach on the fire in a saucepan with a little broth, two or three tablespoonfuls for a small measure; stir, add as much gravy, an ounce of butter, a teaspoonful of flour, salt, stir two minutes, and serve.

Au jus in Winter.—When prepared as above, put it away in a bowl in a cool place, for one day; then set it back on the fire in a pan, add a little butter and a little broth, stir and just warm it, when put away again; repeat this for four or five days in succession, and you certainly will have an excellent dish. Some hard-boiled eggs cut in four pieces, lengthwise, may be placed around the spinach when dished, also some *croutons.* Spinach is generally served on a flat dish, and scolloped all around with a knife.

With Sugar.—Proceed as for spinach *au jus* in every particular, except that you put very little salt, and one or two teaspoonfuls of sugar, according to taste. Lady-fingers or pieces of sponge-cake may be placed all around the dish.

A la Crème.—Boil and chop the spinach as directed. Set it on the fire in a saucepan, stir till perfectly dry, but not burnt; add two ounces of butter, and stir again for five or six minutes; then add about two tablespoonfuls of cream to a small measure of spinach; stir again five minutes, take from the fire; add again one ounce of butter, stir two minutes, and serve with hard-boiled eggs or *croutons,* or both. Milk may be used instead of cream when the latter cannot be had, but it is inferior in taste.

With Anchovy.—Proceed as for the above, using a tablespoonful of essence of anchovy instead of cream.

Spinach au Beurre, or à l'anglaise.—Boil and chop the spinach as directed. Put it in a saucepan with butter; set on the fire, stir till the butter is melted and mixed with the spinach, salt to taste, and serve.

Sprouts.—Boil, prepare, and serve sprouts the same as spinach.

Tomatoes are, like sorrel and rhubarb, very healthful.

To blanch.—After they are washed, throw boiling water over them, and then take off and remove the skin.

Stewed, to serve with Meat or Fish.—When blanched as above, put the tomatoes in a stewpan with butter, salt, and pepper, set on the fire and simmer for about forty-five minutes; serve warm all around the fish or piece of meat. Tomatoes may be eaten raw, with or without salt; in no matter what way they are partaken of, they are not yet known to have indisposed anybody. Although great quantities are consumed in this and other countries, still many more ought to be used; they are so easily preserved, that every family ought to have a large provision of them for the winter and spring consumption.

Stuffed.—Soak in cold water one-fourth of a ten-cent loaf of bread, etc.; when perfectly soaked, squeeze it with the hands. Take six tomatoes, as much of an even size as possible, cut the top off; that is, the side opposite the stem, and with a small spoon take out the inside and put it in a bowl, and then turn into a colander to let the liquid part run off. Put about an ounce of butter in a saucepan, and when melted add a small onion chopped; stir, and when nearly fried add also the part of the tomatoes in the colander also chopped; stir half a minute; put in the soaked bread, stir and mix; then salt, pepper,

15*

and grated nutmeg; give one boil more, and take from the fire. Fill the tomatoes with this mixture, dust with bread-crumbs, put a piece of butter the size of a hazel-nut on each, and bake. Just before serving, wet with a little tomato-sauce, broth, or gravy.

Turnips—to boil.—Clean, scrape, and wash well, then put them in a saucepan, either whole or in slices, or cut with a fruit-corer or with a vegetable spoon, add cold water enough to boil them in, a little salt, set on the fire and boil gently till tender; then take off, drain, drop in cold water, drain again, and use.

In Béchamel.—While the turnips are boiling as described above, make a *Béchamel* sauce and turn the turnips in as soon as made; boil gently about two minutes, stirring the while, and serve warm. Do exactly the same with a cream or white sauce.

Au jus.—Boil and drain them as directed above, then put them in a saucepan with a little gravy, set on the fire, stir now and then for about ten minutes, add a teaspoonful of *meunière*, stir again for two or three minutes, and serve warm.

With Sugar.—Cut with a fruit-corer or with a vegetable spoon about a pint of turnips, and boil them till under done, then drain. Put the turnips in a saucepan with two or three tablespoonfuls of broth, set on a good fire, toss occasionally for about ten minutes, then add two or three tablespoonfuls of sugar, toss again now and then for ten minutes longer, and serve. It may take a little longer or less time than described above, according to the state of the turnips; if young and very tender, keep on the fire five instead of ten minutes, and if old, it may take fifteen minutes

Glazed.—Cut the turnips with a vegetable spoon, boil

them for five minutes, and drain them. Put half a gill
of broth in a saucepan with about one pint of turnips and
set on a good fire; toss and stir now and then till done,
and till the broth is all boiled away. If it boils away
before the turnips are cooked, add more and finish the
cooking. When done, sprinkle about three ounces of
sugar on them, stir for about one minute, dish the turnips,
dredge powdered sugar all over, put in the oven two minutes, and serve.

Water-cress.—This contains much sulphur, and is the
greatest anti-scorbutic known. Besides being eaten with
salt or in salad, it may also be stewed in the following
way: Take only the top and the leaves around the stalk;
clean and wash it well; throw it in boiling water with a
little salt, and when cooked drain it well, so as to extract
all the water from it. Put a piece of butter the size of an
egg in a stewpan; when melted, put the cress in, sprinkle
on it a tablespoonful of flour (for three quarts); stir continually with a spoon, boil ten minutes, then add salt, pepper, a little grated nutmeg, and half a pint of broth; boil
ten minutes longer, and serve either alone, or with hard-
boiled eggs on it; cut the eggs in two or four pieces.

Salads.—Salads are seasoned with oil, vinegar, salt,
and pepper, and sometimes with mustard also. The best
oil is that made of olives, but much is sold for olive-oil
which contains more lard than oil. It is impossible to tell
which is pure by the color. Pure olive-oil is of a pale-
yellow-greenish color. It is very easy to tell the pure oil
by tasting, but of course it is necessary to know the real
taste of good oil.

The best vinegar is wine-vinegar, with *tarragon* in it
(*vinaigre à l'estragon*), but it is expensive. Next to it is
cider-vinegar. Beer makes good vinegar, but inferior to

that made with cider. Pyrolignic vinegar is very unhealthy. No one can be too careful in selecting vinegar.
The superiority of the French mustard comes from the
compounds used, and not from the way it is made, as
thought by many. In the French mustard, besides *vinaigre
à l'estragon*, there is white wine, and more sweet-oil than
in any other kind. A good deal of mustard is made here,
and often sold as French, after being carefully labelled.

Salad is made with every species of lettuce; chicory,
cultivated and wild; cabbages, red and white; cauliflowers,
celery, dandelion, corn-salad, purslain, water-cress, etc. If
it were possible to clean the salad by merely wiping the
leaves with a towel, it would be better than washing; but
it must be washed if there is any earth or sand on it. The
salad should be made by an experienced person, who can
judge at a glance what quantity of salt, pepper, oil, and
vinegar is necessary. The quantities cannot be given, as
that depends on the quantity of salad. Chopped parsley
and chives are served on a small plate at the same time
with the salad, as many persons like those spices.

Celery.—When the celery is washed and cleaned, wipe
it dry, cut the white or eatable part (the top or green part
is used for soup) in pieces about one inch long, put them
in the salad-dish with salt, vinegar, and mustard, stir a
little, leave thus about one hour, then add pepper and oil,
move again, and serve.

Lettuce.—Lettuce, and especially Cos or Roman lettuce, must be handled very gingerly, in order not to wilt
the leaves while cleaning and washing. When the head
of the lettuce, especially of Roman lettuce, is hard, it is
not necessary to wash it at all, as when the outer leaves
are taken off, the rest is perfectly clean. Never use the
knife, but break the leaves; put them in the salad-dish;

spread all over the dish, according to taste and fancy, the blossoms and petals (not the leaves) of any or all of the following plants: burnet, wild chiccory, rose (any kind), pink, sage, lady's-slipper, marsh-mallow, nasturtium, periwinkle. Thus decorated, the salad is put on the table at the setting of it, and made when the time for eating it comes. Of these decorative flowers, the handiest are the rose and pink, as at every season of the year they are easily obtained. In spring and summer most of the others can also be had easily.

The salad, thus decorated, is placed on the table at the same time with the soup. It is made while the roast-piece is carved or eaten; the petals of flowers or blossoms are not removed, and, of course, are eaten with the lettuce. The salad is seasoned with salt, pepper, vinegar, and oil. The proportions are two tablespoonfuls of oil to one of vinegar for a salad for three, four, or five persons. It is generally moved round in the dish, so as to impregnate every leaf with the seasoning. It is served immediately after the roast-piece.

Cream may be used instead of oil.

Turnip-rooted Celery (called also Soup Celery).—Clean, wash well, and scrape it carefully; cut it in thin slices, place it in the salad-dish, sprinkle salt, pepper, vinegar, and mustard on it, mix well the whole together, and leave thus from four to six hours. Then throw away the vinegar, or most of it; add very little salt and vinegar, oil, and move well. Serve as above, that is, immediately after the roast-piece of the dinner.

A salad with cabbage, chiccory, corn-salad, or any kind of greens, after being properly cleaned, washed, wiped dry, and cut in pieces if necessary, is made and served exactly like a salad of lettuce described above.

Nasturtium.—This is said to be a native of Mexico; it makes a good salad in summer-time. Make and serve like a salad of lettuce.

Chervil and Sorrel.—In Italy, Spain, and the south of France, they make salad with these two vegetables, half of each, prepared and served like lettuce.

Some persons like a thick sauce with salad; it is made thus: Put a hard-boiled yolk of egg in a bowl, mash it, and then mix with it salt and a tablespoonful of vinegar; when these three are thoroughly mixed, add pepper and oil (about two tablespoonfuls of oil), little by little, stirring and mixing well the while; turn the mixture over the salad, and move as directed above. The mixture may be prepared in the salad-dish, and the salad put in afterward.

Mustard should never be used with lettuce; it is too strong to be eaten with such tender vegetables.

Of Salsify.—In the spring, when the top of the salsify has grown for one or two weeks only, and immediately after the frost is out of the ground, cut it off, split it in four, wash it well, drain it dry, and prepare as a salad of lettuce. The root is prepared as described for salsify, and is never made in salad.

Of Cucumbers.—Peel and slice them, then put them in a vessel, salt every layer, and leave thus in a cool place about one hour, drain them dry and then dress them with oil, vinegar, salt, and pepper; slices of onion may be added, if liked.

Of Beans.—Boil the beans in water with a little salt, drain them dry, and then dress them with parsley chopped fine, salt, pepper, oil, and vinegar.

Of Beets.—Boil the beets in water only till done, and when cool, peel and slice them, and prepare them with pepper, salt, vinegar, and oil. The beets may be baked.

Of Eggs.—Slice hard-boiled eggs, and dress them with chopped parsley, salt, pepper, vinegar, and oil.

Of Lentils.—Proceed as for beans in every particular.

Of Onions.—Bake the onions, then peel and slice them, and dress them with mustard, salt, pepper, vinegar, and oil.

Of Tomatoes.—Wash, wipe dry, and slice the tomatoes; slice also onions and mix with them, the quantity to be according to taste; then season with salt, pepper, oil, and vinegar.

Of Walnuts.—The European walnut only can be used, and as soon as good to eat; that is, before the outer shell dries and opens. Break the nuts in two, take out the kernels with a pointed knife, and place them in a salad-dish, with some juice of grapes not yet ripe; add salt and pepper, leave thus two or three hours, moving now and then, and serve. The edible part will be found very good eaten that way. To persons who have never eaten any, it may appear a strange dish, but let them try it.

Of Potatoes.—A potato-salad is the one that requires the most seasonings, especially oil and vinegar. They are better served warm than cold, although many prefer them in the latter state. When steamed, peeled, and sliced, put them in the salad-dish, with salt, pepper, vinegar, oil, and parsley, to taste. Mix the whole gently and well, and serve. If served very warm, butter may be used instead of oil.

Another.—Add to the above a few anchovies, or slices of pickled cucumbers, or capers, or pickled beets.

Another.—Add to the first some slices of truffles, previously soaked in Madeira wine for ten hours, and also a little of the wine.

Another.—Put a hard-boiled yolk of egg in the salad-dish, with two tablespoonfuls of oil, and mix well so as to make a paste of them; then add two anchovies, a piece of tunny the size of a nutmeg, and half a dozen sprigs of chervil, the whole chopped fine; mix again with the rest; add also a chopped pickled cucumber, mustard to taste, vinegar, and then the slices of potatoes (warm or cold), slices of truffles previously soaked in Madeira wine, a little of the wine also, salt, and pepper; stir and mix again well, and serve.

Apricots, Oranges, Peaches, Pears, Strawberries, Raspberries, Blackberries, Currants, and like Berries, in Salad. —Dust the bottom of a dish with white sugar, put a layer of slices of apricots, oranges, peaches, or pears, or a layer of the others entire, and dust again; repeat the same till the whole is in, then add over the whole a pinch of grated nutmeg, with French brandy or rum to suit your taste, and serve as a dessert.

Cocoa-nut.—Peel it carefully and soak it in brandy for twenty-four hours. A little sugar may be added; serve as a dessert.

Salad Macédoine.—This salad ought to be called "compound salad," as it is made of a little of every thing that can be served in salad, *i. e.*, fish, meat, green and dry vegetables, &c. When the whole is mixed, you add chopped parsley, sweet-oil, vinegar, salt, and pepper; you shake it till your arms are sore, and you have a salad *Macédoine.* Every one should try it; serve as an *entremets.*

Salmon and Turbot.—Cut in slices, place them in a salad-dish, with hard-boiled eggs cut in two, or with some lettuce, and serve as a *hors-d'œuvre,* with salt, pepper, oil, and vinegar.

Of Pineapple.—Proceed as for that of apricots, etc., in every particular.

Of Anchovy.—Clean and bone the anchovies, and then place them in the middle of a dish; chop fine some hard-boiled yolks of eggs and put a string of it around the anchovies; do the same with the whites, and then put a string of chopped parsley around the whites; season with oil and very little vinegar. Serve as a *hors-d'œuvre*.

Pickles and Preserves.—To pickle the fruit, it must be pickled before commencing to ripen, and be sound; the same for vegetables. When the fruit or vegetable is clean, and cut in pieces, if necessary, such as cabbage, have water on the fire, and drop it in at the first boil. If the fruit or vegetable is desired white, add to the water lemon or unripe grape juice. It is necessary to be very careful in blanching, for, if too much blanched or cooked, it will be soft and tasteless; if not enough, it will ferment. As a general rule, it is cooked as soon as it floats, but it can be ascertained by running a skewer or a small knife through it. By putting some fresh spinach-leaves or fresh grape-vine-leaves on the top of the fruit or vegetable, it will keep it more green than without. When blanched, take from the fire and drain. Drop it immediately in cold water, and drain again. When dry, put the fruit or vegetable in jars, cover it with boiling vinegar; season with peppers, pepper-corns, cloves, and tarragon, also some rock-salt. When perfectly cold, seal the jars air-tight, and keep in a dark, cool, and dry closet. Every kind of fruit or vegetables can be pickled in the same way; the only difference is in the time of blanching or cooking, which is according to the nature of the fruit: *apples, string-beans, beets, cabbages, cauliflowers, cherries, cucumbers, lemons, melons, mushrooms, onions, peaches, pears, plums, pumpkins, quinces, radishes, walnuts,* etc., may also be preserved in salt and water, and in the following way: When cooked as above, put them in jars and cover them with very salt water. Seal when cool, and then put the jars in a boiler full of cold water, with straw or rags to prevent breaking them; set on the fire, boil from twenty to thirty minutes, take from the fire, let cool; then take the jars from the water and put away as the above.

Peas and *mushrooms* are almost always preserved in water and salt.

Asparagus is also preserved, but it is so difficult to succeed, that even manufacturers of preserves have given it up.

Tomatoes.—Wash them and then bruise them in a boiler; set on the fire, boil half an hour, and strain, to secure all the juice. Put the juice on the fire, boil till reduced about one-half, let cool, put in jars, seal them, put them in a boiler of cold water, with straw or rags to prevent breakage; set the boiler on the fire, boil twenty minutes, take off, let cool. When perfectly cold, take the jars off, place in a cool, dark cellar, and we warrant that they keep for years. No salt or seasonings of any kind are used to preserve them. When you wish to use them, season to taste.

Tomato Catsup.—To make catsup with the above sauce, you have only to add to it, when in jars, peppers, pimento, cloves, etc.; but it is really not necessary, being too strong for this climate.

Another way.—Take good and well-ripened tomatoes, clean and wash them well, put them in a stewpan and set it on a moderate fire for a while; take from the fire, throw away the water coming from them, and then strain them into a vessel. Put what there is in the vessel back on the fire, and in the same stewpan, and let it reduce about one-half; take from the fire, pour in a crockery pot, and leave thus twenty-four hours; then put in bottles, cork well, and place them in a cold and dry place.

Cucumbers.—The small green ones are the best. Clean them well in cold water with a brush, removing the prickles. Put cold water in a vessel with rock-salt in it, and shake it to dissolve the salt; soak the cucumbers in it for about three days. Take them out and immediately put them in pots or jars with small onions, a few cloves of garlic, pepper-corns, rock-salt, cloves, and a bunch of seasonings composed of bay-leaves, tarragon, and burnet; cover them with boiling vinegar (turn the vinegar on them as soon as it boils), cover the pots or jars air-tight when perfectly cold. Look at the cucumbers every two or three days for the first three weeks, and after that only once in a while. According to the quality of the vinegar or of the cucumber itself, the whole may turn white after a while; in that case throw away vinegar and spices, put new spices in, the same spices as above, except the onions, which you keep with the cucumbers; cover again with boiling vinegar, and cover when cold as before. If they have not been kept too long in that state before changing the vinegar, they will be just as good as if they had not turned white.

EGGS, MACARONI, AND RICE.

EGGS are fit to eat as soon as laid, and the sooner they are used the better. You ascertain if they are fresh with an oonoscope, or by holding them before a light and looking through. There are several ways to preserve eggs, but to do which they must be fresh; as soon as perfectly cold after being laid, they may be preserved. Dissolve gum in water to the consistency of thin mucilage, and with a brush give a coat of it to the eggs; lay them in a box of charcoal dust and keep them in a dry, dark, and cool place. When wanted, they are soaked in cold water for a few minutes, and washed. They are also preserved in hydrate of lime. When boiled hard, let them cool and place them in a dry, cool, and dark place; they will keep for weeks. If wanted warm after that, put them in cold water, set on the fire, and take off when the water is warm.

With Mushrooms.—Cut in strips or fillets four mushrooms, one onion, one clove of garlic, and fry them with two ounces of butter, then add a tablespoonful of flour, stir for about one minute, add also half a pint of broth, same of white wine, boil gently till reduced about one-half, when put in the pan eight or ten hard-boiled eggs cut in dice, or cut the whites only in dice and put in the yolk whole, boil one minute and serve. It makes an excellent dish for breakfast.

With Cheese and Parsley.—Put about two ounces of butter in a saucepan on the fire, and when melted fry in it a tablespoonful of parsley, chopped fine; then add a pinch of nutmeg, salt, pepper, about four ounces of pineapple or Gruyère cheese, grated, and a gill of white wine; stir till the cheese is melted, when you add eight or ten eggs, one after another, stirring the whole time and mixing them with the cheese; serve when done. More cheese may be used, according to taste.

In Fricassée.—Put about half a pound of stale bread with one pint of milk in a saucepan on the fire and boil for two or three minutes, then mash well so as to mix the two together, put back on the fire, stir continually till it makes a rather thin paste, then take off, mix with it six or eight eggs, grated cheese to taste, salt and pepper, put back on the fire, stir, and serve when cooked. Lemon-juice may be sprinkled on just before serving.

A la Lyonnaise.—Chop fine two white onions and fry them with two ounces of butter, then add salt, a pinch of nutmeg, half a pint of broth; boil gently and stir now and then till it turns rather thick, when you add also eight whites of eggs, chopped; give one boil, and serve. Place the eight yolks, whole, all around, and between and alternately a small cake *feuilleté,* and serve warm.

A la Béchamel.—Slice the eggs or cut them in four pieces lengthwise, put them in *Béchamel* sauce, set on a slow fire for two minutes, and serve warm.

Fines Herbes.—Mix well together in a saucepan, and cold, two ounces of butter with a tablespoonful of flour; set on the fire, stir, and when melted thoroughly, add a teaspoonful of parsley and one of chives, chopped fine, salt, pepper, and about a gill of white wine; stir, and boil gently for about five minutes; and turn over hard-boiled eggs in a dish; serve warm. The eggs are served whole, shelled, but not cut.

Piquante-Sauce.—Dish hard-boiled eggs as for *fines herbes*, and turn over them a *piquante* sauce; serve warm. They may be served in the same way with any other sauce.

Stuffed, or à l'Aurore.—Cut six hard-boiled eggs in two lengthwise; take the yolks off the whites; chop them fine with six or eight sprigs of parsley, put both eggs and parsley in a bowl; add salt, pepper, a little nutmeg grated, a piece of the soft part of bread soaked in milk and squeezed, three ounces of butter, mix the whole well. Then with the mixture fill the whites, that is, the place where the yolks were; fill a little more than full, so that all the mixture will go into and upon the twelve halves. Lay in a saucepan a *purée* of spinach or of sorrel, or of any other vegetable, according to taste; lay the halves of eggs on it, the mixture upward; put for ten minutes in the oven, and serve warm.

In Boxes.—Fold note-paper so as to make a kind of square box without a cover; put half an ounce of butter in it with a pinch of chopped parsley; lay it on a gridiron and on a slow fire, break an egg in it, and when nearly done add salt and bread-crumbs, to taste; serve warm when done.

With Cheese.—Prepare as the above; add grated cheese at the same time you add salt and bread-crumbs; finish the cooking, and serve warm.

Au Gratin.—Chop fine six or eight sprigs of parsley, a shallot if handy, or a small onion, half an ounce of the soft part of bread, an anchovy, and then mix the whole well with two ounces of butter; mix again with two yolks of eggs, place the mixture in a tin dish, place on a slow fire, and when getting rather dry break half a dozen eggs over it, dust with bread-crumbs, season with salt and pepper, and when nearly done spread two yolks of eggs beaten, with a teaspoonful of water over the whole, and serve warm.

With Ham.—Prepare as scrambled eggs with the exception that you put in the pan, at the same time you put in the eggs, four ounces of boiled ham cut in dice. Serve the same.

With Milk, Water, or Cream.—These three names are wrongly applied to eggs in many cook-books; they are creams, and not eggs.

Ham and Eggs.—There are several ways of preparing this good dish; the ham may be raw or boiled; in slices or in dice; mixed with the eggs, or merely served under. Fry the ham slightly, dish it and then turn fried eggs over it; or fry both at the same time, the eggs being whole or scrambled, according to taste.

With Asparagus.—Cut in pieces, about a quarter of an inch long, a gill of the tender part of asparagus, throw it in boiling water with a little salt; boil as directed, and drain. Beat eight eggs just enough to mix the yolks with the whites; put them in a stewpan, season with a pinch of grated nutmeg, salt, and pepper; add also a tablespoonful of warm water, set on a slow fire, stir till they are becoming thick; then add four ounces of butter, stir five minutes longer; add the gill of asparagus; simmer about five minutes longer, and serve.

Boiled.—(*See* EGGS IN THE SHELL.)—Put the eggs in boiling water with a little salt, as near as possible at the first boiling; leave from five to ten minutes; take out and put them immediately in cold water; then shell them without breaking them, and use.

With Brown Butter.—Break gently in a plate or dish, and without breaking the yolks, eight eggs; sprinkle salt and pepper on them. Put two ounces of butter in a frying-pan, and on a good fire; when turning brown subdue the fire. Put also, and at the same time, the same quantity of butter in another frying-pan, and on a good fire, and when hot, place the eggs in without breaking the yolks; then spread over the eggs the brown butter you have in the other; take from the fire when you see the whites becoming hard; put them on a dish, pour on them a tablespoonful of vinegar which you have warmed in the pan after having used the brown butter, and serve.

Fried.—Put half a pound of lard in a frying-pan, and on a good fire; when hot, break gently, one by one (being careful not to break the yolk), the quantity of eggs you can put in the pan without allowing them to adhere together; turn them upside down once with a spoon or skimmer; take from the pan with a skimmer as soon as the white part becomes hard, and serve with fried parsley around.

Scrambled, or Mashed.—Beat six eggs just enough to mix the whites and yolks together; put two ounces of butter in a stewpan, and set on the fire; when melted, take from the fire, add salt, pepper, and a pinch of grated nutmeg, then the eggs, also a tablespoonful of broth; put back on a very slow fire, stir continually till cooked, and serve warm.

Sur le Plat.—Butter the bottom of a crockery or tin dish with two ounces of butter; break into the dish and over the butter, gently and without breaking the yolks, six eggs; sprinkle salt, pepper, and grated nutmeg all over, put the dish on a slow fire, or on warm cinders, and when the white is hard, serve. They must be served in the dish in which they are cooked.

In the Shell.—Bear in mind that some eggs cook quicker than others. Put eggs in boiling water for two minutes, if liked soft or underdone; and three minutes, if liked more done. They are generally served enveloped in a napkin.

In Matelote.—Put a bottle of claret wine in a stewpan and set it on a good fire; add to it two sprigs of parsley, one of thyme, a clove of garlic, a middling-sized onion, a clove, a bay-leaf, salt, and pepper; boil fifteen minutes; then take all the seasonings out and have your wine boiling gently; break one egg in by letting it fall gently in order to have it entire, and then take it out immediately with a skimmer, and place it on a dish; do the same with eight eggs; keep them in a warm (but not hot) place. After which put in the wine, without taking it from the fire, four ounces of butter kneaded with a tablespoonful of flour; boil till reduced to a proper thickness, pour it on the eggs, and serve.

With Onions.—Cut in dice three middling-sized onions and put them in a saucepan with four ounces of butter; set it on a moderate fire and stir now and then till the onions are turning yellow, then sprinkle on them a teaspoonful of flour, salt, and pepper; add a pint of warm water and boil gently till rather thick, but not too much so. Put into the saucepan half a dozen hard-boiled eggs cut in four pieces each, lengthwise, boil gently two or three minutes longer, and serve warm.

With Green Peas.—Proceed as for eggs with asparagus, except that you boil a gill of peas instead of asparagus; prepare and serve in the same way.

With Cauliflowers.—Blanch the cauliflowers and proceed as for the above. Eggs are prepared as above, with celery, lettuce, etc.

16

A la Tripe.—Proceed exactly the same as for eggs with onions, except that you use milk or broth instead of water.

A la Neige, or Floating Island.—Beat four (or more) whites of eggs to a stiff froth. Put in a tin saucepan one pint of milk and one ounce of sugar, set on the fire, and as soon as it rises put lumps of the whites into it with a skimmer, turn the lumps over after having been in about half a minute, leave them in another half minute, take them off with a skimmer also, place them on a sieve to allow the milk that may be around the lumps to drop. Put in a tin saucepan four yolks of eggs, two ounces of sugar, and mix well; add the milk that has been used to cook the whites, after having strained it, and mix again. Set on the fire, stir, give one boil, take off, add a few drops of essence to flavor; turn into a dish; place the lumps of whites gently on the liquor and they will float; and serve cold. If the liquor is desired thicker, use only half of the milk.

To poach Eggs.—Set cold water on the fire in a frying-pan, with salt and vinegar in it, a tablespoonful of vinegar to a quart of water. As soon as it boils, break a fresh egg in the water or in a small plate, and slide it gently into the water. Then with a skimmer turn the white gently and by degrees over the yolk, so as to envelop the latter in the former, giving the eggs an elongated shape. They may be poached hard or soft—hard when the yolk is cooked hard; soft when the yolk is still in a soft state.

Fondue of Eggs.—Beat well six eggs, and put them in a stewpan with two ounces of *Gruyère*, well grated, and about one ounce of butter; set on a brisk fire, and leave till it becomes rather thick, stirring all the time with a wooden spoon; take from the fire, add pepper, and stir a little; turn over on a warm dish, and serve. This is a very favorite dish in Italy, and also in Switzerland, where it originated.

To beat Whites of Eggs.—Have a convenient basin; break the eggs gently; allow the whites to fall in the basin and retain the yolks in the shell. This is very easily done by breaking the shell about the middle, opening slowly so as to let the white fall, and at the same time retain the yolk in one of the halves of the shell; if some white remains, turn the yolk from one half into the other, and *vice versa*, till the whole of it has fallen. Then add a very small pinch of salt to prevent the curdling of the eggs; commence by beating slowly; beat faster and faster, till they form a stiff froth. They are well beaten when, placing a twenty-five and a ten-cent silver piece on the top, they are firm enough to bear them. If the pieces sink, beat again. Always beat eggs in a cool place, they will rise better and faster. (*See* EGG-BEATER.)

Basin.—Pay no attention to the old prejudice and belief that metal is not good to beat eggs in. The best and easiest for family use, in which one as well as a dozen whites of eggs can be easily whisked, is of block-tin, and can be made by any tinsmith. It has the shape of an ordinary goblet or tumbler if the foot is cut off, the bottom being round. Size: six inches deep from the centre of the bottom to the top; eight inches in diameter at the top, and only six inches in diameter where the bottom commences (or five inches from the top); the basin being broader at the top than at the bottom, and the bottom being one inch deeper in the centre than on the sides.

Omelets—how to beat the Eggs.—Break in a bowl the quantity of eggs you want, or as many as there are persons at the table; beat them well with salt and pepper, by means of a fork. A little grated nutmeg may be added, if liked. The adding of milk to the eggs makes the omelet soft.

To make it.—Always have a brisk fire to make an omelet; the quicker it is made the better, and the less butter it requires. If possible, have a frying-pan to make omelets only in; keep it in a clean place and never wash it if you can help it; by warming it a little before making the omelets and wiping it with a coarse towel, you can keep it as clean as can be without washing. To wash it causes the omelet to adhere to it while cooking, and injures its appearance. Commence by beating the eggs, then put the butter in the frying-pan, about two ounces for eight eggs; set on the fire and toss gently to melt the butter as evenly and as quickly as possible, else some of it will get black before the whole is melted. As soon as melted, turn the beaten eggs in, and stir and move continually with a fork or knife, so as to cook the whole as nearly as possible at the same time. If some part of the omelet sticks to the pan, add a little butter, and raise that part with a knife so as to allow the butter to run under it, and prevent it from sticking again. It must be done quickly, and without taking the pan from the fire. When cooked according to taste, soft or hard, fold, dish, and serve warm.

It is *folded* in this way: run the knife or fork under one part of the omelet, on the side nearest to the handle of the pan, and turn that part over the other part of the omelet, so as to double it or nearly so; then have an oval dish in your left hand, take hold of the frying-pan with the right hand, the thumb upward instead of the fingers, as is generally the case in taking hold of a pan, incline the dish by raising the left side, place the edge of the pan (the one opposite to the handle) on the edge of the dish, turn it upside down—and you have the omelet on the dish, doubled up and sightly. Cooks do not succeed in turning out a decent omelet generally, because they cook it too much, turn it upside down in the pan, or because they do not know how to handle the pan.

In holding the pan as it is generally and naturally held, that is, with the palm of the hand resting on the upper side of the handle, it is impossible for anybody, cook or other, to dish the omelet properly without extraordinary efforts; while by resting the thumb on the upper part of the handle, the fingers under it, the little finger being the nearest to the pan, it is only necessary to move the right hand from right to left, describing a circle and twisting the wrist, so that, when the pan is turned upside down, the fingers are up instead of downward, as they were when taking hold of the pan.

An omelet is called soft if, when you commence to fold, only about two-thirds of the eggs are solidified; and hard, when nearly the whole of the eggs are solidified. With a good fire it takes only about four minutes to make an omelet.

By following our directions carefully, it will be very easy to make an omelet, and make it well and sightly, even the first time, and will be child's play to make one after a few days' practice.

With Apples.—Peel two or three apples, cut them in thin, round slices, fry them with a little butter, and take them from the pan; then put a little more butter in the pan, and when hot, pour in it six beaten eggs, in which you have mixed the slices of apples; cook, dish, and serve as directed above.

With Asparagus.—Cut the eatable part of the asparagus half an inch in length, throw them in boiling water with a little salt, drain them when cooked, and chop them fine; beat them with eggs and a little milk; have hot butter in a frying-pan on a good fire; pour the eggs in, tossing continually till done, and serve on a dish as directed.

With Bacon.—Put two ounces of butter in a frying-pan; when melted, add two ounces of bacon cut in dice; when turning brown and very hot, pour in eight eggs, beaten as directed above; toss the pan nearly all the time till done, and serve as directed.

Au naturel.—Beat five eggs, with salt and pepper, as directed. Put about an ounce of butter in a frying-pan on the fire, and when melted, turn the eggs in; cook, dish, and serve as directed.

Aux Fines Herbes.—Proceed as for *au naturel* in every particular, except that you beat with the eggs a tablespoonful of chopped parsley, or parsley and chives, when handy; cook, dish, and serve in the same way.

Célestine.—Beat eight eggs as directed. Dip the point of a small kitchen knife in water and cut with it little lumps of butter the size of a pea and of any shape; about two ounces of it, drop them in the eggs and beat a little to mix, then melt butter in a frying-pan and cook, dish, and serve as directed.

In the Oven.—When the omelet *au naturel* or *Célestine* is cooked enough to commence folding, put the frying-pan in a quick oven for about one minute and serve. The omelet swells and does not need folding, but if it gains in bulk, it loses in taste.

Jardinière.—Chop fine, parsley, chives, onions, shallots, a few leaves of sorrel, and a few sprigs of chervil; beat and mix the whole well with beaten eggs; cook, dish, and serve as directed. It requires a little more butter than if made with eggs only.

With Cheese. — Grate some pine-apple or *Gruyère* cheese, about two ounces to four or five eggs, and mix and beat it with the eggs; then make the omelet as directed.

With Kidney.—*Sauté* as directed, till about half done, part of a beef or calf's kidney, or one sheep's kidney, and mix it with beaten eggs. Cook and serve as directed. It makes an excellent dish for breakfast. The kidney may be cooked till done, and when the omelet is to be folded in the pan, put five or six tablespoonfuls of the kidney on the middle of the omelet, fold, dish, and serve as directed. When dished, none of the kidney is seen, being under the omelet.

With Mushrooms.—Cut mushrooms in pieces, and mix them with beaten eggs; then cook and serve them as directed. This also makes an excellent dish for breakfast, especially if made with fresh mushrooms.

With Sorrel.—Make an omelet *au naturel* or *Célestine*, and serve it on a *purée* of sorrel. The same may be served on a *purée* of tomatoes or onions.

With Lobster.—Cut two ounces of boiled lobster in small dice, mix it well with beaten eggs, and cook and serve as directed.

With Sugar.—Mix well the yolks of eight eggs with two ounces of fine white sugar and a pinch of salt, and beat well the whites; then mix well yolks, whites, and the rind of half a lemon, having the latter chopped very fine. Put four ounces of butter in a frying-pan, and set it on the fire; when melted, pour the eggs in, and toss and stir as directed. Then dust a dish with fine white sugar, put the omelet on, then dust again the upper side with the same;

have ready a red-hot shovel, or any other flat piece of iron, pass it over the top of the omelet, so as to color it while melting the sugar, and serve warm. The whole process must be performed quickly. The sugar may be beaten with the eggs whole; both ways are good; it is only a question of taste.

With Rum.—Make an omelet with sugar as above, and when on the table, pour a gill or so of rum on it, set fire to it, and let it burn as long as it can, taking slowly but continually with a silver spoon the rum from the sides, and pouring it on the middle while it is burning, and until it dies out by itself; then eat immediately.

With Truffles.—Slice four ounces of truffles, beat them with six eggs, a little milk, and a little salt and pepper. Put in a frying-pan four ounces of butter, and set it on a good fire; when melted, pour the eggs in, toss almost continually till done, and serve as directed for omelets.

With Ham.—Cut four ounces of ham in small dice, and set it on the fire in a frying-pan with about two ounces of butter; stir, and while the ham is frying, beat six eggs and turn them over the ham in the pan when the latter is fried; stir with a fork, to cook the eggs as quickly as possible; turn the part of the omelet nearest to you over the other part by means of a fork, and serve like an omelet *au naturel.*

With Boiled Ham.—Proceed as for the above in every particular, except that you mix the ham with the eggs after the latter are beaten; put the mixture in the frying-pan, and finish as the above.

With Salt Pork (called omelet au Lard).—Beat half a dozen eggs with a fork. Cut four ounces of salt pork in dice, set it on the fire in a frying-pan, and when nearly fried turn the eggs in; stir, and finish as other omelets.

Lean or fat salt pork (according to taste) may be used, or both. If it is all lean, use some butter, otherwise it will burn.

Soufflée. — Put in a bowl four ounces of pulverized sugar with four yolks of eggs; then with a wooden spoon mix well and stir for two minutes; add a few drops of essence to flavor. Beat the whites of four eggs to a stiff froth in another bowl, and when you see that they are beaten enough, turn two tablespoonfuls of the yolks and sugar into them, and while still beating, but not as fast; then turn the rest of the yolks and sugar into the whites, and mix gently with a wooden spoon. Butter a tin or silver dish, turn the mixture into it, smooth or scallop with the back of a knife, dust with sugar, and bake in an oven at about 310°. It takes about twelve minutes to bake.

Another.—Mix well six yolks of eggs with four ounces of sugar; beat the six whites to a stiff froth and mix them with the rest, add some lemon-rind chopped very fine or grated. Put four ounces of butter in a crockery dish, set on a moderate fire, and when the butter is melted pour the eggs in; stir with a fork, and as soon as you see some of the mixture becoming hard, place the dish in a hot oven for about five minutes; take off, dust with sugar, and serve.

Macédoine, or à la Washington.—Make four omelets of four eggs each, one with apples, one with asparagus or sorrel (according to the season), a third with *fines herbes*, and the fourth *au naturel;* you serve them on the same dish, one lapping over the other. It makes a fine as well as a good dish.

This omelet, or rather these omelets, were a favorite dish with the Father of his Country; they were very often served on his table when he had a grand dinner. It is also

16*

served with the four following omelets: *au naturel*, with salt pork, *fines herbes*, and with cheese.

With Oysters. — Blanch a dozen oysters, drain, and beat with the eggs, and then proceed as directed.

With Tunny, or any kind of smoked or salt Fish. — Beat the eggs as directed, using little or no salt; then chop the fish fine, mix and beat it with the eggs, and cook as directed. It requires a little more butter than if there were no fish. A few drops of lemon-juice may be added when dished.

With Sweetmeats. — Make an omelet *au naturel*, and when ready to be folded in the pan, place on the middle of it two or three tablespoonfuls of any kind of sweetmeats, then fold and serve.

Omelets are served as *entremets* after the vegetables, and at breakfast. All but four are served as *entremets*, and all are served at breakfast; the four excepted are: with bacon, ham, salt pork, and kidneys. By using different kinds of sweetmeats, an infinite number of omelets can be made, and, except the *soufflée*, they are all made alike.

Macaroni. — This excellent article of food is now as well known here as in Europe. The harder the wheat the better the macaroni. The manufacturers of this country use Michigan flour in preference to any other.

To blanch. — Put about three pints of cold water and a little salt on the fire, and at the first boiling drop half a pound of macaroni into it; boil gently till tender but not soft. It takes about twenty minutes to boil it, according to quality. A little butter, about two ounces, may be added in boiling. As soon as tender, turn it into a colander, and it is ready for use.

Au Gratin. — Blanch the macaroni, and when drained put it on a tin or silver dish, and mix with it a *Béchamel* sauce; add salt, pepper, two or three ounces of butter, a little nutmeg grated, about four ounces of grated cheese, either pine-apple, *Gruyère*, or Parmesan; dust with bread-crumbs, put about eight pieces of butter the size of a hazel-nut here and there on the top, set in a warm but not quick oven till the top turns rather brown, and serve warm as it is, that is, in the dish in which it is. If in a tin dish, put it inside of another dish, and serve.

A l'Italienne.—Blanch half a pound of macaroni and drain it. Put it in a saucepan with four ounces of butter, and mix well by stirring the butter in the warm macaroni. Then add also three or four tablespoonfuls of gravy; mix again half a pint of tomato-sauce and grated cheese, as for *au gratin;* set on the fire, stir, add salt to taste; keep on the fire for about ten minutes, stirring now and then, and serve warm.

Napolitaine.—This is the most expensive way of preparing macaroni. Wealthy Italians have it prepared with beef *à la mode* gravy only, or gravy made especially for it, with good lean beef cut in dice, and using as many as twelve pounds of meat to make gravy for one pound of macaroni, the meat being prepared as boiled beef afterward, but it can be prepared with ordinary gravy.

Blanch four ounces of macaroni and drain as directed, then put it in a saucepan with two ounces of butter, salt, pepper, a little grated nutmeg, and set on the fire; stir till the butter is melted, and then add grated cheese as directed for *au gratin*, and half a pint of gravy; stir and mix for about ten minutes, and serve. Macaroni requires much butter; the quantity of cheese is according to taste; some put weight for weight of macaroni, butter, and cheese. It is also prepared in a mould (*en timbale*) for *chartreuse;* it is macaroni *Napolitaine*, when every thing is mixed with it; instead of leaving it ten minutes on the fire, put it in the mould, set in the oven for about fifteen minutes, turn over a dish, and serve warm. In using much cheese, the macaroni will preserve the form of the mould when served.

In Croquettes.—Proceed as for rice *croquettes.*

Rice—to boil.—Wash half a pound of rice in water and drain it; put it in a saucepan with one quart of broth taken from the top of the broth-kettle, and before having skimmed off the fat; set on the fire, boil gently for about fifteen minutes, or till rather underdone, and put on a very slow fire to finish the cooking. Water and butter may be used instead of broth. If the broth is absorbed or boiled away before the rice is cooked, add a little more to keep it moist; add salt, pepper, and nutmeg to taste, and it is ready for use.

Another way.—When boiled, place it in a slow oven to dry it, and then pour over it, little by little, stirring the while, four ounces of melted butter.

Another.—Wash half a pound of rice in cold water and drain it. Put it in a saucepan with two quarts of cold water, salt, and the juice of two lemons; boil six minutes, and drain; put it in a saucepan then with about six ounces of melted butter; mix, cover the pan well, and put it in a slow oven for about half an hour; take off and use.

Rice may be boiled in several different ways, or rather with several ingredients. To the above ways, in India or other southern countries, they add, besides salt and nutmeg, a teaspoonful of curry-powder to a pound of rice. In Italy they add slices of ham, sausage, saffron, and even Parmesan cheese. When cooked, chopped truffles may be added at the same time with the butter. Oil is sometimes used instead of butter.

In Border.—When thus prepared, take it with a spoon and place it all around the dish, leaving room in the middle to serve a bird, and then serve warm.

Another way.—When prepared as above, put the rice in a mould for border; the rice must be rather dry and the mould well buttered. Press on it so as to fill the mould well, then put it in an oven at about 350 deg. Fahr. for ten or twelve minutes. Take off, place a dish on the mould, turn it upside down, and remove the mould. The inside of a mould, for border, is plain, but the outside and bottom are scalloped; the bottom makes the top of the rice when served. There is an empty place in the centre to hold a bird.

Cake.—Butter a mould well and then dust it with sugar. Prepare rice as directed for *croquettes*, and instead of spreading it on a dish to cool, fill the mould about two-thirds full with it, and bake in a warm but not quick oven for about half an hour. Serve on a dish. The mould may be prepared with sugar only in this way: put pulverized sugar into the mould, set it on a rather slow fire, and when turning rather brown turn the mould round and round, so as to have it lined all over with sugar; bake as above, turn over a dish, remove the mould, and serve hot or cold, with or without a sauce for puddings.

In Croquettes.—Wash four ounces of rice in cold water and set it on the fire with a pint of milk and the rind of half a lemon; when done or nearly so, the milk may be boiled away or absorbed by the rice; add a little more to keep the rice nearly covered with it. When done, take off and mix with it two tablespoonfuls of sugar, two ounces of butter, two tablespoonfuls of milk, three yolks of eggs, a little pinch of salt, and the same of nutmeg—the latter, if liked. Put back on the fire for one minute, stirring the while. Spread the mixture on a dish and let cool. If the *croquettes* are for *breakfast*, the above may be done the evening previous. When cold, stir the mixture, so as to mix the upper part with the rest that is less dry. Put it in parts on the paste-board, about a tablespoonful for each part. Have bread-crumbs on it, roll each part of the shape you wish, either round, like a small sausage, or flat, or of a chop-shape. Then dip each *croquette* in beaten egg, roll in bread-crumbs again, and fry in hot fat. (*See* FRYING.)

To shape them, roll each part round at first, and with a few bread-crumbs; then with a knife you smooth both ends, while you roll them round with the left hand; the two must be done at the same time. When fried and in the colander, dust with sugar, and serve as warm as possible. *Croquettes* are generally served in pyramid. A napkin may be spread on the platter, and the *croquettes* served on it.

In Fritters.—When a rice-cake is cold, it may be cut in pieces, dipped in batter for fritters, fried (*see* FRYING), dusted with sugar, and served hot.

Soufflé.—Prepare rice as directed for *croquettes*, and when ready to be spread on a dish, add a few drops of essence to flavor; have five whites of eggs beaten to a stiff froth, and mix them gently with it; butter a mould well, fill it two-thirds full with the mixture, dust with sugar and set in a warm but not quick oven, and serve as soon as brown and raised. It takes from fifteen to twenty minutes. If the oven is warmer under the cake than on the top, it would be necessary to place something under the mould, the cake rises better and is lighter. This cake, like every *soufflé*, must be served promptly and before it falls.

With Fruit.—This dish is excellent, sightly, easily made, and can be varied infinitely. The rice is prepared as for *croquettes*, and is used when ready to be spread over a dish to cool. The fruit, if it be *apples, pears, plums*, etc., is stewed. One or several kinds may be used for the same dish. It is served warm or cold, according to taste. Place a layer of stewed fruit on a dish and then a layer of rice over it; another layer of the same or of another stewed fruit, and over it a layer of rice. Place as many layers as you fancy, imitating a pyramid, and you have a fine dish.

Rice-water.—This being often prescribed by doctors against diarrhœa, we will give the receipt for it. See that the rice is clean, but do not wash it. Put one pint of rice in a pan with a quart of cold water, and boil gently till the rice is quite soft or a little overdone; if the water boils away, fill up with cold water so as to have the rice always covered by it. When done, mash it through a colander, put back on the fire, add water to make it thin or thick, according to prescription; as soon as warm, sweeten to taste with sugar or honey, and take cold or warm, also according to prescription.

Nouilles.—Put four tablespoonfuls of flour on the paste-board; make a hole in the middle, and break two eggs in it, add a pinch of salt, and knead well; then roll down to a thickness of one-twelfth of an inch; dust it slightly with flour; cut it in strips about an inch wide; then cut these strips across, so as to make fillets one inch long and one-eighth of an inch broad. Spread the strips on a sieve for half an hour, to dry them a little. Put cold water and a pinch of salt in a saucepan, and set it on the fire; at the first boiling throw the *nouilles* in, boil two minutes, stirring occasionally; drain, throw them in cold water and it is ready for use. It may be kept in cold water half a day. *Nouilles* are used to make soup, and are prepared in the same and every way like macaroni.

SWEET DISHES.

THESE are served both as *entremets* and *dessert*. Many are *entremets* at a grand dinner, and *dessert* at a family dinner. As the name indicates, sugar is one of the most important of the compounds used to prepare them. It is used in syrup, the making of which is generally more difficult than the rest of the operation.

The *father of cooks*, the great CAREME, divides syrup, or the "cooking of sugar," as he calls it, and as every practitioner has called it since, into six degrees; each one corresponding to the six different states into which the sugar passes, while on the fire, from the time it begins to boil to that when it begins to turn *caramel* or burned.

A copper pan is the best and handiest of all; it can be done in another, but it is more difficult; the sugar turns brown before being thoroughly cooked or reduced. Always use good loaf sugar. If it be necessary to clarify it, do it in the following way: for five pounds of sugar, put the white of an egg in a bowl with half a pint of water, and beat well with an egg-beater; then turn into it nearly three pints of water, stir, put away half a pint of it to be used afterward. Then add to the rest five pounds of sugar, in

lumps, set on a rather slow fire, and as soon as it comes to
a boil, mix with it the half pint put away, little by little,
skimming off carefully the while, and when no more scum
gathers on the surface, strain through a towel and commence the working. If the sugar does not require to be
clarified, that is, when it is good white sugar, set five
pounds of it on the fire, in a copper pan, with nearly two
quarts of water, and skim off carefully as soon as the scum
gathers. It may be stirred a little to cause the sugar to
melt evenly, but as soon as it commences to boil, stop stirring, else it will turn white and stringy. It passes from
one -state or degree to another in a very short time, and
must be watched closely. It is at the *first* degree when,
by dipping a piece of wood into it so as to retain a drop
of it at the end, and which you touch with another piece
of wood—if, by pulling them apart, slowly and immediately, instead of separating it at once, it forms a thread, but
that soon breaks. It marks then 34 at the hydrometer.
It is at the *second* degree when, by repeating the same process, the kind of thread formed does not break as easily as
the first. It marks then 36. It is at the *third* degree
when, by dipping a skimmer in it, holding it horizontally and striking it on the pan, then blowing on it, it
forms small bubbles. It marks 39 at the hydrometer. It
is at the *fourth* degree by trying again with the skimmer
after a short time, and when, instead of forming bubbles,
it will fly away like threads. It marks then 41. The
fifth degree is when, by dipping a piece of wood in the
sugar and quickly dipping it also in a bowl of cold water,
shaking it at the same time and then biting it ; if it breaks
easily between the teeth, but at the same time is sticky, it
has attained the fifth degree, and marks 44. A few boil-
ings more and it is at the *sixth* degree, and by trying in the

same way as the preceding one, it will break under the teeth, but will not stick to them. Above 44 the mark is uncertain, the syrup being too thick; it passes from that state to that of *caramel;* is colored, and would burn immediately. When that happens, make burnt sugar with it according to direction.

Apples au Beurre.—Peel and core the apples with a fruit-corer. Cut slices of stale bread about one-quarter of an inch in thickness, and then cut them again of a round shape with a paste-cutter and of the size of the apples. Spread some butter on each slice and place an apple on each also. Butter a bakepan, place the apples· and bread in, fill the hole made in the middle of the apple to core it with sugar; place on the top of the sugar and on each a piece of butter the size of a hazel-nut, and set in a warm, but not quick oven. When about half done, fill the hole again with sugar and a pinch of cinnamon, place butter on top as before, and finish the cooking, serve warm. When done, they may be glazed with apple-jelly and put back in the oven for two minutes; the dish is more sightly.

Flambantes.—Lay apples in a saucepan, after being peeled and cored, add sugar to taste, and water enough just to cover them, also a stick of cinnamon, and set on a rather slow fire, and leave till done. Take them from the pan carefully and without breaking them; place them on a tin or silver dish, forming a kind of pyramid or mound; turn the juice over them, dust with sugar, pour good rum all over, set it on fire, and serve immediately and warm. As soon as on fire it is placed on the table, and the host must baste with the rum so as to keep it burning till all the alcohol is exhausted, then serve.

The following cut represents either a dish of apples *flambantes* before being in flames, or apples with rice.

In Fritters.—Peel, core, and cut apples in slices, and then proceed as directed for fritters.   Serve hot.

With Wine.—Proceed as for apples *flambantes* in every particular except that you slice the apples, and instead of pouring rum over, you pour Madeira wine, and do not set it on fire.

Meringuées.—Peel, quarter, and core half a dozen apples; set them on the fire in a saucepan with two tablespoonfuls of water; stir occasionally till done, then mix with them two or three tablespoonfuls of sugar, and wnen cold put them on a tin or silver dish; arrange them as a mound on the middle of the dish.   Beat three whites of eggs to a stiff froth, and mix three ounces of pulverized sugar with them; spread two thirds of that mixture all over and around the apples, smooth it with a knife; then put the other third in a paper funnel, and by squeezeing it out, decorate the dish according to fancy.   You may squeeze some small heaps of the mixture here and there, over and around the dish, or squeeze it out all around, giving it a rope-like shape.   Dust with sugar, and put in an oven at 250 degrees for twenty to twenty-five minutes. Serve warm in the dish in which it has been baked.

Charlotte.—Peel, quarter, and core six apples; put them in a pan with two tablespoonfuls of water, cinnamon, and stew till done, when add three or four ounces of sugar, mix gently so as not to mash the apples, let cool. Butter a mould well, line it, bottom and sides, with strips of stale bread, about one quarter of an inch thick, one inch broad, and of a proper length for the mould. Fill till about half full with some of the apples, then put a rather thin layer of any kind of sweetmeat on the apples; finish the filling up with apples; cover with pieces of stale bread, bake in an oven at about 340 degrees for about twenty minutes, turn over on a dish, remove the mould, and serve hot.

With Sweetmeats.—Prepare apples *au beurre*, and when ready to be served, fill the hole with any kind of sweetmeats or with currant-jelly. Serve warm.

In Pine-Apple.—Core the apples with a fruit-corer and then peel them with the scalloped knife (the peels are used to make syrup or jelly), place them tastefully on a dish, so that they will form a pyramid, filling the place where the core was with sugar and a little cinnamon; then pour a little apple-syrup on the whole, and bake. When done, pour a little more syrup over, and serve cold or warm.

Apple-Syrup.—Peel, quarter, and core four or six apples, of the pippin variety; cook them well in about a pint of water, a wine-glass of brandy, and a pinch of grated cinnamon; when well cooked, put them in a coarse towel, and press the juice out; put it in a stewpan and set it on a good fire; add a pound of loaf-sugar, take the foam off with a skimmer a little before it boils, and boil about five minutes; take from the fire, let cool, bottle it, corking well. It may be kept for months. Syrup with pears, pine-apple, etc., is made in the same way.

Blanc-Mange.—Set on the fire in a block-tin saucepan one quart of milk with the rind of a lemon and two table-spoonfuls of sugar; stir occasionally to melt the sugar.

Then mix about six ounces of corn-starch with half a pint of milk in a bowl. As soon as the milk rises, take it from the fire; take off with a skimmer the rind of lemon, and the skin that has formed on the top of the milk; put the milk back on the fire; turn the corn-starch into it, stir continually and very fast till it is very thick. It will take hardly a minute to get thick. Turn into a mould wetted with cold water and put away to cool. When perfectly cold, serve with the following sauce : Mix well in a tin saucepan two ounces of sugar and two yolks of eggs, then add half a pint of milk and mix again ; set on the fire; stir continually, give one boil; take off; let cool, and serve.

Blanc-Manger.—Throw in boiling water two ounces of sweet almonds and the same of bitter ones, or pour boiling water over them, and then skin them as soon as the skin comes off easily. Pound them well with four ounces of sugar, lay the whole in a pan with about a pint of water, set on the fire, and when on the point of boiling, take off and strain. Put in a tin saucepan about a pint of milk, the strained juice, an ounce of gelatin, a little rind of lemon, and a little nutmeg, both grated ; set the whole on a moderate fire ; simmer just enough to melt the gelatin and mix it with the rest, and then strain. Wet a mould with cold water, put the mixture in it, set it on ice, and serve when cool. It may be served with a sauce like the above.

Charlotte Russe.—Wipe a mould well, see that it is dry, and then line the bottom and sides with lady's-fingers, or sponge cake cut in pieces about the size of a lady's finger. Commence by lining the bottom, placing the pieces so as to form a star or rosette, or plain, according to fancy. Then place some of them upright all around, rather tight, and even with the top of the mould. Fill with cream, well whipped, sweetened, and flavored with essence; place the mould on ice, and when ready to serve, place a dish on it, turn upside down, remove the mould, and serve as it is, or decorated.

To decorate.—Make a paper funnel, fill it with cream, or icing (sugar and white of egg worked), then spread some all over the top according to fancy; it is quickly done and is sightly. The mould may also be filled with some other cream; as *crème légère, crème cuite,* etc.

Charlotte à la Chantilly.—It is a *Charlotte* made exactly as the above one, but filled with *crème à la Chantilly.*

A la Polonaise.—Make a sponge cake, cut it transversely, dip each piece in cream (any kind) and then place them back where they were so as to give the cake its original form as near as possible. When thus re-formed, cover it with cream, dust with sugar, and decorate with any kind of sweetmeats. Besides the sweetmeats that are placed here and there all around, some currant-jelly may also be used to decorate. Place on ice for some time, and serve.

Italian.—Peel, quarter, and core about a quart of pears and set them on a rather slow fire, in a saucepan with half a pint of white wine, sugar, cinnamon, and lemon-rind. While they are cooking, line a mould as for *Charlotte Russe,* remove the lemon-rind, and fill the mould with the pears; place it on ice when cool, turn over on a dish, remove the mould, decorate with icing, or cover entirely with apple-jelly, and serve. It is also made with *génoise* cake instead of sponge cake.

Française.—This is prepared and served like a *Charlotte Russe,* with the exception that it is filled with *blanc manger* or *fromage à la crème* instead of cream.

Of Fruit.—This is made of cherries or any kind of berries; cherries must be stoned carefully. Dip the fruit in wine-jelly as soon as the latter is cool, but not firm, and line a mould with it. By having the mould on ice it will be more easily done. Fill the mould with cream, as for *Charlotte Russe,* place on ice, and serve as soon as congealed. When the mould is taken from the ice, dip it in warm water a few seconds, place a dish over it, turn upside down, remove it, and serve immediately. A *Charlotte* of fruit is sightly enough without decorations; it requires some time to make it, but it is worth the trouble, being a handsome as well as a good dish.

Another.—Line a mould as for the above. Put one ounce of gelatin in a bowl with about three tablespoonfuls of water and leave it so for about half an hour. Mix well together in a saucepan four yolks of eggs and three ounces of pulverized sugar, add about three tablespoonfuls of milk, and mix again: set on the fire and stir for about three minutes, add the gelatin, stir again, give one boil, and put away to cool a little. Beat four whites of eggs to a stiff froth, turn the above mixture into them, mix gently again; fill the mould with the whole, place on ice till perfectly cold. When cold, turn upside down on a dish, remove the mould, decorate as the preceding one, and serve cold.

Cheese with Cream—(Fromage à la Crème).—This is made in different ways; sometimes with soft curds only, or with curds and cream, or with cream only when very thick. Gelatin dissolved in a little water may also be added. The curds or cream, or both, are beaten with an egg-beater, sweetened to taste with sugar, and flavored with essence. To make it more sightly, when beaten and flavored, it is moulded, placed on ice to make it firm, and then turned over a dish, the mould removed, and then served. Any kind of essence may be used to flavor it, such as vanilla, *fleur d'oranger*, rose-water, violet, etc.; it may also be made with coffee, tea, chocolate, orange, lemon, etc. Put a few drops of very strong coffee, or tea, or chocolate at the same time with the sugar and essence.

With orange or lemon, rub them on a piece of sugar, which you pound and use to sweeten the cheese. Three or more different ones may be made with a quart of curds; for instance, flavor one third of it with essence, another third with coffee or chocolate, and the other with orange. The colors will be different also. It is an excellent and refreshing *entremets* in summer-time. Cheese may also be flavored with pine-apple cut in very small dice and mixed with it instead of essence.

Compotes, or Jams.—How to make syrup for Compotes. —Common Syrup.—Put a pound of loaf-sugar in a crockery stewpan, with a pint of water, a wine-glass of brandy, and a pinch of well-grated cinnamon; set it on a slow fire, boil gently for ten minutes, skimming off the foam; then take from the fire and let cool; bottle it; cork it well and keep it to use when wanted. It may be kept for months in a cool and dry place.

Stewed fruit of any kind is called either *compote* or jam. They are first peeled and cored and then cooked with sugar, water, and sometimes cinnamon, or cloves, both in powder and according to taste; also lemon-juice or rind to taste. Cinnamon agrees well with any kind of apples, but is not liked by every one in every kind of fruit. The fruits may be cooked and served whole, in halves, or quarters, or mashed, according to fancy and taste. The proportions of water and sugar are also according to taste, or according to the nature or state of the fruit. Sour apples require more sugar than sweet ones, unripe berries require more also than ripe ones. The preparation is very simple; not being prepared to keep, they are served as soon as cold. They may be served warm, but they are certainly not as good. When there is not syrup (juice) enough, pour some of the above over the fruit, or some apple-syrup. The peels and cores of the apples may be used to make syrup, together with those of pears.

While peeling, coring, or cutting fruit, drop each in cold water, else it changes color and is unsightly.

When cold, the *compote* may be put in a mould; turn over a dish, remove the mould, and serve. Several kinds may be served on the same dish as well as one; being of different colors, the dish is more sightly, and quite as good. Loaf-sugar is the best.

Instead of cooking them with water, etc., as directed above, put some syrup on the fire, and as soon as it boils, drop the prepared fruit in it, and boil slowly till done.

Of Apples.—Quarter, peel, core, and put apples in a stewpan with a gill of water for two quarts, sugar and cinnamon to taste; when done, dish them, pour the juice in the stewpan all over, and serve cold. If there is not juice enough, add some apple-syrup.

Of Apricots or Peaches.—Take two quarts of apricots or peaches and cut them in two, remove the stones. Throw them in boiling water for two minutes and take off; drop in cold water and take out immediately, then skin them. Put about half a pint of water in a crockery pan or in a well-lined one, and at the first boil put the peaches in, with sugar to taste; boil gently till done, turn the whole over a dish, and serve cold. If there is not juice or syrup enough, add a little common syrup.

17

Of Blackberries, Currants, Raspberries, Strawberries, and other like Berries.—Prepare syrup of sugar, and when at the second, third, or fourth state, throw the berries in; boil from one to five minutes, according to the kind, take from the fire, and serve when cold.

Of Cherries.—Cut off the stalks of the cherries about half their length, wash well and drain them. Put them in a stewpan in which there is just enough syrup at the first degree to cover them; boil slowly till cooked, and serve.

Of Oranges.—Peel four oranges, and divide each carpel without breaking it, and then throw them in syrup of sugar at the fourth or fifth degree, and boil slowly three or four minutes; take from the fire, let cool, and serve.

Of Pears.—Peel the pears, cut the stem half its length, put them in a stewpan with a little sugar, a few drops of lemon-juice, a pinch of cinnamon, and a little water. Set on a moderate fire, and at the first boiling add two gills of claret wine. Simmer till cooked, then put the pears only on a dish; set the stewpan back on the fire, add to the juice in it about the same quantity of syrup of pears or of syrup of sugar at the third degree, boil fifteen minutes longer, pour the whole on the pears, and serve warm or cold.

Of Lemons.—Peel the lemons, cut them in pieces, remove the seeds, and proceed as for that of oranges, boiling a little longer.

Of Pine-Apple.—Peel and cut in slices, put them in a crockery pan, with a little water and sugar, set on a good fire, and finish and serve like apricots.

Of Plums.—Throw the plums in boiling water, and take them out when half cooked; put them in a crockery stewpan, with a little water and a little sugar; simmer till cooked, place them on a dish, pour some common syrup on, and serve when cold.

Of Quinces.—Quarter, peel, and core the quinces; throw them in boiling water for five minutes; take out and drain them; put them in a crockery stewpan, with four ounces of sugar for every pound of quinces, a few drops of lemon-juice, a little water, and a pinch of grated cinnamon; set it on the fire, simmer till cooked, place them on a dish, pour some common syrup on them, and serve cold.

Of Chestnuts.—Roast about one quart of chestnuts, remove the skin and pith, lay them in a pan with half a gill of water and four ounces of sugar; set on a slow fire, toss now and then till the sugar and water are absorbed or evaporated, turn over a dish, dust with sugar, and serve warm or cold. A few drops of lemon-juice may be added just before dusting with sugar.

Cold Compote.—Wash strawberries and raspberries in cold water, drain dry, and place them on a dish. Pour boiling common syrup or boiling currant-jelly all over; let cool, and serve.

Of Cranberries.—Put one pint of water in a tin saucepan, with six ounces of loaf-sugar, the rind of half a lemon, and set it on the fire; boil down until, by dipping a spoon in it, it adheres to it. Then throw in it about one pint of cranberries; boil about twelve minutes, stirring now and then, take off, let cool, and serve.

Another.—After having boiled ten minutes in the same way as above, and with the same proportions of sugar, cranberries, etc., take from the fire, mash through a fine colander or sieve, put back on the fire, boil gently five minutes, let cool, and serve.

Creams or Crèmes au Citron (with Lemon).—Put one

pint of milk in a tin saucepan with the rind of a lemon;
set on the fire, and as soon as it rises place an iron spoon
in it and boil gently five minutes; take from the fire.
Mix well in a bowl four ounces of sugar with four yolks
of eggs, then turn the milk into the bowl, little by little,
stirring and mixing at the same time. Strain the mixture
and put it in small cups; put the cups in a pan of boiling
water, boil gently for about ten minutes, and put in the
oven as it is, that is, leaving the cups in the water. The
cups must not be more than half covered with water, else
the water will fly into it. It takes from ten to fifteen
minutes to finish the cooking in the oven, according to the
size of the cups. Take them from the oven when the
crème is rather firm, except a little spot in the middle, and
which you ascertain by moving the cups.

Any one with an ordinary amount of intelligence can
make creams as well as the best cooks, after having tried
only two or three times. When you know how to make
one, you can make fifty, just by using different flavorings.

Au Café (*with Coffee*).—The stronger the coffee the
better the cream. The most economical way of making
strong coffee is: when you intend to have cream with
coffee for dinner, put the first drops that fall, when you
make the coffee for breakfast, into a glass; put it immediately in cold water, and as soon as cool cover it with
paper, which you tie around it with twine, and use when
you make the cream.

Always use good fresh milk and fresh eggs. As soon
as the whites of the eggs are separated from the yolks, put
them, together with the shells, on ice, and use the next
day to clarify your jellies, or to make icing, etc. A little
care is a great saving in the kitchen.

Put one quart of milk in a milk-pan on the fire and

take off as soon as it rises. While the milk is on the fire, mix well together in a bowl eight yolks of eggs with half a pound of sugar, and coffee to flavor; then turn the milk into the mixture, little by little, stirring the while; when the whole is thoroughly mixed, strain it. Put the mixture in cream-cups, place the cups in a pan of boiling water— enough water to half cover them; boil slowly for about ten minutes, put the pan and cups in a moderately-heated oven, and take off when done. It takes from ten to fifteen minutes to finish the cooking, according to the size of the cups. It is done when the whole is solidified except a little spot in the centre, which, by moving the cups, will shake somewhat. Serve cold.

With Burnt Sugar.—Put two ounces of sugar in a small tin pan, with a tablespoonful of water, set on the fire, and boil till burnt and of a light-brown color; take off, and put it in a stewpan with a pint of milk, four ounces of white sugar, a few drops of rose or orange-flower water; boil ten minutes, stirring occasionally; take from the fire, beat the yolks of two eggs, and one entire, put in the pan and mix the whole well, then strain, after which you put the mixture in small cream-pots for that purpose; place them in a hot but not boiling *bain-marie*, and as soon as it thickens take them out, dust them with fine white sugar, let cool; place them on ice for about fifteen minutes, and then it is ready to be served.

With Chocolate.—Put in a stewpan and on a moderate fire six ounces of chocolate, three tablespoonfuls of water, three ounces of white sugar, stir now and then with a wooden spoon till melted; then pour in it, little by little, a quart of good fresh milk; boil ten minutes, take from the fire, and mix in it one egg well beaten with the yolks of five others; strain through a fine sieve, put in cream-pots or cups, place them in a hot but not boiling *bain-marie*, take off as soon as it thickens, dust with fine white sugar, let cool, place on ice for about fifteen minutes, and use.

With Orange.—Use orange-rind, and proceed as for lemon-cream in every other particular.

With Tea.—Proceed with strong tea as for cream *au café* in every other particular.

With Essence.—Make cream *au café*, with the exception that, instead of using coffee to flavor, you use a few drops of vanilla, rose-water, orange-flower water, violet, cinnamon, etc.—any kind of essence, to taste.

With Cinnamon.—Beat well together in a bowl about an ounce of potato-starch, a teaspoonful of cinnamon, four eggs, four ounces of sugar, and milk enough to make a rather liquid batter. Turn the mixture into a mould, which put into a pan of boiling water for fifteen minutes, then place in the oven till cooked. Serve cold.

Cuite.—Put two ounces of sugar in a tin pan with two eggs, and mix well; then add an ounce of flour, little by little, mixing the while; then, in the same way, add also about a pint of boiled milk; set on the fire, stir continually till it turns rather thick; take off, flavor with essence to taste, let cool, and serve or use for filling.

Frangipane.—Set one pint of milk on the fire. Mix well together in another pan three tablespoonfuls of sugar, two of flour, three eggs, three macaroons crumbled, and as soon as the milk rises, turn the mixture into it, little by little, stirring and mixing the while; keep stirring about three minutes; take off, add a few drops of essence to flavor; turn into a bowl, let cool, and it is ready for use. It may be made without the macaroons.

With Almonds.—Make as the above, with the exception that you use sweet almonds, chopped fine, instead of macaroons.

With Hazel-nuts.—Proceed as above, using hazel-nuts instead of almonds.

Légère.—Mix well together in a tin saucepan five yolks of eggs and five ounces of sugar; add four tablespoonfuls of milk, and mix again. Set the pan on the fire, and stir continually till it turns rather thick; take off, and add a few drops of essence; turn into a plate or dish and let cool. When cold, beat five whites of eggs to a stiff froth; have somebody to pour in the whites, and, while you are still beating, about two tablespoonfuls of the cold mixture, and stop beating. Then turn the rest of the mixture into the whites, and mix the whole together gently; do not stir too much, but move round and round with a wooden spoon, and it is done. If it is stirred too much, it may become too liquid. It makes an excellent and light cream.

Patissière.—Beat four whites of eggs to a stiff froth, and then mix about one ounce of pulverized sugar with them. Put four yolks of eggs in a bowl with half a gill of milk, and beat well till thoroughly mixed. Put in a saucepan about two ounces of pulverized sugar, with a teaspoonful of potato-starch (*fecula*), and two-thirds of a gill of milk, and mix the whole well; then add the eggs and milk, and beat the whole well with an egg-beater. Set the pan on a rather slow fire, stir continually with a wooden spoon till it turns rather thick, and then turn the four whites and sugar into the pan also, little by little, stirring the while, and take off when thoroughly mixed. As soon as off the fire, add essence to flavor, and about one-quarter of an ounce of gelatine, dissolved in tepid water. Serve, or use to fill when cold.

Renversée.—Make cream with tea, coffee, or chocolate, and instead of turning the mixture into cream-pots, turn it into a mould lined with burnt sugar; place the mould in boiling water for about fifteen minutes, place it in the oven to finish the cooking, turn over a dish, remove the mould, and serve cold. To line the mould, put two or three tablespoonfuls of pulverized sugar in it; set it on a slow fire, and when the sugar is melted and turning brown, move the mould round and round to spread the sugar all over; then put the cream in it.

Sweet Cream.—We mean here the oily substance which forms a scum on milk; also called *whipped cream.* It is used to make Charlotte Russe, to fill *meringues, choux,* or cream-cakes, etc.

Put a pint of good thick cream in a bowl, and if the weather is warm, place the bowl on ice for half an hour, then beat the cream with an egg-beater till stiff and thick. If the cream does not become stiff after having beaten it fifteen or twenty minutes at the longest, it is not good, or it is too warm. Good cream may rise and become stiff in five minutes. When beaten, add to it about four ounces of pulverized sugar, which you mix gently with it, not stirring too much; add also a few drops of essence to flavor. If wanted very stiff, add also, after the sugar, half an ounce of gelatin, melted in a little tepid water. When beaten and mixed, if not used immediately, it must be put on ice.

Chantilly.—It is the above cream flavored with *fleur d'orange* (orange-flower water), or with essence of violet.

Ice Cream.—Made with cream it is richer than with milk. With eggs it is better and richer than without, and those that advocate it without eggs, either have no palate, or do not know how to use them in making it.

The addition of starch, fecula, arrow-root, flour, meal, etc., spoils it. The proportions are, to a quart of milk or

cream: from four to six eggs; from eight to fourteen
ounces of pulverized sugar; essence, or chocolate, or fruit-
jelly to flavor and color. Our receipt is for six eggs and
fourteen ounces of sugar to a quart of milk.

Set the milk on the fire, and when it comes to a boil,
mix well half the sugar and the essence with six yolks
and three whites of eggs; beat the three other whites separately to a stiff froth. As soon as the milk rises, take it
from the fire, put half the sugar in it and stir to melt it,
then turn the mixture into it also, little by little, beating
the while with an egg-beater; set on the fire, and take off
at the first boiling. While on the fire it must be beaten
gently, as, if it is allowed to boil, the eggs may curdle.
As soon as off the fire, mix the three whites with the rest,
beating with an egg-beater, just enough to mix the whole
well; put in cold, salt water to cool, and then freeze.

The smaller the ice is broken and mixed with plenty
of rock-salt, the quicker it freezes.

Custard.—Put four yolks of eggs in a bowl, then
sprinkle flour on them, little by little, stirring and mixing well the while with a wooden spoon, and when the
mixture is rather thick, stop sprinkling flour, but sprinkle
milk, and mix again in the same way till the mixture is
liquid; add sugar and essence to taste, beat the four
whites to a stiff froth, mix them gently with the rest;
butter a mould well, fill it about two-thirds full with the
mixture, and set in a warm but not quick oven. Serve as
soon as out of the oven. If intended to be served cold,
omit the whites of eggs.

Fritters.—These are made with every kind of fruit, when
ripe, peeled and stoned, or cored when necessary, and according to the kind. The fruit is used whole, such as strawberries and the like; or in slices, such as apples, pears, etc.;

17*

or in halves, like peaches, plums, etc. It may be used as soon as prepared; or may be soaked a few hours in a mixture of sugar, brandy, or rum, and lemon-rind.

Have *batter for fritters* made in advance, and while you are preparing the fruit heat the fat (*see* FRYING), dip each fruit or each slice in batter, drop it in the fat, stir and turn over, and when done, turn into a colander, dust well with fine white or pulverized sugar, and serve as warm (or rather as hot) as possible. Even the best fritters served cold make a very poor dish. Besides fruit, the blossoms of the acacia and those of the violet make the most delicate fritters.

With Bread or Pain perdu.—Set one pint of milk on the fire with two ounces of sugar, and the rind of half a lemon, stir now and then, and when it rises add a few drops of essence to flavor, then take off and soak in it slices of bread, cut with a paste-cutter and about half an inck thick. When well soaked, drain; dip them in beaten egg, roll in bread-crumbs, and fry and serve as fritters.

Glazed Fruit — Oranges glazed.—Oranges or any other fruit glazed, when mounted in a pyramid, is called *croque en bouche.*

Peel the oranges; then divide the carpels and free them from the pith, and put them away in a warm place for a few hours; they may be left over night. Cut very fine wire in pieces about eight inches long, bend each piece at both ends, forming a hook; then run one end or hook through the carpel of orange, and hang it on a stick placed on something horizontally. In order not to spill any of the juice, hook the orange near the edge of that part that was the centre of the orange before being divided, and as the other end of the wire forms a hook also, it is easy to hang it.

Prepare syrup of sugar, and when at the sixth degree

take it from the fire, dip each carpel of orange into it and hang it again, and so on for the whole. As soon as dry enough to handle them, which takes hardly half a minute, pull off the wire and serve when perfectly cold.

To mount them in pyramid is not difficult, but requires time. When they are cold, prepare again the same syrup of sugar as above, and take it from the fire. While the sugar is on the fire take a tin mould, a plain one, larger at the top than at the bottom, and slightly grease it with sweet-oil. A convenient size for a family is, seven inches high, six inches broad at the top, and only four inches at the bottom.

Place one carpel of orange, resting on the bottom of the mould, along the side and the edge upward; as soon as the sugar is out of the fire, dip one of the two ends of another carpel into it, the edge only, and immediately place it as the first one, and touching it. The syrup being hot and liquid, the two pieces will adhere; do the same with others till you have one row around the bottom. Commence a second row as you did the first, but this time the first carpel you place must be dipped in sugar, in order to adhere to the first row, and all the others must also be dipped so as to adhere not only to the first piece placed, but also to the first row; and so on for each row till the mould is full, or till you have as much as you wish. As soon as cold, place a dish on the mould, turn upside down, and remove the mould. You have then a sightly dish, but not better than when served only glazed.

Another way to make it.—Grease with oil your marble for pastry, place the same mould as above over it but upside down, that is, the broader end down; grease the outside also with oil. Then place the rows of carpels of oranges all around outside of it, and in the same way as described above. The *croque en bouche* is more easily made this last way, but it is more difficult to remove the mould. Mould and fruit must be turned upside down carefully, after which the mould is pulled off.

If the syrup gets cold, it hardens, and cannot be used; in that state, add a little water and put it back on the fire, but it is difficult to rewarm it; generally it colors and is unfit. When that happens, make burnt sugar with it, or a *nougat.* It is better and safer to make a little of it, just what can be used before it gets cold, and if not enough, make some a second and even a third time. While the sugar is hot, and while you are dipping the fruit in it, be careful not to touch it, as it burns badly. In glazing the fruit first, some syrup falls in taking it from the pan to the stick; place your marble board, greased with oil, under, so that you can pick it without any trouble and use it.

Chestnuts, glazed.—Roast the chestnuts, skin them well, then hook, dip, and hook again on the stick as directed for pieces of oranges. A pyramid also may be made, and a sightly one it makes.

Cherries.—They must be picked with their stems, and by which you tie two together with a piece of twine. See that they are clean and dry, and have two sticks instead of one, placed parallel, about two inches apart, in order to prevent the two cherries from touching, when hung, as they would immediately adhere. Proceed for the rest as described for oranges.

Pears.—Small, ripe pears are excellent glazed; peel them, but leave the stem on, and then proceed as with cherries in every particular.

Strawberries or any other Berries.—The berries must be picked with the stem. Wash them in cold water, drain, dry, or wipe carefully, and then proceed as for cherries in every particular. A more delicate dish than strawberries or raspberries glazed cannot be made.

Grapes.—When clean, proceed as described for cherries.

Plums.—Take plums, well ripened and with the stems on, and proceed as with cherries.

Prunes.—Soak the prunes in tepid water, and when dry, hook them like carpels of orange, and finish in the same manner.

Currants.—When clean and dry, tie two clusters together, and proceed as for cherries.

Pine-Apple.—Cut pine-apple in dice, and proceed as described for carpels of orange.

Iced Fruit.—As a general rule, the more watery the fruit the more reduced the syrup of sugar must be. If it is not reduced enough, small pieces of ice, formed by the water of the fruit, will be found while eating it. The fruit must be ripe. It is done also with preserved fruit. It is impossible to tell exactly the degree or state of the fruit and syrup without a hydrometer.

The following *preparation* may be added to the fruit, or to *punch*, as soon as it begins to freeze; it is not indispensable, but gives it more body: Put one pound of loaf-sugar in a copper pan with two gills of cold water, set on the fire, stir now and then till it comes to a boil, then boil till it is at the fifth state or 43°, and take off. Beat four whites of eggs to a stiff froth, flavor with essence of vanilla, and turn the sugar into the eggs, little by little, but do not stop beating until the whole is in. Then move the mixture gently round with a spoon for about a minute, and it is ready for use.

With Peaches, Apricots, or Plums.—The following proportions are for one pint of juice. Peel and stone the fruit carefully, then mash it through a sieve into a bowl. Make one pint of syrup of sugar at 32°, and when cold turn it into the bowl and mix it with the pint of juice, add the juice of a rather large orange and a little of the rind grated, mix again, freeze as directed for ice-cream, and serve.

With Currants, Lemons, Oranges, Pears, Pine-Apples, Strawberries, and other Berries.—Proceed as for peaches in every particular, except that you press the juice of the currants and berries through a towel instead of mashing them through a sieve, and that you use the syrup at 44° for them also; the others are peeled and cored or seeded.

With Melons.—Proceed as for peaches, except that you add to the mixture a little *kirschwasser*.

With Preserved Fruit.—Use the syrup at 30°, and proceed as for peaches in every other particular.

Iced Coffee.—Make strong coffee, and when cold mix it with the same volume of thick cream, sweeten to taste, freeze, and serve.

Iced Chocolate.—Break in pieces about four ounces of chocolate, and set it on a slow fire in a tin pan, with two tablespoonfuls of water; when melted take it from the fire, add a gill of warm water, and work it with a spoon for five minutes; then mix it with the same volume of syrup of sugar at 30°, freeze and serve. The syrup is used when cold.

Iced Tea is made as iced coffee.

Sweet Jellies— Wine Jelly.—Soak two ounces of gelatin in a gill of cold water for about half an hour. Put in a block-tin saucepan three eggs and shells, three ounces of sugar, one quart of cold water; beat a little with an egg-beater to break the eggs, and mix the whole together; add also a few drops of burnt sugar, same of essence, rum, according to taste, from half a gill to half a pint, then the

gelatin and water in which it is; set on a good fire, stirring slowly with an egg-beater, and stopping once in a
while to see if it comes to a boil, when, stop stirring, keep
boiling very slowly for two or three minutes, and turn into
the jelly-bag, which you do as soon as clear; the process
requires from two to three minutes. While it is boiling
take a few drops with a spoon, and you will easily see when
it is clear. Pass it through the bag three or four times,
turn into a mould, put on ice, and when firm, put a dish
on it, turn upside down, remove the mould, and serve.

Jelly Macédoine.—Make the same jelly as above, and
pass it through the bag also; put some in a mould, say a
thickness of half an inch, have the mould on ice; then, as
soon as it is firm, place some fruit on that layer and according to fancy; and, with a tin ladle, pour more jelly
into the mould, but carefully and slowly, in order not to
upset the fruit you have in; continue pouring till you have a
thickness of about half an inch on the fruit. Repeat this
as many times as you please, and till the mould is full;
vary the fruit at each layer, and especially the color of the
different kinds. The color of the jelly may also be changed
at every layer, by mixing in it more burnt sugar, some
carmine or cochineal, some green spinach, a little in
one layer and more in another. Any kind of ripe fruit
can be used: strawberries, raspberries, stoned cherries,
grapes, apples cut in fancy shapes; also peaches, bananas,
etc.

Cold Wine-Jelly.—Put two ounces of gelatin in a bowl
with a piece of cinnamon and a pint of cold water, and
let stand about an hour. Then pour over about a quart
of boiling water, and let stand about four minutes. After
that, add two pounds of sugar, the juice of three lemons,
a pint of sherry wine, and half a gill of brandy. Stir to

dissolve the sugar, and turn the mixture into a mould through a strainer; place on ice, and serve as the above jellies.

Soufflés.—Put in a bowl four tablespoonfuls of potato-starch with three yolks of eggs, one ounce of butter, and a few drops of essence to flavor. Turn into it, little by little, stirring the while, about three gills of milk; set on the fire, stir continually, and take off at the first boiling. Stir continually but slowly. As soon as cold, beat three yolks of eggs with a tablespoonful of cold water, and mix them with the rest. Beat four whites of eggs to a stiff froth, and mix them also gently and slowly. Butter a mould well, fill it about two-thirds full, and bake in a warm but not quick oven (about 300° Fahr.). Besides being flavored with essence, *soufflés* may be flavored with coffee, lemon, orange, etc., according to taste. Generally, *soufflés* are served under the name of the object used to flavor them, such as *soufflé au café* (*soufflé* flavored with strong coffee), etc. They are all made in the same way as the above one, with the exception that they are flavored with strong coffee as above, and used instead of essence, or strong tea, chocolate, etc., or with a little jelly of different fruit, or with roasted chestnuts well pounded, instead of potato-starch, etc.

A hundred different kinds of *soufflés* can be easily made by following the above directions.

Apples, fried.—Peel and cut in small dice, dropping them in cold water till the whole is ready. Then fry with a little butter till about half cooked, when add a little water and sugar to taste; finish the cooking, take from the fire; beat a yolk of egg with a teaspoonful of cold water and mix it with the apples; serve warm. Proceed in the same way with *pears.*

Peaches baked.—Cut peaches in two, remove the stone, and with a paste-cutter cut some slices of bread, and place them in a buttered bakepan with half of a peach on each, the skin downward; dust well with sugar, put a piece of butter the size of a kidney-bean on each, place in a rather slow oven; dish when cooked, turn the juice over, if any; if none, a little syrup of pears, and serve warm.

Do the same with *apricots, plums,* and slices of *pine-apples.* The slices of pine-apples may be soaked in *kirsch-wasser* for twenty-four hours before using them.

Prunes, stewed.—Wash them in cold water if necessary. Soak them in tepid water for about two hours, and set the whole on the fire; boil gently till half done, when add sugar to taste, a gill of claret wine to half a pound of prunes, and serve either warm or cold when done. If the water boils away too much, add more.

Currants, Blackberries, or other Fruit, for Dessert.—Beat well the white of an egg with a little water; dip the fruit in, and roll it immediately in some fine-crushed sugar; place it on a dish, and leave it thus five or six hours, and serve.

A more sightly and exquisite plate of dessert than a plate of currants dressed thus, cannot be had.

Besides all our receipts, any kind of fruit may be served for dessert, according to the season; also any kind of cheese; also fruits preserved in liquor.

Berries with Milk or Cream.—Nearly every kind of berries, when clean, may be served with milk or cream, and sugar to taste.

With Liquor.—They may also be served with brandy, rum, *kirschwasser*, whiskey, etc., and sugar.

Marmalades, or Preserves of Fruits—Of Apricots or Peaches.—Boil two pounds of peaches for a minute, take off and drop them immediately in cold water. Drain and skin immediately, cut in two and remove the stone. Crack two-thirds of the stones and throw the kernels in boiling water; leave them in till the skin comes off easily; skin them well and cut them in small pieces, length-wise. Lay the peaches in a pan, with about a pound and a half of sugar, set on the fire, boil about twenty minutes, stirring the while with a wooden spoon; a few minutes be-fore taking from the fire, put also the kernels in the pan; then turn in pots or jars as soon as off the fire. Cover well when cold, and keep in a dry and cool (but not cold) closet.

Of Plums.—Proceed as for the above.

Of Pears and Quinces.—Quarter, peel, and core the fruit, put it in a pan, and proceed for the rest as directed for peaches, except that you use sweet almonds instead of kernels.

Of Blackberries, Cherries, Currants, Raspberries, and other like Berries.—Wash the fruit in cold water, drain, dry, and mash it through a sieve placed over a saucepan; when the juice and pulp are in the pan add the same weight of loaf-sugar as that of juice, which is easily ascertained by weighing the pan first; set on the fire, skim it carefully; it takes about half an hour to cook; then put in pots and let cool; cut a piece of white paper the size of the inside of the pot, dip it in brandy, put it over the fruit, cover the pots, and place them in a dry and cool closet.

Of Grapes.—Select well-ripened grapes and pick the berries. Put them in a thick towel, and press the juice out, which you put in a copper or brass saucepan, set on a good fire, and boil till about half reduced. Skim off the scum, and stir now and then while it is on the fire. Then add about half a pound of loaf-sugar to a pound of juice, boil again fifteen or twenty minutes, take off, put in pots or jars, cover or cork well when cold, and put away in a dark and cool closet.

Candied or Comfited Fruit.—The best state of the fruit to be candied is just when commencing to ripen or a little before. It must be picked in dry weather, and be sound; the least stain is enough to spoil it soon after it is preserved.

Peaches.—Make a cut on the side of the fruit and remove the stone without bruising it; then skin it carefully and drop it in a pan of cold water. When they are all in, set on the fire, boil gently till they float. There must be much more water than is necessary to cover them, in order to see easily when they come to the surface. Then take them off carefully, with a skimmer, and drop them in cold water and drain. When drained, put them in a pan, cover them with syrup of sugar after it is skimmed and clarified. (*See* SYRUP OF SUGAR.) The syrup must be boiling when turned over the fruit. Set on the fire, give one boil only, and turn the whole into a bowl, which you cover with paper, and leave thus twelve or fifteen hours. After that time, drain, put the syrup on the fire, the peaches in the bowl, and at the first boiling of the syrup, turn it over the fruit, cover the bowl with paper, and leave about as long, that is, twelve or fifteen hours.

Repeat the same process three times more, in all five times. The last time the syrup must be at the first state as described for syrup of sugar. Inexperienced persons will do well to try at first with a few fruits, and go through the whole process, after which it will be comparatively easy.

Every one is awkward in doing a thing for the first time, and does not do it well, however easy or simple it may be. That is the reason why societies of farmers make better preserves than other people; they teach one an other; and besides, no one is allowed to touch the fruit before having seen it done several times.

Candied fruit, as well as preserves, get spoiled by fermentation, if not cooked enough; by moisture, if kept in a damp place; or by heat, if kept in a warm place.

When the last process has been gone through, leave the fruit in the bowl about twenty-four hours; then put it in jars, cover air-tight, and put away in a dry and cool closet. It may also be drained, dried on a riddle in a warm place, and kept in boxes. A wooden riddle or screen is better than a metal one. They may also be put in decanters, covered with brandy or other liquor, and corked well. When preserved in brandy, it is not necessary to remove the stone; they may be covered with half syrup and half brandy.

Plums.—Pick them just before commencing to ripen, and cut the stem half way. When clean, but neither stoned nor skinned, prick them around the stem with a fork, drop them in cold water, set on the fire, add a gill of vinegar to three quarts of water, and take from the fire as soon as they float. Drain, put them in a bowl, pour boiling syrup of sugar over them, and proceed as directed for peaches, that is, cover and pour the syrup on them five times in all. They are kept like peaches also, either in jars, dried, or in brandy.

Pears.—After being peeled and the stem cut off half way, they may be preserved whole or in quarters. In peeling them, they must be dropped in cold water with a little lemon-juice to keep them white. They are picked just before commencing to ripen. When ready, put cold water and the juice of a lemon to every two quarts in a deep pan, and drop the pears in, set on the fire and boil gently till well done; take off, drain and drop in cold water, which you change two or three times and without stopping; then drain again, place them in a large bowl, and then proceed as for peaches. They are kept like peaches also.

Apples.—Proceed as for pears, except that apples are cooked much quicker.

Pine-Apples.—Peel, slice, and drop the fruit in cold water; add a little sugar, set on the fire and boil gently till done, when drain and drop in cold water and drain again. Put them in a bowl, and proceed as for peaches for the rest, with the exception that they are kept in jars only, and not dried or put in brandy.

Chestnuts.—Skin the chestnuts and put them in cold water on the fire, and take off when tender; then remove the under skin or white envelope or pith. Place them in a bowl, and proceed as for peaches for the rest.

Oranges.—Drop oranges in boiling water and take off when the rind is tender, and when a darning-needle can be run through it easily. Drain and drop them in cold water. After two or three hours drain, cut in slices, and put them in a bowl; then proceed as for peaches, except that they are kept in jars only.

Quinces.—Peel, quarter, and core quinces just before they commence ripening, drop in boiling water; drain them when done, and drop them immediately in cold water. As soon as cold, take them off, drain and put them in a bowl. For the rest, proceed as for peaches, with the exception that they are only kept in jars, but neither dried nor put in brandy.

TO PRESERVE IN BRANDY.—Besides the dried fruits above described, several may be preserved in brandy, without being cooked and soaked in syrup of sugar.

Cherries.—Pick them when fully ripe, see that they are clean, and put them in decanters with cloves, pieces of cinnamon, and entirely covered with brandy; cover well, but do not cork, and leave thus two weeks, at the end of which, place a colander over a vessel and empty the decanters into it; pass the liquor through a jelly-bag, mix it with some syrup of sugar at the second degree, turn over the fruit which you cover with it, and cork the decanters well when perfectly cold. Keep in a dark, cool, and dry place.

Do the same with strawberries and other like fruit.

Fruit Jellies—With Apples or Quinces.—Peel, core, and cut in small pieces two quarts of good apples or quinces, lay them in a stewpan with a clove well pounded, and the juice of half a lemon; cover with water, set on a moderate fire, and boil slowly till well cooked. Turn into a jelly-bag, or a thick towel under which you place a vessel to receive the juice, and when it is all out, put it in a stewpan with three-quarters of a pound of sugar to every pound of juice; boil to a jelly.

As soon as done put it in pots or jars, let cool, cut a piece of white paper the size of the inside of the pot, dip it in brandy, put it over the jelly, cover the pot well, and place in a dry, cool closet, but not too cold. What remains in the bag may be used to make a *compote*. Watch the process carefully, skimmer in hand, to skim off the scum, and stir now and then, lest it should burn.

With Apricots, Peaches, Plums, etc.—After having taken the stones out, cut them in four pieces, and proceed as for apple-jelly above in every other particular.

With Blackberries, Currants, Grapes, Raspberries, or other like Berries.—Put the well-ripened berries in a coarse towel and squeeze all the juice out of them, which you

put into a stewpan with as many pounds of loaf-sugar
as there are of juice, and finish as directed for apple-jelly.
A little rum or essence of rose, or any other, according to
taste, may be added just before taking from the fire.

Punch.—Put a saltspoonful of black tea in a crockery
pot, with one clove, a little cinnamon, and the rind of a
lemon cut in pieces; pour on the whole half a pint of boiling water; let it remain thus five minutes, and strain.
Put a bottle of rum or brandy in a crockery vessel, with
twelve ounces of loaf-sugar, set the rum or brandy on fire,
and let burn till it stops. Then mix tea and rum together,
and it is ready for use. It is drunk cold or warm, according to taste. When wanted warm, if made previously, set it on a moderate fire, in a tin or crockery kettle.

It keeps very well if carefully bottled and corked
when cold.

Another way to make it is to mix the rum or brandy
with the tea without burning it. It is warmed, used, and
kept like the above. The quantity of water may be reduced or augmented, according to taste, and so also the
sugar.

Another.—Grate the rind of a lemon and of two
oranges on a piece of sugar, the yellow part only, and put
it in a bowl with cold water to dissolve it; then add two
gills of pine-apple syrup, essence of vanilla, a pint of claret
wine, a pint of Catawba, Sauterne, or Rhine wine, a pint
of Champagne, and a gill of brandy; sweeten to taste;
strain, put on ice for some time, and serve.

Another.—Put a pound of sugar in a bowl with a gill
of water to dissolve it; then add the juice of three
oranges, a little rind grated, a bottle of Champagne and
one of Catawba or Sauterne wine; strain, place on ice for
some time, and serve cold.

Roman Punch.—Make iced lemon with one quart of juice, same of syrup as directed, then mix with it the juice of four oranges, some lemon and orange rind grated, and about three gills of rum (or according to taste); also, if liked, the preparation used for iced fruit. Then put the mixture in the freezer, stir while freezing, and serve. It must not be frozen hard, as it is better when served rather liquid and frothy. It may be made with any other liquor, if preferred.

Punch is served either after the *entrées* or after the *relevés* of fish, according to taste.

PASTRY.

Of all the branches of the science and art of cooking, pastry, if not the most difficult, requires the greatest care. An inferior piece of meat makes an inferior dish, but still it can be eaten without danger : but inferior pastry can hardly be eaten; or, if eaten, it is indigestible. We will recommend our readers to be very careful about proportions; it would not make a great difference for some kinds, but for others, putting too much or too little of one or more things would certainly result in failure. It is very important to have good materials. New flour is very inferior for pastry; it must have been ground for at least three months. Always keep it in bags, and in a dry and well-ventilated place. Sift before using it. Use fresh eggs, good butter, and good pulverized sugar.

The most important of all is the oven, for, supposing that you have used good materials, have mixed them well, if not properly baked, every thing is lost, materials and labor. Supposing that you have a good oven, there is still a difficulty—and if the last, not the least—the degree of heat. Some require a quick oven, as puff-paste, *choux*, etc.; others a warm one, and others a slow oven, as *meringues*, biscuits, etc. By putting the hand in the oven you can tell if it is properly heated, but it requires ex-

18

perience, and even practitioners are often mistaken; therefore, the easiest way is to have a thermometer in the oven.
It may be placed in the oven of every stove or range; it
is only necessary to bore a hole on the top of the range
or stove, reaching the oven, and have a thermometer with
the bulb inclosed in a brass sheath, perforated, long
enough to reach the oven, and of the size of the hole
bored—the glass tube being above the top of the range.

Pastes.—There are several kinds of paste. Puff-paste
is the most important; it can be made very rich, rich, and
less so; and several hundred different cakes can be made
with it. Small cakes are called *petits fours.*

The next in importance is the *pâte-à-choux;* then the
paste for meat-pies, sometimes called *pâte brisée.*

Puff-paste requires care, but is easily made; *pâte-à-
choux* must be well worked.

Puff-paste.—To make good puff-paste, good flour and
butter, free from salt or sour milk, are indispensable.
It must be made in a cool place. Take half a pound of
good butter and knead it well in a bowl of cold water; if
fresh and not salt, the kneading will take the sour milk
out of it; if salty, it will remove the salt, then put it in
another bowl of cold water and leave it till it is perfectly
firm, and then use. When the butter is ready, put half a
pound of flour on the paste-board or marble, make a hole
in it, in which you put a pinch of salt, and cold water
enough to make a rather stiff dough. It requires about
half a pint of water, knead well, make a kind of ball with
the dough, and put it on a corner of your marble or paste-
board. Take the butter from the water and knead it on
the board, to press all the water out of it. Give it the
shape of a large sausage; dredge the board slightly with
flour, roll the butter over only once, as it must take very

little of it, dredge both ends of the piece of butter with flour also, then by putting one end on the board and pressing on the other end with your hands, you will flatten it of a rather round shape, and till of about half an inch in thickness. Put it thus on the corner of the board also. Immediately after having prepared the butter, take the dough and roll it down, of a round form also, and till large enough to envelop the butter in it easily. Remember that during the whole operation of folding and rolling the paste down, you must dust the marble or pasteboard with flour, very slightly and often; do the same on the top of the paste. It is done in order to prevent the paste from adhering to the board or to the rolling-pin. It must be dusted slightly, so that the paste cannot absorb much of it, as it would make it tough. Have a slab of marble or slate ; it is much easier than wood, and cooler.

When the dough is spread, place the butter right on the middle of it. Turn one side of the dough over the butter, covering it a little more than half way; do the same with the opposite side, the dough lapping over that of the first side turned ; do the same with the side toward you, and also with the side opposite. Dough stretching easily when pulled, and contracting easily when let loose after having pulled it, you have now still four corners of the dough to bring over the butter and in the same way as above, and by doing which, you give to the whole a somewhat round form, and also have the butter perfectly enveloped in the dough. Place the rolling-pin on the middle of the paste, horizontally, and press gently on it so as to make a furrow; do the same from place to place, on the whole surface, making furrows about an inch apart. Repeat the process again, this time placing the rolling-pin right on the top of each elevated line ; and again, repeat it a third time, also placing the pin on each elevated line. Now do exactly the same contrariwise. Then, roll the paste down, gently, evenly, to a thickness of about one fourth of an inch, and of a rectangular shape. Fold it in three by turning over one-third of its length toward the other end, and thus covering another third of it; fold or turn over the remaining third, so as to cover the first third turned over. Roll it down again of about the same thickness as above, but without making furrows in it; give it also the same rectangular shape, taking care to make the length of what was the width, *i. e.* extending it the longer way in an opposite direction to that of the first time, so that the ends will be what the sides were. Fold in three as before, put it on a plate and set in a refrigerator for from ten to twenty minutes. Take hold of it again, roll down as above, fold in the same way also, and put away for ten minutes. You roll down and fold from four to six times, not counting the time you envelop the butter in the dough. In cold weather, and when the butter is firm, fold and roll only four times; but in rather warm weather, fold and roll six times. If it is too warm, it is of no use to try with butter.

Puff-paste may be made without stopping; that is, without putting it away in a cool place for some time; but it is better to let it rest; it is lighter and rises better. When finished, it can be used immediately; but it is better also to put it in a plate or dish, cover it with a towel, and put it in a refrigerator for from twelve to twenty-four hours. Although it must be kept in a cool place, do not put it near enough to the ice to freeze. It may be kept thus for two or three days.

Puff-paste with Beef-Suet.—Take half a pound of fresh beef suet, the nearest the kidney the best; break it

in small pieces with the hands, at the same time removing
the thin skin and fibres as much as possible; put it in a
bowl of cold water and knead well till it is rather soft;
take it off, mash and bruise it well on the paste-board with
a rolling-pin; knead it again like butter; roll it in flour
like butter also, and proceed as above for the rest, and with
the same proportion, weight for weight of flour and beef-
suet, but it requires more salt. Beef-suet being more firm
than butter, puff-paste can be made with it during summer, but it must be eaten immediately, being very inferior
after a while.

The proportion of butter and flour may be varied.
Weight for weight makes the real puff-paste, and very
rich. If less butter is used it will not rise as much, but is
excellent nevertheless, and is more handy to make different
cakes, such as short-cakes with fruit. Therefore puff-paste
may be made with the following proportions: to one pound
of flour, use fourteen, twelve, ten, eight, or even four ounces
of butter or suet. Another way is to mix one or two eggs
in the flour, water, and salt before rolling it down. When
eggs are used, it requires less water. Envelop the butter
in it in the same way.

Allumettes.—Cut strips of puff-paste of any length,
about three inches wide and about one-fifth of an inch in
thickness; mix well together, and for about three or four
minutes, one ounce of sugar and about half the white of
an egg; spread this mixture over the strips of paste, so
as to have a rather thin coat of it; then cut the paste
across, so as to make small strips about one inch broad
and three inches long. Bake in an oven at about 400
deg. Fahr.

Feuillettés.—Roll puff-paste down to a thickness of
from one-eighth to one-half of an inch in thickness; cut

it in pieces of any size and shape, according to fancy, with a knife or with a paste-cutter; glaze the top only with egg, and bake in an oven at about 450 deg. Fahr.

Feuillettés à la Condé.—Roll and cut the paste exactly as for the above; then, instead of baking it, fry it in hot fat (*see* FRYING); turn into a colander when fried, dust with sugar, and serve as warm as possible.

Pommées.—Line the bottom of a bakepan with puff-paste, about one-eighth of an inch in thickness; spread stewed apples over it of a thickness of one-quarter of an inch; cover these with another thickness of puff-paste; prick the cover all over with the point of a knife, and bake in an oven at about 400 deg. Fahr. When baked, cut it in square pieces, dust with sugar, and serve hot or cold, according to taste.

Porte-manteaux.—Cut strips of puff-paste of any length, about three inches broad, and one-eighth of an inch in thickness; spread on the middle of the strips, and lengthwise, some frangipane, or stewed apples, or any kind of sweetmeats, of the size of the finger. Then turn one side of the paste over the frangipane or sweetmeats, glaze the border with egg (we mean by "the border," about half an inch in width, measuring from the edge); then turn the other side over it so that the glazing will cause the two pastes to stick together. Thus it will be only a little over an inch broad and about half an inch thick. Cut the strips across in small pieces about two inches long, glaze the top with egg, and then bake in an oven at 400 deg. Fahr.

Tartelettes.—Roll some puff-paste down to a thickness of about one-sixteenth of an inch; cut it, with a paste-cutter, of the size of small tin moulds, and place the pieces in the moulds; put about a teaspoonful of frangipane in each; place two narrow strips of paste across each, which strips you cut with a truckle; bake in an oven at about 380 deg. Fahr.

Tartelettes (sweet).—Proceed as for the above in every particular, except that you use any kind of sweetmeats or jelly instead of frangipane.

Cake Pithiviers.—Roll some puff-paste down to a thickness of about one-eighth of an inch; cut it round and place on a baking-pan; if the pan be square or rectangular, cut a round piece that will go in easily; cut a strip of paste about one inch broad, glaze with egg the border of the paste in the pan, place the strip all around, and then glaze it also. Fill the middle with the following mixture: pound four ounces of sweet almonds and mix them well with half a pound of sugar, two ounces of butter, four yolks of eggs, essence to flavor, and four macaroons chopped. Cut another piece of puff-paste round, and of the same size as the other; dust it slightly with flour, fold it gently in four; the piece then will have two straight sides and a circular one. With a sharp knife make three cuts in each of the two straight sides through the four thicknesses of the paste, and about half an inch in length. Make another cut through the paste also, representing half of the figure 8, right in the middle of the piece of paste, commencing half an inch from the border of the circular side and in the middle of it, and going toward the point, so that when the paste is open there are sixteen cuts in it. Place the paste still folded on the paste and mixture in the pan, the circular side on the border and the point right in the middle; open it gently, and the whole will be covered. Glaze with egg, and put in an oven at from 430 to 460 deg. Fahr. The same cake may be filled with a frangipane, and prepared as the above for the rest.

Rissoles (also called Fourrés).—Cut round pieces of puff-paste about three inches in diameter; wet the edge with water, put a teaspoonful of compote or any kind of sweetmeat on one side of it, then fold the paste in two, so as to cover the sweetmeat; pinch the paste around to cause it to adhere, in order to envelop the sweetmeat; you have then a cake of a semicircular shape. Glaze with egg, bake in a quick oven, dust with sugar, and serve.

Galette du Gymnase.—Make puff-paste with half a pound of butter to a pound of flour, and when done as directed, knead it. Then roll it down to the thickness of about one-fourth of an inch, cut it in strips of any length and about an inch and a half wide, glaze with egg, bake in a quick oven, about 420 deg. Fahr. The two ends of the strips may be brought together and joined, forming a crown. The same *galette* is made with trimmings of puff-paste, kneaded and rolled as above.

Fanchonnettes.—These are made with the same puff-paste as the *galette* above; then cut it in round pieces, place them on small moulds, fill them with any kind of sweetmeats and frangipane, with almonds, half of each; bake, dust with sugar, and serve. Instead of frangipane, spread raisins over the sweetmeats, or almonds, peanuts, hazel-nuts, etc., all cut in small strips, lengthwise; you make then an infinite number of different small cakes.

Fans.—Make some puff-paste with equal weight of flour and butter, fold and roll it down six times, and put in a cold place. Leave it of a thickness of about one-quarter of an inch; cut it with a sharp knife in pieces of a rectangular shape, about four inches long and two broad, which cut again in two, across and from one corner to the other, so that you make two pieces of a right-angled triangle shape. Place the pieces on their sides in a bakepan, on their sides, far apart, and bake in a very quick oven. When done, dust with sugar, and serve.

Vol-au-vent and *bouchées* for the day's use are baked early in the morning. They are warmed in a slow oven just before filling them.

Vol-au-vent.—A *vol-au-vent* is made with puff-paste and filled with oysters, meat, etc., when baked; that is, when the cake is baked and emptied, it is warmed in the oven, filled, and served warm. It is made of an oval or round shape. When made small it is generally of a round shape, but when made rather large it is generally of an oval shape. When the puff-paste is ready to be used, roll down to any thickness from one-quarter to three-quarters of an inch; cut it with a sharp-pointed knife of the size and shape you wish, then with the same knife cut what is called the cover, *i. e.*, make a cut all around, about half an inch from the edge or border, and about one-third through the paste, leaving two-thirds of the thickness of the paste uncut. This operation is called marking out the cover. Glaze the top of the paste with egg, and bake it in a very quick oven, about 500 deg. Fahr. In glazing, be careful not to glaze the sides or allow any egg to run on the sides; it would prevent the paste from rising. Some drawings may be made on the cover with the back of a knife, according to fancy: leaves, for instance, are very easily imitated; it is only necessary to run the knife on the paste, without cutting it. When in the oven, do not look at it for at least seven or eight minutes, for in opening the door of the oven it might cause the paste to fall, and even after that time open and shut the door quickly; take off when properly baked. When the oven is hot enough it takes about twelve minutes, and even less time when the *vol-au-vent* is small.

18*

Take from the oven when baked, and immediately run the point of the knife all around and in the same place as you did before being baked, which place is well marked. Thus you cut off the cover and remove it, then remove also all the unbaked paste that is inside of the *vol-au-vent*, so that you have left what may be called a shell. Keep it then till the oysters or meat are ready to put in it. About five minutes before the filling is ready, put the shell or baked paste in a slow oven to warm it, turn the filling into it, enough to fill it entirely; place the cover on the top, and serve warm. The unbaked paste removed from the inside is baked, and makes an excellent cake, though not a sightly one.

Another.—Cut a piece of puff-paste the same as for the above one, that is, either round or oval, and of the size you wish. Instead of marking a cover, glaze the border with egg. It is understood here by "the border," a space about three-quarters of an inch broad and all around it, the space being measured from the edge toward the centre. Then cut a strip of puff-paste about three-quarters of an inch broad, long enough to cover the place or space glazed, which strip you put all around the first paste, and you then have a border. The place between the two pastes being glazed, they will adhere in baking. Then also glaze the upper side of the border carefully with egg. With a knife or fork, prick the paste, inside of the border only, in ten, fifteen, or twenty places, according to the size of the *vol-au-vent*, and in order to prevent that part from rising as much as it would if not pricked. Bake in the same oven as the above—a very quick one.

A *vol-au-vent* thus made is deeper than the first one, having two thicknesses of paste. Generally there is little or no paste (unbaked) to remove; having pricked the centre, it prevents it from rising and bakes it evenly, but if there is any, remove it. A cover may be made by cutting a piece of puff-paste of the size of the *vol-au-vent* and baking it separately. It may be decorated with the back of the knife as the above one, and made convex on the top by baking it on a piece of tin. It is warmed, filled, and served the same as the above.

A *vol-au-vent* is filled with the following:

With Oysters.—The quantity is according to the size of the *vol-au-vent*. Blanch one quart of oysters. Put two ounces of butter in a saucepan, set it on the fire, and when melted add a tablespoonful of flour; stir, and when turning rather yellow add also about a pint of milk, and the liquor from the oysters; stir, and as soon as it turns rather thick put the oysters in, taking care to have them free from pieces of the shell. Give one boil, add salt to taste, two yolks of eggs, stir again, turn into the warm paste, place the cover on, and serve warm.

With Lobster.—Prepare the lobster as for *bouchées*, fill the shell with it, and serve warm.

With Cod-fish.—Prepare fresh cod-fish *à la Béchamel*, fill the *vol-au-vent* or shell with it, and serve warm.

With Turbot.—Proceed as for cod-fish in every particular.

With Eels.—Fill the *vol-au-vent* with eels, oyster-sauce, or in *poulette*, and serve warm.

With Chicken.—Fill with a chicken or part of a chicken in *fricassée* or *sauté*.

With Livers and Combs of Chicken.—Prepare combs and livers of chicken in *fricassée*, the same as a chicken, fill the *vol-au-vent* with them. Serve hot.

With Sweetbreads.—Cook the sweetbreads as directed, and fill the *vol-au-vent* with them. Serve warm.

With Veal.—Fill the *vol-au-vent* with veal in *blanquette*, in *ragout*, or in *bourgeoise*, and serve. It is generally filled with what has been left the day previous, as it requires very little for a *vol-au-vent.*

With Brains.—It may be filled with brains of calf, pig, sheep, or veal; prepared in *poulette*, or stewed.

With Rabbit.—Fill it with part of a rabbit *sauté.*

It may also be filled with any other *meat* or *fish*, according to taste, and being cooked previously.

With Fruits.—Fill the *vol-au-vent* with any kind of stewed fruit, jelly, sweetmeats, etc. It may be only filled, or the fruit may be dressed in pyramid inside of it.

Bouchées.—*Bouchées*, or *petites bouchées*, as they are sometimes called, are small, round *vol-au-vent*, served warm. They are also called *bouchées de dames* and *petites bouchées.* Roll puff-paste down to a thickness of about one-quarter of an inch, cut it with a paste-cutter of any size, mark the cover, and bake in an oven at about 450° Fahr. A good size is about three inches in diameter. When cut, take another paste-cutter about two inches in diameter, place it on the piece of paste; press on it just enough to mark the place where it was, but not enough to cut the paste, remove it and then the cover is marked; that is, you have a circle on the top of the paste, half an inch from the edge all around. Glaze with egg and bake. Make one for each person. Immediately on taking them from the oven, cut off the cover with a sharp-pointed knife. That is easily done; it is only necessary to follow the mark made with the paste-cutter, which is just as visible as before baking. Remove the cover and then carefully take out some unbaked paste inside of the *bouchée*, fill with lobster prepared as directed below, put the cover on, and serve as warm as possible.

The Filling.—Cut some flesh of boiled lobster in dice. Put two ounces of butter in a saucepan and set it on the fire; when melted, add a tablespoonful of flour, stir for about one minute, and add also broth (the quantity must be according to the number of *bouchées*, but we will give here the quantity necessary for five or six *bouchées*), about three gills, also salt, pepper, then the cut lobster; stir now and then for five or six minutes, and use.

Of Oysters.—Prepare, fill and serve exactly as the above, except that you fill with oysters prepared as for *vol-au-vent*, instead of filling with lobster.

Of Cod-fish.—Fill the *bouchées* with cod-fish, prepared *à la Béchamel*, and serve warm.

Of Eels.—Have some eels prepared either in *poulette* or oyster-sauce, fill the *bouchées*, and serve warm.

Of Turbot.—It is filled with turbot *à la crème* or *à la Béchamel.*

It may also be filled with any kind of *fish*, prepared *à la Béchamel*, *à la crème*, in white sauce, oyster-sauce, etc.

Of Truffles.—Cut the white flesh of a chicken in dice, prepare it as a chicken *sauté*, using truffles but no mushrooms, fill the *bouchées* with it and serve warm.

Of Purée of Chicken, or *Bouchées de Dames.*—It is filled with some *purée* of chicken, and served as warm as possible.

Do the same with a *purée* of game.

Of Bobolink.—Prepare and clean twelve bobolinks as directed for birds, put a teaspoonful of truffles, cut in small dice, in each bird, for stuffing; sew the incision, and bake or roast the birds. Put each bird in a *bouchée*, and serve warm. A more delicate dish cannot be made.

The same may be done with any kind of *small bird.*

Bouchées are generally served on a napkin and on a dish, in pyramid.

Pâte à choux.—Weigh four ounces of flour, to which add half a teaspoonful of sugar. Put two gills of cold water in a tin saucepan with two ounces of butter, and set it on the fire, stir a little with a wooden spoon to melt the butter before the water boils. At the first boiling of the water, throw into it the four ounces of flour and stir very fast with the spoon, holding the pan fast with the left hand. As soon as the whole is thoroughly mixed, take from the fire, but continue stirring for about fifteen or twenty seconds. It takes hardly half a minute from the time the flour is dropped in the pan to that when taken from the fire. The quicker it is done, the better. When properly done, nothing at all sticks to the pan, and by touching it with the finger it feels as soft as velvet, and does not adhere to it at all. Let it stand two or three minutes, then mix well with it, by means of a spoon, one egg; then another, and so on; in all four. It takes some time and work to mix the eggs, especially to mix the first one, the paste being rather stiff. They are added one at a time, in order to mix them better. If the eggs are small, add half of one or one more. To use only half a one, it is necessary to beat it first. Let the paste stand half an hour, stir again a little, and use. If it is left standing for some time and is found rather dry, add a little egg, which mix, and then use.

Beignets Soufflés—(*also called Pets de Nonne*).—Make some *pâte à choux;* take a small tablespoonful of it, holding the spoon with the left hand, and with the forefinger of the right cause the paste to fall in hot fat on the fire (*see* FRYING), turn over and over again till fried, then turn into a colander, dust with sugar, and serve hot. In frying, the paste will swell four or five times its size, and by dropping it carefully and as nearly of a round shape as possible, the cakes will be nearly round when done.

Choux or Cream Cakes.—Make some *pâte à choux;* have a buttered bakepan, and drop the paste upon it in the same way as you drop the *beignets* above; glaze with egg, and bake in an oven at about 380° Fahr. When baked and cold, make a cut on one side, about two-thirds through, the cut to be horizontal, a little above the middle, then, by raising the top a little, fill the cake, which is hollow, with one of the following creams: *whipped, Chantilly, cuite, frangipane,* or *légère;* dust with sugar, and serve.

The same. with Almonds.—Blanch sweet almonds and cut them in small strips, lengthwise; then, when the *choux* are in the bakepan and glazed with egg, spread the almonds all over, bake, fill, and serve as the above.

Saint Honoré.—Make some *pâte à choux.* Then put four tablespoonfuls of flour on the paste-board with two of sugar, one egg, one ounce of butter, salt, and a pinch of cinnamon; mix and knead the whole well; roll the paste down to a thickness of about one quarter of an inch and place it in a bakepan. Put a dessert-plate upside down on the paste, and cut it all around the plate with a knife; remove what is cut off and also the plate. Spread some *pâte à choux,* about a teaspoonful, all over the paste left in the bakepan, about one-sixteenth of an inch in thickness; put some of it also in the pastry-bag, and by squeezing it out, make a border with it about the size of the finger; prick the middle of the paste in about a dozen places with a fork and inside of the border; glaze the border with egg, and then bake in an oven at about 400° Fahr. While the above is baking, make very small *choux* (about the size of a macaroon), and bake them also. When both are baked, and while they are cooking, make some *crème légère,* fill the inside of the cake with it, so as to imitate a sugar-loaf or mound, about four inches in height, smooth it or scallop it with a knife. Put twc tablespoonfuls of sugar and two of water in a saucepan, set it on the fire, toss the pan occasionally to boil evenly, and till it becomes like syrup. Do not stir too much, else it will turn white and somewhat like molasses-candy. It is reduced enough when, by dipping (not stirring) a little stick in it and dipping it again immediately in cold water, the syrup-like liquor that has adhered to it breaks easily and is very transparent. It must be as transparent as glass. As soon as reduced thus, take from the fire and use. Dip the top of each small *chou* in it, holding the *chou* with a small knife stuck in it; place a piece of candy (generally, sugar-plums of various colors are used) on the top of each *chou;* place them apart and around the *crème légère,* and upon the border of the cake, with one a little larger than the others on the top of it; serve cold. This cake is as good as it is sightly.

Eclairs.—Eclairs are also called *petits pains* or *profiterolles au chocolat.*

Eclairs au Chocolat.—Make some *pâte à choux* as directed above, and put it in the pastry-bag with tube No. 1 at the end of it. Force it out of the bag into a baking-pan greased with butter. By closing and holding up the larger end of the bag and by pressing it downward, it will come out of the tube in a rope-like shape and of the size of the tube. Draw the bag toward you while pressing, and stop when you have spread a length of about four inches. Repeat this operation till the baking-pan is full or till the paste is all out. Leave a space of about two inches between each cake, as they swell in baking. Bake in an oven at about 370 degrees. When baked and cold, slit one side about half through, open gently and fill each cake with the following cream, and then close it. Cream: put in a block-tin saucepan three tablespoonfuls of sugar, two of flour, four yolks of eggs, and mix well with a wooden spoon. Add a pint of milk, little by little, and mixing the while; set on the fire, stir continually till it becomes rather thick, and take off. Have one ounce of chocolate melted on a slow fire in half a gill of milk, and mix it with the rest, and use. Put one ounce of chocolate in a tin saucepan with a teaspoonful of water, and set on a slow fire; when melted, mix with it two tablespoonfuls of sugar, stir for a while; that is, till it is just thick enough to spread it over the cakes, and not liquid enough to run down the sides. A thickness of about one-sixteenth of an inch is sufficient. The cakes may either be dipped in the chocolate or the chocolate may be spread over them with a knife. Serve cold.

Eclairs au Café.—It is made exactly like the above, except that you mix with the cream three tablespoonfuls of strong coffee, instead of chocolate and milk.

Eclairs au Thé.—It is made like the preceding one, with the exception that strong tea is used instead of strong coffee.

Eclairs à la Vanille.—Proceed as for the above, but mix a teaspoonful of essence of vanilla in the cream instead of tea.

Eclairs à l'Essence.—The meaning of *éclairs à l'essence* is, that a few drops of any kind of essence are mixed with the cream instead of chocolate and milk, and prepared and served like the others.

Eclairs aux Fraises.—Instead of filling the cakes with cream, fill them with strawberry-jelly, and for the rest proceed as for *éclairs au chocolat.*

Eclairs aux Groseilles.—Made like the above, but filled with currant-jelly.

Do the same with *apple, blackberry, cherry, grape, peach, pear, plum, quince, raspberry jelly,* etc.

Petits Pains à la Reine.—*Eclairs* are so called when filled with marmalade of peaches in which sweet almonds chopped fine have been mixed previously.

Petits Pains à la Rose.—Like the above, and by adding a few drops of essence of roses to the marmalade.

Petits Pains à l'Essence.—Like the above, with any kind of essence : *pink, violet, geranium,* etc.

Biscuits in Boxes.—Make some square boxes with sheets of white paper ; fill them about two-thirds full with the same mixture as for lady's fingers, dust with sugar, and bake in a slow oven ; serve cold.

With Almonds.—Mix well together with a wooden spoon four yolks of eggs with four ounces of sugar (pulverized), add three ounces of flour and mix well again. Beat the four whites to a stiff froth, and then have somebody to turn the mixture into them while you finish beating, and then mix the whole gently but well. It must not be stirred too much. Have two ounces of bitter almonds well pounded, with a teaspoonful of sugar, and mix them with the rest. Butter small moulds, turn the mixture into them, filling about two-thirds full, glaze with egg, dust with sugar, and bake in an oven at about 300 degrees Fahr. ; serve cold.

With Chocolate.—Make some biscuits like the above, omitting the almonds, and flavoring them with a few drops of essence of vanilla. When cold, glaze them with chocolate, the same as described for *éclairs*, and serve.

With Essence.—Make biscuits with almonds or without, as the above ones, and flavor them with any kind of essence, or with orange and lemon rind grated.

Glazed.—When the biscuits are baked, glaze them

with icing, and serve cold. These are sometimes called *biscuits à la royale.*

Of Rheims.—Mix well in a bowl six yolks of eggs with six ounces of sugar, with a wooden spoon. Add and mix with the above five ounces of flour and lemon-rind grated; beat four whites of eggs to a stiff froth, and mix them also with the rest. Butter small moulds, turn the mixture into them, and bake in a slow oven, about 300 degrees Fahr. These are often made of the shape of lady's fingers. They are excellent eaten with wine.

With Filberts.—Put ten or twelve ounces of filberts or peanuts in a mortar with a few drops of orange-flower water and about half the white of an egg; when reduced to a paste, mix well with it four ounces of sifted flour, eight ounces of fine, white sugar, the yolks of two eggs well beaten, and the whites of four eggs whisked to a froth; when the whole is properly mixed, put it into a well-buttered mould, which place in a moderately-heated oven; watch it carefully, take out when cooked, which is easily known by the color it assumes.

Biscuits with hazel-nuts, peach, or other kernels, may be made in the same way; that is, using them instead of filberts.

Lady's Fingers.—Mix well together with a wooden spoon four yolks of eggs and four ounces of pulverized sugar, then add three ounces of flour and mix well again. Beat four whites of eggs to a stiff froth; have somebody to turn two tablespoonfuls of the mixture into the whites as soon as beaten enough, and which you mix with the egg-beater, then turn the rest of the mixture in, mixing gently with the wooden spoon. This must be done rather quickly, to prevent the whole from turning liquid. Put the mixture in the pastry-bag with tin tube No. 1 at the end of it, squeeze it out in sticks about four inches long into a baking-pan slightly buttered and dusted with flour, or on a piece of paper placed in the bottom of the pan; then dust them with sugar, and bake in a rather slow oven. They must not change in the oven, that is, they must not spread or swell, showing that the oven is too hot or too slow, or that the mixture has not been properly prepared. They must be like small sticks, round on the upper side and flat underneath. They are sometimes called *biscuits à la cuiller.* They are used to make a *Charlotte Russe,* or eaten with wine.

CAKES.—*Almond.*—Blanch, skin, and pound well one ounce of sweet almonds and the same of bitter ones, which you mix with eight ounces of pulverized sugar, six of flour, two eggs, a tablespoonful of brandy or rum, and a pinch of sugar. When thoroughly mixed, add five yolks of eggs, mix and stir for five minutes, then add also and mix half a pound of melted butter. Turn the mixture in small moulds, well buttered, and bake in a rather slow oven. Some almonds cut in small pieces may be spread over just before baking; or, when baked, some icing may be spread over. Serve cold. This is also called *Nantais cake.* Instead of almonds, use filberts, hazel-nuts, currants, peanuts, or raisins.

Fourré.—This is made with puff-paste and cream, or puff-paste and different mixtures placed inside of it, such as *Pithiviers cake* and fruit-pies.

Anchovy.—Knead four ounces of flour with two ounces of butter, a little salt, and a little water. Clean four anchovies and put them in vinegar for five minutes; then cut them in small pieces, put them in a bowl, and cover them with sweet-oil; leave them thus ten minutes.

Roll the paste thin, then place a little more than half of it on a tart-dish, raising it all around with the thumb and forefinger ; cover the paste with the anchovies, and these with the remainder of the paste, after having cut it in square pieces ; spread some of the oil in which were the anchovies on it, bake in a warm oven, baste now and then with a little of the oil, and serve warm.

Apple.—Stew eight or ten apples and mash them through a sieve. Put them in a saucepan with about two ounces of butter and eight of sugar, set on the fire for five minutes, take off, let cool, and then mix with it five or six eggs, one after another. Turn the mixture into a buttered mould, which you place in a pan of boiling water, then boil slowly about half an hour, turn over a dish, and serve warm or cold.

Hard.—Put half a pound of flour on the paste-board and make a hole in the middle; put into it three ounces of pulverized sugar, three ounces of butter, two eggs, a pinch of cinnamon, a few drops of essence, and knead the whole well, dust the board with flour, roll the paste down to a thickness of about one-fourth of an inch, cut it in pieces with a paste-cutter, of any shape ; beat one egg with a teaspoonful of sugar and glaze the pieces with it ; with a piece of wood draw leaves or flowers on each, and bake in an oven at about 360 degrees Fahr. They are eaten cold at tea.

Heavy or Gâteau de Plomb.—Proceed as above with one pound of flour, a pinch of salt, one ounce of sugar, four yolks of eggs, one pound of butter, half a pint of cream ; when rolled down as above, fold in two or four, and roll down again ; repeat the process four times. Then place it in a bakepan and put in a hot oven. Serve cold at tea.

Milanais.—Put one pound of flour on the paste-board

and make a hole in the middle, in which you put half a pound of butter, same of sugar, two eggs, a pinch of salt, and a quarter of a gill of rum. Mix and knead to a rather stiff dough with cold water. Spread it and roll it down to a thickness of about one-eighth of an inch. Glaze it with egg, dust with sugar and bake in a rather quick oven. When cold, cut it in two, spread some *compote* of peaches or of apricots on one half, put the other half over it, cut in pieces according to fancy, and serve.

Rum Cakes.—These are made with sponge cake cut with a paste-cutter, some sweetmeats or jelly is placed on the middle, then it is dusted with pulverized sugar, watered with rum, and then placed in the oven for about two minutes. These cakes have several names, according to the kind of sweetmeat used.

Savarin.—Put one pound of flour on the paste-board and make a hole in the middle; put into it four ounces of sugar, and make a hole again; then put in the middle four eggs, twelve ounces of butter, one and a half gills of milk; mix and knead the whole well; then mix again in the whole four ounces of leaven prepared as directed; butter a mould, dust it with sweet almonds chopped; put the mixture in it; put in a warm place (about 78 degrees Fahr.) to rise, and bake in an oven at 430 degrees Fahr. It will take about two and a half hours to rise. The mould must not be filled, else it will run over in rising.

Sauce for Savarin.—Put four ounces of sugar and half a pint of cold water in a block-tin saucepan, set it on the fire and boil till reduced about one-third; then add from one-half to one gill of rum (according to taste), give one more boil, and turn over the cake. Baste the cake with the sauce till the whole is absorbed by it. Serve warm or cold.

Sponge Cake.—Mix well together in a bowl six yolks of eggs with four ounces of sugar; add four ounces of flour and mix again, add also a few drops of essence, then whisk six whites of eggs to a stiff froth and mix them again with the rest. Butter a mould, put the mixture into it, not filling it more than two-thirds full, and bake in an oven at about 320 degrees. Sponge cake may be cut in pieces and used to make a *Charlotte Russe*, instead of lady's fingers.

Apple Dumplings.—Quarter, peel, and core the apples, and cut them in pieces, then envelop them in puff-paste with beef-suet, boil till thoroughly done, and serve warm with sugar, or with apple or wine sauce. It may also be served with sauce for puddings.

Buckwheat Cakes.—Make a kind of thin dough with tepid water, yeast, buckwheat flour, and a little sugar and salt, let rise, and fry with butter. Serve hot with sugar, or molasses, or butter.

Corn Cakes.—Mix well in a bowl two eggs with two ounces of melted butter, a pint of corn-meal, salt and sugar to taste. While mixing set milk on the fire, and as soon as it rises, turn it into the mixture, little by little, stirring and mixing the while, and till it makes a kind of thick dough. Butter well a shallow bakepan, put the mixture into it, and bake.

Crullers.—Mix well together and work with a wooden spoon, in a bowl, one egg with two ounces of melted butter and half a pound of pulverized sugar; then add salt, cinnamon, nutmeg, a few drops of essence, and one pound of flour, and mix again; add also milk, little by little, stirring and mixing at the same time, enough to make a thick batter. Divide the mixture in parts and fry in hot fat. (*See* FRYING.)

Doughnuts.—Mix well together in a bowl four eggs with half a pound of sugar, add two or three ounces of melted butter and mix again, then mix with the whole, about one pound of flour and boiled milk enough to make a rather thick dough, season and mix well with the whole, nutmeg, cinnamon, and a few drops of essence. Cut in fancy pieces with a knife or paste-cutter, and fry in hot fat. (*See* FRYING.) Dust with sugar, and serve hot.

Muffins.—Mix well together on the paste-board one pound of flour and three eggs, then add and mix again milk enough to make a thin dough, a little yeast and salt. Put away to rise; divide in parts and bake.

Pound Cake.—Take a large bowl and put in it one pound of melted butter and one pound of pulverized sugar, and mix the two thoroughly together with a wooden spoon; then add and mix well also with them, three eggs previously beaten with a saltspoonful of nutmeg and cinnamon, half of each. When the eggs are mixed, add also half a pound of flour, mix well again; then add six well-beaten eggs, and mix; then another half pound of flour, a few drops of essence of rose, half a gill of Sherry wine, a liquor-glass of brandy, four ounces of citron, and half a pound of comfited fruit, chopped fine. Beat and mix as well as possible. Butter a mould, dust it with fine bread-crumbs, turn the mixture into it, and bake in a warm but not quick oven. It takes about two and a half hours to bake. As soon as cold, serve it. It may be glazed with sugar, or sugar and white of egg.

Short Cake.—Cut puff-paste, made with a pound of flour and six or eight ounces of butter, in square or round pieces, bake; when cold, spread sweetened strawberries on, then cover with another cake, spread strawberries again on it, etc. Strawberry-jelly may be used.

Plum.—Mix well in a vessel a pound of sugar with a pound of butter, and then again with eight eggs, one at a time, also half a pound of raisins, half a pound of flour, a little rum, and a little yeast. Line a mould with buttered paper, turn the mixture into it, not filling it more than two-thirds full, place it in a warm but not quick oven for nearly two hours, remove the mould, and serve hot or cold.

Tea Cake.—Put half a pound of flour on the pasteboard, and in the middle of it a pinch of salt, half an ounce of sugar, two eggs, four ounces of melted butter, and cold water enough to make a rather stiff paste. Knead well, roll down to about a quarter of an inch in thickness; cut it in pieces with a knife or paste-cutter; moisten the top with water by means of a brush, dust with sugar, and bake in an oven at about 370 degrees Fahr. Serve cold.

Viennois.—Make some biscuits in boxes, and when cold, cut off a little piece on the top, in the centre, which place you fill with peaches or apricots in *compote;* put two together; serve cold.

With Jelly.—Proceed as above in every particular, using currant or raspberry jelly instead of *compote.*

MEAT-PIES.

Pâtés de Viande.—Meat-pies are made in moulds without bottoms and which open in two, or are made of two pieces joined and fastened together with two pieces of wire. The size of the mould and that of the pie are according to taste. A pie may be made and filled with a reed-bird, or with a quail, or a partridge, or prairie-chicken, or with a dozen of them. We will give the receipt for one prairie-chicken.

19

Pâté of Game.—Bone a prairie-chicken as directed for birds, and cut it in about half a dozen slices or pieces. Grease the mould with butter and put it in a baking-pan. Put one pound of flour on the paste-board and make a hole in the middle; place in it six ounces of butter, one egg, a pinch of salt, and about one gill and a half of cold water, and knead the whole well. Roll it down to a thickness of about one-quarter of an inch, and of a rectangular shape; fold in two, and roll down again. Repeat this from six to twenty times; that is, till the paste is soft. The last time roll it down to a thickness of one-third of an inch, and give it as round a shape as possible. Dust the upper side slightly with flour, fold in two in this way: turn the side farthest from you on the other, so that the side of the paste nearest to you will be somewhat round, and the opposite one will be straight. By pulling with the hands the two ends of the straight side toward you, it will make it somewhat round also; then, take hold of the paste exactly in the places where you were pulling; put it in the mould with the side nearest to you on the top; open it gently, and with the hands spread it so that the bottom and sides of the mould will be perfectly lined with it. With a sharp knife cut the paste even with the top of the mould. Line the sides of the paste with thin slices of fat salt pork. Mix in a bowl one pound and a half of sausage-meat with two eggs, salt, pepper, a pinch of cinnamon and one of nutmeg; place a layer of this mixture about half an inch thick on the bottom of the paste; then a layer of thin slices of fat salt pork; one of slices of prairie-chicken; again a layer of sausage-meat, one of salt pork, etc., layer upon layer, till the mould is nearly full, finishing with a layer of sausage-meat, and giving to the top of the *pâté* a convex form, but leaving a space of

about half an inch unfilled all around, so that the top of
the *pâté* will be about one inch higher than the sides, and
half an inch higher than the sides of the mould and paste.
The cover of the *pâté* is made with the same paste as the
bottom and sides, or with puff-paste.

Roll the paste down to a thickness of about one-eighth
of an inch. Glaze the sides of the paste in the mould
with egg; that is, the space (half an inch) left unfilled;
put the paste for the cover on the *pâté;* press it gently
against the other paste with the fingers in order to cause
the two pastes to adhere; with a sharp knife cut off the
paste even with the mould. Make a hole in the middle and
on the top of the cover about one inch in diameter; cut
five pieces of paste about three inches square, dust them
slightly with flour; place them one upon another on your
left thumb, keeping it erect; then with the right hand take
hold of the pieces, bringing the edges together so that the
top will form a ball; with a sharp knife make two cuts
across and through the five pieces; form a kind of stem
as if you were to imitate a mushroom with these pieces,
and plant the stem in the hole; when baked it looks
like a flower. Glaze the cover with egg; cut strips of
paste in different shapes with a knife or paste-cutter, place
them on it according to fancy, and bake in an oven at
about 390 degrees Fahr. The strips of paste may also be
glazed with egg. It will take about two hours to bake.
As soon as cold, cut the cover all around and remove it;
fill the empty places with meat or calf's-foot jelly and put
it on the dish. Chop some of the same jelly, put some
all around it and on the top; cut some of it also in fancy
shapes with a knife or paste-cutter; place it all around
the dish and on the top of the *pâté*, and serve.

The cut following represents a plain pie; that is, without any decoration, and immediately after having removed the mould.

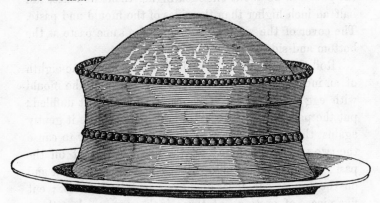

Another, or Rabbit-Pie.—Chop very fine and separately one pound of veal, one of beef, one of lean fresh pork, three of rabbit or hare, and three of fat fresh pork. Mix the whole well together and season with salt, pepper, cinnamon, cloves, and nutmeg, all grated or in powder. Line a mould with paste as directed above, put a layer of the mixture in the mould about one inch thick, place on it slices of truffles, if handy and liked; then another layer, truffles, etc., till the mould is full. If filled without truffles, it is not necessary to put layer after layer. Cover also as above, and bake in a moderately heated oven, about 320 degrees Fahr. It takes from five to six hours to bake.

Another, or Prairie-chicken Pie.—Skin a prairie-hen (or several) and bone it. It is not necessary in boning it for a pie to proceed as directed for boned turkey, but merely to remove all the bones in the easiest and quickest manner; you cannot spoil the flesh, as it is to be chopped. Weigh the flesh when free from bones and skin. Weigh as much of each of the following: ham, salt pork, and calf's liver. Grate the salt pork and chop the three others very fine, and then pound the whole. Season with salt, pepper, cloves and nutmeg, both grated, a pinch of cinnamon and chopped parsley; mix with the whole two or three eggs, one at a time, in order to mix better. Line a mould with paste as directed above; line the paste with thin slices of salt pork, fill it with the mixture, and cover, bake, finish, and serve exactly the same as the preceding. For two prairie-hens it will require about three hours to bake. Slices of truffles may also be used; they are mixed at the same time with the eggs and seasonings.

With Cold Meat.—When the paste is placed in the mould as directed above, line it with thin slices of salt pork, then put a very thin layer of sausage-meat, prepared also as above, then fill with butcher's meat, poultry, and game, having previously removed all the bones, and cut the meat in strips; the greater the variety, the better the *pâté*. Put a little of each kind of meat used in a mortar, say from one ounce to a pound, with parsley, thyme, bay-leaf, salt and pepper; pound the whole well and then mix with one egg, half a gill of white wine, or a liquor-glass of brandy, to every pound of meat. Fill the hollow places with the mixture, to which you may add a little gravy or broth if it is not liquid enough. Place thin slices of salt pork on the top, cover with paste as described above, cook and serve as above also.

Meat-pies, as seen above, are made with every kind of meat; with one or several kinds at the same time, according to taste.

Wines and liquors may be used, it is only a matter of taste. The cover may be placed with only a hole in the centre, instead of decorating it.

By using in turn butcher's meat, poultry, and game, an infinite number of different *pâtés* can easily be made.

Terrines (*Terreen, or Tureen*).—A *terrine* differs from a meat-pie in this, that instead of using a tin or brass mould and lining it with paste, a *terrine* (French word for terreen) is used, and is only lined with thin slices of salt pork, and closed with its cover. It is filled, cooked, and served in the same way as a meat-pie.

Timbale.—The name *timbale* is given to a meat-pie when made in a straight tin mould, lined as a *terrine*, and covered with a tin cover. A *terrine* or *timbale* keeps longer in winter than the pie.

Pains de Gibier (*Pains of Game*).—This means, loaves of game. It is a *terrine* made with any kind of game, of one or of several kinds, with the exception that birds are boned and filled (*see* DIRECTIONS FOR BONING), before placing them in the terreen; also, before covering the terreen, place a piece of buttered paper all around, so as to have it as nearly air-tight as possible when covered. Bake as above, and as soon as out of the oven remove the cover; put a piece of tin, sheet-iron, or wood on the top, large enough to cover the meat, but not the border of the terreen. Place some weight on it in order to press the meat down, and leave thus over night. The weight and piece of tin are removed, the terreen is wiped clean, the cover placed on it, and it is then served, or served on a dish. It keeps very well in winter time, and many are imported from Europe, especially those made like the following:

Another.—Cut four ounces of boiled beef-tongue and one pound of truffles in large dice. Put about two ounces of salt pork in a frying-pan on the fire, and when fried, add about six ounces of the flesh of prairie-hen, cut in pieces, four prairie-hens' and four chicken livers, eight in all; stir, and when turning rather brown, add also chopped parsley, salt, and pepper; stir again for two or three minutes, and take off. Put in a mortar one pound of flesh of prairie-hen, baked and chopped; one pound and a quarter of fat salt pork, and about four ounces of *panade*. Pound the whole well and put it in a large bowl. Then pound well also the six ounces of prairie-hen flesh and eight livers with twelve yolks of eggs and a wine-glass of Madeira wine, and put in the bowl also. Add to it the tongue and truffles, and mix the whole well, adding game-gravy, or meat-gravy if more handy, about a gill of it, season to taste with salt, pepper, nutmeg, and cloves, grated. Bay-leaf and thyme, well pounded, may also be used, if liked. After being pounded, the whole may be mashed through a sieve, but it is really not necessary. Then place the mixture in one, two, or three *terrines*, cook, and serve as above.

Another.—Take the flesh of six prairie-hens when cooked, and pound it well. Pound also eight livers, fried; four of prairie-hens and four of chickens; put flesh and livers in a saucepan with gravy, set on a slow fire, and as soon as warm, add to it, little by little, and stirring continually, about three-fourths of its volume of good butter. When all the butter is in, take from the fire, mix one pound of truffles cut in dice with it; put the mixture in one or more terreens; cover, bake, and serve as above.

Terrines and *pains* are sometimes made with poultry, and in the same way as those of game.

Fish-Pies.—These are made in the same way as meat-pies, using cooked fish instead of meat, but putting fish only inside of the paste. When done it is filled with *coulis of fish* instead of jelly. Serve as a meat-pie. The fish must be free from bones.

Fruit-Pies.—Pies are made with paste and fruit or vegetables. The under-paste may be made of trimmings of puff-paste, or of the paste hereafter described, but the top is always made of puff-paste. The paste on the top may cover the fruit entirely, or it may be only strips running across, according to taste and fancy. The fruit is used raw or cooked previously, according to kind; if it requires longer cooking than the paste, or if it requires to be mixed or mashed, it must be cooked previously.

Under-Paste.—Put one pound of flour on the pasteboard with six ounces of butter in the middle of it; also two ounces of sugar, two eggs, and cold water enough to make an ordinary paste, neither too stiff nor too soft. Roll the paste down to a thickness of one-eighth of an inch, spread it on a tin dish or bakepan, buttered slightly, raise the borders a little or place a strip of puff-paste all around it; put the fruit in the middle, then cover with a thin piece of puff-paste or place strips of it only over the fruit, and bake in a rather quick oven, about 390 degrees Fahr. The strips of paste are cut with a paste-cutter (caster-like) and placed across; one strip may also be placed all around. When trimmings of puff-paste are used for the under-paste, when placed on the tin or bakepan, prick it in about a dozen places with a fork to prevent it from rising. To place a border around the paste, you have only to cut a strip of it about half an inch wide, wet the paste with water by means of a brush, that is, the edge or place where you are going to put it; then take hold of the strip, place one end of it on the paste and run it all around till you meet the end, cut it off and stick the two ends together by wetting them also. When the border is placed, then put the fruit in the middle; if the fruit is not cooked, it must be mixed with sugar and essence, or cinnamon, or nutmeg, according to kind; if cooked, that is, stewed, or in *compote* or in jelly, it is sweetened and flavored.

The following are used to make pies : *apples, apricots, cherries, currants, blackberries, cranberries, gooseberries, grapes, mulberries, oranges, peaches, pears, pine-apples, plums, quinces, raspberries, lemon, rhubarb, prunes, whortleberries,* etc. It is better to stone the fruit before using it. Pies are decorated in the three following ways:

1. When you use cooked fruit, put a thin layer of rice (prepared as for *croquettes*) on the paste, then a layer of stewed fruit; then the strips over, and bake. Two or three layers of each may be used.

2. When baked, spread over the pie some syrup of apples, of pears, or syrup for *compotes.*

3. Just before serving, spread some *crème légère* on the top, tastefully and fancifully, by means of a paper funnel, or with the pastry-bag.

Tarts and Tartelettes.—These are small pies. Instead of using a tin dish or a bakepan, you use small tin moulds, such as for *madeleines,* and proceed exactly as for pies.

Mince-Pie.—Every thing used to make a mince-pie is chopped fine, and the spices are used in powder. Prepare paste as directed for meat-pies, and make it either with or without mould. Proportions : to three pounds of beef add six pounds of beef-suet, one pound of currants, one of prunes, one of raisins, and one of apples, the rind of two lemons, two ounces of citron, and one pound of any kind of comfited fruit; nutmeg, mace, cinnamon, cloves, and sugar to taste; also wine or brandy, or both, to taste. Bake in a moderately heated oven. The fruits may be used candied or fresh, the apples fresh or dried, it is a matter of taste. Twenty kinds of fruits and meat

19*

may be used as well as three or four; there are no rules
to make a mince-pie, since its compounds are not used to
be tasted at all separately, but as a whole.

Pot-Pie.—Make a paste with one pound of flour, two
ounces of butter, two ounces of beef-suet (the latter prepared as directed for puff-paste), a little salt and water,
enough to make a rather stiff paste; roll it down to a
thickness of about a quarter of an inch and fold it in three
and roll down again; repeat the process half a dozen
times, the last time leaving it rolled down and of the
thickness above mentioned. Line the sides of a pot with
it, lay slices or strips of salt pork on the bottom of the
pot, then fill it with strips of meat, any and every kind
(slices of potatoes may be added, if liked); season with
salt, pepper, nutmeg, and cinnamon; fill with water or
broth; cover with some of the same paste; cover the
pan and boil gently till done. When the cover of paste
is laid on, make a hole in the centre to let the steam out,
and to fill up with water or broth if it boils away. Run
a sharp-pointed knife or a skewer through, to ascertain
when done. Serve warm. Proceed as above either for
butcher's meat, chicken, and other domestic fowls, or
game.

PUDDINGS.—Puddings are made of several materials
and in a hundred different ways. Some are cooked by
boiling, others are baked, and some are both boiled and
baked. Puddings for inhabitants of cities ought to
be made as light as possible. For persons working outside and at manual labor, it does not matter, because their
food passes through the system in a short time. It is
very well known that the poorer class of Americans eat
too much pudding and pie. Many do it for economy,
others for convenience. The former are mistaken, and the

latter are blamable. Puddings and pies cost more in the end than meat properly and carefully prepared. We do not mean to do away with them entirely, but we advise every one to do with puddings as with every thing else, "use, but do not abuse." "Pies, cakes, and sweetmeats, are universally known to be poisoning to children, and the mothers who give them are conscious that they are purchasing the momentary smile of satisfaction at the risk of after-sickness, and perhaps of incurable disease."— PETER PARLEY.

The above needs no commentary; we only recommend it to the consideration of young mothers.

For Convenience.—We have taken the trouble to put questions about it to over three hundred mothers, wives of mechanics or of employés at a comparatively small salary, and we are sorry to say, that more than ninety per cent. gave us about the same answer—they make and cook cakes in one day, enough to feed the whole family for three days, to save the trouble of cooking every day. We cannot see where the trouble can be for a good wife and mother to prepare her husband and children's dinner.

Pudding-eating is an English custom; but, before following a custom of another country, people ought to consider if that custom or fashion (whatever it is) has not been introduced into that country by necessity, which is the case of pudding-eating in England and in some parts of Holland.

In England, where the fog is nearly perpetual, the stomach requires to be filled with something heavy, something that will stay there till the next meal, and very often longer than that.

It is well known that in England farm hands, or other persons working in the open air, eat six times a day, and have pudding at least three times; they drink home-brewed beer, which is very heavy, and very rich also. Let any one here, in this pure, clear atmosphere, eat six times a day, have pudding three times, with a pint of home-brewed beer every time, and see how he will feel in the evening. We beg all, who may doubt our observations, to try the experiment.

Pastry in general, no matter how light it may be made, lies heavier on the stomach than any other food, and is very difficult of digestion. There are thousands of persons that have never had any indigestion but of pastry. Children like pastry very much; this is easily understood; as their young stomachs digest very rapidly, they crave food oftener than grown persons. Pastry being easier to have at any time than any thing else, it is given to them; and from habit in youth arises the liking when grown up. The stomach, being accustomed to it from infancy, may digest it better, but it is always at the expense of the whole system; the stomach must work hard, too hard in digesting it; whence come dyspepsia, weakness, and finally consumption, or debility, or any other sickness of the same kind.

The cut below represents a pudding (any kind), made

in a mould, scalloped, and hollow in the middle ; any kind of mould may be used for puddings.

Bread-Pudding.—Soak half a ten-cent loaf in milk for about an hour, and squeeze it with the hands ; place the bread in a bowl and mix well with it a gill of milk, three tablespoonfuls of sugar, one ounce of citron, cut rather fine, four ounces of raisins, four ounces of melted butter, four yolks of eggs. Then beat the four whites of the eggs to a stiff froth and mix them with the rest. Grease a mould well with butter, dust it with bread-crumbs, turn the mixture into it, and bake. The mould must not be more than about two-thirds full. About 400 degrees Fahr. is the proper heat for a bread-pudding. It takes about forty minutes to bake. Serve with a sauce for pudding, hot or cold, according to taste.

Cabinet Pudding.—A cabinet pudding is made in any kind of a mould and of any size, with sponge-cake or lady's fingers. Butter a mould well; if the butter is too firm, warm it so as to grease the mould better. Slice some citron and cut it in lozenges or of any other shape, according to fancy, and place tastefully on the bottom of the mould ; place some raisins all around also. It is not necessary to cover the bottom with them, but have some here and there, imitating flowers, stars, etc. Then put over them a layer of sponge-cake, cut in strips of any length and about half an inch thick ; on this layer place some citron, some comfited (candied) fruit of one or several kinds, and all cut in dice, also some raisins ; then another layer of cake, some more fruit, and so on, till the mould is full. After having placed the citron and raisins on the bottom, it is not necessary to put the rest in with care or order, but merely fill the mould with them and so that they are all mixed up. Set about a pint of milk on

the fire and take it off as soon as it rises. Mix well in a
bowl three ounces of sugar with three yolks of eggs, then
turn the milk into the bowl, little by little, stirring and
mixing the while, and pour the mixture over the cake,
fruit, etc., into the mould. The above quantities of milk,
sugar, and eggs are for a middling-sized pudding, and it
will be very easy to make more or less, according to the
size of the pudding. The mixture must be poured over in
sprinkling, and it must nearly cover the whole within
about half an inch. It must not be poured too slowly,
for, the cake absorbing the liquor pretty fast, you would
have too much of it if you were filling as directed above ;
we mean filling till the mould is nearly full. Place the
mould in a pan of cold water so that it is about one-third
covered by it, set on the fire, and as soon as it boils, place
the whole, pan and mould, in an oven at about 380 degrees Fahr., and bake. For a middling-sized one it takes
about one hour. When done, place a dish over the mould,
turn upside down, remove the mould, and serve with a
sauce for puddings.

With Vermicelli.—Blanch four ounces of vermicelli,
drain and drop it in cold water and drain again. While
the vermicelli is cooking, put about a quart of milk in a
saucepan on the fire with two ounces of sugar and a piece
of lemon-rind, stir now and then to dissolve the sugar, and
as soon as the milk rises, take it from the fire, remove the
lemon, then turn the vermicelli into it, put back on the
fire, add a tablespoonful of butter, stir continually, and
when the vermicelli is well cooked, take off, mix well
with the whole four eggs and sugar to taste. Turn the
mixture into a well-buttered mould, place it in a pan of
boiling water, boil slowly for ten minutes, then place as it
is, pan and mould, in a moderately-heated oven to finish

the cooking. It will take from fifteen to twenty minutes. Proceed as above with *macaroni, tapioca,* etc.

Plum-Pudding.—Break with the hands, in small pieces, about twelve ounces of the soft part of good and well-baked bread, not too fresh, but not stale, and grate it. Clean twelve ounces of raisins and currants, half of each. Cut in small dice four ounces of citron and four ounces of candied orange-rind. Chop fine the rind of a lemon. Butter a towel slightly and dust it with flour, slightly also. Take twelve ounces of good fresh beef-suet, remove the fibres and skin as well as possible, and chop it rather fine with three or four ounces of flour, and which put in a large bowl. Mix with it seven eggs and half a pound of sugar. It is believed by many that brown sugar is better than white, but it is only a belief, if not a prejudice. Add and mix again the bread, the raisins, and currants, the citron, and orange-rind. Having the whole thoroughly mixed, add half a gill of French brandy or Jamaica rum, a little salt, the lemon-rind, half a gill of cream. or a little milk, and a little grated cinnamon. Place the mixture on the towel, and tie it as fast as possible, giving it a round shape. Drop the towel in boiling water, and boil for from four to five hours. Some boil a plum-pudding as long as seven hours. It may also be boiled in a mould for that purpose, but it is easier in a towel and quite as good. When taken from the water, remove the towel, cut a little piece of the pudding off, tó make it stand better on the dish. The place cut off is generally where the towel was tied, being the less smooth. The cut following shows a plum-pudding boiled in a towel.

Serve with a sauce for puddings. The sauce may be served in a boat, or spread all over the pudding. When served the second day, or cold for supper, it is cut in slices; some Jamaica rum is poured over it, then set on fire, basting as long as it burns, and serve. It is generally burnt on the table, but the rum may be poured over in the kitchen. The cut below represents a whole one with rum around it and on fire.

Biscottes.—Put half a pound of flour on the paste-board and make a hole in the middle of it; put in the hole four ounces of sugar, one ounce of butter, three yolks of eggs, and a few drops of essence to flavor the cakes. Mix and knead the whole well with the hand. When like dough, roll it under your hands and bring it to a rope-like form of about three-quarters of an inch in diameter; cut it in pieces about two inches long; roll again with the hand so as to make a ball of each; then roll again with both hands so as to give each piece a round, elongated, olive shape; that is, smaller at each end than at the middle. Put them in a baking-pan, greased with butter; glaze each piece well with egg and a little sugar beaten together, then, with a sharp knife, which you dip in flour, make a cut on the top and into each cake, lengthwise, about three-quarters through, and bake in an oven at 350 degrees Fahr. Serve cold. It is an excellent cake for tea as well as for dessert.

With Almonds.—Add to the above mixture one ounce of pounded almonds.

With Filberts or Hazel-nuts.—Add to the mixture

for *biscottes*, one ounce of filberts or hazel-nuts, pounded well.

Brioche.—Mix together on the paste-board, one pound of flour, six eggs, one pound of butter, four ounces of leaven prepared as directed, and tepid water enough to make a rather soft dough, then beat well. The longer it is beaten the better, and the lighter the *brioche* will be. By beating we mean—take hold of the dough with the right hand, raise it and then throw it with force on the board and in the same place where it was; repeat that till it comes off your hand without any of the paste sticking to it. Put the mixture in a tin vessel, set it in a warm place (about 78° Fahr.) for about two hours to rise, and then put immediately on ice to cool. When cold, put it back on the paste-board, cut off about one-fourth of it. Make a kind of crown with the larger piece, but not a very large one; let the hole in the middle be about three inches in diameter. Then give the other piece a rope-like shape, about three-quarters of an inch in diameter; place it over the crown, giving it the shape of a star, and bake in an oven at 430°. Serve warm, without sauce.

Baba.—Mix together and beat as for a *brioche*, one pound of flour, ten eggs, one pound and a quarter of but-

ter, four ounces of raisins, four ounces of citron, four
ounces of leaven, about half a pound of different kinds of
fruits, preserved in syrup or candied, all cut fine; put to
rise, let cool, shape, bake and serve as a *brioche*.

A *baba* may be baked in a mould; the cut on the previous page represents one.

Croquignolles.—Put in a bowl four ounces of flour, a
teaspoonful of sugar, a pinch of salt, half a pound of
butter, four whites of eggs, and a few drops of essence;
mix the whole well so as to make a very stiff paste. Then
put the mixture on the paste-board, and roll it in a rope-
like form about half an inch in diameter; then cut it in
pieces about half an inch long, glaze with yolk of egg,
dust with sugar, and bake in a warm but not quick oven.
Serve cold at tea.

Galette.—Knead together half a pound of flour, six
ounces of butter, two eggs, and a pinch of salt; roll it
down to a thickness of a quarter of an inch, put in a bakepan in the oven, and when nearly done, take off; mix well
together one egg with a gill of cream and an ounce of
butter, while the *galette* is in the oven, spread the mixture
over it, put back in the oven, finish the cooking, and serve
cold at tea.

Génoises.—Put in a large bowl six ounces of flour,
eight of sugar, two eggs, a liquor-glass of brandy or rum,
and a few drops of essence; mix and stir the whole well
for three minutes, then add two more eggs, stir and mix
one minute longer, add again four eggs and continue stirring one minute longer. Melt half a pound of butter in
another bowl, and mix with it about two tablespoonfuls
of the mixture; when, turn into the other bowl and mix
the whole well together. Butter a bakepan, spread the
mixture in it, and bake in a rather slow oven (about 300°

Fahr.). When the top is well baked, turn it over and finish it. When cold, cut the whole in strips about two inches long, then again across so as to make pieces of a lozenge-shape, and serve as it is or with a *sauce for puddings*.

The same, with Almonds.—Pound well four or six ounces of sweet almonds, place them in the bowl with the rest, and then mix, bake, and serve as the above one.

Do the same with *bitter almonds, hazel-nuts, peanuts, filberts,* and *raisins ;* flavor with any kind of essence.

With Chocolate.—When the cake is cut in pieces, glaze it as directed for *éclair au chocolat.*

With Sweetmeats.—When the cake is cut in pieces, with a sharp-pointed knife, cut off a part of each piece, on the top and right in the centre, so as to make a small hole, which you fill with any kind of sweetmeat or with any *cream*, and then serve. When thus served, they are called under several names.

Macaroons.—Throw into boiling water for five minutes ten ounces of sweet almonds, and two ounces of bitter ones; skin them well; put in a mortar, and pound them to a paste, adding a few drops of the white of eggs during the process. Grind well also a pound of white sugar, with the quarter of a rind of lemon well grated ; then mix well together almonds, sugar, and the whites of two eggs. Make balls of any size with it; put the balls on a piece of paper, beat the yolk of an egg with half a gill of water, and glaze the top of the balls with it by means of a brush ; put them in a slow oven; it will take about fifteen minutes to cook them.

Macaroons with Chocolate.—Melt on a slow fire and in a tin pan three ounces of chocolate without sugar (known as Baker's chocolate) ; then work it to a thick paste with one pound of pulverized sugar, and three whites of eggs. Roll the mixture down to a thickness of about one-quarter of an inch; cut it in small round pieces with a paste-cutter, either plain or scalloped; butter a pan slightly and dust it with flour and sugar, half of each, place the pieces of paste or mixture in and bake in a hot but not quick oven. Serve cold.

Madeleines.—Mix well together in a bowl three ounces of sugar, three of flour, and two eggs, then again one ounce of melted butter and a few drops of essence to flavor. Butter slightly small tin moulds, dust them slightly also with flour and sugar, half of each, turn the mixture in, filling the moulds only two-thirds full, and bake in an oven at about 340°. Serve cold.

The same, with Almonds.—Chop rather fine some sweet almonds, and when the mixture is in the moulds as described above, spread the almonds over them; bake, and serve as above.

Do the same with *hazel-nuts, filberts, peanuts,* or *raisins.*

Meringues or Kisses.—Put half a pound of pulverized sugar in a plate, beat six whites of eggs to a stiff froth as directed, then have somebody to sprinkle the half pound of sugar into the eggs, and while you are still beating, which must be done in two seconds; stop beating and mix gently with a spoon, not by stirring but by turning the whole upside down several times. If it is stirred too much, it may turn too liquid. Put the mixture in the pastry-bag, with tin tube No. 2 at the end of it; spread the mixture on paper in a baking-pan, in oblong cakes about three inches long; dust them with pulverized sugar, and put in an oven at from 220° to 230° Fahr. It requires some time to dry them, about one hour. As soon as taken from the oven, place one in your left hand, the top downward; press gently on the under side which is up, with the first finger of the right hand, so as to make a hollow; put in that hollow twice as much cream as is necessary to fill it; place another cake prepared alike over the cream; so that the two will be united and kept together by the cream; do the same with the rest; place them tastefully on a dish; dust them with sugar, and serve. They are generally filled with *whipped cream*, but may be filled with *crème légère* or *crème cuite.* They may also be filled with *crème Chantilly.*

Swiss Meringue.—Instead of squeezing the mixture out and spreading it in oblong cakes, make a crown of it, then another and another, four in all, dust and bake in the same way; place them on a dish, one above the other, and fill the middle of the dish with cream as above. Serve cold. The mixture may also be placed on paper by the spoonful, but they are not as sightly as by means of the pastry-bag.

Zephyrs.—Proceed as for meringues as far as mixing the sugar with the whites of eggs, when mix also with both a few drops of cochineal. Put the mixture in the pastry-bag, with tin tube No. 1 at the end of it. Squeeze the mixture out and spread it on paper in a baking-pan, in different shapes: dentilated, convoluted, overlapping, waved, etc., according to fancy, about three inches and a half long. Bake in same oven as meringues, and serve when cold, as they are.

Nougat.—Throw a pound of sweet almonds into boiling water for five minutes; skin them well, and when cool cut them in four or five pieces lengthwise; then melt a pound of fine white sugar with two spoonfuls of water, in a copper or crockery pan, and on a good fire, stirring all the

time with a wooden spoon; when well melted, put the
almonds in; keep stirring about five minutes longer, take
from the fire, add a little of the rind of a lemon well
grated, oil the mould, put it on the corner of the range in
a warm but not too hot place; put the almonds and sugar
in the mould, and little by little take off when of a brown
color, turn on a plate, remove the mould, and serve.

Pancakes.—Make a thin paste with one pound of flour,
four eggs, two tablespoonfuls of sweet-oil, one of French
brandy, a little salt, the necessary quantity of lukewarm
water and milk, about half of each; let it remain thus
two or three hours at least; then put about an ounce of
lard, butter, or oil in a frying-pan, and set it on a brisk
fire; when hot, put some of the paste in it with a ladle,
spread the paste so as to cover the bottom of the pan;
fry on both sides, place it on a dish, dust it with fine
white sugar on both sides, and serve warm.

Buckwheat and other pancakes are made in the same
way.

Waffles.—Make a thin paste with eight ounces of flour,
six ounces of pulverized sugar, two eggs, a few drops of essence to flavor, half a liquor-glass of brandy or rum, and
milk. Warm and butter both sides of the mould, put some
of the paste into it, close it gently, set it on the fire, turn
over to heat both sides equally, dust them with sugar
when done, and serve either warm or cold. It takes hardly
a minute for each with a good fire.

BREAD.

It is next to an impossibility to bake bread in a small
oven; half the time the bread is too much or not enough
baked. In cities, where good baker's bread can be bought,
it comes as cheap as it can be made at home, if not cheaper,

and saves a great deal of time and labor. It is not difficult to make good bread with good flour. There are several ways of making and of using yeast. Some are better
than others; but many, though differently manipulated,
bring about the same results. The only difficulty is the
baking of it. Bakers can almost always bake bread properly, having large brick ovens. If they do not bake their
bread enough, which is generally the case, it is not because
they cannot, but because under-baked bread is heavier,
and people, especially the poorer class, buy it in preference
to the other; judging by the weight, they think they have
more of it for a certain sum of money. Under-baked
bread is difficult of digestion. (*See* FOOD.)

The best bread is made with the best wheat-flour, all
that can be said by anybody to the contrary notwithstand-
ing. Rye, corn, and barley bread are excellent, and may be
partaken of by those whose constitution, occupation, etc.,
allow it. In every thing, bread included, the people, or
what may be called "the million," are wiser than *soi-di-
sant* philosophers; and if oat-meal or Indian-meal were
better than wheat-flour, they would be dearer. To describe or discuss the innumerable methods of making
bread would require several volumes. We have perused
carefully hundreds of them; they nearly all differ theo-
retically, but practically, when practical (which is not
always the case), they amount to about the same thing.
We think that the only difficulty, if difficulty there be, is
in the use of the yeast, the making of the same, and the
baking. Chemical processes for rising will never equal
the processes of nature and time. Many bakers do not
use the yeast properly, their bread being sour or musty;
some sweeten their bread, to disguise an inferior quality of
flour, or as an antidote to sourness or mustiness.

Bread gets dry after a while, and is inferior in quality and taste. The lighter the bread the better, although many do not think so. The belief may come from the fact that the lighter bread is the more porous, and therefore the quicker it evaporates and loses its taste. Warm bread, besides being injurious to the teeth, is difficult of digestion. When perfectly cold, let it stand in a dry place, neither cold nor warm, for one or two hours, and use. We give below the best methods of making bread—French bread, or rather good light bread, for we do not see that it is more French than Chinese or American, as long as it can be made everywhere with good flour; it is certainly the best for inhabitants of a large city, and especially for those having a sedentary occupation. Let us apply the proverb to bread as well as to every thing else: "Feed me with food convenient for me."—*Bible.*

Mix well together one gill of good strong yeast with half a pound of flour, so that it makes a rather stiff paste. Knead so that you shape it like a ball. Make two cuts with a knife on the top, across and about one-quarter of an inch deep; then place the paste in a bowl of tepid water (milk-warm), the cuts upward. After it has been in the water for a few minutes it will float and swell; let it float about two minutes, when take off and use. Put six ounces of flour on the paste-board, and make a hole in the middle; put into it the yeast prepared as above, tepid water enough to make an ordinary dough, and salt to taste. Knead well, shape according to fancy, put in a warm place (about 78 deg. Fahr.) to rise, and bake. It requires about six hours to rise.

Another.—Wash and clean thoroughly half a pound of potatoes, and then steam them with the skins on. Mash them well with half a pint of flour, about half a pint of tepid water, and half an ounce of salt. When thoroughly mixed, put away in a warm place (about 78 deg. Fahr.) for one hour. Then add and mix with it half a pint of good yeast, and put away in the same place for about nine hours. It may take a little longer than nine hours or a little less, but it is very easy to know, and in this way : after a while it will rise slowly and gradually for some time, and then begin to fall; as soon as it begins to fall, mix a little tepid water with it and strain through a sieve; throw away potato skins and eyes; mix what is strained with two pounds of flour and tepid water enough to make an ordinary dough. Put it away again in the same place until it cracks on the top, which will take place in about an hour. Then put six pounds of flour on the paste-board, and make a hole in the middle; put into it a little tepid water and the dough when cracked; knead the whole well with water enough to make an ordinary dough, salt to taste. To knead it well, it is necessary to raise the dough or part of it, and then throw it back on the paste-board with force. The more the dough is kneaded, the better and lighter the bread. Then shape the loaves, let rise, and bake in a very quick oven.

To shape.—Divide the dough, as soon as kneaded, in as many parts as you wish to make loaves; then knead each part, one after another, so as to make a kind of ball; then, by rolling and pulling it, give it an elongated, sausage-like shape. A pound loaf can be made a foot and a half long, as well as four inches; it will only be narrower and thinner, and will have more crust. When the dough is thus elongated, take a round stick or a small rolling-pin, place it on the top of the dough, right on the middle, lengthwise, and then press on it and roll just a little, to and fro, so as to make a kind of furrow in the middle.

20

Have a towel well dusted with flour, place the dough on it upside down, that is, the furrowed side under; let rise as ordinary bread; turn it into a pan, but so that the furrowed side will be up (the side that was down in rising must be up in baking); dust the furrow well with rye-flour to prevent the paste from closing, so that the top of the loaf will be concave instead of convex when baked.

Another.—Steam half a pound of potatoes and mash them well; then mix them immediately and while hot with about a pint of flour, a quart of water, and half a pint of good strong yeast. Leave the mixture six hours in a rather warm place, then strain through a sieve, pressing the potato-skins so as to squeeze all the liquid out of them. Immediately add to the strained mixture flour enough to make ordinary dough, which you knead a little, and let stand as it is from one to two hours and a half, according to temperature. Knead then with it about six pounds of flour, salt to taste, and tepid water to make ordinary dough, and leave it thus two hours, then shape in the same way as the above; put it to rise in the same way also (it will take from one to two hours, according to temperature); dust with rye-flour, and bake.

French bread may be shaped like other bread, round or square; it is just as good.

Rolls, or rather French rolls as they are generally called, are made, shaped, and baked in the same way.

It is a mistake to call *bread* certain mixtures of flour, soda, and milk; or flour, milk, and butter, etc.; it is no more bread than a mixture of carbonic acid, water, alcohol, molasses, vitriol, etc., is wine. No one can give a name to such a mixture except chemists.

BILLS OF FARE.

Dinner-Time.—On account of the various occupations of members of the same family, this is often the first and only time of the day that sees them all assembled. It is the dinner that mostly supplies the waste that the system has undergone for twenty-four hours. Being taken after the day's work is over, it gives to the stomach time to digest (mind and stomach never working at the same time). (*See* Food, Economy, Coffee, and Tea.)

The dinner, being the most substantial meal of the day, requires more preparation than any other meal; the bill of fare of it should, therefore, be made the day before, or at least early in the morning. It should always be made between the mistress or master of the house and the cook; written and hung in the kitchen, near the clock. The first thing to put down is what may be left from the preceding day, and also what may be in the larder; then what is wanted in butcher's meat or poultry, or both; the fish or game, or both, and which, with vegetables, are according to the market. It is then one of the duties of the cook to make a list of what is wanted as accessories; such as flour, eggs, sugar, spices, etc.

Besides the above, it is also the duty of the cook to send the dishes to the table in their regular order; for, if the whole dinner is sent at once, all the dishes have to be eaten at once also, else the last get cold and are unpalatable, or, by mixing them, they are rendered tasteless, as the flavor of one neutralizes (if it does not destroy) the taste of another.

To make models of bills of fare is not difficult, but to follow them is nearly impossible; hardly one in a hundred would suit any one.

Bills of fare vary according to the season of the year, and therefore to the produce in the market.

We will try to give another, and we think a better way of making them to suit everybody, every purse, and at any time.

A dinner, no matter how grand, is composed of three courses, and seven kinds of dishes.

The first course comprises dishes of four kinds, viz.: potages, *hors-d'œuvres, relevés, and entrées.*

The second course comprises dishes of two kinds, viz.: *rots* and *entremets.*

The third course comprises dishes of one kind, the dessert.

The number of dishes of each kind is generally according to the number of guests.

It may also be according to the importance of the occasion for which the dinner is given; to the honor the giver or givers wish to show the personage or personages invited; to the amount of money they are willing to spend. etc.

The following table shows how many dishes of each kind are to be served at dinner to a certain number of persons:

For..	2	4	6	10	16	20	30	40	50	60	80	100	Persons.
Serve	1	1	1	2	2	2	4	4	4	6	8	8	Potages.
"	2	2	2	4	4	6	6	10	10	12	12	16	Hôrs-d'œuvres.
"	1	1	1	2	2	2	4	4	4	6	8	8	Relevés of fish.
"	1	1	1	2	2	2	4	4	4	6	8	8	" of meat.
"	2	2	2	4	4	4	8	8	8	12	16	16	Entrées.
"	1	1	1	2	2	2	4	4	4	6	8	8	Rôts.
"	1	1	1	2	2	2	4	4	4	6	8	8	Salads of greens.
"	2	2	2	4	4	4	8	8	8	12	16	16	Entremets.
"						2	2	2	4	4	4	8	Large side pieces of Relevés & Entrées.
"								2	2	4	4	6	" cakes.
"	4	4	4	8	8	8	16	16	16	24	32	36	Plates of Dessert.

The above table shows the number of dishes, but more than one dish of the same kind can be served; for instance, four kinds of potages, *relevés,* etc., are served for forty; but two or four dishes of each kind can be served.

The size of the *relevés* and *rôts* should be according to the number of guests.

It is just as easy to select dishes for a small family-dinner as for a grand one; two, three, four, or more dishes can be selected; for instance, you select a potage, an *entrée* or *rôt,* or both, one vegetable or a sweet dish, or both; and one or as many plates of dessert as you please.

Have a bouquet on the middle of the table, if possible, or at least a basket of fruit. Flowers during dinner have the same effect as music after it; they soften the manners, and gently and sweetly gratify the senses.

To simplify and render the making of bills of fare easy, we have divided the different dishes into seven parts, each part being in the order the dishes of which must be served, and representing the seven kinds of dishes composing a dinner. By this means you select the dish or dishes which suit you, and which you can procure in any or all of the seven parts, and your bill of fare is made, and more to your liking than any steward on earth can do.

Order of dishes.—1. *Potages.* 2. *Hors-d'œuvres.* 3. *Relevés :* of fish, and then of meat. 4. *Entreés :* beef,

mutton, lamb, veal, fish, poultry, and game last.   5. *Rôts :*
of meat, and then of fish.   6. *Entremets :* salads of greens,
vegetables, eggs, macaroni, sweet dishes, and cakes.   7.
Dessert : cheese the first.

First part, or *Potages.*—Any kind coming under the
head of potages or soups.

Second part, or *Hors-d'œuvres.*—These are small
dishes placed on the table as soon as the soup-dish is removed or even before, and which are removed just before
serving the sweet dishes of the *entremets.* They are passed
round after every dish, on account of being considered
more as appetizers, as repairers of the natural waste of animal life. Very little of them is partaken of at a time;
they are *anchovies ; artichockes,* raw; pickled *beets ; but-*
ter ; caviare ; cervelas ; raw cucumbers ; figs ; every kind
of *fish,* salted, smoked, pickled, or preserved in oil; every
kind of *pickled fruit ; horse-radish ; horse-radish butter ;*
melons ; broiled *mushrooms ; olives ;* raw and pickled
oysters ; steamed *potatoes* served with butter; *radishes*
and butter; *sardines ; saucissons ; sausages,* salt and
smoked, but not fresh; salted and smoked *tongue ; tunny ,*
walnuts in salad.

Third part, or *Relevés.*—*Relevés* are composed of fish
and large pieces of meat. A fish served whole is always
a *relevé ;* in pieces, it is an *entrée.* Pieces of *beef, mutton,*
and *pork,* roasted, are always served as *relevés.* At a
family dinner the *relevé* is almost always a fish. The
other pieces of meat that are served as *relevés* are : *bear,*
buffalo, boiled and corned *beef, leg* and *saddle* of mutton,
quarters of lamb, large pieces of *veal ;* also all *vol-au-vent*
of meat and of fish, *boucheés* and *fish-pies.*

Fourth part, or *Entrées.*—These comprise every dish
of *meat,* except poultry and game, when roasted; every

dish of *fish* not served whole; also *pâtés de foies gras*, *sour-krout*, *snails*, *meat-pies*, *terrines*, *pains* of game and of poultry. The dishes of *meat* mentioned in the *relevés* may be served as *entrées* at a family dinner. The order of the dishes is described above.

Fifth part, or *Rôts.*—*Poultry*, *game*, and *fish*. At a family dinner, *lamb* and *veal* are often served as roasted pieces, especially at seasons when there is no game, and poultry is scarce.

Sixth part, or *Entremets.*—The following are served as *entremets*: all *salads* of greens; all dishes of *vegetables*, of *omelets*, except four, viz., with bacon, salt pork, ham, and kidneys. Also dishes of *macaroni*, of *rice*, *eggs à la neige*, all *sweet dishes* (sweet dishes are also served as *dessert*), and *cakes;* such as *baba, brioche, génoises, madeleines, savarin,* and sponge-cake.

Seventh part, or *Dessert.*—The dessert comprises ripe *fruit, sweet dishes* (these are also served as *entremets,* according to taste), *pastry* (except meat-pies, *terrines,* and *pains*), *salads* of fruits, and *cheese.* The latter is always served the first (*see* CHEESE). After cheese, there is no rule for serving the other plates of dessert; it is according to each one's taste.

Punch is served after the *entrées* or after the *relevés* of fish, according to taste.

Early Breakfast.—We are of opinion that everybody ought to eat as little meat as possible, and drink no wine, beer, or any other liquor at an early breakfast, no matter what the sex or age may be, except when prescribed by the physician in case of sickness, debility, etc. The food may be selected from the following: *bread* and *butter, eggs, omelets,* fried *fish,* fried *vegetables, sardines,* and *fruit,* according to the season.

As for meat, in case it should be eaten, it ought to be cold, such as fowl or veal, cooked the day before.

Muffins, and other cakes or pastes, served warm, are very bad for the stomach and teeth.

The beverage ought to be either coffee, with milk, chocolate, cocoa, choca, or cold water, but do not by any means drink tea at breakfast; it is too astringent.

Although cold meat is not by far so injurious as warm meat for breakfast, it ought, nevertheless, to be as little partaken of as possible, and especially by the young.

Late Breakfast, Lunch, Tea, and early Supper.—At these meals the following dishes may be served:

Every dish served as a *hors-d'œuvre, calf's* head and feet, bear *hams, head-cheese, eggs* cooked in any way, *omelets, mutton* chops, *veal* cutlets, fried *fish*, ripe *fruit*, boned *birds, ham*, cold *meat* of any kind, *oysters, pâté de foies gras, salads* of chicken, or any other birds, and of lobster, *sandwiches, sardines*, fried *vegetables, sweet dishes*, and *pastry*.

Late Supper.—This being the last meal taken before retiring, persons should be careful about what they eat then, especially those who take no bodily exercise, or retire soon after it. Some are not aware that their rest depends nearly, if not entirely, on what they have eaten at supper. The lighter the food the better; such as fried *fish*, *sardines, lait de poule, bavaroise*, well-ripened *fruit*, a *cream*, a little *iced fruit, fruit-jelly, prunes*, etc.

The gastronomical or hygienic rule to be observed in eating, it will be seen, is therefore, after the soup and *hors-d'œuvres*, to commence with the heaviest or most substantial dishes, and to finish with the lightest. The rule is just the opposite for wines. Here we must commence with the lightest, and end with those which contain the most alcohol, and are consequently the heaviest.

INDEX.

———◆———

20*

THE END.

COOKERY AMERICANA
AN ARNO PRESS COLLECTION

Each of the following titles includes an Introduction and Revised Recipes by Chef Louis Szathmáry.

Along the Northern Border: Cookery in Idaho, Minnesota, and North Dakota. New York, 1973.

Cooking in Old Créole Days by Célestine Eustis. New York, 1904.

Cool, Chill, and Freeze: A New Approach to Cookery. New York, 1973.

Directions for Cookery, in Its Various Branches by Miss Eliza Leslie. 31st edition. Philadelphia, 1848.

Fifty Years of Prairie Cooking. New York, 1973.

Hand-Book of Practical Cookery by Pierre Blot. New York, 1869.

High Living: Recipes from Southern Climes. Compiled by L. L. McLaren. San Francisco, 1904.

Home Cookery & Ladies' Indispensable Companion: Cookery in Northeastern Cities. New York, 1973.

The Improved Housewife, or Book of Receipts by Mrs. A. L. Webster. 6th edition. Hartford, 1845.

The Kansas Home Cook-Book. Compiled by Mrs. C. H. Cushing and Mrs. B. Gray. 5th edition. Leavenworth, Kansas, 1886.

Midwestern Home Cookery. New York, 1973.

Mrs. Porter's New Southern Cookery Book by Mrs. M. E. Porter. Philadelphia, 1871.

One Hundred Recipes for the Chafing Dish by H. M. Kinsley. New York, 1894.

Six Little Cooks by Elizabeth Stansbury Kirkland. Chicago, 1879.

Southwestern Cookery: Indian and Spanish Influences. New York, 1973.

ARNO PRESS, 330 MADISON AVENUE, NEW YORK, N.Y. 10017